THE ETERNAL WISDOM OF

|| DNYANESHWARI ||

D1737152

Dr. Vassant V. Shirvaikar

The Eternal Wisdom of

‖ DNYANESHWARI ‖

Dr. Vassant V. Shirvaikar

ZEN
PUBLICATIONS

The Eternal Wisdom of Dnyaneshwari

First Edition: April 2013

PUBLISHED BY

ZEN PUBLICATIONS
60, Juhu Supreme Shopping Centre,
Gulmohar Cross Road No. 9, JVPD Scheme,
Juhu, Mumbai 400 049. India.
Tel: +91 22 32408074
eMail: info@zenpublications.com
Website: www.zenpublications.com

Book Design: Red Sky Designs, Mumbai

ISBN 13   978-93-82788-08-9

PRINTED BY
Repro India Limited

CONTENTS

Sadguru Shri Shankar Maharaj

AUM

Sarve Bhavantu Sukhinah

Sarve Santu Niramayah

Sarve Bhadrani Pashyantu

Ma Kashchit Dukha bhagbhaveta

Om Shantih! Om Shantih! Om Shantih!

AUM

Oh Lord! May all be happy.

May all be free from misery.

May all realise goodness and

may no one suffer pain.

Peace ! Peace ! Peace !

PREFACE

It is more than seven centuries ago that Dnyaneshwar Maharaj wrote *Bhavarthadeepika* the commentary on *Bhagvad-Gita* on the instructions of his Guru and elder brother Nivruttinath (older only by two years) at the age of nineteen (though some say fifteen) years of age, but it is now better known as Dnyaneshwari after the author. It is written in *ovi* style verse traditional for Marathi religious literature.

Nivruttinath wanted this commentary to bring the philosophy of *Bhagvad-Gita* to common man, even a rustic. In those times, not only Vedic literature but most of the religious philosophical literature was in Sanskrit which only learned Brahmins knew and therefore outside the reach of common man. Most of such literature even otherwise was inaccessible to non-Brahmins leave alone a rustic farmer as the following lines from the eighteenth Chapter of *Dnyaneshwari* show:

The Vedas are full of Knowledge but there is none more miserly because they speak only with the first three castes. Others like women, shudras etc., who suffer tortures from this world, are not allowed under their shelter. I feel that in order to remove these earlier mentioned faults and with the intention of giving benefit to all, the Vedas have reappeared in the form of the Gita. Not only that, the Vedas are available to anybody through the Gita when its meaning enters in the mind, by listening to it or by reciting it. (18:1456-1460).

Greatness of *Dnyaneshwari* lies in the fact that it brought the philosophy of *Gita* and by that the philosophy of the Upanishads to common man. It became very popular; the *ovis* from it were and are even today melodiously sung in many households. *Dnyaneshwari* is regularly read in many households as part of their religious routine in spite of the fact that hardly anybody completely understands the seven centuries old Marathi language which is very much different from that spoken today. Fortunately, many prose translations are available and that satisfies the need of the curious who wish to understand the philosophy of *Gita* which by itself is also difficult to understand.

Dnyaneshwari became so popular that many people made copies (in pre-printing days it had to be by hand) for their use. But during this process many copies were produced with corrupted text. It was Saint Eknath who three centuries later collected many copies and prepared a corrected text which is what is available today. Fortunately unlike Ramayana and Mahabharata there is no indication that anybody has added his own text to the original.

In *Dnyaneshwari* Dnyaneshwar Maharaj explains each of the seven hundred *shlokas* of *Bhagvad-Gita* in detail through a number of *ovis* making skilful use of examples, similes and metaphors pertaining to natural phenomena and life situations familiar to the rural folk in Maharashtra. The 700 *shlokas* of *Gita* are explained in 9032 *ovis*. One wonders how an orphaned boy in his teens could know so much about lifen human traits and nature.

My real contact with *Dnyaneshwari* came quite late in life when I was about 58 years old and retired from service. I had purchased a copy of *Dnyaneshwari* (with a prose translation in Marathi by B. A. Bhide, published by Dhavale publications) as far back as in 1953 when I was twenty years old studying for the M. Sc. (Physics) course and later was engrossed in my job as a research scientist. This did not permit a mood conducive for reading spiritual literature of serious type. I did try once or twice to read it but could not go beyond the first few verses because it did not grip the interest. But that changed 37 years later when sometime in 1990 I received instructions to read and summarise the teachings of *Dnyaneshwari* in an easy language. That was how my closer acquaintance with the great work started.

It was difficult at first to understand *Dnyaneshwari*. The language of *Dnyaneshwari* is the eighth century old Marathi which most people do not understand well today. Also verse cannot express ideas as clearly and categorically as prose does. Fortunately, the Bhide book is quite comprehensive in that, it also gives *ovi*-by-*ovi* a prose translation as well as the corresponding original *Gita Shloka* (verse) and its Marathi translations by various saint poets in verse style viz., *Samashloki* of Vamanpandit, *Arya* of Moropant and *ovi* of Mukteshwar. This facilitated the understanding of the meaning not only of each *Gita* Shloka but also subject matter of the *Dnyaneshwari* verses. This was a great advantage to me because I have never learnt Sanskrit. The language of the Bhide book prose is somewhat archaic so I also consulted other Marathi prose translations, typically by Shri Keshavraomaharaj Deshmukh, a great spiritual person which is also in slightly archaic language and another by the scholar Mr. M. R. Yardi which is in a modern Marathi style. Later, I also consulted the English translation by another spiritual person, the Late Swami Umanand, the well-known *yogini* and disciple of Swami Muktanand of Ganeshpuri Siddhashram.

My assigned task was to make a composition to explain *Dnyaneshwari* that could be easily understood but I had to understand it first. I found myself confused while I read the text. Then I realized that this was mainly because Dnyaneshwar Maharaj had written this commentary with an objective that a common man, even a rustic farmer of his times, should understand it. Towards this end, he has used numerous similes and illustrative examples from common life and nature. For a modern reader one or two such similes and examples would have sufficed, but Dnyaneshwar Maharaj had chosen to use multiple similes and examples. It was those that were distracting the thread of logical philosophical thought. But for a modern educated and far better reader these extra similes etc., are not only superfluous but distracting. The first task therefore was to filter out the text to exclude them.

While selecting the text, following norms were used: (i) Most introductory verses like obeisance, praise of deities and guru were omitted. (ii) Where the meaning was clear without the help of similes or illustrative examples, these were omitted. (iii) Wherever multiple similes or illustrative examples are used, only one simile or example was retained and that too only if its use was needed to understand the meaning. When total tally was taken in the end, it was found that 5752 verses out of the total of 9032 verses used in this text were related to the philosophical aspect. That is quite a distraction and justifies selecting only the philosophical part for translation. The translation part itself was not very difficult because I was familiar with the language and terminology used in the spiritual texts both in English and Marathi. However it took some time before all the text could be translated and written into the computer.

Most translations of *Dnyaneshwari* are sequential *ovi*-by-*ovi* translations. As is well known the structures of Marathi and English sentences are different. In Marathi a sentence has its verb towards the end while in English the verb comes in the earlier part of the sentence immediately after the subject. Thus the sequential *ovi*-by-*ovi* translation of material spread over several *ovis* creates a structural difficulty. In this book therefore translation has been presented for a cogent group of *ovis*. I also decided to break the text into paragraphs with topical headings and sub-headings making the text easier to follow and also to provide the corresponding *ovi* numbers.

The laborious process of copying and translating into English gave me a good dividend. I had to understand the meaning first before translating it into English. That plus the time spent in translating and writing into computer gave me a lot of time for imbibing the *Dnyaneshwari* philosophy and prevented my glossing over the text. I could now really perceive the skill with which Dnyaneshwar Maharaj has presented *Gita* to the layman and my respect for the great philosopher and *yogi* increased tremendously. I still wonder how Dnyaneshwar Maharaj, in his teen age could know so much about the ways of the nature and behaviour of man of all strata. I had no doubt that such a book could not have been written without a Divine inspiration and backing.

When I started reading *Dnyaneshwari* and reached the second chapter *it was as if the doors of a treasure vault were opened to me.* Here one reads about the perishable body, the immortal soul even after death, the relation between the body and soul, the rebirth as another individual after death, the birth and death cycle and how one's actions *(karmas)* bind an individual to it, how only Self-Realization can make the individual free from the cycle and *how not logical arguments and reading books but only meditation can lead one to Self-Realization.* Though today I take these ideas for granted, at that time I was under the influence of what I had read in Puranas (our main source of ethical education), which speak of *Paapa* (sin) and *Punya* (merit) and corresponding ideas of *Narak* (hell) and *Swarga* (heaven) where one is relegated after death depending upon your account of the sins (bad *karmas*) and merit (good *karmas*) with Chitragupta the chartered accountant of Yamaraj the god of death. Like everybody else I used to think that sin cancelled by a merit. Also that people are reborn as man, an animal or even as a tree after spending your time in these two places.

But *Dnyaneshwari* changed those ideas. I learnt that you have to be reborn not only for suffering for the bad *karmas* but enjoying the fruits of the good *karmas*; the algebra of plus cancelling the minus does not work. Birth-death cycle continues as long as *karmas* are not nullified. Also, any amount of reading religious philosophy does not help, meditation is the only way. But the best idea I liked is that *while Puranas talk about heaven after death Dnyaneshwari (i.e. Gita) speaks of liberation while one lives provided one has achieved Self-Realization,* and that is permanent unlike a spell in heaven (or hell). So that brought me back from the dream world of heaven and hell to the real world of liberation while living, a most practical approach and an excellent target.

Dnyaneshwari is a guide to Self-Realization which is synonymous with *Moksha* or liberation. Unlike many sectarian religious texts that insist upon following only their own spiritual path, *Gita/ Dnyaneshwari* offers four different paths viz. the *Path of Knowledge, the Path of Action, the Path of Yoga and the Path of Devotion (Bhakti).* The seeker can choose a path depending upon his mental make-up. *Gita* classifies persons based upon the relative predominance of the three attributes *Sattva (purity, goodness, knowledge etc.), Rajas (movement, desire, passion etc.)* and *Tamas (lethargy, darkness, ignorance etc.)* in man. A person with predominance of *Sattva* attribute goes to the Path of Knowledge and *Bhakti* while a person of predominant *Rajas* attribute is more suited to the Path of Action, which may also include the Yoga Path. This classification must have been based on the observed diversity of human nature.

The classification of spiritual paths in four types has a modern psychological basis as pointed out by Yardi based on the works of Carl Jung. Yardi points out in the introduction to his book "Bhagvadgita – a Synthesis", that modern psychology classifies persons broadly as *introvert* and *extrovert*. The former can be further classified as *intellectual introvert* and *emotional introvert*. The path of knowledge is suitable to the intellectual introvert, the way of action to the extrovert and the way of devotion to the emotional introvert. The introvert seeker, through the grace of his Guru, controls the mind through discipline and yoga and gradually gives up desire and ego, until they no longer interfere with the development of the higher consciousness. The four paths are not mutually exclusive. Every path is intermixed to some extent with the other three. Especially, the element of *Bhakti* or devotion is always present in the other three paths. *Dnyaneshwari* gives guidance for all these paths.

While *Bhakti* path is suitable for all levels of people, educated or otherwise, as long as they are emotionally suited for it the Path of Knowledge can be taken up only by intellectuals. It is the intellectual component of the society: Scientists, engineers, business managers, planners, writers and educated politicians who lead the society and can improve it, a work they can do better with a spiritual background. For such people *Dnyaneshwari* is a wonderful guide, it teaches about discrimination between good and evil and also warns against the trap of book knowledge in which an intellectual can fall due to ego.

Regarding the guidelines about the Path of actions it is told that one should always follow one's own *Dharma* i.e. the code of righteous conduct prescribed for one's caste i.e. status in the society and do one's righteous duties without the pride of being the doer and without expecting the fruits thereof and offering them to God. We have also the wonderful advice for a happy frame of mind by developing an attitude of equanimity towards success and failure.

In Chapter 4 we have a promise from God that whenever society is troubled by evil people and *Dharma* (the sense of righteousness) is on the decline, He takes birth as an *avatar*, punishes the wrongdoers and re-establishes the *Dharma*. Actually this promise had created a doubt in my mind about why there were no *avatars* during the atrocities committed by Hitler and the communist dictators. Apparently I had not studied *Dnyaneshwari* properly. I came across the explanation in Chapter 10 and realised that this promise should not be taken literally but considered to mean that such crisis always brings forth a leader with superior qualities who restores the order: "Actually the splendour of the universe is within him. The signs by which one can recognise such a person are that the whole world bows to him and obeys him. Persons with these signs are my *Avatars*, and to say that a particular *Avatar* is better than the other is committing a sin because I am the entire universe. (10:308-312)." This put my doubts at rest. And it also told me that *Dnyaneshwari* is not a book just to be read and kept aside but should be read and consulted often.

We have also His promise in Chapter 9 that "I serve those who have completely surrendered to Me, …. and thus, with extreme faith meditate on Me and worship Me. **When they accepted the path of My worship, at that time itself the responsibility of taking their care in all respects fell on Me and I was compelled to do what they should have done for themselves.** Just as mother bird takes complete care of her babies who have not yet developed wings and lives only for them, I also take care of My devotees who have kept complete faith in Me……I give them whatever they want and having given, I guard it also for them. I provide maintenance to all those who give themselves to Me completely. (9:335-343)."

Whenever I read His following promise in the context of a devotee on deathbed it brings tears to my eyes: "Were I to come to my devotees only when they remember Me at the time of their death, then of what use is their worship? Do I not, purely out of compassion, rush to any person who prays for my help in their distress? But if I were to wait until my devotees also pray before I go to them then who would like to be a devotee? I must rush to them the moment they remember Me otherwise I will not be able to bear the burden of their devotion. It is for this reason, i.e. to pay the debt of their devotion that I go to the devotees to serve them at the time of death. In order that weakness of their bodies does not cause them distress, I keep them bound to the state of Self-realisation, make their mind calm and steady and thus bring those dear ones to Me. (8:124- 134)."

There are parts of *Dnyaneshwari* which may surprise a traditionally minded person. It is imprinted on a traditional Hindu mind from childhood that performance of religious rites pleases

God. He fears very much the displeasure of God on account of the sufferings that he thinks might bring on to him. He falls prey to the suggestions of the priests and astrologers to perform various kinds of worship and when they fail to bring forth the promised results he performs some more rites enriching only the priest. But see what Shri Krishna has to say about such a person in Ch 13:

"He reaches the height of happiness when he gets the thing he likes and he sinks due to sorrow when he gets what he does not like. However highly intelligent one may be, if he worries because of favourable and unfavourable circumstances, then in reality he is an ignorant person. (13:805-806). He may be devoted to Me but that devotion is with a material objective in mind. He makes a show of My devotion but keeps his sights on pleasures. If he does not get them after being devoted to Me, then he gives up the devotion saying that the talk of God etc., is all lies. Like an ignorant peasant he sets up different deities and after failing with one he goes to the next. He joins that Guru tradition where there is a great pomp and show, receives Guru-*mantra* from him and considers others as ordinary. He behaves cruelly with living creatures but showers special love on a stone idol. But his love is not steady in one single place. He makes my idol and installs it in one corner of the house and he himself goes on pilgrimage to places of other deities. He offers devotion towards his family deity and on auspicious occasions he worships other deities. After installing me in the house he makes vows to other deities. On the day of *Shraaddha* he belongs to the forefathers. He worships cobras on *Nagpanchami* day as much as he worships Me on *Ekadashi* day. On *Chaturthi* day he becomes a devotee of Ganapati and on *Chaturdashi* day he avers, "Oh Mother Durga, I am a devotee of only you." He leaves the daily rituals and incidental actions during *Navaratri* and sits for the reading of Navachandi and on Sunday gives an offering of Khichadi to the deity Bahiroba. Then on Monday he rushes to *Shivalinga* for offering *Bel* leaves and thus he somehow manages to perform the worship ritual of all deities. That devotee performs the worship ritual of all deities without taking rest for a moment just like a prostitute who demonstrates her love for all the people in the town. Such a devotee who rushes every now and then to different deities is ignorance reincarnated. (13:810-823).

Shri Krishna calls such a person an ignorant person. Now in contrast see what he has said in Ch 9.

"Therefore one must give up the love of the material body, consciousness about his qualities and pride about his possessions and surrender himself completely to Me. (9:381). Then, when the devotee offers Me a fruit from a tree with boundless love I anxiously spread My palms to receive it and eat it without even waiting to remove the stem. If he offers Me a flower, I should really smell it but overcome by his love I put it in My mouth and taste it. But why talk of flower? Even if he offers a leaf I do not bother to see whether it is fresh or dry and eat and savour it. And may be even that leaf is not available, but there is no dearth of water which is available free. But when that devotee offers that water with complete devotion, then even if it was free, I feel as if he has built immense temples for Me,..... *I only look at the devotion and accept the offering without differentiating between rich and poor, big and small.* Really speaking, fruit, flower, leaf etc. are only a means of manifesting the devotion and are useless unless offered with the feeling of devotion. Therefore I am telling you an easy way. Do not permit yourself to forget Me. (9:382-397)"

But unfortunately even those who read *Gita/Dnyaneshwari* regularly do not follow Shri Krishna's advice.

I later learnt from Yardi's book mentioned earlier that Shri Krishna had learnt this philosophy from his Guru Rishi Ghora Angirasa who was opposed to the priestly influence of the Vedic religion with its elaborate *Yajna* rites to propitiate gods and was bent towards the Vedanta philosophy of the Upanishads. *Pancharatra* philosophy which is based upon *Bhakti* was also coming into vogue in his times. All this has found its way into the *Gita*.

We have Chapter 6 that speaks about *Kundalini* power generally dormant at the base of one's spine, how it can be awakened through meditation and yogic posture, the consequent processes inside the body and the spiritual experiences that may be experienced by the practitioner. This is probably the first book that discusses this aspect in detail. This must have been based upon Dnyaneshwar Maharaj's own experiences since he belonged to Nath Panth where *Hathayoga* is practiced. The lineage in the Nath Panth starts from Adinath i.e. Lord Shiva. The genealogy of disciples in Nath Panth is Adinath – Macchindranath – Gorakshanath – Gahininath – Nivruttinath – Dnyananath (Dnyandeo or Dnyaneshwar Maharaj). Dnyaneshwar Maharaj humbly ascribes the credit of his work to all his above seniors with himself being merely instrumental.

Dnyaneshwar Maharaj was very devoted to his Guru, his own brother only two years older in age. This is how he elaborates on the importance of a Guru:

"Then, with great love in his heart he meditates on the form of his Guru. By installing that form in his pure heart he himself becomes the articles of worship or he installs his Guru like *Shivalinga* in the temple of bliss situated in the premises of Knowledge and bathes it with the nectar of meditation....... He offers his Guru the food of non-duality, and taking him to be *Shivalinga* serves as its priest. (13:385-390)........ the extreme love I have in my heart for my Guru compelled me to expand on this topic. I am praying him to accept it and give me an opportunity to serve him so that I shall be able to explain this book further in a better way." (13:453-460)

In *Gita/Dnyaneshwari* every spiritual seeker following any of the four paths is a *yogi* who need not be afraid that his efforts may go waste if he dies before achieving Self-Realization. Shri Krishna assures that:

"Had he practised yoga then he would have attained liberation before death. But because of lack of speed he had to stop in the middle. But liberation is reserved for him. He is reborn in a religious family and starts gaining spiritual wealth. People in such family observe morals, speak clearly and truthfully and behave as prescribed in the Scriptures. (6:441-445). Or he is reborn into the family of a *yogi* of high level..... Due to the mature intellect he knows all branches of knowledge easily. (6:451-454). His intellect develops further from the point of his death in the earlier lifetime and he is able to grasp mysterious subjects and even difficult things told by a Guru. (6:457, 459)...... Somehow, yoga practice also comes easily to him and he can attain the state of *Samadhi* effortlessly. (6:460-461). He attains *Siddhis* even while he is an acolyte."

We thus see that *Dnyaneshwari* does not ask you to worship God but to *offer your love and devotion* to Him and assures of a reciprocal love from Him. The deep humility and compassion of Dnyaneshwar Maharaj can be seen in **Pasayadan** or prayers for grant of grace (towards the end) in which he does not ask anything for himself but for the entire universe and especially those unfortunate people who have slipped into sinful ways.

Another notable peculiarity of *Dnyaneshwari* is that many religious texts promise wealth, progeny and other worldly benefits to the reader. *Dnyaneshwari* does not. It concerns itself only with Self-realisation for which instead of prescribing a sectarian path as many spiritual books do it offers four different paths from which an aspirant can choose depending on his own personal makeup.

I do feel a little guilty having deprived the reader of the poetry of the *Dnyaneshwari*, but probably the end justifies the means and an interested reader can always get a copy of the English Translation by M. R. Yardi published by Bharatiya Vidya Bhavan (which is also available on the Web now).

On the other hand the filtered text with *headings and sub-headings* as given in the present work is convenient to read and grasp quickly without distraction. It is in fact most suitable for readers from the intellectual and professional class (like scientists, engineers and managers mentioned earlier) who may not have much time at their disposal. As mentioned earlier, individuals of this category are in a position to lead people and shape the society to a better standard. The leadership qualities are a Divine manifestation which one can use for betterment of mankind. It is this class of persons that should read works like *Dnyaneshwari* and bring the principles of the Art of Living with ethics and respect to the members of society.

Many people think that following a spiritual path requires giving up family life and become a *sanyasi,* but this is a misunderstanding. Mere ochre clothes do not make one an aspirant or even religious. The spiritual desire has to be in the mind. Spiritual path is open to anybody so interested irrespective of one's religion, caste, creed, and gender or marital status. Many great saints were householders.

I was surprised to read in the book "Am I a Hindu" by E. Viswanathan, written for the America-born Hindu children of Indian origin, that many *Shaivaites*, especially in south India, feel that Shiva has been given a secondary position in the Bhagavad-Gita. They feel that in *Gita* the ultimate principle or Brahman is identified with Vishnu and not with Shiva and therefore they shun *Gita* thinking it to be a Vaishnavaite. Dnyaneshwar Maharaj has put following words in Krishna's mouth in the twelfth chapter: "Only a true Guru like Lord Shiva can explain this respect towards devotion, but praising Lord Shiva is like praising Myself. (12:207-217)." This shows the unity between Shiva and Shri Krishna. The *Anushasan Parva* of Mahabharata says that Shri Krishna during his lifetime himself worshipped Shiva and had propitiated Lord Shiva to obtain a boon of a son from Rukmini and again from another wife Jambavati. Thus the above attitude is uncalled for and narrow minded because all scriptures advise not to differentiate between Shiva and Vishnu. According to a story in *Skanda Purana* Shri Krishna was born as a result of a boon from Lord Shiva to a cowherd boy in the kingdom of Ujjain that Shri Krishna will be born to his mother in a later birth.

I thank my good friend Mr Dietrich Platthaus from Essen, Germany also a fellow physicist who gave critical suggestions during the translation. This work was ready in February 1999 and has been on the internet since February 2000. Currently it is available at the URL *vvshirvaikar@dj6qo.de* owned by Mr Platthaus. The German translation made by him has already been published in Switzerland.

I must acknowledge the full support given during this work by my wife Venu (whom we address by her maiden name Damayanti), herself a keen devotee of Shri Shankar Maharaj.

This translation after putting it on the internet led to many friendships with spiritually minded persons and many are still in contact. The questions they asked on various aspects made me think and learn. But the best contact has been that of Mrs Meera Seth who is a feature writer for the magazine *Businessworld*. She took the lead in the publication of this work as a book by approaching Mr. Yogesh Sharma of Zen Publishers for its publication which Mr. Sharma readily agreed and guided towards its publication. She also kindly offered to critically go through the text and suggest improvements. I gratefully thank her for finding time to do all this in spite of her busy schedule, as a service to Him. The improved language can be credited to her and the numerous informative and explanatory footnotes are also due to her critical queries and suggestions.

I also appreciate Mr Sharma's quick response and his positive encouragement for the task and thank him for the support. I am full of admiration for the editing and the get up he has given to the book.

I offer this work at the feet of my Guru Shri Shankar Maharaj because of whom this work started and whose blessings have made all this possible.

December 28, 2012   *Vassant V. Shirvaikar*
                                                                    Pune

The Translations

A Brief History

❧

This work of translating **Dnyaneshwari – The Philosophical Part** was taken up in 1990 and was completed in about 1999. In February 2000 after the Internet came into widespread use, a web version was put at the URL: *www.hinduweb.org/home/dharma_ and_philosophy/vshirvaikar/Dnyaneshwari*. The text was quite popular. Unfortunately the Website managers of Hinduweb stopped access to it after some time making it impossible to upload updates. The Web pages were transferred to the the Geocities platform offered by Yahoo! at URL: *http://www.geocities.com/vshirvaikar* until Yahoo! discontinued Geocities in 2009. The Webpages were then transferred to the present URL: *www.vvshirvaikar.de* at the domain owned by my good friend Mr. Dietrich Platthaus from Essen, Germany.

The German translation of the above made by Mr. Platthaus in 2000 which is also on the Web, has been published in book form by Ms Marion Musenbichler for Anamcara Verlag, Rotenboden 228B, FL-9497 Triesenberg in Lichenstein, Switzerland.

The original English translation is now being published by Mr. Yogesh Sharma, Publisher of Zen Publications, Mumbai.

Saint Dnyaneshwar
A Brief Biography

〜◆〜

Saint Dnyaneshwar was the second of the four children of Vithalpant and Rukminibai Kulkarni, a pious couple from the village Apegaon near Paithan (old Pratishthan) in Maharashtra on the banks of River Godavari. This story dates back to the 13th century.

Vithalpant studied *Vedas* and *Shastras* and became well versed in them at a very young age. Being extremely pious and detached towards worldly matters he spent much of his time on pilgrimage. During one of the pilgrimages he visited Alandi about 30 Km from Pune and camped in the local Hanuman temple. Sidhopant, a local Brahmin, was very much impressed with the youth and thought of him as a suitable match for his daughter Rukmini. He met Vithalpant and after making enquiries proposed the marriage. Not having any interest in setting up a family, Vithalpant declined but because of instructions received in a vision, he later consented.

After marriage Vithalpant remained at Alandi for some time but due to his lack of interest in family life his father-in-law took him to his parents in Apegaon where Vithalpant's father Govindpant and mother were happy to see their married son. Unfortunately both passed away shortly thereafter leaving the family responsibilities to Vithalpant who could not make two ends meet owing once again to his disinterest in worldly matters. Finally Sidhopant took the couple back to Alandi under his care. But that did not make any difference to Vithalpant who one fine day went for a bath to the river and instead of returning home, went to Varanasi.

In Varanasi, Vithalpant met a great saint Ramanandaswami. Suppressing the fact that he was a married person he requested Ramanandaswami to accept him as a disciple and to initiate him into the holy order of *sanyas*. Now, according to the rules, a married person cannot become a *sanyasi* unless his wife permits him. The ritual of adopting the *sanyas* requires undergoing the rituals performed for a dead person. All his past is thus erased and he is given a new name. Vithalpant was renamed as Chaitanyashram.

One-day Ramanandaswami set upon a pilgrimage to Rameshwar in the South. On the way halted at Alandi. While he was camping there Rukminibai who now spent her time in worship and other spiritual pre-occupations to drown her grief, went to meet Ramanandaswami who uttered the words of blessing to her, *"Putravati Bhava!"* or "May you have children". Rukminibai started laughing at these words and when asked to explain told the Swamiji the situation that her husband had deserted her. Swamiji probed her and realised that the description of her husband fitted his disciple Chaitanyashram.

According to the *shastras*[1] he too was to blame for having initiated Vithalpant. He immediately abandoned the pilgrimage and returned to Varanasi and accosted Chaitanyashram who confessed to his guilt. He ordered Chaitanyashram immediately to return to his wife and start a family.

Vithalpant returned to Alandi, but was excommunicated from

---

1 *Generally meaning texts on rules of religious and social behaviour as contained in various Smriti books like Manusmriti, Yajnyavalkyasmriti and Parasharsmriti. (Today the term is also used to mean subjects like science.)*

the Brahmin community because it was unheard of and against *shastras* to abandon *sanyas* and adopt family life again. Vithalpant managed to spend his time in the study of *Vedas* and *Shastras*. In the course of time four children were borne to the couple: Nivrutti in the year 1269, Dnyandeo (Dnyaneshwar) in 1271, Sopan in 1273 and the fourth a daughter Muktabai in 1275.[2] Everything was fine until Nivrutti was seven years old which is the time when a boy of Brahmin parentage has to be invested with the sacred thread and be inducted as a Brahmin. He approached the Brahmins of Alandi to be permitted to perform the thread ceremony but the conservative orthodox community refused.

In a state of extreme distress Vithalpant went to Triambakeshwar (near Nasik) with his family for performing worship at the Shiva temple. Triambakeshwar is one of the twelve Jyotirlingas or luminary lingas of Lord Shiva.

One night, while they had gone for performing *pradakshina*[3] (circumambulation) of the temple they encountered a ferocious tiger (in thirteenth century the area was a deep forest). The members of the family ran helter skelter and were dispersed. Nivrutti wandered into a cave in the Anjani Mountain where Gahininath, one of the nine famous Nath yogis was staying for some time. Gahininath was attracted towards Nivrutti and in spite of his young age initiated him into Nath sect. Gahininath assigned him the *mantra* 'Ramakrishna Hari' and instructed him to propagate devotion to Shri Krishna. That is how Nivrutti became Nivruttinath. The matter of excommunication did not affect this because the Nath sect does not bother about caste or religion and though socially it may be observed it is ignored in spiritual matters.

---

2 *Bhide gives the dates as Nivrutti 1273, Dnyaneshwar1275, Sopan 1277 and Muktabai 1279. Sacchidanandbaba who recorded Dnyneshwari as it was told to audience mentions that it was completed in 1290 making Dnyneshwar Maharaj only 15 years old which appears to be not quite right. The dates given in the text are based up on an Abhang of a contemporary female saint Janabai.*

3 *It is customary to circumambulate or go round a temple or idol in clockwise direction one or more times during a visit to a temple.*

All the four children were very intelligent and pious. They studied the *Vedas* and *Shastras* under their father but because they were excommunicated they could not join the Brahmin community or study in schools run by them. In desperation Vithalpant went to Apegaon and appealed to the Brahmins there who, after studying the *shastras* opined that death was the only atonement for the sin. In a hopeless state of mind Vithalpant and Rukminibai abandoned their children at Apegaon, travelled to Prayag and drowned themselves in the River Ganges.

The orphan children somehow grew up begging for dry alms from sympathetic people, which they would cook and eat. In the course of time they too approached the Brahmin community of Paithan to accept them as Brahmins after whatever purification rites necessary but the Brahmin community refused. However, considering the excellent behaviour of the children and their learning they permitted them to live in the community on the condition that they will observe celibacy and produce no progeny. This was in the year 1287 when Dnyandeo was sixteen years old.

About this time Nivruttinath initiated Dnyanadeo into the Nath sect and instructed him to write a commentary on the *Gita*. Thus we have a unique situation of an eighteen year-old Guru instructing his sixteen-year-old disciple to write something which was to become the hope of humanity.

The children moved to Nevase, a village in Nagar district on the banks of river Pravara. There Dnyandeo began his commentary on the *Gita*. He used to give a discourse on it to a group of seekers, some of them belonging to the Nath sect but many were followers of the path of devotion. A local devotee by name Sacchitanandababa wrote down whatever Dnyandeo said. A prominent person among the audience was the saint Namdeo known for the miracle where Vithoba the presiding deity of Pandharpur had eaten the food offering brought by Namdeo when he was a mere boy. Dnyandeo and Namdeo had met earlier at Pandharpur and developed mutual friendship.

There is a legend regarding the above mentioned Sacchitanandababa. On the day when Nivruttinath, Dnyandeo etc. entered Nevase, Sacchitanandababa had died. His wife Soudamini wanted to commit *Sati* and was accompanying his body to the cremation ground. Somebody suggested that a saint had come and she should get his blessings before going as *Sati*.[4] She found Dnyandeo sitting in meditation under a tree. She bowed to him and he blessed her with the words *"Akhand Saubhagyavati Bhava"* meaning, "May you never be a widow". When he came out of meditation he realised the odd situation but praying to God and Guru and using his powers he brought back Sacchitanandababa to life. The latter remained his devotee for life.

Dnyandeo started work on his commentary, which he called *Bhavarthadeepika* (pronounced: Bhaavaartha-deepika) in the year 1287. He finished it two and half years later, in 1290 when Dnyaneshwar Maharaj was 19 years old. By that time he had developed a great friendship with Saint Namdeo who was a devotee of Vitthal or Vithoba. He had also realised that the path of *yoga* on which the Nath sect lays a great stress could not be easily followed by everyone and the path of devotion was a key for all seekers irrespective of his or her caste, creed or gender. Perhaps he was influenced in this by Namdeo who was a tailor by profession and therefore by definition, belonged to the Shudra caste.

Shortly after the completion of *Bhavarthadeepika*, Dnyandeo joined the *varkari*[5] movement probably under the influence of Namdeo and virtually became their leader. The *varkari* sect is essentially a subset of the *bhakti* movement (hence called *varkari-panth*). They worship Vithoba or Vitthal which is a name derived

---

4 *Practice of wife immolating herself on the funeral pyre of her dead husband during cremation. This cruel system has been banned by the British.*

5 *The word Vaarkari means 'Pilgrim' (Vaari- going on pilgrimage, kari – one undertaking it). The Vaarkari movement as a practice was available during the time of Dnyanadeo, but it gained a lot more from his writings and teachings after his Samadhi, since he too was an ardent worshipper of Vithoba.*

from Vishnu. The main place of pilgrimage for the *varkaris* is the temple of Vithoba and Rakhumai (Rukmini) at Pandharpur in Maharashtra. The peculiarity of this deity at Pandharpur is that it wears a crown with *Shivalinga* on it, thus linking the Shaivaites and Vaishnavaites.

The *varkaris* follow a discipline wherein it is considered essential to visit the Vithoba temple at Pandharpur at least twice a year, on the two *Ekadashi* (11th day by lunar calendar) in *Ashadh* (which falls sometime in August) and *Kartik* (which falls sometime in November) months. They do the pilgrimage of foot all the way from their homes to Pandharpur.

Subsequent to the *Bhavarthadeepika,* Dnyandeo wrote *Amritanubhava,* again in verse form dealing with spiritual and devotional topics. As the name suggests, it is the experience of the nectar of devotion and presents his own Divine experiences unlike *Dnyaneshwari* which is a commentary on another book. Both *Dnyaneshwari* and *Amritanubhava* are holy texts for the *Varkari* sect today.

Dnyandeo then accompanied Namdeo and several others who followed the path of devotion (*bhakti* maarg) like Savata Mali, and began a pilgrimage of all the holy places of North, East and West India. Immediately after returning to Alandi (in 1296), Dnyandeo expressed his desire to leave his body by taking *samadhi.* He chose the thirteenth day of the dark fortnight of *Kartik* (sometime in November) for the final *samadhi.* People gathered and there was a final round of bhajans etc. Dnyandeo embraced his brothers and sister and close friends like Namdeo. With tears in their eyes, the people of Alandi watched him as he entered the cave and sat in the yogic posture. The cave was then sealed with a stone and Dnyandeo left his body by *yogic* process. He was only 21 years of age at this time.

Within a year and a half of this event Nivruttinath, Sopan and Muktabai also left the material world. Sopandeo took *samadhi* at Saswad near Pune. Nivruttinath travelled with his sister on a pilgrimage along Tapi River where both were caught one day in a thunderstorm. In the roar of thunder, rain and lightning, Muktabai vanished without trace. Soon after, Nivruttinath took *samadhi* at Triambakeshwar near Nasik.

Thus came about the end of an unusual family that enlightened the world spiritually and continues to do so even today. All the children were highly spiritually evolved. Muktabai, even as she was in her teens became Guru to a highly accomplished *yogi* named Changdeo who was believed to be several centuries old.

Thus ended the short lifetime careers of the four children, who seem to have been born for the specific task of bringing the Vedic philosophy and *Bhakti* movement to common man.

Muslim invasions of India began soon after this. This affected the religious and spiritual life of Hindus, drawing a spiritually golden era to an end. During this period, it became progressively difficult to venture upon *vari* and pilgrimages. But copies of Dnyaneshwari were preserved by many families and were read regularly. In the course of copying and probably due to the additions of their own words, (as is common to copying manuscripts) many copies with such errors entered the circulation. Three hundred years later, in 1584, Saint Eknath collected several available copies and after careful study, prepared a good copy (what we call 'critical edition' today) as free of corrupt text as possible. Even today, some copies bear small differences, typically different words (and hence the meaning) and also the number of *ovis*. But that is not a very serious matter except to a historian.

Mahabharata War
A Backdrop

Gita is supposedly the advice given by Shri Krishna to Arjuna on the first morning of the famous 18-day Bharata or Mahabharata war on Kurukshetra battleground. The causes of the family feud and the consequent war lie in the events which had occurred couple of generations earlier and expose the fickleness as well as the greatness of man. It goes to show how apparently normal events can have far-reaching consequences. Readers may please note that what follows has been written from a historical standpoint and not from mythological standpoint to which the pious are generally exposed.

THREE GENERATIONS EARLIER

The appropriate point to start this history would be the late 12th century BC when king Shantanu, 98th in the lineage of the lunar dynasty of the Aryan kings (according to the corrected dynasty lists compiled by P.L.Bhargava, See Ref (PB-VA) in Bibliography), ruled Hastinapur situated about 60 Km NW of New Delhi, on the banks of the Ganges. This was the end of Vedic period, Shantanu's brother Devapi who opted to become a *rishi* wrote the last of the hymns of Rigveda which is in the tenth Mandala. The roots of the Mahabharata war may be traced to King Shantanu's two marriages.

Shantanu's first marriage: Once, when Shantanu went hunting, he came across a beautiful woman and fell in love with her. She agreed to marry him on the condition that he would never question her actions. He agreed. In the following years, she gave birth to seven children every one of whom, as soon as it was born, she would take to the river and drown. Shantanu became sad but could not question her because of the mutual agreement. However, when the next child was born he secretly followed her and stopped her from drowning the child which was a boy. She revealed that she was the River Ganga personified and had to drown the first seven children because of a curse. The eighth child was to have survived and was to be handed over to Shantanu but now that he had broken his promise she would leave him taking the son with her. Ganga left with the son but returned him to Shantanu when he grew to be a youth well versed in all branches of knowledge and in martial arts. The boy was named Devavrata and grew to be a brave warrior and a wise person, well versed in the code of righteous behaviour (i.e. *Dharma*). It was expected that he would succeed Shantanu, but events took a different turn.

Shatanu's second marriage: Shantanu once came across a fisherman's daughter named Satyavati and fell in love with her. Her father agreed to give her in marriage to Shantanu on the condition that it would be her son who shall succeed him on the throne. Shantanu refused but was depressed in spirit. When Devavrata noticed this and found the reason he coaxed his father into the marriage. In order that his father be able to keep the promise regarding the succession to the throne, Devavarata himself denounced his right to the throne. Besides he took a vow that he would remain a celibate and would not get married so as to eliminate any chance of successors being born to him. This vow was so severe that Devavrata was called by people as Bhishma or severely frightening. Even today a serious vow is termed *Bhishma-pratidnya* or vow of Bhishma. Thus Shantanu married Satyavati. In return Shantanu gave a boon to Devavrata that he would die only when he wished it so. One may trace the root cause of the Mahabharata war to these events caused by Shantanu's lust.

Pandu and Dhritarashtra: Shantanu had two sons from Satyavati. The elder son died in a battle. The second son Vichitravirya was a weakling but Bhishma supported him having the welfare of Hastinapur at his heart. In order to get Vichitravirya married Bhishma invaded Kashi and won three daughters of the king of Kashi. One of them, Amba, prayed that she was already in love with another prince and was let go. Vichitravirya was thus married to the two remaining princesses Ambika and Ambalika. Vichitravirya however died without a son and heir to the throne. By the custom of those days it was permissible to breed a son through the brother of the husband and the heir would be considered as legal. This system was called *Niyoga,* meant not for pleasure but only towards the goal of procreation. There was no living brother to Vichitravirya but before her marriage to Shantanu, Satyavati had a son from the Rishi Parashara, grandson of the great Rishi Vashishtha (according to Bhargava *loc cit* this Parashara was not Vashishtha's grandson but a descendent of real Parashara.) This son was the famous great Rishi Vyasa who edited the Vedas, wrote Puranas and after the Mahabharata war composed the book *Jaya* which is the precursor to the epic Mahabharata. Satyavati, in consultation with Bhishma, called upon Vyasa to beget children for the two wives of the late Vichitravirya in order to have a successor to the throne. Unfortunately the elder son Dhritarashtra was born blind while the second son was anaemic and was therefore named Pandu. At the request of a slave of the palace, Vyasa also begot a son from her. This was Vidura who later turned out to be a great learned sage and played a significant role in the affairs of the kingdom.

PANDAVAS AND KAURAVAS

Because Dhritarashtra was blind, Bhishma who was the regent, made Pandu ascend the Hastinapur throne. Pandu had two wives,

Kunti, daughter of King Ugrasen of Yadava clan and Madri, the daughter of the king of Madra in Punjab. Kunti was thus the sister of Vasudeva, Shri Krishna's father. Pandu had three sons from Kunti and two from Madri. Kunti's sons were Yudhishtira (or *Dharmaraja*), Arjuna (or *Partha*) and Bhima. Madri's sons were named Nakul and Sahadeva.

Dhritarashtra was married to Gandhari the princess of Gandhar (now Kandahar in Afganistan). In deference to her husband's blindness Gandhari covered her eyes throughout her life by tying cloth over them. They had hundred sons known as the Kauravas and a daughter. The eldest son was Duryodhana who was very ambitious and cunning. His second son was Duhshasana who was also like his elder brother. These brothers hated the Pandavas because they were better in character and valour and were liked by all.

The Pandavas: Actually Pandu was not the real father of these sons. Legend goes that before her marriage, Kunti had served the great Rishi Durvasa who gave her a boon of a *mantra*, which she could use to invite any deity for getting a child. (Pandu was anaemic and unable to bear children so Mahabharata seems to have used this mythical legend as a good ruse to legalise Kunti's and Madri's children as Pandu's. But note that this system called Niyoga was socially and legally accepted in those days. Pandu and Dhritarashtra were themselves borne by Niyoga from Maharshi Vyasa and they or the Pandavas were never considered inferior in any way because of this. Also considering the qualities of the five sons there is no doubt that their real fathers were no ordinary persons.) Immediately after she received the boon from Rishi Durvasa, Kunti tried the *mantra* out of curiosity and invited the Sun God though she was still unmarried and a virgin. He came in person and gave a son to Kunti. Kunti was frightened and secretly put the baby in a basket and left him afloat in the river. He was found by a charioteer and was named Karna and was also known as Radheya after his foster mother Radha. When Karna grew up he joined the Kauravas and was very close to Duryodhana. Karna played a major role in the

Mahabharata war and led it after Bhishma retired from the war after getting seriously injured. Karna is considered as one of the greatest characters of the Epic Mahabharata, a legendary generous person thrown by fate into the Kaurava camp in spite of being the eldest of the Pandavas and never wavering in his allegiance to Duryodhana, even when the secret of his birth was revealed to him. He was as good as Arjuna in war and had to be killed by a trick arranged by Shri Krishna. Thus traditionally, one speaks of only five Pandavas. According to the above legend Yudhishtira the eldest of the Pandavas was born from Yama the god of death, Arjuna from Indra the king of the gods and Bhima from Vayu the wind god. After getting these three sons, on Pandu's instructions Kunti gave the *mantra* to Madri the other wife of Pandu. Madri invited the twin gods Ashwinikumars and hence she got twin sons Nakul and Sahadeva.

Pandu's death and Dhritarashtra's enthronement: Pandu died while he was in forest. Madri committed Sati by burning herself on the funeral pyre. Probably because Yudhishtira the eldest son of Pandu was too young, Bhishma now enthroned Dhritarashtra in spite of his being blind.

After Pandu's death Kunti returned to Hastinapur with her sons the Pandavas and stayed with their uncle Dhritarashtra where they studied along with the Kauravas the *Shastras* and the marshal arts, especially archery under the royal Guru Dronacharya.

Kauravas' enmity: The Kauravas always bore jealousy and animosity towards the Pandavas who were liked by all due to their excellent skills and personal qualities. Yudhisthira was known for his truthfulness and morals while Bhima was very strong even as a child and became an expert in wielding the club or mace. Arjuna was the best archer with unsurpassed skill with bow and arrow and was the most favourite student of Dronacharya. Duryodhana also was an expert with the mace. The Kauravas out of jealousy always tried to create trouble for the Pandavas and even made unsuccessful attempts to kill them by poisoning and by burning them. The feud between the Pandavas and the Kauravas grew as the boys reached adulthood.

Pandavas marry Draupadi: Kauravas, especially Duryodhana and Duhshasana once tried to poison Bhima but failed due to his strong constitution. Another time they plotted to burn all of them alive by inviting them to a house, which they had especially built with inflammable materials. The Pandavas escaped but to create a false impression that they had died and thus avoid further attempts on their life, they had to travel around incognito, posing as Brahmin mendicants, hiding from the Kauravas lest they would be murdered. During this incognito stage they reached the kingdom of Panchala where a competition was held by the king Drupada for choosing a bridegroom for his daughter Draupadi or Panchali (also known as Krishnaa since she was dark complexioned). The competition consisted of hitting the eye of a revolving fish with an arrow while taking aim through its reflection in water. While going around for alms the Pandavas reached the venue of the competition. The difficult test was won by Arjuna. The Pandavas returned to their home with the princess Draupadi. Their mother, not knowing that Arjuna had won a princess, instructed them to share the gains equally among the five brothers. As they could not go against her command all five of them married Draupadi. (There are other examples of polyandry mentioned in the Puranas. But note that there are tribes in the northern hill regions of India where polyandry is still practised. Since social customs are well merged with religion it is difficult to change such practices.) Draupadi's time was divided equally among the brothers and there does not seem to be any complaints. Shri Krishna was a cousin of Pandavas and always supported them. He was especially close to Arjuna. Draupadi considered Shri Krishna as her brother while Arjuna was married to Shri Krishna's sister Subhadra for which again Shri Krishna was responsible.

Pandavas get Indraprastha: When Pandavas became older they asked for their share of the kingdom. Dhritarashtra who was heavily under the influence of his sons and Duryodhana in particular, initially refused but finally had to give in and gave them a small piece of kingdom nearby. This was a forest land (Khandava forest) which Pandavas cleared and established the capital of Indraprastha which is also now part of New Delhi. People were very happy in their kingdom. But this made the Kauravas more jealous.

Pandavas lose kingdom in gambling: The Kauravas advised by their maternal uncle Shakuni, the king of Gandhara, hatched a plan by which Pandavas would lose their kingdom in a gambling bout since it was not possible to win against Pandavas in any normal battle. It was considered the duty of a Kshatriya not to refuse to a duel or a gambling game. Taking advantage of this custom, Duryodhana invited Yudhishtira for a gambling bout. Pandavas did not know that they were going to use loaded dice, Yudhishtira who was known for his righteousness and truthfulness lost all he had including the kingdom. Duryodhana then challenged him to continue to play by putting on bet the liberty of his brothers, which was also lost. Thus the brave Pandavas became slaves to the Kauravas. Now that the Pandavas were slaves the Kauravas unfortunately dragged Draupadi (who was under menstruation at that time) by hair into the court where the game was being played. Duhshasana even tried to undress and molest her. Unfortunately all this was happening under the eyes of Bhishma and the other elders who had to keep quiet for keeping the unity of the kingdom and to whom Duryodhana would not have listened anyway. The episodes created a big furore in the court and it was finally decided that Pandavas should be condoned from being slaves and instead they should be banished to forest for twelve years and after that for one more year they should remain incognito. If they were identified during the incognito period then they were again to go to forest for another twelve years. Pandavas had to accept this proposal and they left the kingdom with Draupadi for the forest.

Coming out of incognito period: Twelve years passed during which Kauravas tried to give a lot to trouble and humiliate the Pandavas but every time they failed. During the thirteenth year they went incognito to King Virat as servants under different guises. Draupadi also remained as a servant to the queen in the palace. Kauravas tried to discover their whereabouts but could not succeed. But towards the end of the incognito period, Kauravas raided Virat's kingdom to loot his cattle wealth when Arjuna, seeing that Virat's army would be defeated, took part in the battle and defeated the Kauravas. Thus, Arjuna was discovered. However that day was also the end of their one-year incognito period. Virat, happy with the victory and finding the mighty Pandavas on his side gave his daughter Uttara in marriage to Arjuna's son Abhimanyu cementing the friendship.

Pandavas, once they were out of the incognito period, immediately claimed their kingdom back. But things were not so simple. They had completed one lunar year (354 days) but Kauravas insisted they were meaning solar year (365 days). This dispute was not resolved and finally it was decided that only a full scale war would decide the question of inheritance. To give Kauravas a final chance Shri Krishna tried in vain to mediate but the Kauravas were blind with arrogance and power. They even tried to arrest Shri Krishna. War became inevitable. But this was not a sniper war of today. Both parties conferred regarding the date of the war as well as the rules. Among the rules was that the war was to start every day at sunrise and the warriors were to stop fighting at sunset. Thus the Mahabharata war is called a *Dharmayuddha* or a war fought according to the rules of *Dharma* or a code of conduct.

Decision of war: Both parties sent calls to their friends, relatives and supporters and people came from as far away as Afganistan in the northwest which had Aryan kingdoms as well as from the east and the south. The venue of the war was Kurukshetra not far from New Delhi. (You may find it on a map of India). Shri Krishna played an interesting role in the war. Both Duryodhana and Arjuna went to meet Shri Krishna for his assistance in the war. Both reached his palace early morning and waited for Shri Krishna to wake up.

Proudly, Duryodhana sat near his head while Arjuna sat humbly at his feet. When Shri Krishna woke up he first saw Arjuna and asked what he wanted. Thus the discussion started. Shri Krishna said that he himself would support one side and lend his army to the other. He also said that he would not handle any weapon during the war. Duryodhana opted for the army while Arjuna opted for Shri Krishna. Shri Krishna acted as Arjuna's charioteer during the war and saved him many times from death. He was an intelligent and shrewd strategist and it is mainly this shrewdness which made Pandavas win the war. Bhishma and Dronacharya fought on Kauravas side as their duty but their heart was with Arjuna and Yudhishtira. However they did not become lax in their duties. The tales of the war and how Shri Krishna's tricks saved Pandavas is interesting and legendary but that is a different topic.

Arjuna Feels Remorse

On the morning of the first day of the war, both armies were facing each other. Before the war was to start, Arjuna asked Shri Krishna, his charioteer to take the chariot to the centre between the armies in order to have a look at the warriors gathered there, because it was necessary to know with whom he was going to fight. Shri Krishna did so and indicated to Arjuna his elders like his great-granduncle Bhishma, his guru Dronacharya and other kings.

When Arjuna saw among both the armies his elders, brothers, cousins, uncles, friends and relatives and even grand-children (According to C. V. Vaidya, at the time of this war Arjuna was 65 years old, Shri Krishna 83, Dronacharya 85 and Bhishma was more than 100 years old; Shri Krishna's father Vasudeo was 140 years old. However according to Dr Pattnaik, Yudhishtira ascended the throne when he was 127 years old when Krishna was 125 years old and Arjuna 2.5 years younger than Yudhishtira. It appears that people lived long in those days). The reality of fighting his own kith and kin, especially his grand-uncle Bhishma and Guru Dronacharya faced him. He realised that genocide was going to occur for the sake of winning the kingdom. In a despondent mood, overcome with grief and compassion Arjuna said to Shri Krishna,

"By seeing all these friends and relatives gathered here for war, I am feeling un-nerved and my mouth has gone dry. I am feeling confused. I do not think we will gain by killing these friends and relatives. The persons for whose benefit we desire the kingdom are those who have come here to sacrifice their life and wealth. I can see that this war will destroy many family lineages and when I see the horror of this destruction, how can I ignore the sins of that destruction? Such destruction leads to the destruction of morals. I am wondering how we became ready to commit this sin in the first place!" So saying Arjuna kept down his bow and sat quietly.

This was a shock to Shri Krishna. He said to Arjuna, "How did these thoughts of compassion, unbecoming to an Aryan come into your mind in this time of crises? Shed this weakness and get ready for the war."

But Arjuna did not move. He said, "How can I strike persons like Bhishma and Dronacharya whom I should actually worship? The blood will be on my hands. I am really confused and am not able to think what is right and what is wrong. Consider me your disciple and advise me what is proper." And then Arjuna fell silent. Shri Krishna then gave him the advice on duties of a person towards himself, the society and God. This advice presented as a dialogue between Arjuna and Shri Krishna is the *Gita*. It convinced Arjuna that he has to fight the war more as his *dharma* (righteous conduct and duty) as a Kshatriya (warrior caste) rather than for the gains of the kingdom. Thus convinced, he picked up his bow and arrows and got up to fight the war.

Dhritarashtra, being blind could not participate in the war. Mahabharata (Sauti's addition) tells us that he requested Shri Krishna that he should be able to learn about the events of the war. Maharshi Vyasa granted Divine sight to Dhritarashtra's charioteer Sanjaya so that he could see the events of the war and describe them to Dhritarashtra. Thus Dhritarashtra and Sanjaya also knew the contents of *Gita* almost at the same time as Arjuna. But blinded by love for his sons it had no effect on Dhritarashtra. What he was interested in was only whether his sons were winning or not.

EPILOGUE TO THE MAHABHARATA WAR

The war lasted for eighteen days. Only survivors were the Pandavas, Duryodhana, Dronacharya's son Ashwathama, Kripacharya, Kritavarma, Shri Krishna and a few others. Duryodhana went into hiding but was discovered and killed by Bhima in a mace fight.

Kauravas and their allies were thus completely decimated. It was one of the greatest genocide in history were young strong blood vanished. All Pandava's sons died so there was no heir to the hard won kingdom. Ashwathama as a revenge on behalf of the Kauravas tried to kill the foetus of Abhimanyu's child (Arjuna's grand child) but Shri Krishna by his yogic powers made it survive. Thus Pandavas had an heir after all. His name was Parikshit. Bhishma who had a boon of dying by his own will waited in injured condition until Uttarayana, the northward travel of the sun started. (Currently it starts on December 21. Yudhishtira became the king and reigned for 36 years.

Just towards the end of his reign, there were bad omens occurring in Dwaraka. One day men of Yadava clans Vrishni and Andhaka arranged for a picnic at Prabhas Patan where excellent food and liquor was arranged. Uddhava, the great devotee of Shri Krishna did not like it and left on a pilgrimage. Except Shri Krishna, all Yadava men including Balarama became drunk and started fighting among each other. Shri Krishna, though he did not drink, also took part in the free for all fight in which the survivors were except Shri Krishna, his father Vasudeva, brother Balarama and two more Yadavas Babhru and Daruka. Even Krishna's sons died. Balarama had quietly left the scene earlier. Leaving Vasudeva (father) to look after the grieving ladies Shri Krishna left the place with the two Yadavas out of whom Babhru died on the way. Shri Krishna and Daruka wandered in the forest in search of Balarama who was found sitting under a tree. He had already left his body by yogic powers. Asking Daruka to fetch Arjuna from Hastinapur to take care of Yadava women, Krishna wandered into the forest (near Somnath in Gujarat state, Western part of India), and sat under a tree sad and depressed at the tragedy. While sitting under the tree he was shot by an arrow in the leg by a hunter who mistakenly thought he was shooting a deer. Thus Shri Krishna died after an illustrious career at the age of about 118 years according to Vaidya and 161 according to Dr Pattnaik. He was cremated at Prabhas on the bank of the river Patan nearby. There is small temple depicting Shri Krishna sitting under a tree and the hunter bowing before him at a place about 10 Km from Somnath temple in Gujarat.

When the news of Shri Krishna's death came the Pandavas felt like orphans. When Arjuna arrived in Dwaraka to take care of the Yadava women as per the message from Shri Krishna, father Vasudeva handed him over the grieving women and left his own body. Arjuna was given the task of escorting the widows of the Yadavas to Hastinapur. After Arjuna left Dwaraka with the women Dwaraka was swallowed by sea. While Arjuna was escorting them the Abhir tribes on the way in Punjab-Rajasthan region attacked him and took the women away. Arjuna had no power left as he was now old. He returned to Hastinapur shamefaced and very soon all the brothers went to the forest for passing their last days as was the custom in those days. Parikshit succeeded the throne.

Hindu tradition believes that Kaliyuga began with the death of Shri Krishna. Mahabharata war is therefore a chronological landmark for historians. The orthodox Hindu tradition puts the start of the Kaliyuga at 3101BC said to be based on a single unsubstantiated statement of the famous astronomer-mathematician-philosopher Aryabhatta, however historians put it much earlier, some at 1400 BCE and some at 1100 BCE based on Dynasty data.

Prelude To *Bhagvad-Gita*

War between Pandavas and Kauravas became inevitable when Duryodhana refused to return to the Pandavas their kingdom which they had lost to Kauravas in a rigged gambling game. Krishna's failed efforts of reconciliation put a final seal on the inevitability of war. Kings came to Hastinapur with their armies in support of their favourite side. While Krishna let Duryodhana have his army, he himself chose to stay with Arjuna as his charioteer vowing that he himself would not wield any weapon in the war. Bhishma the grand- uncle and Dronacharya the marshal arts teacher of both Pandavas and Kauravas fought on Kaurava side out of their sense of duty but their heart was with the Pandavas, especially Arjuna and Yudhishtira. Both sides agreed on the date and the rules of war for, this was to be a *Dharmayuddha* or a war fought according to the rules of *Dharma* (the righteous code of conduct). Maharshi Vyasa gave Sanjaya, a counsellor to Dhritarashtra, the power of Divine sight by which he could see the events of the war and describe it to the blind king.

The huge armies of both the Pandavas and Kauravas marched to Kurukshetra at sunrise facing east and west respectively, all eager to fight. On Shri Krishna's advice Arjuna prayed and obtained grace and support from goddess Durga.

On Arjuna's request Shri Krishna placed his chariot between the two armies, in order to have a look at the warriors gathered there. Observing the Kaurava army, and among them his own grand-uncle Bhishmacharya and Guru Dronacharya, Arjuna now faced the reality of fighting his own kith and kin. He realized that genocide was inevitable for the sake of winning the kingdom. In a despondent mood, overcome with grief and compassion Arjuna kept down his weapons and refused to fight. He told a shocked Shri Krishna that he was confused and requested to be considered his disciple and advised about what is proper." And then Arjuna fell silent.

Krishna then gave an advice to Arjuna about one's righteous duties, impermanence of life and how to be happy by becoming one with God and adopting an attitude of equability. This advice is now famous as *Bhagvad-Gita*. Now on to *Bhavarthadeepika* or *Dnyaneshwari*, the commentary on the advice that is *Gita* written by Saint Dnyaneshwar:

Notes For The Readers

1. *In the original Gita/Dnyaneshwari both Shri Krishna and Arjuna are mentioned by various names e.g. Krishna as Vaasudeva, Madhava etc., and Arjuna as Partha, Kaunteya etc., but for convenience we shall refer to them throughout in this translation only as 'Shri Krishna' and 'Arjuna'.*

2. *Author's comments and explanatory notes have been given as numbered footnotes. The sources of information on which these are based are given in the Bibliography at the end of the book. Inside the headline text these sources are indicated by letters in a bracket e.g. with corresponding reference against the listed source. E.g. (SR-B) indicates the source: "Bhagvadgita" by Dr S. Radhakrishnan; similarly (HW-LL) indicates the book "Life before Life" by Dr. Helen Wambak.*

3. *The numbers inside the brackets within and at the end of each paragraph are the chapter number and the ovi numbers. E.g. (1:115-120). means ovis 115-120 in Chapter 1.*

4. *Gita Shloka corresponding to each set of ovis may found from the tables in the* **APPENDIX - GITA SHLOKAS CORRESPONDING TO DNYANESHWARI OVIS**

1
Arjuna's Despondency

~∞~

OBEISANCE

Obeisance to the Supreme Soul who is in the form of *AUM* and whom only the Vedas can describe. My obeisance to you who are the Self and can only be experienced.[1] Oh God, you are Ganesha, who enables everybody's intellect to understand everything. Thus says this disciple of Shri Nivruttinath.[2] (1:1-2).

(Dnyaneshwar Maharaj in *ovis* (1:3-84)describes in beautiful poetic style the form of Ganesha, the God of Knowledge and remover of all obstacles comparing each part of the body to some branch of knowledge. He then offers obeisance to Sharada,[3] the Goddess of learning and then praises his Guru, Nivruttinath, ascribing to him the credit for initiating the work and providing strength, enthusiasm and sense of devotion for fulfilling this immense task. He then extols the qualities of the *Gita*, which even great Rishis read respectfully and enjoy.

---

1 *That is Self or Atman or Soul cannot be seen or sensed by any of the senses. It can only be experienced.*
2 *See the Biography of Dnyaneshwar Maharaj elsewhere in this book.*
3 *Also known as Saraswati the goddess of learning.*

From *ovi* (1:85) onwards is described the situation on the battlefield of Kurukshetra on the opening day of the war between the Kauravas and the Pandavas. Dhritarashtra, father of the Kauravas, being blind had requested Maharshi Vyasa to enable him to get the news about the war sitting at home. Maharshi Vyasa then empowered Dhritarashtra's charioteer, Sanjaya with Divine vision that would enable him to see the events on the battlefield and describe them to the blind king.)

Overcome by the love for his sons, Dhritarashtra asks Sanjaya to describe the situation on the battlefield of Kurukshetra where his sons and the Pandavas have gone to fight each other. (1:85-87)

Sanjaya replied, "There is a furious stir in the Pandava army like the waters at the time of the Great Flood. It is arranged in many strategic formations and looks terrifying. (1:88, 91).

But Duryodhana looked at it with scorn and approaching Dronacharya, his teacher, he remarked, "Look at the various strategic formations of the Pandava army. It is Drishtadyumna, son of Drupada whom you taught and made an expert in the military arts, who has arranged these formations. (1:92-95). There are other warriors also in their army with strength and capability comparable to those of Bhima and Arjuna. They include the great warrior Yuyudhan, Virat and the great chariot-warrior Drupada. Also come for the war, are Chekitan, Dhrishtaketu, Kashiraj, Uttamouja and the great king Shaibya. Abhimanyu the son of Subhadra looks like a younger image of Arjuna. Other sons of Draupadi as well as many other warriors have also come." (1:99-102).

Now I shall mention the names of the warriors fighting on our side too. Here is our Grand-uncle Bhishma with a capability as bright as sun. This brave Karna is like a lion. Then we also have the powerful stalwarts like Kripacharya, Vikarna, Ashwathama, Samitinjaya, Soumadatti and innumerable other warriors. (1:103-108, 109). Besides, Grand-uncle Bhishma has been appointed the chief of our army. His strength imparts this army the appearance of a fort. Who can face this army? On the other hand the Pandava army is very small, yet it appears huge to me. On top of it, that colossus Bhima has become the chief of their army." (1:115-120).

After talking thus to Dronacharya, Duryodhana addressed the rest of the army and calling upon them to arrange themselves in proper formations, for their own protection and the protection of their great chariot-borne warriors, enjoined them to obey Bhishma. He also asked Dronacharya to protect Bhishma and give him as much respect as they gave him, since the strength of the entire army depended on Bhishma. (1:121-125). Hearing this, Bhishma was pleased and gave a battle cry and blew his conch, which frightened both the armies. (1:130).

Now listen to the happenings in the Pandava army. (1:137). Shri Krishna whose love for his devotees is paramount, is acting as Arjuna's charioteer out of love for him. Shri Krishna blew his Panchjanya conch which silenced the war cries of the Kaurava army. This was followed by the terrible sounds from Arjuna's conch and the conches of the other Pandavas. Other warriors like Drupad, Kashiraj, Arjuna's sons, Satyaki, Dhrishtadyumna, Shikhandi, Virat etc., also blew their conches, the sounds from which shook the earth. (1:142-143, 146-153). The disoriented Kaurava army was brought under control by their leaders who began to shower arrows on the Pandava army. (1:164-166).

Feeling satisfied, Arjuna eagerly glanced at the army and when he saw the Kauravas ready for war he slowly picked up his bow. Then he asked Shri Krishna to take his chariot and place it in the middle of the two armies so that he could observe the great warriors who have come there to fight. He said, "I must know with whom I must fight. These Kauravas generally are of evil nature and though they are eager for war they lack courage." (1:167-173). Thus reporting Arjuna's speech to Dhritarashtra, Sanjaya further described,

ARJUNA'S DESPONDENCY

"Oh King, Shri Krishna brought the chariot in between the two armies where Bhishma, Dronacharya and other kings were waiting. Observing them, Arjuna said, "Shri Krishna, look. These are all our own family members and teachers." Hearing this, Shri Krishna was startled and thought, "What is this that has entered Arjuna's mind?" But he kept quiet. (1:174-179). Arjuna saw his teachers, grand-uncle, relatives and friends, sons and grandsons too. Arjuna was shaken. Compassion arose in his mind and his warrior nature left him. (1:180-182). He said to Shri Krishna, "I see only our friends and relatives here. They have come here for war but will it be proper for us also to do the same? I am confused and my bow has fallen from my hands. (1:194-198). If we have to kill the Kauravas then why should we not kill my own brothers too? Both belong to our family. (1:207). It will be improper to fight this war. (1:209). I am not interested in winning the war. What is the use of enjoying the pleasures after killing these people? (1:210-211). I shall be burdened with the sin of killing my family members. (1:228)." Thus raving, Arjuna said that he was not going to touch any weapon in this war because he found it to be improper. (1:233). The body, for the pleasures of which one wished for the kingdom (of Hastinapur), was itself short-lived, he said. When we know this why should we not loathe it? (1:263). Overcome with grief, Arjuna jumped from the chariot and threw his bow and arrows on the ground. Tears started flowing uncontrollably from his eyes. (1:268, 272).

Dnyaneshwar Maharaj says, "Listen in the next chapter how Shri Krishna advises a grief stricken Arjuna on the meaning of spiritual goal." (1:274).

2

The Path of Knowledge

∾⊗∾

Dnyaneshwar Maharaj now goes on to explain the cause of Arjuna's sorrow:

Shri Krishna Consoles Arjuna

Shri Krishna said, "Arjuna, first think whether this kind of talk and behaviour on the battlefield becomes you. Realise who you are and what you are doing. (2:6). What has come over you? What is it you are feeling sorry about? It is not like you to bother about irrelevant matters and to give up courage. (2:7-8). You who are famous for unqualified bravery are crying! (2:11). Do not let your mind be overcome by weakness. Gather your courage and come to your senses. Leave this foolishness, get up and take your bow and arrow. What use is compassion on the battlefield? You are an intelligent person. Then why don't you realise that compassion during a battle is of no use? It will only harm your name in this world and make you lose the rewards of the world beyond.[1] (2:17-20). This kind of compassion is of no use during the time of war. Is it only now that you have realised that Kauravas are your relatives? Did you not know that earlier? Is this dispute a new thing in your

---

1 *It was the belief in those days that a Kashtriya warrior dying on the battlefield attains heaven.*

life? It has been a usual affair between you and the Kauravas. (2:23-25). Due to this delusion you will lose the standing you have gained so far and not only will you lose everything in this world but in the next as well. A true warrior should keep away from the weakness of heart, because for a Kshatriya it is his downfall." (2:27-28).

Arjuna however repeated his pleas saying that he could not be so ungrateful as to fight with and kill his own teacher (i.e. Dronacharya) to whom he owed all his battle skills and who was like a father to him and therefore fit to be worshipped. Finally, when he realised that Shri Krishna was not listening to his pleas, he said he felt confused and prayed to Shri Krishna for proper advice consistent with *Dharma*[2] (code of righteous conduct) adding that Shri Krishna was like his teacher, brother, parents, family deity and saviour. (2:30-68).

BIRTH DEATH CYCLES ARE NATURAL

Shri Krishna then said, "Arjuna, I am really surprised at what you are doing. You call yourself knowledgeable but you do not let go of your ignorance. And when I try to teach you something you lecture on ethics.[3] (2:91-92).

"Tell me, is this universe sustained only because of you? If that is so, then what people say about the universe that it has been in existence from time immemorial must be false. Is what everybody says about the creation that 'All creatures are created by the one and only God,' all wrong? Has the situation now become such that what is born is created by you and what has died has been killed by you? And that the Kauravas will be destroyed only if you wish it so? Or that they will remain immortal if you decide not to kill them because of your ego? Perhaps there is delusion in your mind

---

2 Dharma *though in today's popular understanding means religion, really means the code of conduct in our daily life and in society. It is also sometimes used to mean one's natural tendency.*
3 *What is presented here from Ovis (2:91-229) is the Vedanta philosophy from the Upanishads.*

that people die because you are the one who causes death? Arjuna, birth and death are things established from time immemorial and are natural occurrences, then why should you feel sorry for them for no reason? (2:94-100). Arjuna, persons of discrimination know that both birth and death are delusions and do not lament either of them. (2:102). The feeling that "this is born" or "that has died" is created because of *Maya*,[4] otherwise the basic underlying principle, which is Brahman, is indestructible. Wind causes ripples on water, which then takes a wavy shape, and when wind dies, water becomes flat, then what was created and what got destroyed? (2:105-107).

Consider the obvious example of the body. Changes occur with age in the same body. First there is childhood in the body. It goes and youth comes; but when one state goes and the other comes the body itself is not destroyed. In the same way changes occur in an individual life, the difference in this case being that one body goes and is replaced by another, but the Consciousness (soul) does not get destroyed. He who understands this does not suffer grief due to the delusion of life and death. (2:108-110).

SENSE PLEASURES ARE CAUSE OF DELUSION

The reason why people do not realise this is that man is a slave to the senses. His mind, being caught in sensual pleasures, leads to the delusive feelings of happiness and sorrow. Enjoyment of sense pleasures leads to feelings of happiness and sorrow and the sense objects take control of the mind. There is nothing steady about sense objects. Sometimes they give pleasure and sometimes pain. For example, praise gives pleasure while criticism causes unpleasantness; hard objects are unpleasant, soft objects give pleasure, etc. (2:111-114). This leads to the ignorance about the true nature of the Self in this life. (2:118).

---

4 *Maya is the power of God through which He creates and sustains the universe according to Vedanta philosophy. Since according to Vedanta the universe is an illusion, the term Maya is also used sometimes for illusion.*

People get trapped by the sense organs (eyes, ears, tongue, nose and skin) and when they experience the feelings like hot and cold etc., they develop likes and dislikes and then get subjected to the feelings of pleasure and pain. Nature of the sense organs is such that it makes them feel there is nothing better than sensual pleasures of the body and mind. And these sense objects (which cater to the sense organs) are impermanent like a mirage. Therefore you should dissociate yourself from them. (2:119-122).

Pleasure and pain do not touch a person who is not influenced by these sense objects, nor has he to go through rebirth. Keep in mind that he who is not trapped by the sense objects is totally indestructible. (2:123-124).

ULTIMATE PRINCIPLE - THE BRAHMAN

Arjuna, I am going to tell you about one more thing which sensible people realise. In this world, which is pervaded by *Maya*, there is a mysterious principle about which all philosophers agree. (2:125-126). When a man of Knowledge[5] ponders over what is universe etc., matters related to the material world get eliminated and what remains for him to think about is only that principle which is the Self (or Soul).[6] Having come to a definite conclusion about what is truth and what is untruth, he is oblivious to an impermanent thing like the body. Careful thinking leads to a conclusion that whatever is impermanent and delusive is inconsequential and what is permanent is fundamental. He who created this universe is devoid of attributes like colour or form. He is all-pervading and beyond birth and death. He cannot be destroyed even if you want to. On the other hand, bodies are naturally perishable; therefore it is proper that you, Arjuna, should fight. It is not you who is their destroyer and they also are not destructible only by you. If you think

5 In this book spiritual knowledge (of the Brahman or Self) is spelled with capital K.
6 Atman in Sanskrit, Atma in Marathi

otherwise then that is because of your ignorance. (2:131-138).

Things seen during a dream appear real while the dream lasts but once we wake up we realise that they were not real. You too are only experiencing a similar illusion due to the effect of *Maya*. (2:139-140).

SOUL IS IMMORTAL

Even if the body dies, the Soul *(Atman)* does not die. Therefore do not extend your impression about the death of the body to the Soul. (2:141). Just as a person discards his old clothes and wears new ones, similarly the Soul, the master of the Consciousness discards one body and occupies another.

This Soul is without birth, is permanent, eternal, pure and without form. It cannot be cut by weapons, cannot get drowned even in floodwaters, fire cannot burn it and wind cannot suck it. This constant and eternal Soul totally pervades everything. It cannot be understood by reasoning but can be experienced only through meditation. This infinite supreme entity is inaccessible to the mind and is unobtainable through implements or techniques. It is unbounded and superior to all living and nonliving things. It is without the three attributes,[7] timeless, beyond shape and form and all encompassing. Arjuna, if you are able to realise this Soul that exists inside all then all your sorrows will disappear. (2:144-151).

And even if you were to consider the Soul to be destructible there is no reason for you to feel sorry, because like the flow of the Ganges, the cycle of creation, existence and dissolution continues perpetually. (2:152-153). These three states, are ever applicable to all living beings. Your sorrow in this context is therefore improper because this natural cycle has been going on since time immemorial.

---

7 *Attributes or gunas : Attribute or guna means a qualification. All worldly objects, entities or actions are supposed to have three attributes in different proportions. The attributes are: Sattva, the attribute of purity, goodness, knowledge etc.; Rajas, the attribute of movement, desire, passion etc.; and Tamas, the attribute of lethargy, darkness, ignorance etc. Attributes are discussed in detail in Chapters 14, 16 and 18.*

(2:155-156). Birth and death are inevitable. (2:158).

WHAT IS BORN DIES AND IS REBORN

Sant Dnyaneshwar continues....

Whatever is born perishes and is later born again. This wheel of life and death has been going on perpetually from time immemorial like the cycle of sunrise and sunset. At the time of the big deluge these three worlds also get destroyed. Therefore beginning and end are inevitable. (2:159-161).

Prior to birth creatures have no form. They acquire it after birth. When they die they certainly will not reach another state but only return to original state of the previous formlessness. The form you see between the birth and the death is the projection (an *illusive* image) of Brahman due to the influence of *Maya*. (2:164-166). All creatures acquire a form due to the effect of *Maya*, therefore why should you shed tears over something which does not exist in the first place? Instead, you should think about the eternal Soul *(Atman).* (2:168-169).

Those who develop a love for this Soul *(Atman)* are not influenced by sense-objects. They become detached and dispassionate and live a hermit's life. With the Soul or Self as their goal they observe constraints like celibacy and penance. (2:170-171). Many have attained a state of steadiness of mind and by concentrating on that pure Self, have lost all thoughts about the material world. Many have developed such detachment and become constantly engrossed with It (i.e. the Self) while singing its praises. Some have left their "I am the body" feeling while some have become one with It (Self). Just as the river flow merging into the ocean does not revert, similarly superior yogis, once their intellect merges with the Soul become one with It and they are not reborn. (2:172-176). This all-pervading Brahman exists within everybody. It cannot be destroyed even if you want to. It is the cause of birth and death of every creature, then why should you feel sorry? (2:177-178).

DHARMA- THE RIGHTEOUS CODE OF CONDUCT

Have you forgotten your *Dharma* (the code of righteous conduct or duty) which guides one through one's life? (2:180). *Swadharma* (i.e. your own *Dharma* or *Dharma* applicable to oneself) is never to be given up whatever may happen to the Kauravas or to you. If you forsake your own *Dharma* (i.e. that of a Kshatriya or warrior) and show compassion, will that compassion save you? This fountain of kindness is inappropriate during a war. (2:182-183). *Self-interest is harmed if one does wrong things at the wrong time.* Therefore come to your senses in time and attend to your *Swadharma.*[8] Behaving as prescribed by *Swadharma* never leads to any blemish. (2:185-186). All desires get fulfilled if you follow *Swadharma*. For you Kshatriyas (warrior caste) there is nothing more proper than fighting. (2:188-189). Such opportunities of war come to Kshatriyas as a result of a lot of merit. (2:194). If you avoid this war and grieve over wrong things then it is as good as self-destruction. (2:196). If you forsake *Swadharma* then you will be burdened with sin and the blemish of failure will not be erased for ages. (2:201).

And how are you going to leave this battlefield? Your enemies will not understand that you are giving up the enmity out of a clean and kind heart. They will surround you and shower you with arrows and then your kindness will be of no help to you in escaping. Even if you do escape and survive, living that life will be worse than death. (2:202-205).

8 *Swadharma means (Swa= self) one's own Dharma or the code of (righteous) conduct that is applicable to you depending upon your social or institutional status. In Vedic times there were no castes but after the fair skinned Aryans merged with the darker skinned non-Aryans the term Varna (colour) was introduced to differentiate between them. Brahmins (priestly duties), Kshatriya (warriors) and Vaishya (traders, farmers and other professions) Varnas were Aryans while the dark Varna non-Aryans were assigned menial duties and were called Shudras. While in Vedic times people of the three (upper) Varnas could change their professions, slowly the Varna which began to be called caste came to be determined by parental caste. Shastras defined duties for each caste (See 18:818-900). Swadharma therefore means here personal and social duties of one's Varna and not that of one's religion e.g. Arjuna was a Kshatriya and his duties were to fight to protect people.*

You have gained exceptional fame (2:211) and these Kauravas are afraid of you. (2:215). That fear [they have towards you] will not remain if you retreat. (2:217). And even if you want to run away they will not let you. They will catch you and put you to ridicule. Instead of hearing all that slander and feel broken-hearted, why should you not defeat them by fighting bravely and then enjoy the throne? And even if you were to die fighting then you will naturally attain the kingdom of heaven (which is due reward to those warriors who die fighting). Therefore do not waste your time in thinking, pick up your bow and arrow and be ready for war. (2:218-221)

Practice of *Swadharma* removes all past blemishes. Why should you then have an apprehension that you are going to commit sin? (2:222). It would be a sin only if you act with the desire of fruits in mind even if the act itself was as prescribed according to *Swadharma*. If you fight as a *Kshatriya* with a desireless attitude towards the fruits then there is no sin involved. (2:224-225)

Equanimity towards Happiness and Sorrow: One should not feel ecstasy by happiness nor feel aggrieved by sorrow. Neither should one think about gains and losses. One should not keep thinking in advance about whether one would win or die in this war. One should quietly accept whatever comes to his lot while acting according to *Swadharma*. Actions performed with this attitude do not lead to any blemish, therefore Arjuna go and fight with determination. (2:226-229)

YOGA OF INTELLECT (BUDDHIYOGA)

What I have told you so far is the Yoga of Knowledge of the *Sankhya* philosophy. Now I shall tell you about the Yoga of intellect (of *Karmayogis*).[9] (2:230). By following this yoga of intellect you do not miss the worldly pleasures and at the same time you are also assured of liberation. As mentioned earlier in connection with *Swadharma*, one should perform one's duties but without bothering about the fruits of his actions. He who is endowed with this attitude

---

9 *Karmayogi is a person who does his duties as part of his Dharma.*

of performing his duties without the desire of the fruits thereof becomes immediately free of all encumbrances (that lead to birth and death). (2:233-235).

An intellect which is not touched by the thoughts of sin or merit (i.e. desireless intellect, because it is the desire that leads to worry/anxiety about sin and merit), which is extremely subtle and steady and not stained by the three attributes *Sattva*, *Rajas* and *Tamas*, destroys the fear of the material world if it (that intellect) illuminates the mind even slightly, by virtue of the merits of earlier births. (2:236-237)

Righteous and base intellects: Even if this righteous intellect were to be present only slightly, it should not be considered as unimportant. This righteous intellect, which leads one towards God, is very rare. (2:238-239). This unique, righteous intellect, in the world, has no other goal than attainment of God.[10] All other types of intellect are corrupted intellects that are affected by passions and in which persons without discrimination get enraptured.

Therefore Arjuna, such persons without discrimination may attain heaven, earth or hell but never the bliss of the Self (2:241-244).

These persons establish the greatness of Vedic rituals quoting the Vedas in support, but perform them with the desire of fruits in mind. They say that one should be born on this earth, perform the rituals like *yajna* and then enjoy the consequent pleasures of heaven. (2:245-246). They perform all the rituals rigorously as prescribed but they do one unfortunate thing. By keeping the pleasures in heaven as their goal they forget the very God in whose name they conduct the rituals. (2:249-250). Like cooking excellent food and then selling it for money, they sell the *Dharma* for the benefit of pleasure. Therefore I say that people who spend their time in debating on the meaning of the Vedas shelter a corrupted intellect. (2:254-255).

Attributes of the Veda constituents: Vedas (which comprise of

10 *"Attainment of God" means Self-Realization.*

13

Samhitas, Brahmanas, Aranyakas and Upanishads.) are definitely associated with the three attributes Sattva, Rajas and Tamas. Upanishads and other philosophical works should be considered as having the Sattva attribute.[11] The rest, which discuss rituals and other exercises for attainment of heaven, have the Rajas and the Tamas attributes (gunas). These gunas are the cause of pleasure and sorrow and you should not harbour them in your mind. Discard these three attributes, do not speak of "I" and "mine" and keep the bliss of the Self-realisation firmly in your mind. (2:256-259).

Though Vedas tell many things and suggest many rituals, you should choose only that which is beneficial for you.

After deep thinking I came to the conclusion that it is proper for you to avoid evil deeds and perform actions as prescribed in the Shastras[12] but without the desire for fruits thereof. Do your duty as per your own Dharma with a desireless attitude. (2:260-266). But when you are fortunate enough to have achieved success, do not get exhilarated by it nor feel sorry if for some reason you are not successful. Whatever work that was undertaken, if it reaches completion then it is fine but if it does not, then also it is all right. (2:268-269). Whatever work one does, when it is performed as an offering to God, then it automatically becomes complete. (2:271). A balanced attitude of mind towards both successful and unsuccessful actions is hailed as the best state of Yoga. Equanimity of mind, where mind and intellect work together, is the essence of yoga. (2:272-273).

---

11 *Attributes of Vedas etc. Vedic Samhitas involve rites (for yajnas) therefore they are assigned Rajas. If the rites are for evil purposes then they would be assigned Tamas. But Upanishads lead to the (pure) Brahman hence is assigned Sattva. Attributes are discussed in detail in Chapters 14, 16 and 18. (See also earlier footnote on attributes).*

12 *Shastra or Dharmashastra denotes rules particularly those related to righteous behaviour as given in texts like Manusmriti, Parasharsmriti etc. written by various rishis to guide people. Now-a-days the term is used to mean a scientific discipline as in rasayanshastra = chemistry but that is not applicable here.*

PATH OF ACTION OR *KARMAYOGA*

The path of action appears to be of lower status in comparison with the *yoga* of *intellect*. But one achieves success in the yoga of intellect only through actions when performed with a desireless attitude, because negation of the actions (by doing them without desire of fruits thereof) leads naturally to the state of yoga.[13] Therefore Arjuna, steady your mind with the help of this yoga of intellect, giving up the desire for fruits of your actions. Those who followed this yoga of intellect transcended this material world and were liberated from the entanglement into sin and merit. Such people, even though they do perform their duties, they reject the fruits thereof and therefore are liberated from the birth and death cycles and reach the eternal state of bliss. Arjuna, you will become like that when you give up your delusion and your mind becomes dispassionate. Then the very pure mystical Knowledge will rise within you. In this state, the thoughts of gaining more knowledge or remembering whatever was learnt in the past do not arise. Then, the intellect which was wandering due to the influence of sense-organs will easily become steady in the Supreme Soul. When the intellect becomes steady, you will reach a state of *Samadhi*, the steady quiet bliss and only then you will attain the state of yoga. (2:274-284).

STABLE INSIGHT AND STABLE INTELLECT

Arjuna then asked, "Shri Krishna, who should be called a person of *stable insight (Sthitapradnya)* and how one may recognise him. Also, what are the characteristics of a person who may be called a person of *stable intellect (Sthirabuddhi)*? And how to recognise a person who perpetually enjoys the state of *Samadhi*? In what state does he remain and what does he look like? (2:287-289).

Shri Krishna replied, "The strong desire for sense pleasures

---

13 *Here it means oneness with God or Brahman.*

carried in the mind is what comes in the way of the bliss of the Self. He who is always contented and whose desire for sense pleasures (which is the cause of the downfall of persons), has left him for good and who is always immersed in the bliss of the Self should be considered as a *person of stable insight (Sthitapradnya)*. (2:291-293).

Desire and anger vanish naturally from the mind of a person who remains unperturbed even when faced with all types of distress and who is not led astray by the lure of pleasure. Having reached a state of perfection he is totally free of fear. Freed of these restraints he has reached oneness with the Brahman. Such a person should be considered as a person of stable intellect. (2:294-296).

Such a person always behaves with impartial attitude towards all. This nature of his having constant equanimity and compassion towards all creatures never changes. He is never enthralled by happiness from good things nor disheartened by sorrow from the bad. He who remains absorbed in the Supreme Self, being bereft of feelings of happiness and sorrow, should be considered as a *person of stable insight (Sthitapradnya)*. And he, who is in complete control of his sense organs, should be considered as *a person of stable intellect*. (2:299-300).

CONTROLLING SENSE ORGANS

And Arjuna, I shall tell you an interesting thing. Seekers practice restraint and give up sense-pleasures; but they too can get entangled in various types of sense-pleasures if while restraining the ears, eyes etc., they fail to restrain the tongue. (2:303-304). One can restrain oneself from all sense-pleasures except that of the tongue. One cannot forcibly restrain the pleasure of the tongue because our life depends on food. But when a seeker attains Self-realisation, the tongue naturally gets controlled and since the "I am the body" feeling has left him he forgets all sense-pleasures. (2:307-309).

These organs cannot be brought under control by any other

means.[14] Because even those who constantly try to conquer them and keep their minds under control by observing strict rules and restrictions, are harassed by them. Such is the power of these organs! Even in the case of yogis, the sense objects appear in the form of *Riddhi-Siddhis* (Occult powers) gained by them and rule their minds through the organs. If a *yogi* is caught in their clutches then he deviates from his study of yoga, such is the strength of the organs. (2:311-314).

Therefore Arjuna, he who leaves all desire for pleasures, controls his organs and is not allured by the sense-pleasures is alone worthy of the trust set by yoga i.e., steadiness of intellect. Such a person has the knowledge of the Self and never forgets Me.[15] (2:315-317).

On the other hand, he who outwardly gives up sense-objects but keeps on thinking about them must be considered as entangled in the materialistic world. (2:318). A slightest trace of desires remaining in the mind destroys discretion. (2:320). Mere memory of these sense-pleasures creates desire for them in the mind of even a detached person. Passions then arise in the mind and where there is passion there is also anger. Anger leads to thoughtlessness. Thoughtlessness leads to loss of memory and then the intellect is engulfed by the darkness of ignorance. The intellect then suffers and loses direction. Thus, the loss of memory leads to confused intellect and this in turn destroys all knowledge. In this way, even occasional memory of the sense-pleasures can lead to such downfall. Therefore, when these sense-pleasures are totally removed from the mind, anger and hatred are automatically destroyed. When anger and hatred are destroyed then even if the organs become engaged in the sense-pleasures they do no harm. (2:321-332). Such a person is detached towards sense-objects, free of desire and anger and remains engrossed in the bliss of the Self. (2:334). He who thus remains absorbed in the Self may be considered without doubt to

---

14 *It is implied that external means like rituals, fasts etc., though they may help discipline the mind, cannot be of any use in controlling the five senses. Only internal means like meditation is useful for the purpose.*
15 *Shri Krishna now presents himself as Bhagwan or God.*

have a stable intellect.

Be Cheerful: Worldly sorrows do not enter a cheerful mind. (2:338). How can a person feel unhappy when his heart is cheerful? The mind of such a person remains naturally focused on God. Like a flame in a windless air, that person with stable intellect achieves the yogic state and becomes united with Brahman. (2:339-341).

A person, in whose mind the thoughts of this yoga do not take root, gets entangled in the trap of sense objects. The intellect of such person is never stable nor does he desire it to be stable. If there is no feeling of stability in the mind then how can he achieve peace? Just as a sinner cannot attain liberation, similarly where there is no love for peace there is no happiness either, even by chance. (2:342-345). Therefore instability of mind is the cause for sorrow and therefore it is best to control the sense organs. (2:347).

Persons who submit to the demands of the sense organs do not really transcend the material world, though outwardly it may appear to be so. (2:348). Even a person who has attained Self-realisation, is trapped in the sorrowful consequences of the material world if he pampers the sense organs. Therefore what better achievement is there than conquering the sense organs? (2:350-351). He whose sense organs obey his commands may be considered has having a stable insight. Now listen to another characteristic of such a person who has reached perfection. (2:353-354).

YOGI (THE MAN OF PERFECTION) IS ALWAYS AWAKE

When all creatures are in a state of sleep regarding Brahman he is ever awake to it and he shuts his eyes at the (material) things for which everybody else struggles.[16] Such a person should be recognised as a great sage free of attachments. (2:355-356). He is not bothered about whether or not he has achieved the *riddhi-siddhis*

---

16 *A common man is not aware about Brahman being in him and does not bother about it but a yogi is always aware of it.*

(occult powers). (2:360). Satiated with Self-realisation, he remains in the state of bliss of the Self and goes about in the world in that state, bereft of ego and all desires.

Recognise him truly as a person with stable insight. (2:366-367). This is what is called the extreme state of Brahman experienced by the dispassionate people who effortlessly become one with It. Once they become one with Brahman then there is no question of their mind suffering and becoming an impediment in the way of reaching the state of the Brahman at the time of physical death. (2:368-369).

3
Path Of Action

~~∞~~

*D*nyaneshwar Maharaj now continues the commentary on this *Chapter 3 giving guidance on how and with what kind of attitude one's duties should be performed.*

ARJUNA IS CONFUSED

At this stage Arjuna asked Shri Krishna, if he was against action, then why was he asking Arjuna to fight. (3:3)

JNANAYOGA AND KARMAYOGA - BOTH HAVE COMMON GOAL

Shri Krishna said, "While I was telling you about the *Buddhiyoga,* naturally I also told you about *Sankhya* philosophy. But it is I who has expounded both from time immemorial. Through the practice of *Jnyanayoga* (the Yoga of Knowledge) of the *Sankhyas* a seeker attains Self-realisation and becomes one with Me immediately. *Karmayoga* (Yoga of Action) is a slow-speed path in which a seeker diligently practices actions according to *Swadharma* and attains liberation at an appropriate time. A

Jnanayogi (i.e. follower of *Jnanayoga)* is like a bird who can fly to and eat directly the fruit (of Self-Realization) on a tree while an ordinary human being *(Karmayogi i.e. a follower of Karmayoga)* is like a man who has to laboriously climb the tree, branch after branch, to get at it. Both paths, though outwardly different, lead to the same result. But which path to follow depends upon the capability of the seeker.[1] (3:33-44)

IMPORTANCE OF ACTION

Abandoning action is not non-action: If instead of doing the prescribed actions[2] first, one says that "I am abandoning actions like a *Siddha*",[3] then that will not at all constitute non-action for him. Because it is foolish to think that non-action is the same thing as not doing the duties that have fallen to one's lot. (3:45- 46). As long as one is in his body and has desires, actions cannot be abandoned; certain natural duties (like earning livelihood, preparation of food, eating, having progeny etc.) have perforce to be performed. But the actions become non-actions when one is ceaselessly content.[4] Therefore one who wants to achieve non-action should never give up the prescribed actions. (3:47-50)

It is *Maya*, which controls the material universe. (See the note regarding *Maya* at 2:105 -107). Therefore, to say that 'I shall do this and not do that' is ignorance. Even if one stops doing one's duties, the organs have to continue with their own natural duties. (3:53-54). Then what is it that one is giving up? (3:58) Therefore, a person under the control of nature or *Maya* cannot give up action. (3:63)

---

1 *Here Shri Krishna discusses only two paths: path of Knowledge and path of Action. There are two more paths, Path of Yoga discussed in Ch 6 and Path of Devotion which are mentioned in chapter 7.*

2 *Prescribed actions are those prescribed by Swadharma.*

3 *P Siddha is a Yogi who has attained Siddhis (Occult powers) by which he can perform miraculous tasks like levitation, passing through solid material like walls, thought reading etc.*

4 *Satisfaction leads to desirelessness which leads non-actions..*

Some may try to attain the state of non-action by giving up prescribed duties and by controlling the tendencies of their senses. But as long as thoughts about actions continue to occupy their minds they cannot be said to have achieved non-action even though outwardly they may hypocritically pretend to have abandoned actions. Such persons, without doubt, must be considered to be engrossed in sense-objects. (3:64-66).

A Desireless Person

In this context, listen to the characteristics of a desireless person. (3:67). Such a person though outwardly he may behave like others, is internally steady, always absorbed in the meditation on the Supreme Self. Since he is in control of his sense organs he is not afraid of sense-objects and nor does he avoid his duties. While he lets his action-organs do their task he is not affected by the resultant feelings. He is not influenced by delusion or by lust. Since outwardly he behaves like others, one cannot know his inner state. Such a person may be considered as liberated. Such a liberated person should be specifically called a yogi. Therefore Arjuna, be such a *yogi* and let your mind be quiet and free, and let the action organs do their duties. (3:68-76)

Performing Prescribed Duties Is A Ceaseless *Yajna*

One cannot abandon worldly duties. Then why should one indulge in doing prohibited actions? Actions performed with desireless attitude lead to liberation. Actions performed by a person according to his caste as per the directions laid down for the four-caste system lead to his liberation. (3:77-78)

Performance of the duties as laid down by *Swadharma* is equivalent to performing a ceaseless *Yajna* and does not allow sins to enter the mind. One who leaves *Swadharma* and prefers improper actions gets bound to the worldly birth and death cycles. (3:81-82)

Brahmadeo's Advice

Shri Krishna then told Arjuna the following old legend:

When Brahmadeo[5] created this world, he created at the same time both humans and the code of behaviour or actions (*Dharma*) for them. But the code was subtle and men could not understand it. So they asked Brahmadeo, "On what basis do we exist here?" (3:86-87)

Act as per the code: Brahmadeo replied, "I have already set the code of actions depending upon your *varna*. Let your actions be guided by it and your wishes will be fulfilled with ease. You need not trouble your body by performing *Vratas* (observance of austerities like fast, sometimes with rituals) and penances. You need not go far away for pilgrimage. You need not observe yoga and similar techniques, penance with desire or *mantra* and *tantra* techniques. Do not worship other gods. Perform the natural *yajna* of doing actions as per the proper code of righteous conduct for you *(Swadharma)* and the actions will become successful. If you worship gods by performing actions as per the code (of *Swadharma*) then the deities will be pleased and give you the desired objects and will sustain you. You will enjoy the good things of life and be happy." (3:88-95)

When you worship the gods by doing actions as prescribed by *Swadharma*, the deities will be pleased with you and there will develop a mutual love between both of you. (3:96-97).[6]

---

5 *The term Brahmadeo is used instead of Brahmaa (the god) to avoid confusion with the term Brahman which is also sometimes called Brahma.*

6 *What is meant in short is that performing actions as per the code (Swadharma) is a yajna that amounts to worship of God. By so doing you please the appropriate gods who in turn undoubtedly will look after your welfare and bless you with your needs.*

Violators of code shall be punished: And Brahmadeo also warned that, "But if any person, after thus gaining wealth becomes lusty and influenced by the tendencies of the sense objects behaves arrogantly and does not use the wealth to worship God through performance of his duties, does not give offerings to Fire and donate food, does not show devotion to the Guru, does not welcome guests and satisfy [i.e. look after] his community, and by thus neglecting duties remains infatuated with wealth and gains, will face many calamities, lose his wealth and will not be able to enjoy it. (3:103-108). He who forsakes his duty loses his liberty. Fate punishes him considering him to be a thief[7] and snatches everything from him. (3:111-112). Even if he asks for mercy he is not set free up to the end of time. (3:115). Therefore one should always be alert and follow one's duty with commitment." (3:118)

Utilisation of Wealth: Brahmadeo further said, "He who, with desireless mind spends his wealth for the duties prescribed by *Swadharma*, worships his Guru, well-wishers and Fire, and after performing *Shraaddha*[8] of forefathers and other yajna rituals through the hands of Brahmins, partakes of the remaining food along with his family, gets his sins washed and becomes free of all blemishes. (3:119-123). Therefore wealth earned by actions according to *Swadharma* should be spent according to *Swadharma* and whatever remains should be enjoyed with satisfaction. (3:124-125)."

Food a form of Brahman: Shri Krishna continued, "But those sinners who, by considering themselves to be only the body and not the soul, do not see the sense-objects as anything other than means of enjoyment and who instead of considering the earned wealth as the material for *yajna*, use it selfishly for their own pleasures, (for example) prepare tasty food and consume it themselves, actually consume sin. (3:125-129).

All wealth is a means of *yajna* in the form of *Swadharma*-based

---

7 *Not ploughing back the rewards into the world/society is considered theft.*
8 *Shraaddha is the ritual worship and offering of food to dead parents and forefathers.*

actions and should thus be offered to God. Instead, these fools prepare various types of food only for themselves. The food fulfilling a *yajna* is no ordinary thing. It is actually a form of Brahman because life of all creatures depends upon it. (3:130-133).

Creatures grow by food, food grows by rain, rain falls because of *yajna* and *yajna* is performed by actions which are prescribed in the Vedas which themselves have originated from the indestructible Brahman.[9] Therefore the Brahman pervades all the living and non-living objects. Thus, the basis of the *yajna* performed by actions is the immortal Vedas. Thus, Vedas permanently reside in the prescribed actions. Thus I have told you in short the background of the *yajna* as part of *Swadharma*. (3:134-138).

Therefore, a proud arrogant person who does not behave properly as per *Swadharma* and instead by evil deeds spends time in physical pleasures is a sinner and burden to this earth. His life and works being fruitless are wasted. (3:139-141).

Duties accompany the body at birth. Duties naturally come with the body i.e. as soon as a person is born, therefore why should one avoid proper actions? Those who avoid the duties even after attaining the human body are ignorant. (3:141-144).

But the actions do not bind one who is always engrossed in the Self even while going about doing his duty because he is satiated with the knowledge of the Self and with that he has finished the duties of this lifetime. Therefore he does not get loaded by his actions. (3:146-147).

Just as the means of satisfaction become irrelevant when one becomes satisfied, the desireless actions according to *Swadharma* are relevant only until one attains the knowledge of the Self. (3:148-149)

Therefore Arjuna, you should control your organs, leave selfish desires, and follow what is prescribed by *Swadharma*. Those who

---

9 *In the ancient Vedic times people performed yajnas to propitiate gods who then caused rain. Yajnas are performed using Vedic Samhitas hence rain, yajna, Vedas which are believed to have originated from Brahman are all interlinked and related.*

follow *Swadharma* with desireless attitude attain Brahman in this world. (3:150-151).

ACTIONS AS AN EXAMPLE TO OTHERS

There is another advantage gained by performing prescribed actions. When we do our duties, others note and follow and thereby they are saved from pitfalls. Particularly those who have attained Self-realisation and reached a perfectly desireless state should perform duties for the guidance of others even after Self-realisation. (3:153-155). If a man of knowledge does not teach others by his actions then how will the ignorant understand and take to good path? It is natural for ordinary people to emulate the actions of the big, thinking them to be the prescribed actions. Therefore one should not abandon one's duties. Especially the saints and similar persons must perform their duties. (3:157-159).

Even God has to set example by actions: Why talk of others? Even I follow this path of actions. I do so not because I am in difficulty or desire anything. You are aware that there is nobody in this world who has reached more perfection than I have. (3:160-162). I carry out prescribed duties in such a way that people get the impression that I do them out of some desire. But I do the duties only because all creatures are dependent on Me and they should not behave wantonly. (3:164-165).

If I were to remain engrossed in the Self after reaching perfection, how would people cope up with life? If people emulate Me in that condition, the entire world will stop functioning. Therefore, a person, particularly a capable person who has attained knowledge should not abandon actions. (3:166-168). A desireless person must attend to actions with the same readiness as one with desire but without posing as somebody special. I am telling this to you repeatedly because it is essential that society be protected in every way and one should never show that he is different from the others. (3:169-171)

Jnanayoga Not To Be Told To The Unfit

Never sing even by mistake, praises of the path of non-action to a person who is fit only for path of action. Such a person should be told the importance of proper actions and guided towards performance of good actions by setting him an example by one's own behaviour. If one performs actions for protecting the society, such actions do not bind him against liberation. In this way even persons of knowledge perform good deeds with desireless and dispassionate attitude for serving people. (3:173-176)

One should not also tell about this profound spiritual path to an ignorant person who, ignoring the fact that all actions are caused by *Maya,* thinks, because of the ego and narrow thinking, that he is the doer. (3:178-179).

Maya, the creator of all actions is absent in a person who has realised Self. Such persons give up I-am-the-body ego, understand the unique relation between the attributes and actions and remain in the body with uninvolved attitude. Therefore even by remaining in the body, the actions do not touch them. (3:181-183). A person who is under the influence of the attributes and acts under the control of *Maya* is alone affected by actions. Because though organs behave according to their own nature with the help of the attributes, he claims the credit for their actions. (3:184-185).

Therefore Arjuna, you perform all the prescribed actions and make their offering to Me but concentrate your attention on the Self. Do not harbour an ego like "This is the action, I am its doer and I am going to do it." Do not go after this body, shed all desires and enjoy or endure whatever comes to your lot. (3:186-188). Those who respectfully accept this firm opinion of mine and behave according to it with faith will be free from the bondage of their actions. (3:192-193).

A wise person should never pamper the organs. (3:202). When the body is controlled by other factors, why should one accumulate the fruits of actions for its sake? (3:205). Ordinarily, the mind experiences pleasure when the organs are provided with the sense-objects. But just as the company of a robber is safe for a short time, only up to the village boundary, the lust residing in the organs leads them to depravity. (3:210-211, 213). The desire for sense-pleasures causes anger and destroys the intellect. Desire and anger are both extremely dangerous; therefore shed their company. Do not let the nectar of experience of the Self be spoilt by even the thought of desire and anger. (3:215-218).

IMPORTANCE OF DHARMA

Dnyaneshwar Maharaj continues: It is advantageous to practice one's own *Dharma*, however difficult, rather than that of others even if the latter may appear attractive. (3:219-220). Would one demolish one's own thatched hut by comparing it to the white mansions of others? (3:223). Similarly, even if one's *Dharma* is painful and difficult to practice, it is that which makes his afterlife happy. (3:225). Therefore for one's own benefit, one should not do actions which may befit others but not to himself. Even if one has to sacrifice one's life for the sake of practising *Swadharma* it is better because it will establish one's greatness in both the worlds. (3: 228-229).

ARJUNA'S QUESTION

At this point Arjuna asked, "Who is responsible for making even persons of Knowledge distort their thinking and go astray?" He also asked other questions broadly in the same vein. (3:232-238)

DESIRE AND ANGER OBSTRUCT LIBERATION

Shri Krishna replied, "Desire and anger dwelling in a person's mind are the two merciless culprits who are responsible for it. They keep people away from Knowledge and devotion. (3:240-241). They rule the whole world by means of delusion etc. They are generated from the *Rajas* attribute in the mind and are the root of the demoniacal endowment. They thrive on ignorance of the mind and are the source of the demoniacal actions. Though desire and anger arise from the *Rajas* attribute, they are favourites of the *Tamas* attribute, which is the main constituent of indiscrimination and delusion. (3:243-244). They operate through hope and delusion. (3:246-247). Desire and anger are closely connected with ego and temptation. Because of them, falsehood and hypocrisy have prevailed over truth and by destroying peace and through the importance given to *Maya*, minds of even saints have been polluted. (3:249-251). They destroy the sense of discrimination, of dispassion and control over senses. They destroy happiness by destroying Knowledge and instil the three forms of torture (personal, external and elemental) in the hearts and minds of people. They are attached to the physical body after birth and reside in the mind and therefore cannot be discovered even by Brahmadeo. They destroy the personality of even a person of Knowledge and nobody can control them. (3:253-256). Pure Knowledge is never completely dissociated from desire and anger and is veiled by them just as a snake entwines a sandalwood root. (3:262). Therefore one should first conquer them in order that Knowledge unfolds and can be achieved. It is however very difficult to do so because the more one tries the more it helps desire and anger to strengthen their hold and because of this even *Hathayogis* are defeated. There is only one method of bringing them under control. (3:264-267)

LOSING DESIRE AND ANGER LEAD TO SELF-REALIZATION

Explaining the importance of ridding oneself of desire and anger as proposed by Krishna, Dnyaneshwar Maharaj says:

Their original residence is in the sense organs from where impetus for action originates. Therefore it is necessary to exercise control on the sense-organs which will restrict your mind from the pleasure-seeking tendency. This will free your intellect and thus they will lose their support. (3:268-269). Once a person gets rid of his anger and desire, he will realise Brahman and enjoy the in whose bliss he will enjoy uninterrupted bliss of Knowledge. This is the secret between a Guru and his disciple and it is also the union of the Self and the Brahman in which he remains perpetually stable. (3:271-272

4

Yoga Of Knowledge

Dnyaneshwar Maharaj continues:

KARMAYOGA IS ANCIENT

Shri Krishna says, "I had taught this Yoga *(Karmayoga)* earlier to Vivaswat[1] (the Sun-deity) But that was long ago. He then told it to Vaivaswat Manu.[2] Manu acted according to it and taught it to

---

1 *Vivaswat: According to the Puranas Rishi Kashyapa married thirteen daughters of Daksha Prajapati, among them Aditi. Vivaswat or Vivaswan is one of the twelve sons of Aditi hence known as Adityas. They are worshipped as deities. Among other Adityas are: Indra, Varuna and Vishnu. Vivaswan is also one of the names of the Sun. It is customary (though confusing) in Puranas to identify a person with a stellar body like a planet or a star when both have the same name.*

2 *Vaivaswat Manu: Vaivaswat was the son of Vivaswan. He was a Manu or leader of mankind and is therefore known as Vaivaswat Manu. Some historians credit him for saving mankind (meaning Aryan tribes) from floods from their habitat in the Hindukush mountains and settle them on the banks of rivers Indus and Saraswati (now dessicated). Vaivaswat Manu's time is put by historians at about 3100 BCE though according to Purana chronology his time is about 1.65 billion years (Note: Man evolved only about 50,000 years ago.) (PB-VA)*

Ikshwaku.[3] In this tradition many royal Yogis came to know it but there does not seem to be anyone who knows about it at present. This is because people, having become more attracted towards carnal pleasures, forgot about the Knowledge of the Self. Having gone astray in their beliefs they came to think that carnal pleasures are the highest kind of happiness. (4:16-21). How will the ignoramus who have not ever experienced an iota of dispassion and who do not understand what discrimination is, attain me? I do not know how this delusion grew, but a lot of time was lost with the result that this yoga was forgotten on this earth. Arjuna, what I explained to you was that yoga. This yoga is like a life-secret, but how can I conceal it from you? (4:25-28).

ARJUNA'S DOUBT

At this, Arjuna raised a doubt by asking Shri Krishna, "You are living today and Vivaswat lived in ancient times. Then how could you have told him this Yoga?" (4:32-40).

SHRI KRISHNA REMEMBERS ALL *AVATARS*

Shri Krishna replied, "It is natural for you to think you did not exist at the time Viwaswat was existing. What you do not know is that both you and I have gone through many births. You have no memory of them but I remember all My incarnations. (4:41-43)

---

3 *Ikshwaku was the eldest son of Vaivaswat Manu. He is the founder of the lineage of Aryan kings known as the Solar dynasty (Suryavansha) because this lineage is supposed to originate in Vivaswan which is also a name of the Sun. Great kings Ambarish, Bhagirath, Raghu and Shri Rama belong to this lineage. (Vaivaswat Manu's daughter Ila married a Rishi named Budha who was son of Soma the son of Rishi Atri. Ila's son was Aila or Pururava the founder of another lineage of Aryan kings known as the Lunar Dynasty (Soma- or Chandravansha) because Soma is also a name of the moon. Great kings like Janhu, Bharata, Pandavas, Kauravas and Shri Krishna belong to this lineage.*

"I TAKE BIRTH TO PROTECT THE GOOD IN EVERY ERA"

Though not tainted by birth (i.e. subject to birth-death cycles), I do take birth and assume form by means of *Maya*,[4] but this does not affect My remaining untainted by destruction, form and attributes. (4:44-46). I take birth to protect My devotees and destroy ignorance whenever wickedness defeats righteousness because it is the tradition from early times that I should protect the *Dharma* (righteousness) appropriate to the particular age *(Yuga)*,.[5] (4:49-50). Then I eliminate the wickedness and erase the stains of the sins and by bringing together the *Dharma* and ethics, remove the lack of discrimination. The whole world then fills with happiness; *Dharma* reigns in the world and devotees are full of *Sattva* attribute. Whenever I take birth, sins vanish and merit rises. I take birth for these tasks in every *Yuga*.[6] Only persons of knowledge know this

4 *Maya is the power of Brahman and inseparable from through which It creates. In Sankhya philosophy the corresponding entity is called Praktiti and in Shaiva philosophy it is called Shakti.(See Ch 7, 8 and 13 for discussions on these.)*

5 *Yuga is a period of time. According to Puranas there are four yugas: Krita (or Satya), Treta, Dwapar and Kali (with supposedly decreasing moral standards). These are respectively 4, 3, 2 and 1 times 1200 Divine years where one Divine year = 360 Divine days and one Divine day = one solar year. This increases the length of the yugas 360 times leading to unrealistic time scales. Shri Yukteshwar, Guru of Swami Paramhansa Yogananda, however has proposed a different system which uses 1200 solar years as the length of the shortest yuga. According to him, the most recent ascending Kali Yuga began in 499 AD and we are presently in the ascending Dwapara Yuga since 1599 AD, with consequent advances in human culture and knowledge. According to Shri Yukteshwar, the error was made in the Puranas and this occurred during the dark years of Kali Yuga when scholars misinterpreted the scriptures. Thus, by Shri Yukteshwar's hypothesis, we are right now not in Kaliyuga at all but in Dwapara Yuga. However, here we shall use only the traditional definition of a yuga. (SY-HS) Bibliography.*

6 *Some readers may ask about why there was no avatar when the world was tortured by Hitler and the World War II or when innocent people were tortured in Russia and China under the communist rules. But the explanation may be found in paragraph (10:308-312). This promise has to be taken not literally but to mean that such crisis always brings forth a leader or leaders with superior qualities who restores the order. "Actually the splendour of the*

secret of mine. (4:51-57)

He who understands that I am not attached to anything, that I take birth though I am birthless and perform actions though I am actionless, is liberated. Though he may be in his body yet he is not bound by it. He comes to Me when his body dies. (4:58-59).

GRACING DEVOTEES ACCORDING TO PERCEPTION

Those of My devotees who do not bother about the past or the future are not affected by anger and desire. They become one with Me and spend their life only for serving me. Those who are immersed in the knowledge of the Self by becoming unattached become one with Me and then there is no difference between them and Me. (4: 60-63)

I grace people according to the manner in which they express their devotion to Me. It is the natural tendency of man to do My *upasana* (worship). But through ignorance or due to delusion, most people think of Me in many different forms though I am one and the only God. *I am without name but they assign different names to the different forms which they consider as deities. I am all pervading but they qualify My forms as superior or inferior.* (4:66-70). They worship these deities with desire in their minds. People do gain fruits from such worship, but actually those are fruits of their actions, there being nothing other than actions that can give fruits. (4:71-73). I am the witness to the worship of all these deities but each worshipper gets the fruits according to his attitude. (4:76)

---

universe is within him. The signs by which one can recognise such a person are that the whole world bows to him and obeys him. Persons with these signs are my Avatars. Thus we see that the world leaders who put an end to the tyrannies should be considered as a kind of partial Divine manifestation if not a full avatar.

Four Castes

Though all persons are alike, I have divided them into four types according to their qualities and actions. Thus the four castes have been created. The actions prescribed for each caste have been determined taking into account the combination of their natural tendencies and qualities. Therefore even though the four castes have originated from me, I am not their creator[7] and one who understands this is liberated from the ties of the actions. (4:77-81).

The past seekers who understood this performed their actions with desireless attitude which led to their liberation. (4:82-83).

Thoughts Of Actions Involve

Even wise persons are puzzled about the significance of action and non-action. Therefore it should not be interpreted as per one's likes or dislikes but thoughtfully. (4:84-85). The actions of even spiritually very powerful persons have turned out to be driven by desires because of wrong notion of non-action. (4:87). I shall now explain this to you. (4: 88)

Action is that which naturally leads to the formation of the universe and its meaning should be understood first. One should also understand the appropriate action for each caste and the fruits thereof. One must also understand the nature of the prohibited actions so that one does not get involved in them. This world is

---

7 *Many people wonder how God could create castes and thus differentiate among his own children. Natural tendencies and qualities, though they govern the nature of a person's actions are not created by God. But in a community the nature of these actions is used to define duties and classify them into definition of castes. Like, if a person is brave then his duty would be to fight and protect and he is classed as a Kshatriya; a studious, thinking person inclined to study and contemplate and also take up activities related to God would be classed as a Brahmin and a person with tendency to trade would be classed as a Vaishya. Thus a person, in a way, is himself responsible for his caste. Basically, castes should not be birth-related but that is what has developed historically. Many ancient sages advise that caste should be determined by actions and not birth. (See also footnote on Swadharma in Ch 2)*

governed by actions therefore the scope of actions is very mysterious. (4:89-92)

A PERFECT PERSON

Now listen to the characteristics of a person who has reached perfection. Such person does not consider himself to be the doer even as he performs actions and does not hold expectations about its fruits. he has no other reason for actions apart from a sense of duty. It may then be considered that non-action has been well ingrained in such a person. Such a person should be considered as an enlightened person and one who has understood the meaning of non-action. (4:93-95). He who, knowing that performance of his actions is unreal from the point of view of the Self, realises Self, is really free of the burden of action. (4:98). He enjoys the worldly pleasures without being attached to or being affected by them. And even by remaining in one place he not only travels through the universe and becomes himself the universe. (4:101-102).

He who is not averse to actions nor is drawn to them and is not tainted by the ambitious thoughts like "I shall do this" or "I shall complete this" and has offered all his actions to the fire of Knowledge should be considered as Supreme Brahman itself. (4:103-105).

He is not bothered about his person, is desireless about the fruits of his actions and is always in a state of bliss. He is always content but constantly seeks the experience of the Self. (4:106-107). Shedding expectations and ego, he experiences more and more the sweetness of the bliss of the Self. Therefore he is happy with whatever comes to his lot. He does not say that this is mine and that is somebody else's. The very actions he performs merge into him because he does not see anything other than Self in this world. How can actions affect such a person? (4:108-112). There is no doubt that such a person is liberated in all ways, he remains actionless even while doing actions and attributeless even though outwardly he may appear to have attributes. (4:114). Since he considers action itself as Brahman all his actions become non-actions and therefore he remains unattached to them. (4:121

YAJNAS

Now Shri Krishna tells about various kinds of *Yajnas. (Note that traditionally a Yajna needs a fire in which various sacrificial offerings are made.)*

Some people give up indiscrimination from their nature and attain maturity; then adopting dispassion they practise yoga. This is their *yajna* in which they indulge day and night. *Only those who have sacrificed the ignorance and offered it along with their mind as an offering in the fire of (i.e. with the help of) his Guru's advice*[8] *should do this yajna.* (4:122-123).

Dnyaneshwar Maharaj now expounds on other kinds of yajnas that can lead to Self-Realization.

Daivayajna: A *yajna,* performed in the fire of Yoga with the intention of attaining Self by propitiating gods like Indra[9] is called *Daivayajna.* (4:124)

Brahmayajna: Some others follow the path of knowledge to attain Brahman. This is also a type of *Yajna* in which Brahman (Knowledge) itself is burnt as an offering in the fire of Brahman itself until Knowledge and the knower become one with the Brahman. This is called *Brahmayajna.*[10] (4:125)

Yajna of Self-control: Some burn their desires and ambition born of the five sense-organs in the fire of detachment burning in the

---

8 *In the original text Dnyaneshwar Maharaj mentions Guru's advice as Guru vakya. (Vakya means sentence). This may be a mantra or general advice on spiritual effort. Often this is also loosely called Guru-mantra.*
9 *Derived from the term Deva or god.*
10 *These two yajnas are mentioned in the Gita Shloka 4:25 which is translated as "Some yogis worship the deities alone while others offer sacrifice itself by the way of sacrifice in the fire of Brahman." This is difficult to understand in original but Dnyaneshwar Maharaj has expanded upon it.*

mind uttering the *mantra* of *"Aham Brahmasmi"*[11] or I am the Brahman. (4:125-129)

Guru-mantra: Some others, with dispassionate attitude and the continuous chanting of the *mantras* given by their Guru, began lighting the fire of knowledge (of the Self) and after avoiding the pitfalls of occult powers *(Siddhis)* achieved the first spark of Knowledge. The fire intensified after controlling the mind. Burning the desires and family ties in this fire and through control of breathing *(Pranayama)* they became one with the Brahman. What remained is the bliss of the knowledge of the Self. (4:131-139)

These are all different types of *yajnas* but with a common goal. (4:140).

There are other types of *Yajnas* also e.g. *Dravyayajna* or offering of wealth, *Tapoyajna* or performing penance, and *Yogayajna* or practising Yoga. Some offer words i.e. speech as *Yajna,* which is called *Vagyajna.* Others offer their learning to attain Brahman and that is called *Dnyanyajna.* (4:141).

Arjuna, all these *yajnas* are difficult and laborious. But persons who control their senses and practice yoga can perform them because they have sacrificed their ego. (4:142-143).

Pranayama: There are still others who practice *Pranayama* i.e. Breath control. Such yogis are called *Pranayamis.* (4:145). Some others use a technique called *Vajrayoga* in which diet is controlled and *Prana* is sacrificed into *Prana.*[12] All these persons who shed the grime from their mind by various *yajnas* have liberation as their

11 *This is one of the four mahavakyas or great expressions selected by Adi Shankaracharya for the logo expressions for the four Shankaracharya Maths. This mahavakya from Brihadaranyaka Upanishad is assigned to Shringeri Math. Other three expressions are: Pradnyanam Brahma. (Aitareya Upanishad); Tatvamasi. (Chandogya Upanishad); Ayamatma Brahma. (Mandukya Upanishad). (UP-BU), (UP-AI), (UP-CU), (UP-MA), Bibliography.*

12 *Prana means life-force. See note regarding Pranas at (6:192-200).*

goal. (4:146).[13]

ATTAINING BRAHMAN BY *YAJNAS*

Thus, all these people perform these various *yajnas* with the intention of attaining liberation and with their help, wash away the impurities of their mind (4:147). After the ignorance about the Soul (Self) is burnt away, its pure form alone remains and then any difference between the sacrificial fire and the performer of sacrifice vanishes. Thus the intention of the performer is fulfilled; sacrifice ends and all actions get nullified. Then the thoughts or imaginations do not enter the mind, the duality ends and with the ultimate Knowledge that alone remains, they experience the unification with the Brahman. (4:148-151).

Others lead a wasted life: But those, who after being born (as humans) do not practice yoga or perform *yajnas* or practice self-control have an unworthy life in this world and their status in the after-world need not even be mentioned. (4:152-154). All these *yajnas*, which Vedas describe in detail are possible only through actions and when one understands this then those actions do not bind him. (4:155-156).

Dravyayajnas inferior to *dnyanayajnas:* The *yajnas* broadly described in the Vedas needing external actions (like burning materials in fire) lead you only to attaining heavenly plane.[14] But

---

13 *Reader must have realized that all these yajnas basically imply sacrifice of weaknesses like attachment to worldly pleasures by various means like development of dispassion, yogic methods and following Guru's advice.*
14 *In the Vedic days the it was believed that by good karmas and behaviour according to dharma an individual earns merit (Punya); the reward for earning punya was living in heaven (Swarga) the abode of the gods where one can spend his time in pleasures such as dinking nectar and enjoying the dance of the heavenly nymphs (Apsaras). This enjoyment was set off against the amount of merit and when it was exhausted the individual had to take birth on the earth according to his record of past deeds or karmas. The introduction of Brahman by Upanishads toward the end of the Vedic times changed this concept. Present day belief is that even if the Swarga and associated pleasures were true they are only temporary and do not*

these are all *dravyayajnas* i.e. *yajnas* involving wealth and are very inferior to the *dnyanayajnas* or *yajna* of knowledge. (4:157-158)

SERVING SAINTS GIVES KNOWLEDGE

Krishna continues: If you desire to gain this most superior Knowledge then you should serve saints in every way. They are the depositories of knowledge and service is the gate to it. Therefore capture it by serving them. Then make your obeisance to them with all you have, and shedding your ego, be their servant. Then ask them questions about whatever you wish to know and they will explain it to you. Once you understand it, desires will not enter your mind. You will lose all your fears and be fit to attain Brahman and will see everything including yourself as My form Thus your delusion will vanish once you get the favours of a true Guru. (4:164-170)

KNOWLEDGE IS INCOMPARABLE

This knowledge is so powerful that it can remove the ignorance in your mind even if you are a worst sinner or full of illusion and delusion. There is nothing else in this world comparable to Knowledge and as encompassing. (4:172-174). This Knowledge cannot be compared with anything except itself just as if one asks what the taste of nectar is, then the answer is: like nectar and nothing else. Now I shall tell you how to gain that Knowledge. (4:180-185).

PEACE COMES WITH KNOWLEDGE

Knowledge seeks him who is fed up with sense-pleasures in preference to the pleasure of Self-realisation, who does not bother

---

liberate one from the birth and death cycle. The aim of spiritual efforts should be the attainment of liberation through Self-realization. This way one attains a permanent bliss even while one lives. (This is what Gita is all about)

about the sense organs, who does not allow desires enter his mind, does not feel responsible for the things which occur naturally and who has become happy by faith. Peace resides in the mind of such a person. Once the Knowledge becomes firm in his mind he attains self-realisation and peace reigns in his mind. He sees peace wherever he casts his glance and duality like "this is mine" and "that is another person's" vanishes from his mind. (4:186-190).

UNINTERESTED PERSON'S LIFE IS MEANINGLESS

What meaning does the life of a person not interested in Knowledge have? Death is preferable to such a life. (4:192). A person may not have gained knowledge but if he shows even a little interest then there is some hope that he will gain it. But if he does not then he will be surely afflicted by doubts. (4:194-195). One who is thus afflicted by doubts can be definitely considered as lost to the happiness in this world as well as the next. (4:198). A doubting person does not differentiate between truth and falsehood, proper and improper, beneficial and harmful. (4:200). Therefore there is no greater sin than to doubt.[15] [Author's Note: Specifically, not finding answers to doubts and thus attaining Knowledge] The one means of destroying it is Knowledge. (4:202-203). Therefore Arjuna, get rid of the doubts in your mind. (4:208).

---

15 *Once a person is caught in the net of doubts there is no firm faith left. Therefore he goes round and round doubting this and that and reaches nowhere. This is a waste of the God-given opportunity to obtain liberation and same as doubting God which is a sin. But to make use of that opportunity he must make efforts to remove his doubts in the first place.*

5

Renunciation

⤜✦⤛

*D*nyaneshwar Maharaj now explains about the true meaning
of action and non-action.

ARJUNA'S DOUBT

Arjuna is now confused and asks Shri Krishna. "First you told
me to give up actions and now you are insisting on actions. (5:2).
Which of these two paths is more effective? (5:6)

KARMAYOGA AND *KARMASANYASA*
ARE SAME IN EFFECT

Shri Krishna said, "Both *Karmasanyasa* (renouncing actions)
and *Karmayoga* (performing actions without desire for fruits) lead
to liberation. But it would appear that *Karmayoga* is clearer and
easier to follow for everyone, big and small. If one thinks carefully
then it would be clear that the fruits of *Karmasanyasa* are also
gained automatically through this path of action. I shall now tell
you the qualities of a *sanyasi* and then you will realise that both
paths are the same. (5:14-18).

QUALITIES OF A *SANYASI*

A *sanyasi*[1] does not grieve about his gains or losses and does not crave for what he has not received. His mind is steady as a mountain. A person whose mind is free from feelings of "me" and "mine" is forever a renunciate (*sanyasi*). In this state of his mind he is dissociated from the fruits of actions and he is ever happy. Such a person does not have to leave his home, family and possessions to become a *sanyasi* because he is already dissociated from desires in his mind.[2] (5:19-22). He whose intellect is free from desires does not get caught in the bindings of actions. A person attains the qualities of a *sanyasi* (renunciate) only when desires are given up. Therefore both *Karmasanyasa* (renouncing actions) and *Karmayoga* (performing actions without desire for fruits) are the same. (5:23-25). Only ignorant persons who do not understand anything about the *Jnyanayoga* of the *Sankhyas*[3] and *Karmayoga* think that they are different but those who have experienced Self know that they are not different. (5:26-28). One who follows the *Karmayoga* path soon attains the bliss of the Brahman but one who cannot succeed[4] in it wastes his efforts and cannot be a real

1 A sanyasi is one who has renounced the householder's worldly life. In India, a person who is or becomes disinterested in or averse to the worldly way of life or one who thinks that such life may come in the way of his spiritual progress becomes sanyasi by adopting the status of sanyasa (renunciation). This requires a formal ceremony performed by his Guru (teacher) in which death rites of the aspirant are performed and his past is buried. He is assigned a new name and given an ochre dress to distinguish him apart. A sanyasi must live by begging for alms and is not supposed to remain at one place for more than three nights (except in the rainy season) lest he develop an attachment for the place. He must spend his time in pilgrimage, spiritual studies and contemplation of God under the guidance of his Guru.

2 A person with an attitude of detachment is a real sanyasi at heart even if he does not wear ochre clothes.

3 The Samkhya philosophy mentioned here, according to Dr Radhakrishnan is the philosophy from the Upanishads (which is really Vedanta philosophy) presented in Ovis 91-229 in Ch 2 and not that proposed by Rishi Kapila which is discussed later in Ch 8. (SR-B)

4 i.e. performs actions but with the desire for fruits thereof.

sanyasi (renunciate). (5:32-33).

ATTITUDE OF A NON-DOER IS NECESSARY

A person who has kept his mind free of *(I am the body)* delusion and by purifying it with the help of Guru's *mantra* merged it in the Self, becomes the Self. (5:34). A person who, after getting rid of desires, has become Consciousness (Brahman) itself, pervades the expanse of the three worlds (i.e. heaven, earth and the nether) through the form of the Self, even by being at one place. (5:36). For such a person language like *"This is done by me"* or *"I want to do this"* becomes redundant and he remains a *non-doer* in spite of his actions; because, such a person is not even conscious of his body even though his outward behaviour and his bodily functions appear to be normal. Then how can he have the ego about his actions? (5:37-38).

When we think about the Almighty God we see that the all-pervading God is apparently a *non-doer*. He creates this expanse of the three worlds but He does not get involved with these actions even if you call Him a *doer*. He raises populations of creatures from the five elements[5] and He is in all but belongs to none. In fact He is not even aware of the creation and destruction of the world. (5:76-79). He assumes form by taking birth[6] but His formlessness is not affected. Therefore to say that He creates, maintains and destroys is rooted in ignorance. (5:81-82).

When this ignorance is totally destroyed, then delusion is no more and the non-doing nature of God becomes clear. Once a person is convinced in his mind that God is a non-doer then the

---

5 *Five elements or Principles: Indian philosophy postulates the world to be made of five principles or elements: Earth, Water, Air, Fire and Sky or Space. This is as per the understanding of the thinkers at the beginning of human civilisation who could analytically identify the three states in which matter exists. When seen from the modern physical point of view, the first three are the three states of matter namely solid, liquid and gaseous states. These elements are not the chemical elements like hydrogen, oxygen, carbon etc. which to modern count are more than 100, about 92 of them occurring naturally. The fourth element represents the energy while the fifth is the space. But this does not change the basic arguments of the observant ancients.*
6 *As an avatar.*

fundamental idea that "He is not different from me" is naturally established. Once this sense has arisen in the mind then he does not see himself different from anything in the three worlds and considers the world to be as liberated as he himself is. (5:83-85). Such persons have a sense of equability towards everything in this world, (5:88). Such men of Knowledge do not notice differences between different creatures. (5:93-95). Listen now to the characteristics of the person who possesses this sense of equability. (5:102).

INDIFFERENCE TO SUCCESS OR FAILURE

One who is not affected by the success or failure (or gains and losses) of his actions is a person with sense of equability. He is the Brahman personified. (5:103-104). Due to the limitless internal bliss of the Self he is not attracted towards the external worldly pleasures. (5:105-106). These impermanent worldly the sense pleasures that have given the appearance of truth (reality) to this worldly delusion of *Maya*. (5:126).

Persons who have controlled passions totally, are not at all aware of the sorrows born out of sense-pleasures. (5:129). They are internally filled with bliss. But the pleasures attract only those who have not experienced this internal bliss. (5:110). The pleasures of the sense-objects are verily sources of misery from start to end, but ignorant people cannot do without them. (5:120). It is these people who are addicted to manner of their enjoying that bliss, is unusual. They are not aware that they are the enjoyers because they are in a state of egolessness and oneness with the Supreme. (5:131-133). This Bliss of the Self is the best, is indestructible and limitless. Only the desireless persons are worthy of it. (5:146). If you ask how these persons reach this stage while still living,[7] it is because first they give up the pleasures with dispassion and concentrating at the point between the eyebrows and while controlling the breath *(Pranayama)*, they meditate with their eyes turned backwards.

7 Here Krishna gives brief but specific instructions on how to meditate.

(5:151-153). Thus their mind turns inwards and through the state of *Samadhi*[8] they take the life-force and the mind upwards towards the experience of Brahman. When mind dissolves, all desires and ego also dissolves. Therefore he who experiences the bliss becomes one with Brahman while still living. (5:155-157).

〰️

---

8 *A thought-free state reached during meditation.*

6

Meditation

~∞~

In this chapter Dnyaneshwar Maharaj first continues to discuss Krishna's elaboration on the essential oneness of Karmayoga and Karmasanyasa; in the later part, though Gita discusses briefly only the Dhyanayoga (yoga of meditation) Dnyaneshwar Maharaj goes beyond it and brings to the common man the technique of awakening of Kundalini power as practiced by yogis, he himself being a Natha yogi and hence having experienced its effects:

YOGI NOT DIFFERENT FROM A SANYASI

Shri Krishna further said, "Yogi *(Karmayogi)* and *sanyasi* are both the same in their pursuit and intention. You may think they are different but on careful thinking you will find that they are same. Except for the differences in names it is clear that (Karma) yoga is the same as *sanyas* and from the spiritual point of view there is no difference at all between the two. (6:39-40). It is an accepted principle that he, who performs actions but does not get attached to the fruits thereof, should only be considered as a yogi. (6:43). He who performs actions appropriate to his caste/ position and circumstances, but does not maintain the ego about his being the doer and does not permit the desire for the fruits (of the actions) to touch his mind, is a *sanyasi* and doubtless is a *yogi* also. (6:45-47)

On the other hand, he who, forsakes the regular routine duties and incidental duties[1] (like propitiating ancestors etc.) considering them to be restrictive and instead, immediately gets himself involved in other actions, gets himself into unnecessary problems. Why should one give up the burden of family life only to burden oneself with the life of a renunciate? Therefore, one who remains within the prescribed code of actions by doing daily fire rituals[2] etc. enjoys automatically the yogic bliss. (6:48-51)

Shastras have stated that *Sanyasi* is a *yogi* because it is only when the desire goes that the essence of yoga is achieved. (6:52-53)

YOGI SHOULD NOT ABANDON ACTIONS

One who follows the Yoga path[3] should not give up the path of actions. By assuming proper posture and breath-control, by steadying the intellect, controlling the organs and keeping them away from the sense-pleasures, he should turn the consciousness inwards and meditate by continued abstraction of mind *(Dharana)*. This will lead to elimination of the tendencies towards materialistic actions. Then the means *(sadhana)* becomes one with the goal and one becomes steady in the state of *samadhi*. By practising thus the *yogi* reaches perfection. Now listen to the characteristics of such a perfect person. (6:54- 61)

---

1 *Every individual has to perform certain daily duties like bath, eating, worship etc. which are routine actions (Nityakarma) but he has also to do certain incidental (Naimittic) actions like welcoming a guest or performance of rites on special occasions or day. These are further discussed in Ch 18.*

2 *This does not mean everyone should perform fire rituals like agnihotra and other Vedic rites. It is only implied that an individual should not abandon routine and incidental duties that come to his lot.*

3 *Now onwards, Yoga does not mean karma yoga as in the earlier text but means Yoga of Meditation. In a way yoga is also a type of action.*

A perfect person: Sense objects do not enter his mind[4] and he is engrossed in the Knowledge of the Self. He is not excited by the pleasures and sorrows in the world nor is he enticed by pleasures. Even if he has to perform actions he does not care about the fruits thereof. His actions are just sufficient for the survival of the body; at other times, he is oblivious to other actions. Such a person may be considered as settled in yoga. (6:62-65)

ARJUNA'S DOUBT

Arjuna then wondered and said, "Please tell me as to who gives him this capability?" (6:66).

THE HARMFUL EGO

Shri Krishna replied, "In this state of oneness who can give what and to whom? (6:67).

It is due to ignorance that a person dreams of life and death. But when he wakes up he realises that the dreams were unreal and becomes aware of the truth that he himself is the Brahman. We harm ourselves by the unnecessary 'I-am-the-body' ego. (6:68-70).

One should give up this ego thoughtfully and benefit by becoming one with Brahman. Really speaking, by being infatuated with the body, one becomes one's own enemy. (6:71-72). An individual himself is Brahman but his intellect does not believe it. (6:75). A person who nurtures desire becomes his own enemy. On the other hand, he who does not bother about these bindings is the real knower of the Self. (6:80).

For a person who has conquered his mind and calmed his desires the Supreme Self is not very far. When wishful thoughts disappear from the mind the individual becomes Brahman. (6:81-82). When the false ego vanishes completely he becomes one with

---

4 *i.e. he never thinks of sense-objects and pleasures.*

the Brahman already present within him. The thoughts of hot and cold, happiness and sorrow, honour and insult are not possible in such a person. Just as whatever comes in the path of the sun gets illuminated, whoever comes in the path of such a perfect person becomes like him. The thoughts that these deeds are good and those are bad do not enter his mind because he has become one with the Brahman and is devoid of duality. When he ponders over the nature of this world he finds that it is unreal and when he searches for the reality he experiences that that reality is he himself. When he later tries to determine whether he is bound by space and time or by the all-pervading, all his efforts stop because now his feeling of duality with Brahman vanishes. One who has conquered his senses while remaining in his body has automatically reached the level of Brahman. Such a person should be called a *yogi* and the master of his senses. The differences like big and small do not enter his mind and a lump of earth, a precious stone or gold are the same to him. (6:84-92). Then how can ideas about friend and foe, relative or stranger come to his mind? (6:94). Everything in this world appears as Brahman to him. One who has experienced that this world is pervaded by Brahman is a person with vision of equability towards everything. (6:100-101). Even thinking about such a person, makes one become like that person. (6:104). But there is no limit to the praise of such a person. (6:111)

ARJUNA ASKS FOR ADVICE

Arjuna then expressed his desire that though he does not have the qualities of saints in him and perhaps he is not yet fit to understand the importance of these characteristics (of a perfect yogi), Shri Krishna's advice might make him fit to become one with Brahman. (6:138-140). Shri Krishna, realising that this is the opportune time to tell him about the practice of Yoga, told Arjuna as follows: (6:151)

ADVICE ON THE PRACTICE OF YOGA[5]

"What I am going to tell you now is about that Yoga path which is the king among all yoga paths, therefore listen carefully. By this path one gains innumerable fruits of detachment through deliberate actions. Lord Shiva is even now a follower of this path. Some Yogis tried other ways to attain Brahman but getting wiser by their experience they had to turn to this straight path of Self-realisation after which they made rapid progress. A person who has discovered this path forgets his hunger and thirst and is unaware when the day dawns or the night falls. Every step in this path opens towards the mine of liberation. Whether you go eastward or westward the progress on this path occurs quietly and definitely. (6:152-159). Now I shall tell you the details; but they are useful only if you practice them. (6:163).

Selection of location: First of all a suitable place should be selected

5 *The original Gita text Shlokas 10 – 15 instruct briefly on how to seat in proper posture and meditate by concentrating on the tip of the nose and turning mind towards God. Shlokas 16-32 briefly instruct on control of diet and attitudes until he becomes one with Self (God) and becomes steady in thought. In Dnyaneshwari however, very detailed instructions on the selection of place and seat and posture are given. These instructions (Ovis 6:163-327) lead to the awakening of the Kundadlini force that is dormant at the base of the spine in every individual. He describes the Divine experiences one can get from this awakening and how the yogi not only achieves Self-realization but also attains siddhis (Occult powers). These are no doubt personal experiences of Dnyaneshwar maharaj who was a Nath yogi. This probably is the first time that these techniques have been brought to the common man.*

Shaktipat technique of Siddhayoga: During last century, Shaktipat system of awakening kundalini has become popular. In this system a competent Guru, after testing an aspirant disciple and if satisfied, uses his own powers to awaken his (or her) Kundalini even from a distance kilometres. After this awakening yogic processes automatically start within the disciple's body at regular times. It may take years however to reach the state when it reaches the final stage of Sahasrara. Yogis attached to Gulavani Maharaj Math in Pune and Swami Nityananada Ashram at Ganeshpuri in Vajreshawari near Mumbai have such powers. (VS-DT) Bibliography for the practice. One should get a feeling of happiness on sitting there and a feeling that he should not leave the place. One's sense of dispassion should increase while sitting there. Saints should have occupied that place earlier, the effects of which are still felt through a feeling of satisfaction, courage and zeal. The practice of yoga should occur naturally by sitting there and the beauty of the surroundings should give one the experience of the bliss of the Self. Even an atheist should feel like doing penance *(tapas)* there. (6:163-167)

That place should be beautiful and pure. It should be inhabited only by seekers and be away from crowds of ordinary people. Plenty of roots and fruit-laden trees should be available throughout the year and water, especially from natural fountains, should be available even in dry season. It should enjoy mild sun and cool breeze. It should be so thickly wooded that not only wild animals but even bees and parrots cannot enter. But there may be a few water birds around and perhaps a cuckoo and occasional peacock also. Arjuna, one should carefully search for such a place looking for a secret cave or a temple of Lord Shiva. (6:171-179).

Preparation of the seat: After selecting one of the two places (cave or temple), one should sit there alone for a long time and check whether or not the mind becomes calm. If it becomes calm then one should prepare a seat there. The seat should be made of *darbha* grass[6] over which one should put a deerskin and cover it further by a clean washed cloth. The seat should be level and not too high or too low from the ground. If the seat is too high it will make the body unstable and if too low then the body will touch the ground. In short the seat should be steady and comfortable. (6: 180-185).

Stabilising the mind: Then one should sit there concentrating the mind and remember his *Sadguru* (True guru). The Guru must be remembered until the mind is filled with *Sattvic* (pure) feelings so that one's ego gets blunted, mind is rid of thoughts of sense-objects and the organs do not stir. One should remain in this state until it is

---

6 *Kind of grass used in worship rituals.*

experienced that the mind has merged with the heart. In this state the body automatically becomes steady and the vital airs *(pranas)*[7] in the body coming together. After remaining in this state the mind stabilises, interest in worldly affairs gets inhibited and one attains the state of deep trance *(samadhi)* effortlessly as soon as one sits on the seat. (6: 186-191).

Yogic posture and Chakras: Now listen carefully to the details about the yogic posture. First sit with the calves of the legs pressed against the thighs and keeping the left leg on the other leg at a slight angle, press the right sole steadily on the anus, keeping the sole of the left foot naturally pressed on the right foot. Pressing the heel tightly at the centre of the space between the anus and the base of the generating organ, one should balance the body on it. Keeping the two ankles straight he should lift the base of the spinal column. This will make the whole body balanced and supported on the heel. This is the characteristic of posture of the *Mula Bandha*[8] (the knot at the root or base), also known as *Vajrasana*. Once this posture is successfully achieved then the downward path of the *Apana* part of the vital breath, gets blocked and it starts receding inside. (6:192-200).

Then cup both palms and rest them on the left leg, which will make the shoulders rise. The head automatically gets in between them. The eyes then remain in half-closed state and the sight turns inwards. Even if it turns outwards it can look only up to the tip of

---

7 Pranas: Prana means life. Prana also means vital breath and hence called Prana vayu. There are five classes of Prana, all arising from the main Prana and each having a specific function in the life processes in the body. The main types are: Prana (breathing and circulatory system), Apana (eliminating waste products), Udana (speech and sound), Samana creation of auras) and Vyana (muscular movements). There are also five more secondary pranas: Naga, Kurma, Krikala, Devadatta and Dhananjaya. That makes 10 pranas. (VL-AHR)

8 Bandha is loosely translated as knot but effectively they are kind of gates that control the flow of the pranas. Mula, Jalandhar and Odhiyana are postures in the three parts of the body that affect the flow of the pranas and the nerve system.

the nose. The desire to look around vanishes. Then the neck gets contracted and the chin presses against the chest hiding the throat. This posture of the neck and chest is called the *Jalandhar Bandha* or knot. (6:201-208).

Then the belly becomes flat and the navel gets raised. The posture of the part of the body between the navel and the anus is called *Odhiyana Bandha* or knot. (6:209-210).

Thus the Yoga practice starts with the external parts of the body while the thoughts, desires and other affairs of the mind vanish. He is not aware anymore of hunger and sleep. (6:211-213).

Awakening of *Kundalini*: The *Apana* breath then hits the *Muladhar Chakra*[9] situated at between the anus and the generating organ and removes all the impurities accumulated there since childhood. (See the note on the *Chakras* at the end of chapter). Then the *Apana* breath rises to the *Manipur Chakra* situated just below the navel and starts hitting against it. Thus the confined breath stirs the body from inside and removes the impurities accumulated there since childhood. Then the powerful breath enters the abdomen and eliminates the phlegm and bile. Then it reaches the centres of the

---

9 *Chakras are certain nerve centres in the body. Muladhar is the lowermost Chakra located near the base of one's spine near about the sexual organs and at which the Kundalini is located in a dormant state. There are six more Chakras above it: Swadhishtan Chakra located below the navel and a little above the Muladhar; Manipur near the navel; Anahat near the heart; Vishuddha at the throat; Adnya in between the eyebrows. The seventh, not always classed as a chakra, is the Sahasrara or the centre of thousand lotus petals on the vertex crown. Starting from the Muladhar the successive chakras get activated as the awakened Kundalini force rises from Muladhar to Sahasrara each giving unique experiences. Activation of the Chakras accelerates the spiritual progress. In time the seeker whose Kundalini is activated gets liberated from the influence of mundane subjects and finally gets the experience of the Divine. Depending upon the efforts of the seeker and Guru's benevolence the time taken from the awakening and the ultimate realisation may vary between immediate to several years and sometimes lifetimes too. WARNING: The yoga postures described here should not be practiced without guidance from a teacher.*

seven essential elements (viz. flesh, blood, muscles, bones, marrow, chyle and semen), gets rid of the fat, and drives the marrow out from the bones. It cleans the blood vessels and relaxes the organs, which may frighten the seeker, but he should not get frightened. By creating these ailments it throws the diseases out from the body. Then the *Apana* breath brings the solid flesh and bones and the liquid blood together. (6:214-220).

While this goes on the *Kundalini* force awakens by virtue of the heat created by the yogic posture. It was sleeping like a baby cobra coiled in three and half coils near the navel with its mouth facing down, (6:221-223) but now gets awakened due to the constriction by the *Mula Bandha*. (6:225).

Kundalini reaches other Chakras and purifies the body: When it wakes up it opens its mouth and swallows the *Apana* which has occupied the space in the region of the heart. It then swallows the fat and excess flesh from the region of the heart and wherever else it can find flesh. (6:229-231). Then it searches for the palms and soles, tears open the upper parts and searches every joint and organ. It extracts the vitality from the nails, purifies the skin and makes it touch the bones. Then it cleans the insides of the bones and scrapes the interior of the blood vessels with the result that the roots of the hair are burnt. It then drinks off the seven essential elements and makes the body hot and dry. (6:232-235).

It then draws back the *Prana* coming out of the nose and the *Apana* which is inside and when they both meet only the curtains of the six *Chakras* separate them. They would have met except that *Kundalini* asks them, "What business do you have here? Get aside!" The principle is that the *Kundalini* eats off the Earth principle (solid part) and also completely licks off the Water principle (liquid part) from the body and feeling satiated becomes mild and rests at the *Sushumna* (central) nerve in the spine. (6:236-240). In this satisfied mood it vomits the saliva, which becomes the nectar and guards the body. At this stage the heat leaves the body, which now becomes cool from inside as well as from outside because of which the lost strength returns. The flow in the *Sushumna* nerve stops and the functions of the remaining nine *Pranas* also stop. Because of this the body is without action and becomes still. The *Ida* and *Pingala* nerves in the spine meet and the three knots get loosened and the curtains of the six *Chakras* open. Then the vital airs passing through the right and left nostrils (which are designated Sun and Moon respectively) fade to the extent that even a flame will not flicker by them. (6:241-245). At this time, the intellect gets stilled and the remaining fragrance in the *Prana* enters the *Sushumna* nerve along with the *Kundalini*. Then the spiritual nectar (Ambrosia or *Amrit*) situated at the crown of the head spills into the mouth of the *Kundalini* and then gets absorbed throughout the body including the ten *Pranas*. (6:246-248).[10]

Body gets rejuvenated: The skin, which veils the lustre of this nectar but is brightened by it, is shed and all the organs show their bright aura. (6:250, 252-253). Now even Death is afraid of it (the body) and the aging process gets reversed. The *yogi* gets back his lost childhood and he looks like a boy. (6:259-261). He gets bright new nails. He gets new teeth also but they are tiny like a row of pearls. Tiny hairs grow on the body. The palms and soles become red and the eyes become so clean that his vision cannot get confined within the eyelids and even with half-closed eyes the range of his vision reaches the sky. (6:262, 265-267). Though the colour of his skin becomes golden, his body becomes light as air because now there are no earth and water principles in it. He is able to see beyond the seas and understand what is going on in heaven. He is able to understand what is in an ant's mind and he can ride the wind. Even if he walks on water his feet do not get wet. Thus he attains such spiritual powers *(Siddhis)*. (6:268-270).[11]

---

10 *Reader should not think that all this happens at once. The processes mentioned above take place slowly and progressively as the aspirant continues to practice and may take even years.*

11 *Those who have come across yogis may note how young and fresh they look. Some live legendary long lives.*

Divine experiences: Now listen to what happens further. The *Kundalini*, with the help of *Prana* rises up to the heart through the *Sushumna* nerve. (6:271). This *Kundalini* now may be considered as the basis of this universe and of *AUM*, which is the expression of Supreme Soul. (6:272-273). The *yogi* then starts hearing the Divine *Anahat* sound. (6:274). The intellect becomes active consciousness and touches the *Kundalini* power and is now able to hear some of this *Anahat* sound. (6:275). There are ten types of *Anahat* sound and he hears the first type of sound called *Ghosha* and in this basin of *Ghosha* itself sound pictures are then generated which one sees through one's imagination but when the person is not himself where is the imagination? Actually it is impossible to explain where the sound is coming from. (6:276-277). I forgot to tell you one thing that is the *Anahat* sound reverberations near the heart persist as long as Air principle is not destroyed. The reverberations in the Sky principle (space) open the window of the *Brahmarandhra (Sahasrar)* easily. There is another space above the Sahasrar (lotus of thousand petals) where the Consciousness *(Chaitanya)* resides without support. (6:278-280). There the *Kundalini* flashes its energy and by giving an offering of it to the intellect it makes the duality disappear. Now the *Kundalini* drops its brilliance and merges with the *Prana*. At that time it looks like a golden robe shed by a statue of air or like a tongue of lightening. (6:281-284). Thus, when it reaches up to the *Sahasrar*, it looks like a golden chain or a stream of shining water. Then it suddenly vanishes in the space of the spiritual heart and its power dissolves into itself. We should really call it power *(Shakti)* but it is really the life-force which is no longer aware now of any material aspect of the world. In this state things like conquering the mind, holding the breath or meditating do not remain. Having desires or giving them up also stop. Therefore this *Kundalini* may be considered as the melting pot of all the five principles. (6:286-290). Dnyaneshwar Maharaj says, *"Using the body itself to devour the ego about the body is the principle of the Nath Panth* (sect). Shri Krishna has merely mentioned it in the *Gita*, but I have put the details before the audience." (6:291-292)

Siddhis: When the lustre of the power vanishes, the appearance of the body also changes and eyes of common people cannot see the real form of the yogi. Actually the gross body continues to possess the limbs and other organs but it is now made of air principle. (6:293-294). His body can become so light that he is called *Khechar* i.e. one who can travel through space. Once he reaches this stage his body performs miracles because now he has gained *Siddhis.*[12] (6:296). One need not go into the details about these *Siddhis*, main point being that the three principles Earth, Water and Fire have disappeared from within his body. Of the five principles, Water principle has destroyed the Earth principle and Air principle has destroyed the Water principle while in the spiritual heart, the Air principle has destroyed the Fire principle. What remains is the Air principle in the shape of the body. But after some time that too vanishes in the space of the spiritual heart. At this time the *Kundalini* changes its name to *Marut* i.e. wind or air. But until it merges into Brahman its form as power persists. (6:297-301).

Then it breaks the *Jalandhar Bandha* and surges through the throat to the *Brahmarandhra.* With the help of recitation of the basic sound *AUM*, it rises to the *Pashyanti*[13] stage of the sound

---

12 *There eight Siddhis: Anima: reducing one's body to small size, Mahima: expanding one's body to large size, Garima: becoming infinitely heavy, Laghima: becoming almost weightless, Prapti: having unrestricted access to all places, Praakaamya: realizing whatever one desires, Ishtva: possessing absolute lordship, Vashhtva: the power to subjugate all. Advanced yogis are known to possess such powers but they are not to be used indiscriminately. (WK-SI)*

13 *There are four types of sounds – Vaikhari, Madhyama, Pashyanti and Para. Vaikhari sound is the audible sound we hear as words while the rest are progressively more subtle which ordinary persons cannot hear. Tanmatra is the subtle form of a word or sound before it is expressed. It is believed that great sages (like Vyasa) even now guide the affairs of the world and pass instructions in Para state of sound. These are received by yogis including Naths and passed further down successively to lower and lower hierarchy of yogis until the guidance is passed on the people in vaikhari state of sound. (YD-YH).*
Some people may doubt this but Mr Richard Baum, an artist, says regarding the Mother of Pondecherry: "At one point the Mother literally threw me off

and enters the *Brahmarandhra* up to the half of *Tanmatra*. By steadying itself in the *Brahmarandhra*, it embraces the Brahman. The curtain of the five principles is withdrawn and the power meets the Supreme Brahman and evaporates into it along with the Sky principle. (6:302-306).

Thus the soul, which was separated from the Brahman by virtue of acquiring the body, enters the Brahman. At that time thoughts about whether the soul is different from Me (that is the Brahman) does not survive in the mind. (6:307-309). The person now experiences merging of what is described as Sky principle with the sky. This cannot be described in words but has only to be experienced. (6:310-311). Arjuna, understand that this phenomenon is not something explicit which can be understood by listening to words. There is nothing more left for him to know. I can only say that if one is fortunate then one should experience it and be one with the Brahman. (6:316-318). But it is meaningless to talk about it. That (the Brahman) is the root of the universe, the fruit of the yoga, and the energy of the bliss. That is where the forms dissolve. It is the place of liberation and beginning and end disappear there. It is the seed of the five principles and brightness of the Great Effulgence. When the non-believers tortured My devotees, I had to assume My beautiful four-armed form out of It (the Brahman).[14] The great bliss of this state is beyond description. Persons who have realised Self by steadily striving for it have become pure and

---

the couch by her statement that it was she who by disguising herself as the Lord of Nations persuaded Hitler to invade Russia in order to insure Hitler's ultimate defeat and that it was she by means of a hovering force who saved Paris from destruction. In fact, the Mother claims that World War II was an attempt on the part of the Asuras to thwart the WORK, the Supramental Manifestation. In addition, in 1962 when China invaded India and suddenly, despite its seemingly imminent victory, withdrew, the Mother claims that it was her force that caused Peking's sudden about- face."(RB-URL)

14 *This refers to the incarnations (avataras) God had to take to save his devotees from being tortured by the evil people. (e.g. the fourth avatara of Narasimha (half man- half lion) was to save his devotee Prahlada from the tortures from his father Hiranyakashipu.) See footnote in Ch 9)*

reached My status. (6:321-326).

ARJUNA'S DOUBT

Arjuna now gets a doubt whether he himself is fit for practising this yoga. He asks,

"Shri Krishna, I am convinced about the excellence of this yoga practice. But I am not worthy enough to practice it. What I want to ask you is whether anybody would be able to practice it or whether it requires one to be qualified to practice it." (6:333-337).

WORTHINESS FOR YOGA PRACTICE[15]

Shri Krishna replied. "This yoga is a means to liberation. Even an ordinary task cannot be successful unless the doer is worthy and capable of doing it. But the worthiness can be only judged if and when the task is successful. A task that is begun becomes successful only when there is worthiness. But capability is not something one can easily acquire. When a person, by becoming detached performs the prescribed actions then he attains authority. You can use this means to attain worthiness. (6:339-343).

Arjuna, one rule of the yoga practice is that he who does not perform prescribed actions does not become worthy. (6:344). *One who is a slave to the pleasures of the tongue and of sleep does not have the right to practice yoga. Also, one who, out of obstinacy, reduces his diet by suppressing his hunger and thirst and does not sleep properly, cannot control his body. How can such a person succeed in yoga? Therefore one should not pamper the sense-pleasures but at the same time one should not totally abandon them also. (6:344-348).* One should eat but it should be proper and in moderation. One should undertake only a limited number

---

15 *This advice of not complete denial but moderation in habits is one of the best practical advices found in Dnyaneshwari.*

of tasks. One should talk only that much which is necessary, walk within limits and sleep only at proper times. (6:350). Even if one has to stay awake for any reason, it should not be beyond some specific limit. By such regular routine the essential constituents of the body remain in balance. And when the senses are satisfied in proper proportions the mind also remains satisfied. (6:351-352). Once the external organs become regulated the internal happiness increases and the yoga is achieved even without practice. (6:353). One who practices yoga by remaining regular and controlled in his habits experiences the Self. (6:355). A person whose mind becomes steady and remains so until death, may be called a person who has achieved yoga. In this stage his mind may be compared to a flame in windless air. (6:357-358).

GAINS FROM YOGA PRACTICE

A beneficial thing often appears as painful to a person. Otherwise nothing is easier than the practice of Yoga. (6:363). Only with the practice of yoga, by sitting steadily in the posture I described, can the sense-organs be disciplined. Once that is achieved the mind automatically sets itself towards the Soul. When it returns from there and looks back at the Self it realises that "I have been That" all the time. Then it gets immersed in bliss and dissolves in the Self. It becomes one with That (Self or the Brahman) beyond which there is nothing else and which can never be realised through the senses. (6:364-368). In this state, his mind remains steady and his awareness about the body vanishes even if it is afflicted by severe pains. (6:369-371) Because of this indescribable bliss he forgets other things also. Because of the pleasure of the experience of the Self the mind no more remembers the desires and is no longer mindful of the worldly matters. The bliss which adorns the yoga, and which gives satisfaction and Knowledge appears in form[16] by the study of

---

16 *This is somewhat figurative. Just as it is said that a difference between knower and knowable vanishes with attainment of Knowledge, this means that the yogi himself becomes bliss so that bliss has the form of that yogi.*

the yoga and the person who sees (experiences) it becomes of that form. (6:372-374).

ATTITUDES FOR STARTING YOGA PRACTICE

Now Dnyaneshwar Maharaj elaborates on how one can be firm in the matter of yoga practice.

Arjuna, you may feel that this yoga is difficult, but in a way it is very easy. First one should get rid of desire and anger, which arise out of thoughts in the mind. (6:375) Once the sense pleasures are eliminated and organs are controlled, the mind becomes calm. Thus, once dispassion sets in then desires do not enter the mind and the intellect is sheltered by courage. The intellect, once it is helped by the courage, turns the mind towards Self-realisation. (6:375-378)

Even if this does not happen there is another easy way towards Self-realisation. First one should make a rule that a resolution once it is made will not be changed. (6:379-380). If this makes the mind steady then well and good. But if it does not, then let the mind wander freely. Then bring it back from wherever it has wandered. It will then be steady by itself. Once the mind is able to remain steady for some considerable time it will by itself, come towards the Self and when it encounters the Self it will become one with it. The duality will then merge into unification with the Self and the bright light of the union will illuminate the three worlds. (6:381-384). Everything becomes full of Divine energy once the mind dissolves. (6:386)

If you are not able to do even this then listen further. (6:390) One should fix the thought in one's mind that "I am in the body of every being and everything is in Me; that this universe and all living beings are interlinked." (6:391-392). Needless to say that he who sees My presence in every being with the feeling of equality and does not harbour discrimination in his mind based on outward differences between them is undisputedly one with Me. (6:393-394). By not being involved with its affairs he reaches My level through his experiencing of the Brahman even while he is in his body. He who has experienced My all-pervasive nature becomes all-pervasive himself. (6:401-402). I have seen that a person who has experienced Self in the three worlds is himself Brahman by virtue of his experience, even though he goes about normally in his body, with people thinking of him in their own perception as happy or unhappy as the case may be. (6:407-408). Therefore My advice to you Arjuna, is to practice the outlook of equality by which you will see the universe in yourself and be one with it. There is nothing else worth achieving other than this outlook of equality. (6:410)

Arjuna's Doubt On Nature Of Mind

Arjuna now raises a doubt, "Shri Krishna, the path you have told just now will not sustain because of the nature of the mind. It tortures the intellect and weakens the determination and runs away from courage. It creates desires when one is in a state of satisfaction and wanders everywhere. It bounces if suppressed and assists if controlled. Therefore it does not appear possible that the mind would become steady and impart the sense of equality. (6:414-416).

Directing The Mind

Shri Krishna replied, "What you are saying is true. The mind is mercurial. But if one can turn it towards the practice of yoga observing dispassion, then it will become steady after some time. The mind has one good quality and that is, it develops a liking for a thing towards which it gets attracted. Therefore one should make it like the experience of the Self [17] (6:418-420).

Those who are not dispassionate and also do not practice yoga (meditation) would find it impossible to control the mind. But if we do not at all bother about following the techniques of regulated

---

17 *Both by changing the attitude and by continuous yoga practice.*

behaviour *(Yama-Niyama)* and about dispassion, and instead get immersed in sense pleasures and thus do not conquer the mind then how can it become steady? Therefore let your actions be such as to control the mind and then we shall see how it does not become steady. "(6:421-424)

Dnyaneshwar Maharaj now assures that the practice of yoga never goes waste but is carried forward in the next birth too.

ARJUNA'S DOUBT: WHAT IF SEEKER DIES HALFWAY?

Now Arjuna raises one more doubt. He says, "Shri Krishna, I did not know about this yoga until now; therefore I thought that the mind is uncontrollable. But now, by your grace, I have been introduced to the yoga. But I have one more doubt that only you can settle. (6:428-430). Suppose a person, deeply desirous of attaining liberation, gives up worldly pleasures in good faith but has not been able to fully succeed in his spiritual efforts. If such a person dies before attaining his goal then he will have neither the liberation nor the worldly pleasures. Thus in spite of having faith he would have lost both. Please tell me what happens to such a person." (6:431-432).

SEEKER IS REBORN AS *YOGI*

Shri Krishna replied, "Arjuna, can there be anything other than liberation for one who longs for it? He is merely taking rest for some time. And even then, during that rest period, there is such a happiness which even gods do not gain. Had he practised yoga, then he would have attained liberation before death. But because of lack of speed he had to stop in the middle. But liberation is reserved for him. (6:437-440). He reaches with ease the planes which even Indra the king of Gods finds it difficult to attain. But he gets sick of the incomparable enjoyments on these planes and says all the time, 'Oh God! Why are there impediments in My path to liberation?' Then he returns to the earth to be born in a religious family and starts gaining spiritual wealth. People in such family observe morals, speak clearly and truthfully and behave as prescribed in the Scriptures. (6:441-445). For them the Vedas are the living deity, actions are guided by *Swadharma* and discrimination and all thoughts are only about God and their wealth is the family deity. Thus the person happily is born here on the strength of his meritorious deeds. (6:446-448). Or he is reborn into the family of a *yogi* of high level. The person even as a child is already loaded with knowledge because of his past. Due to the mature intellect he knows all branches of knowledge easily. (6:451-454). His intellect develops further from the point of his death in the earlier lifetime and he is able to grasp mysterious subjects and even difficult things told by a Guru. (6:457, 459). His sense-organs come under his control, mind becomes one with the *Prana* the vital life-breath and the *Prana* dissolves in the Consciousness. Somehow, yoga practice also comes easily to him and he can attain the state of *Samadhi* effortlessly. (6:460-461). He attains *Siddhis* even while he is an acolyte.[18] (6:464). He is able to do his spiritual exercises effortlessly because he has reached the shores of Self-realisation after millions of years and after overcoming the impediments of thousands of births. He gets the power of discrimination and putting even that behind in time and going beyond thought he becomes one with the Brahman. (6:465-467). He then gains that indescribable and unfathomable bliss which is beyond words. He becomes the living image of the state of the Brahman, which is the ultimate destination. (6:469-470). He reaches this state while still in his body. (6:480). Consider him as My life-force *(Prana)*. He experiences that he is the *devotee, devotion* and the *deity* of *devotion* all three in one. This union of love between him and Me can be described only as he being the soul in My body. (6:482-485).

---

18 *Beginning stage of a disciple or an aspirant.*

Wisdom And Knowledge

~∞~

KNOWLEDGE, WORLDLY KNOWLEDGE AND IGNORANCE

Shri Krishna said, "Arjuna, you have now understood what yoga is. Now I shall tell you about Knowledge (of the Brahman) and the worldly knowledge. You may perhaps wonder about the relevance of worldly knowledge here. But it is necessary to know about it first because when Knowledge is experienced the intellect puts the worldly knowledge behind. (7:1-4)

"Arjuna, Knowledge is that where the intellect cannot enter, where thoughts stop, and logic does not work. Worldly knowledge is different from this. And ignorance is to think that worldly knowledge is the true Knowledge i.e. Knowledge of the Brahman. Now I shall tell you the method by which ignorance will disappear, worldly knowledge will burn itself leaving nothing behind and Knowledge will be apparent. (7:5-7). Only one in a thousand longs for this Knowledge. And even among those it is rare that somebody will know Me. (7:10). There are millions of people who jump in the floodwaters of desire for Knowledge of the Brahman, but rare is he who manages to swim across to the other bank. Therefore this is no ordinary matter. It is very deep and very difficult to explain but I shall try to explain it to you. (7:13-14).

PRAKRITI

Arjuna, just as our body casts a shadow, this material universe is My projection, *Maya*, manifesting itself through the principles like *Mahat* (universal intellect) etc.[1] It is also known as *Prakriti*. It consists of eight parts and is the one that creates the three worlds. The eight parts are: the five elements earth, water, air, fire and sky, the mind, the intellect and the ego. (7:15-18).

The state of equilibrium of these eight parts is My basic, subtle or *Para Prakriti*. It is also known as the *Jiva* (individual being). It makes the inert active, is the principle of action in the life-force, and makes the mind feel sorrow and temptation. The capability of the intellect to know, is due to association with it. The ego, which originates because of it, runs the affairs of the world with its support. (7:19-21)

---

1 *Brahman creates the universe through Its power Maya as per Vedanta philosophy) or Prakriti as per Sankhya philosophy. The first principle created by Prakriti is Mahat, the Cosmic intelligence, equivalent to the intellect or Buddhi in humans. The next principle is the Ahankara or ego, the sense of self-identity (not personal pride), and the centre in our consciousness from which we think, act and react. This false sense of identity separates one's real Self from everything else and focuses it upon matter leading a person to think, "I am this body, this is mine, and this is for me." This Ahankara is what is responsible for the material universe. Ahankara expresses itself in three universal attributes or qualities: Sattva, Raja and Tama. The mind, the five senses and the sense organs and the five organs of action are born from the essence of the Sattva attribute (the attribute of stability, purity, wakefulness, clarity and light); Sensations, feelings and emotions are caused due to the Raja attribute that represents dynamic movement; The five elements (earth, water, fire, wind and the sky) that form the material world are created from the Tama attribute (the attribute responsible for the tendency towards inertia and lethargy, darkness, heaviness, deep sleep, ignorance and confusion). (VL-AHR)*

CREATION OF LIFE

When this *subtle* (or *Para*) *Prakriti* lovingly creates the gross *Prakriti*, it gives birth to the living beings in the world. Four types of life are produced (*Jaraja* or born through uterus, *Andaja* or born through eggs, *Swedaja* or from sweat e.g. lice etc., and *Udbija* or born through seeds i.e. plants.) Though all these are equally important they belong to different species. There are 8.4 million of such species and their number in each is countless. (7:22-24).

Nature *(Prakriti)* produces these lives in each species with the help of the five elements and controls their population. Nature makes them to be born, to live in the world and then causes them to die and return to the five elements. In this process it demonstrates the working of actions and non-actions by the creatures. (7:25-26). Though it is Nature which creates this expanse of the material world, it is in reality My projection and therefore I am the beginning, middle and the end of this world. (7:28).

Just as the root cause of mirage is the Sun similarly when this visible universe has dissolved and reached the original state, that original state is nothing but Me. Thus whatever is created and destroyed is in Me and I support it from inside and outside. (7:29-32).

Therefore Arjuna, understand that the liquid principle of water, the feeling of touch of the wind, the light of the sun and moon, is Me. The natural fragrance of earth is Me, the sound from the sky is Me and the sound of *Aum* from the Vedas is also Me. The virility in man is Me, the essence of the ego is Me. (7:33-35). The basic energy in the fire is Me. There are different kinds of living creatures in this world who survive on different kinds of food and I exist inseparably in the means for their survival. (7:36-39).

That which expands with the sprouting of the space (Sky) at the time of the creation of the Universe, and swallows the sounds *A*, *U* and *M* comprising the *AUM* at the time of its annihilation; that which does not vanish even after the form of the Universe (which had remained apparent as long as it existed) vanishes at the time of the final annihilation, that formless entity, that self generated seed of the Universe, is Me. I am giving this knowledge to you. You will realise its relevance when you ponder over it deeply and compare it with the *Sankhya* philosophy. (7:40-43). Now I shall explain this knowledge to you in short. (7:44)

I AM EVERYTHING[2]

The penance of the ascetics is My form alone. Understand without doubt that I am the strength of the strong and the intellect in the intelligent. (7:44-45). I am the desire in all creatures by virtue of which the prescribed behaviour (*Dharma*) and earning the livelihood are possible. Though this desire is controlled by the sense organs, self-restraint does not let them go against the prescribed code (*Dharma*) and towards prohibited actions, and hence the prescribed actions come to a successful conclusion and then a worldly person achieves liberation. (7:46-49). How many things like this should I tell you? All this expanse of the material world has been rooted in Me. (7:51)

I AM THE CREATOR OF *MAYA* BUT IT VEILS ME

The feelings of the mind, having the three attributes *Sattva* (purity), *Rajas* (passion) and *Tamas* (sloth) have been created from Me but even so I am not in them. (7:53- 54) [*Simile*: seed gives rise to a tree and then to wood, but this seed is not in the wood]. (7:55-56). But this Nature or *Maya* which is My projection and has been created from Me, veils Me. Therefore creatures do not realise Me even though they have been created from Me. Just as pearls formed from water do not dissolve in it, similarly all living creatures are My own parts and have acquired life due to *Maya*. But though they have been created from Me, instead of becoming one with Me they

---

2 *It often stated that God is in everything. But Shri Krishna avers that He is not in anything but He is everything.*

get blinded by desires due to selfishness. (7:63- 67)

GOING BEYOND MAYA

Arjuna, the problem is how to go beyond this *Maya* of mine and realise Me. (7:68). Whatever steps one takes to cross this river of *Maya*, become harmful. (7:82). Those who try to cross it on the strength of their intellect, get lost. Those who try to cross, using knowledge are completely swallowed by pride. Those who take the help of the *Vedas* are burdened by the ego and are consumed by arrogance. (7:83-84).Those who tried to use their youthful strength were caught in the sexual lust and eventually, becoming old and demented, died sad and frustrated.[3] (7:85-88). Those who perform *Yajnas* get trapped in the wedge of heavenly enjoyment. (7:89). Those who, desiring liberation, perform ritualistic actions get caught in the issues of right and wrong. (7:90). To say that detachment and discrimination are not sufficient and even all round yoga practice also is rarely useful for crossing this river of *Maya*, is like saying that a sick person who neglects to observe diet will get cured. (7:91-92). A person cannot cross this river of *Maya* by his own efforts. (7:96). Only those who are single-mindedly devoted to Me can cross it. Actually they do not even have to cross it because they have rid themselves of the illusion of *Maya* even before they die. (7:97)

Those who are guided by a *Sadguru* (true Guru),[4] those who hold

---

3 *This sentence is superficially confusing. But when we consider the entire set of statements it would mean that anybody trying to use his personal bodily qualities e.g. intellect, knowledge, ritualistic tendency or even using the youthful energy for doing their daily duties get trapped somehow as indicated. This is further clear from (7:96,97) which states that a person cannot cross this river of Maya by his own efforts but should be single-mindedly devoted to God.*

4 *A Guru means a teacher but a Sadguru or true Guru is one who is a Self-realized person and hence qualified to be a spiritual guide. How can a person who has not himself realized Self can guide a disciple towards it? However in the context of Gita, Guru may always be taken to be Sadguru.*

on to their experiences and have taken the route to Self-realisation, those who by shedding the ego, calming the mind, avoiding desires, followed the path of knowledge for ease in attaining unity with the Brahman, leap towards liberation and attain it by the strength of detachment and with the conviction "I am That". But such devotees are very rare. (7:98-102). Except for that one devotee all others are affected by ego and therefore they forget the Self. They remain unaware of their lack of religious observances, are not ashamed of impending degradation and develop the tendency to do what Vedas forbid. (7:103-104)

Arjuna, totally forsaking the purpose of their rebirth, they get engrossed in sense-pleasures and are full of passions with feelings of "I" and "mine". There is no realisation even when pain and sorrow hit them, because their minds are clouded by the effect of *Maya*. Because of this they miss attaining Me. (7:105-107)

FOUR TYPES OF DEVOTEES

The devotees who gained spiritually from their devotion to Me may be divided into four types. *Aarta* (distressed), *Jijnasu* (curious), *Artharthi* (desirous of wealth) and *Jnani* (enlightened). (7:108-109).

Aarta becomes My devotee because of his desire to be rid of his distress. *Jijnasu* worships Me because he wants to know about Me out of an intellectual curiosity. The reason for which the third i.e. *Artharthi* type worships Me is obvious, it is for wealth. But it is fourth type, i.e. *Jnani* who is My real devotee, for he wants nothing but Me for My own sake. He, by the light of his knowledge has destroyed the darkness of duality between him and Me and achieved oneness with Me and even then wishes to remain My devotee. (7:110-112). From his external actions he appears to be My devotee but internally he has become Me and in the light of this knowledge he knows that I am his soul. Therefore feeling satisfied, I too consider him as My soul. How can he who lives realising the signs beyond life be different from Me even when he is in body?

(7:113, 114, 116-118). I like a devotee who comes to Me with selfish motives but the devotee I really love is the *Jnani* type. (7:119).He is nothing but My soul. (7:126).

MY BEST DEVOTEE

Avoiding the obstacles of desire and anger in the wilderness of sense-pleasures he acquires good tendencies and in the company of saintly people he avoids bad behaviour and treads the straight path of righteous actions. How can one who, desireless of fruits of his actions and who treads the path of devotion through hundreds of lifetimes, bother about the goal of those actions? (7:127-129). As he travels alone in the darkness of possessing the body during successive rebirths, the end of the burden of his karmas dawns. (7:130). Now the morning light of the benevolence of the Guru removes the darkness of ignorance, and with the bright illumination from the rays of Knowledge he realises the wealth of equality. (7:131).Wherever he casts his eyes he sees only Me and nothing but Me. Just as water is within and without a vessel that is immersed in it, so is he within Me and I within him and outside him also. But all this cannot be expressed in words. (7:131-134). A great soul like this is rare (7:137).

WORSHIP WITH INTENT

The rest of them worship Me only for the sake of pleasures and get blinded by desires. (7:138). And once they are possessed by the desire for the fruit of their actions, lust enters the heart extinguishing the light of Knowledge. Thus, remaining internally and externally in the darkness of ignorance, they are distanced from Me and start worshipping other deities with all their heart. (7:139-140). Having already become slaves of *Maya* and overcome by lust they worship other deities with elaborate rituals paying elaborate attention to the rules, means and offerings. (7:141-142). But it is only I who fulfil the desire of these devotees worshipping these deities, because I am present in all the deities. However, he does not believe so and therefore he keeps different feelings towards the various deities. (7:143-144). Such devotees do not know Me because they do not come out of their narrow thinking. Though their desires are fulfilled, the fruits of their efforts are impermanent like a dream and only help the continuation of their life cycles. They reach the realm of the deities whom they worship (and the deities are also impermanent). On the other hand, those who choose the path of devotion to Me with their body and mind alone attain on death, oneness with Me who is eternal. (7:147-150). But the common man does not do so and puts himself to loss. (7:151). Why should he not leave the trap of desire of fruits and fly high on the wings of Self-realisation in the sky of Knowledge? Why should he try to measure the immeasurable bliss of the Self? Why should he consider the formless, Unmanifest Me as Manifest and having form? Why should he try to create rituals for reaching Me when I am in all creatures? (7:155-157). Even though I am in the form of light, people are not able to see Me because of their I-am-the-body feeling, since they are blinded by the veil of *Maya*. Otherwise, tell me, is there anything which is not Me? I alone pervade the entire universe. (7:158-160). Arjuna, I was in all the creatures who ever lived were Me; and at this moment all creatures who are living are Me and those who will be born in the future will also be not different from Me. But this is only in a manner of speaking. Actually nothing is born and nothing dies. (7:161-162). All life is illusion. Thus, though I eternally pervade everybody, yet they are still caught in the birth and death cycles. But there is a reason for it. (7:165)

PITFALLS OF DESIRE

Dnyaneshwar Maharaj now expounds on the genesis and culture of Desire:

Desire was born out of ego and body. Due to its combination with hate, the *delusion* that one is *different from soul* was born. This *delusion* was fostered by the ego. Shunning courage and self-control this delusion started growing due to hope. Under the influence of dissatisfaction it got tirelessly engrossed in sense-pleasures and started behaving perversely. It brought impediments in the path of devotion and paved the paths of evil deeds. Because of it people became confused, went astray in life and came under the heavy burden of sorrow. (7:166-171)

But those who are aware of the useless thorns of doubts and do not get caught in the trap of delusion produced by them, who tread the path of unstinted devotion, crush the doubts, avoid sinful actions and with the speed attained through meritorious actions come near Me and thus escape the clutches of desire and anger. (7:171-174). Then they develop a desire to end this saga of birth and death. Sometime or other they succeed in their efforts and attain the perfect Brahman. Having reached their goal and once the novelty of this Self-realisation fades away they find the world full of bliss, gain peace of mind and there is no more need for actions. They then develop a sense of equality and attain unity with Me. (7:175-179).

Experiencing the aspect of My supremacy over the elements they reach My aspect of *Adhibhuta* (Supreme deity). With the impetus of their Knowledge, when they look at Me as the Supreme deity of the sacrifices or the Supreme Soul, they do not grieve death. Otherwise, when death approaches, people feel that a big calamity is about to fall. But nobody knows that those who have become one with Me do not leave Me even when they die. Those who have gained this perfect Knowledge are the real yogis. (7:180-184).

8

The Imperishable Absolute

❦

WHAT IS *ADHIBHUTA, ADHIDAIVATA* ETC.

Arjuna said, "Shri Krishna, please clarify as to what are *Brahman, Karma* and *Adhyatma*. Also explain to me what *Adhibhuta* and *Adhidaivata* are. I am not able to understand what *Adhiyajna* is and what he is in the body. Also tell me how those who have attained control over the mind can know you at the time of their death. (8:1-5)

Shri Krishna replied as follows,

Brahman: That which, in spite of being contained in the porous body does not leak out, that which is subtle but not non-existent, that which has been strained through the fabric of the sky and which, though rare and thin does not fall through the bag of the material world is the ultimate Brahman *(Parabrahman).* (8:15-17)

Adhyatma: The natural state of the principle of the Brahman which takes form but is not created and even after losing it is not destroyed is called *Adhyatma* or Supreme Soul. (8:18-19)

Karma: Different elements like *Mahat*,[1] *Prakriti,* Ego etc. are created from that formless Brahman and the formation of the Primeval Egg *(Brahmanda)* begins. Because of the Primeval thought the Primeval Egg gives rise to countless life species. But though they appear different, the limitless Brahman pervades all of them. It is found that Brahman alone is the root of all these millions of species. *One cannot find who created the world and why it was created but its affairs go on.* But the process of creation of this world continues growing. Thus, the action of creation without creator, which is attributed to the Brahman is called *Karma.*[2] (8:21-29)

Adhibhuta: Now listen to what *Adhibhuta*[3] is. That which is formed from the five elements and which can be sensed because of the five sense organs but is destroyed as soon as it is separated from them is called *Adhibhuta* or principle of existence (life force). (8:30-32)

Adhidaivata (Supreme Being)*: Adhidaivata* is *Purusha*[4] the Supreme Being or the principle of divinity. He enjoys whatever is created by *Prakriti.* He is the one that activates the life force (consciousness), the master of the organs, and one by whose association the thoughts, desires etc. continue to exist even after the body dies. He is actually the ultimate Self, but due to ego, he gets trapped in the struggle of life, and experiences happiness, sorrow etc. Ordinarily understood as the living being, he may be called *Adhidaivata* (Supreme Being) of the body which is made of the five principles. (8:33-36).

Adhiyajnya (Principal Sacrifice)*:* One who causes the I-am-the-body

1 *Universal Intelligence. See footnote in Ch 7.*

2 *Note that this Karma is different from the actions of an individual. In spite of the action of creation God or Brahman is still a non-doer. (See 5:76-89).*

3 *Bhuta means a living being, a creature. Adhi implies whatever is inside. Different sources give different meanings of the word Adhibhuta. E.g. Gita by Gorakhpur Press translates it only as matter, (GP-B). Dr Radhakrishnan translates it as created things. (SR-B) But considering the statement that it is what exists in the body made of panchamahabhutas (five elements) and vanishes when separated from them, it should be the principle of existence or life and not soul because soul cannot vanish.*

4 *The Purusha of the pair Purusha and Prakriti of the Sankhya Philosophy. This is discussed later (13: 949-1036).*

feeling to extinguish is the *Adhiyajnya* (Principle Sacrifice) in the body. Secondly, I am both *Adhibhuta* and *Adhidaivata* but just as pure gold mixed with impurity has to be called impure as long as it is associated with the impurity, this *Adhibhuta* etc., as long as they are veiled by ignorance must be considered different from the Supreme Brahman. Otherwise they are not different. (8:37-41) When the I-am-the-body feeling vanishes, the original unity with the Brahman becomes evident. Where this happens, that *Adhiyajnya* is Me. (8:45) It was by keeping this in mind that I had told you earlier (Ch IV) that all *yajnas* are created through actions. I am opening to you the treasure of liberation where all living things ultimately come to rest. Avoid sense-pleasures by control of the senses with dispassionate attitude. Then attain knowledge by means of the yoga technique using *Vajrasana*, breath and mind control. Once Knowledge merges into the subject of Knowledge, then only the subject, i.e., Brahman, remains. That subject is called *Adhiyajnya*. (8:46-53) As I told you just now, those who know Me as *Adhiyajnya* from beginning to the end consider the body to be a mere cover and dwell in the Self. Such a person does not have awareness about external matters. He who thus becomes one with Me from outside as well as inside, sheds the layers of the five principles from his body automatically. He who is not aware of his body even while living does not feel grief from death. A vessel immersed in water has water inside as well as outside. Does water break if the vessel breaks? Similarly even if body gets destroyed, Brahman continues to be everywhere and therefore how can the intellect which has become one with It get destroyed? Therefore those who remember Me at the time of death become one with me. (8:59-68)

STATE AFTER DEATH

The normal rule is that after death, a person attains that state which is the state of his mind at the time of death. He cannot avoid it. Just as one dreams of things which are constantly in mind while awake, whatever one longs for in life comes to the mind at the time of death and he attains that state. Therefore make a habit of always remembering Me. Consider that whatever you hear, think, see, speak is Me throughout, then I am always with you. I assure you that if you offer your mind and intellect to Me then you will attain only Me. If you have any doubts about this then experience it by practising it. (8:69-80)

Purify your conscious mind by this practice and lead it to the spiritual path. If the mind, which takes one here and there gets engrossed in the Self, then who cares or remembers whether the body exists or not? The mind merges with Consciousness that is solid bliss. (8:81-85)

ATTAINMENT OF BRAHMAN BY YOGA

With the knowledge that the faultless Brahman is formless and without birth and death, that It witnesses all, is older than the sky and subtler than the atom, that the affairs of the world go on by association with It, that It gives birth to all the visible world, that the world lives by It, that It is beyond logic and beyond imagination, that eyes cannot see It even in broad daylight, that like a sunbeam It always appears lustrous to men of Knowledge, that It never sets, he (a person of Self-realisation) who concentrates on It with steady mind at the time of death while outwardly, sitting in the lotus position facing north, with the eternal bliss gained by practising desireless actions *(Karmayoga)*, with the love of Self-realisation and using the yogic techniques mastered for attaining it quickly, he brings the life-force *(Prana)* from the centre *(Chakra)* of fire or energy (i.e. *Manipur Chakra* near the navel) through the central nerve that is the *Sushumna* route to the *Brahmarandhra* or aperture on the crown, where the life-force merges with the sky-principle. The immobile mind and the life force appear outwardly to have merged. But because the mind has become stable and devotion steady, and with the strength of the yogic power, that life-force (which) eliminates the movable and the immovable, enters the centre of the eyebrows and vanishes there. Just as the sound of a bell vanishes in the bell itself, the devotee leaves his body and merges into pure Brahman, which is My lustrous form. (8:86-99).

Akshar And Kshar

It (the Brahman) has been called *Akshar* i.e. immutable or indestructible by knowers of the highest Knowledge, which is the Knowledge of the Self; Whereas, that which men of Knowledge sense and measure by their senses is *Kshar* or mutable. That which is impossible to know is *Akshar*. It is the same as the highest Soul and is above *Prakriti* (Nature). (8:102-103).Only dispassionate persons who have given up sense-pleasures by control of the senses, attain that state which the desireless covet. (8:104-105)

Concentrating On Aum At Death -Time

Arjuna, steady the mind in the heart by breaking the mind's habit to wander. But this is possible only when the senses are controlled with determination. After the mind becomes steady one should meditate on *Aum* and bring the life-force *(Prana)* to the *Brahmarandhra.*[5] Then by concentrating, it should be brought to the boundary of consciousness. Then when *A, U* and *Ma* merge in the half syllable *Ma* it should be made steady in the Consciousness. The uttering of *Aum* then stops and life-force also dissolves in the Consciousness, but the bliss that is Brahman remains. (8:111-117)

Aum is My monosyllable form. He who dies while meditating on it undoubtedly reaches Me and there is nothing more for him to be attained after that. (8:118-119).

I Am The Servant Of Devotees

Arjuna, you may perhaps doubt how one should remember Me at the time of death when the senses are under its shadow and the joy of living is lost. Do not let doubts like "How can one sit

---

5 *See chapter 6.*

up, control the senses and how can one recite *Aum* in the state of mind when it is evident that you are going to die?" trouble you. Because, whoever who serves Me constantly, I become his servant at the time of his death. (8:120-123). Such persons give up sense-pleasures, control their active life and keeping Me in the heart they experience the joy of the Self and thus worship Me by being constantly engrossed in Me and close to Me. *Were I to come to My devotees only if they remember Me at the time of their death, then of what use is their worship? Do I not, purely out of compassion, rush to any person who prays for My help in their distress? But if I were to wait till My devotees pray to Me, before I go to them, then who would like to be a devotee?*[6] I must rush to them the moment they remember Me otherwise I will not be able to bear the burden of their devotion. It is for this reason, i.e. to pay the debt of their devotion that I go to the devotees to serve them at the time of death. In order that the weakness of their bodies does not cause them distress, I keep them bound to the state of Self-realisation, make their mind calm and steady and thus bring those dear ones to Me. (8:124- 134). The devotees also are not sorry to leave their body because they do not have attachment for it. Also, they do not feel that at the time of death I should come to them to take them to Me because they have already become one with Me while they are still alive. (8:136-137). Those who have attained this infinite Me are not reborn. (8:151)

EVEN GODS CANNOT AVOID LIFE CYCLES

On the other hand, even Brahmadeo, who is proud of his Brahmahood cannot escape the life-death cycles. (8:152). One day of Brahmadeo lasts one thousand sets of the four *yugas*, with a similar span for his night.[7] The fortunate persons who dwell in

---

6 *These are very touching words of Bhagwan that indicate his love for his devotees.*

7 *Brahmadeo's one day is called a kalpa at the beginning of which the universe is created and is destroyed at the end of the day. His night is also of the same duration, during which Universe remains in dormant state. 1 Kalpa = 1000*

this *loka* (plane) of Brahmadeo do not return to earth but remain permanently in heaven. Ordinary deities are nothing compared with them. Even their king Indra does not have a life span of even one *Prahara*[8] (3 hours) out of one day of *Brahmaloka*, the best of the fourteen *lokas*.[9] During the length of one day of *Brahmaloka*, fourteen Indras come and go. (8:156-158)

When the day dawns in *Brahmaloka*, the formless Brahman gives birth to the material Universe. (8:160). After four *Praharas*, Brahmadeo's night starts and the expanse of the universe suddenly vanishes and again starts as before at dawn. (8:161). Thus in one day and night of Brahmadeo, the universe is created and destroyed. The vastness of this *Brahmaloka* is such that the seed of this universe is contained in it but even then it is caught in the cycle of life and death. (8:165-166). Actually, the manifested universe created at dawn merges with the unmanifested at night. This state of oneness with the unmanifested is called the state of equality. (8:167-168).

Mahayugas, 1 Mahayuga = 4 yugas i.e. 4,320,000 years; i.e. 1 kalpa = 4320 million years. Fourteen Manus (rulers of mankind) rule during one Kalpa. There is an intervening perioid of 1 Kritayuga length between two Manus during which there is a deluge. The Indra mentioned in the above paragraph actually should be Manu the legendary ruler of mankind. Brahmadeo's life is 100 of his years. All this is to establish that even gods we worship, though they have a longer life span, are perishable and hence have to undergo birth and death cycles. Only Brahman is permanent, and only a person who has realized it is freed from the birth-death cycles.

8 One day-night = 8 praharas i.e. 1 prahara = 3 hrs.

9 Lokas: According to Puranic concept, Brahmadeva created 14 lokas which may be translated as regions of the universe where different types of entities live. There are seven higher lokas the lowest being the earth. These are: 1. Bhuh,(the earth);2. Bhuvah (between the earth and the sun, the abode of Munis, Siddhas; 3. Swah between the sun and the pole star, the abode of gods; 4. Maha, abode of rishis; 5. Jana, abode of Brahma's sons, Sanaka, Sananda, Sanatan and Sanat-kumara; 6.Tapa, abode of deities called Vairagis. (7.) Satya or Brahma. The seven lower than the earth are: Atala, Vitala, Sutala, Talatala, Mahatala, Rasatala and Patala (lowest). There is no rebirth for those from Brahmaloka. See Loka in (EP) Bibliography

BRAHMAN IS MY HIGHEST ABODE

Thus the diversity of the universe is contained in the uniqueness of the unmanifestable. This property is called equality. (8:169). In this state of equality one cannot see similarity or dissimilarity therefore the five elements are not manifested. Once the form dissolves then the worldness of the world vanishes but that from which the world is created remains as it was and is known by the natural name, unmanifestable. One is suggested from the other but they are not two different things. (8:170-172). Both the attributes of manifestability and unmanifestabilty occur in Brahman alone. But Brahman is neither manifestable nor unmanifestable. It is neither eternal nor destructible. It is beyond these two attributes and is axiomatic. (8:174-175). The name *Akshar* itself signifies its indestructibility. It is called the ultimate state *(Paramagati)* since there is nothing beyond it. *But it appears as if it is dormant in this body because it does not do actions nor cause them to be done, but in spite of this, no function of the body stops.* (8:181-183). The affairs of the body like the awareness of the intellect, transactions of the mind, play of the organs and movement of the life-force continue nicely without its [Brahman's] doing anything. (8:186-187).

Since it *(Akshar)* dwells quietly in the body it is known as *Purusha* (Supreme Being or Soul). Since It is loyal to *Prakriti* also it is called *Purusha*. (8:188-189). It is all encompassing and is called by superior yogis as the Supreme Being beyond ego *(Paraatpar)*. *It comes searching for the true devotees and rewards them for their devotion.* (8:190-191). It is the dwelling place of those who believe that the universe is the form of Brahman, it is the place of glory for the ego-less and knowledge to those beyond attributes, kingdom of happiness for the desireless, food served for the contented and protector like a mother to those devotees who do not bother about worldly problems. The path of devotion is the direct approach to It. (8:192-195). There is no rebirth after Self-realisation. It is My highest abode. **I am revealing this secret to you.** (8:202-203).

AUSPICIOUS DEATH TIME FOR *YOGIS*[10]

There is another way of understanding easily the abode where yogis go after leaving their body. If a *yogi* has to leave his body accidentally at an improper time then he has to take rebirth. If a *yogi* leaves his body at an *auspicious* time then the *yogi* attains Brahman immediately but if the time is *improper* then he has to take rebirth. Union with Brahman and rebirth depend upon the time at which death occurs. Listen to what those times are. (8:204-207).

At the moment of death the five elements from which the body is formed, leave it. When a Yogi's death is near, his intellect is not clouded, memory does not become blind and mind also does not die. On the other hand because of the protection by the experience of the Brahman, all the organs remain bright and this brightness lasts until death. But for this to happen it is necessary that the fire principle (heat) is active in the body. (8:208-211). At the time of death, because of aggravation by the harmful airs, the body is filled throughout by phlegm and the intensity of fire in it is destroyed. At such a time there is no vigour in the life-force, then what can intellect do? Therefore without fire (heat) the power of action *(Chetana)* in the body does not survive and the body is like a lump of mud. Under these conditions the *yogi* spends the remaining time of his life in darkness. (8:213-215).In this state how is it possible for him to remember his past spiritual progress (at the time of death) and attain Self? Due to the extinguishing of the power of action in the mire of phlegm he loses his memory and his past spiritual achievements become ineffective prior to death. In short, since the basic support for knowledge is the fire-principle, its strength must be plentiful at the time of death. (8:216-219).

10 *Here, a yogi means not only one who practices yoga and meditates but in general a man of Knowledge, as mentioned in the paragraph (8:220-225). Paths applicable to a yogi and to an ordinary individual (Jiva) are discussed in this and the next paragraphs. Apparently, a man of Knowledge does not necessarily means a self-Realised person as seen from (8:251-252) wherefrom it is clear that such a person becomes Brahman even while he lives and does not have to bother about death to reach there.*

The factors favourable for yogis to leave the body in order to attain Brahman are internally the strength of the fire principle within the body and externally the bright fortnights (of lunar months shwn in Hindu calenders as *Shuklapaksha*) during *Uttarayana*[11] period (the six months period of the northward passage of the sun) and daytime. Knowers of Brahman who leave their body under these favourable conditions become the Supreme Brahman themselves. Arjuna, this is the greatness of the path of yoga, which is the straightforward path to liberation. In summary, the first step in this path is the fire (heat) in the body, the second is the flame of the fire, the third is the time of the day, the fourth is the bright fortnight and the fifth and the last is the six month period of the northward passage of the sun. This is the best condition and is called *Archira Marg*[12] *(path)*. (8:220-225).

INAUSPICIOUS DEATH TIME FOR *YOGIS*

Now I shall tell you about which are the inauspicious times for death. When death approaches, the wind and phlegm in the body get aggravated, darkness spreads in the subtle mind, organs become lethargic, memory gets confused, mind becomes disturbed and life force feels constrained. The fire principle becomes inactive and consciousness of the body becomes engulfed in smoke. (8:225-228). He is neither dead nor in his senses because the life-force is weakened. His body lies motionless waiting for death. Thus the mind, intellect and body get suffocated by the smoke and all his efforts for liberation get wasted. (8:230-231). This internal state of the body together with the external conditions: dark fortnight,

---

11 *During the year Sun apparently moves northward (Uttarayana, uttara = north, ayana = movement) from about December 21 to June 20 and southwards (Dakshinayana) between June 20 and December 21. These are considered as daytime and nighttime of the gods and one solar year is called a day of the gods. The different paths after death for a man of Knowledge and an ordinary person as mentioned here are beliefs expressed in the Chandogya Up. Book V, Ch 10.1-8 and also Brihadaranyaka Up. VI.2.15-16. (UP-CH, UP-BA)*

12 *Gita does not mention Archira path. I have not been able to find the origin. Probably it is derived from Sanskrit Architum=to worship.*

night-time and the months during the southward passage of the sun can only lead to rebirth. A *yogi* who dies under these conditions, because he is a *yogi* goes to *Chandraloka* (Moon plane) and is reborn after some time. (8:232-235). This is the smoky path to rebirth.[13] (8:236). On the other hand *Archira Path* is the best, easy, pleasant and leads to liberation. (8:237)

---

13 In the Chandogya and Brihadaranayak Upanishads (See footnote 10) the return path to rebirth is given as follows: Having dwelt there as long as there is residue (of good karmas), they return by that course by which they come to space, from space into air; after becoming the air, they become the smoke; then mist; then cloud and after having become cloud he rains down. They are born here as rice and barley, herbs and trees, as sesame plants and beans. From thence the release becomes extremely difficult. For, whoever eats the food and sows the seed, becomes like unto him. Persons with good karmas will quickly attain a good birth of a Brahmin or a Kshatriya, or a Vaishya. But those whose conduct has been evil, will quickly attain an evil birth, the birth of a dog, the birth of a hog or the birth of a Chandala. Though a modern man will trash these ideas one must appreciate the inventiveness of the ancients to explain phenomena in an age when there was no scientific thought.

In scientific context, parapsychological research has shown that souls to be reborn attach themselves to the assigned foetus between seventh and eighth months of pregnancy (HW-LL). The late Swami Krishnanand of Bhadran (near Baroda, Gujarat) confirms this through an incident in his life when he was accosted by a yogi at Jagannathpuri who told him that he was going to leave his body in a couple of days and asked him to manage the post death procedures. He further informed that he was going to be reborn in after two months (on 25-2-1954) in his final birth cycle, as a girl in a blacksmith family living in Behala, Calcutta and also that the girl would live only up to age of sixteen. Swami Krishnanand personally went to the family and witnessed these events. When questioned, the yogi explained to Swamiji about the time of attachment to foetus. Until then, the foetus is merely a blank body of blood, bone and flesh, nourished through the mother's soul-force and fed by the building essences through the umbilical chord. It is only after the merger of the astral body with it that the unborn baby begins to experience pain and pleasures and remembers its past lives. After birth, the baby's umbilical cord is cut off and from then onwards it derives the sustaining energy and the life current from the subtle body that has taken over. (SK-TE)

Saicharitra mentions Shri Saibaba telling about his devotee Mrs Khaparde that "In former birth the lady was a merchant's fat cow yielding much milk. Then she disappeared and took birth in a gardener's family, then in a Kshatriya family and married a merchant. Then she was born in a Brahmin family. I saw her after a very long time; let me take some sweet morsels of love from her dish." Saicharitra gives two more instances of humans taking rebirth as animals: in one case two brothers reborn as goats after killing each other out of enmity and the other, two greedy persons, reborn as a frog and a snake. (GD-SS)

BETTER ATTAIN BRAHMAN WHILE LIVING

I have told you about these two paths which have existed from ancient times so that you can benefit from their knowledge. (8:238-239). If a person misses the *Archira* path and falls in the trap of the smoky path then he has to go through the painful stages of rebirth. I had to explain the two paths to you so that the pains of rebirth can be avoided. But whatever falls to his fate is his real path.[14] (8:244-246). Who can tell which path a person will get? Why should there be any path at all to attain Brahman after death? Whether one is dead or alive one is in reality Brahman only. (8:247-248). *Those who attained Brahman while still in the body do not bother about the body or when it is going to die. Why do they have to bother about whether the path is good or bad? (8:251-252).*[15] Therefore Arjuna, be equipped with Yoga so that you attain Brahman. Then it does not matter when and where you shed your body, the unification with Brahman will be eternal. (8:256-257).

MERIT INFERIOR TO BRAHMAN

One cannot compare pure Brahman with the merit gained through study of Vedas, performance of *yajnas* and by donations. (8:261-262).When a great yogi compares the heavenly pleasures with the bliss of the Brahman he finds the former to be inferior compared with the latter. Then, he steps up from the heavenly pleasures to the level of the Brahman. (8:266-267).

---

14 *However, see Shri Krishna's promise in ovis (6:437- 485).*

15 *This is clear from the historical fact that many great yogis, including Shri Saibaba of Shirdi and Shri Gajanan Maharaj of Shegaon left their physical bodies during Dakshinayana period. Shripad Shrivallabh, the first avatar of Shri Dattatreya also took samadhi during the dark half of the month of Ashwin that falls in Dakshinayana period.*

9

Sovereign Knowledge And Sovereign Mystery

~∞∞~

KNOWLEDGE OF SELF AND WORLD

Shri Krishna said, "Arjuna, I shall once more tell you about the root of Knowledge which is the greatest secret in My heart. But you may wonder why I am revealing My secret to you. It is because you are the personification of the sense of devotion and will never ignore what I tell you. Therefore I am eager that whatever is in My heart should enter your heart once for all. (9:34-37).

"One may by all means tell his secrets to a devotee who is of clean mind, of pure intellect, who does not slander others and is faithful. And right now there is nobody else except you here possessing these qualities. Now I am going to tell you about Knowledge of the Self as well as knowledge of the world (i.e. material knowledge). (9:40-42). When these two types of knowledge are obtained, a seeker leaves the worldly affairs to the world and reaches the state of liberation.[1] (9:46).

---

1 *An aspirant must know the impermanent nature of worldly objects and the happiness one might receive from them, which will convince him the importance of the spiritual knowledge that leads to lasting bliss and liberation.*

This Knowledge, which is of highest status, most secret, peerless among the holy things, and the basis of the entire *Dharma* is the best among the best. Once a person gets this Knowledge he has no reason to be reborn. Once the Guru utters it, the disciple easily awakens to the Knowledge of the Self already present within him. (9:47-49). It has another quality. Once obtained it does not get lost. It does not get reduced by experiencing it. Now you may very well ask how is it that people did not get hold of this incomparable knowledge until now. (9:52-53). But you need not have any doubts. (9:56). You see, though I, giver of all types of happiness, am within the hearts of all people, yet under the influence of *Maya* (delusion) they fall prey to the worldly desires. (9:60). Hindered by ego and affection, instead of crossing this stream of the worldly affairs to reach Me, they go on shuttling between the two banks of life and death. (9:62).

If you ask what My nature is, then understand that like the Sun I am always in front of all and not like something which appears now and disappears sometime later. If you ask My expanse, then understand that this whole universe is Me alone, like a tree growing out of a seed. My formless Unmanifest form has taken the form of this universe. Though I am formless, I take form and create this expanse of the three worlds. (9:63-66). All the principles starting from *Mahat* to the body are really created from Me but even so I am not in those principles as I have explained earlier. (9:67, 69).

EVERYTHING IS ME

If you see My form beyond *Maya* without using your imagination then you will realise that My statement that all principles are in Me is false because everything is Me. Thought creates a twilight zone between the ignorance and knowledge. In this twilight zone, the intellect becomes dim and in that dim light, even though I am undivided from everything I appear to be separate from the beings. But once the twilight of thought vanishes then it becomes clear that I am undivided from the beings. (9:71-73). He who imagines beings to be within Me, has those beings only in his imagination, but when the *Maya* which is responsible for the thoughts dissolves, the false existence of the beings also vanishes and what remains is My pure form. (9:79-80). Thought causes illusion of the five elements in undivided Brahman but if the thought is abandoned then one cannot imagine even in a dream that the elements are in Me and I am in the elements. Therefore, to say that I support the elements or that I am in the elements is like talking in a delirium caused by the fever of thoughts. (9:81-83). Therefore Arjuna, the ideas that I am the soul of this universe or I am the support of all creatures are false. It is like the mirage caused by the sun's rays. But just as the sun and its brightness are the same I am also not different from the elements. Did you understand this Divine scheme? Therefore the creatures are not different from Me and I am also not different from them. (9:84-88).

The air appears to be different from the space, which contains it, only if it moves; otherwise it appears to be the same as space. Similarly if one imagines that creatures are in Me then it appears to be so but in a thoughtless state *(Nirvikalpa)* of *samadhi* this illusion vanishes and it becomes apparent that everywhere it is only Me. Existence or otherwise of the beings is due to the imagining about them as separate beings, and once this imagination which originates in ignorance vanishes they also vanish. Therefore understand carefully this Divine scheme. Be a wave in this ocean of Self- realisation and then you will realise that what is pervading this living and nonliving universe is only you. (9:89-93).

Arjuna, has the dream of dualism which you were having vanished? In order that you should not get that dream again you should follow the path of pure Knowledge of the Brahman, which I am going to explain to you. (9:94- 96).

I CREATE EVERYTHING THROUGH *MAYA*

Arjuna, keep in mind that it is only *Maya* which does the

creation as well as destruction of all creatures. (9:97). This *Maya* is also known by the name *Prakriti*.[2] I have already told you that it is of two kinds. (See 7:15) One of them manifests itself in eight forms (Earth, water, air, fire, sky, mind, intellect and ego) and the second is in the form of life. At the time of the great deluge all elements dissolve in *Prakriti* in their unmanifestable form. (9:98-100). At the end of the deluge all that is created by *Prakriti* returns to it. (9:103). Listen to the explanation of the legend about My creating the universe again. (9:105).

When I establish this *Prakriti* it assumes the form of the universe made up of the five elements. (9:106-107). When I establish it, it is like a person waking up from a dream into the wakeful state. Just as when a king builds a city he himself does not have to do anything, likewise, when this universe is created I do not have to do anything. (9:110-111). Once I establish *Prakriti*, the life-forms in the universe develop automatically by its support in the same way as plant-forms sprout and grow from the seeds with the help of the earth. (9:117-118). All life is thus controlled by *Prakriti*, therefore the responsibility for creation of life and its support is not mine. These actions are removed from Me though they originate in Me. How can the actions which ultimately merge in Me, bind Me? (9:122-124). Though the material world created by *Prakriti* has My support I am indifferent to all that and I neither do those actions (of creation etc.) nor cause them to be done. (9:126-127).Though I am in all creatures I have no connection with their actions. (9:129).

This living and non-living universe is created by Me only through the establishment of *Prakriti*; therefore with this logic, I am taken to be the cause of its creation. (9:132). Therefore understand in the light of Knowledge, the Divine principle that all living things are in Me but I am not in them or (going still further), all living things are not in Me and I am not in them. Do not forget this fundamental

---

2 *According to the Vedanta philosophy Brahman creates the universe through Its inseparable power Maya; in Sankhya philosophy the corresponding pair is Purusha and Prakriti. In Shaivaite philosophy the corresponding pair is Shiva and Shakti.*

thing, which is My most guarded secret, which you should enjoy through Meditation after shutting off your sense-organs. Nobody can understand My true nature unless this is understood. Normally, it is thought that this principle is understood through logic but it is useless unless it is experienced. (9:133-137). People speak about Self-realisation without experiencing it but it becomes clear that it was not so and they miss it. (9:139). If you are afraid of this world and you really desire Me then you remember this fundamental thing. (9:140).

DELUSION THAT I HAVE FORM

Some people consider Me as a human being. Those who see Me with gross (materialistic) eyes do not really know Me but these ignorant people confidently say they do. It is their shallow knowledge that comes in the way of real knowledge. (9:142-145).

Those who determinedly got entangled in the worldly affairs but yet try to seek Me, are like a person trying to reach the reflection of the moon in water rather than the real moon; or like a person who drinks rice water and expects the effects of nectar. (9:150-151).

(Now Dnyaneshwar Maharaj ridicules the peoples' practice, done through misdirected attitude and wrong understanding, of treating God like a human being with human attributes instead of the highest power without attributes:)

Because of delusion they consider Me a human being and think that the laws of birth and death apply to Me. Thus, they assign a name to Me who is nameless; attribute actions to Me who is actionless; bodily functions to Me who is without body. They imagine a form for Me when I am formless; social behaviour by Me who is beyond all rules of conduct; a caste to one who is casteless, attributes to one without attributes, limbs to one without any, a measure to the immeasurable Me; location to one who is everywhere. They imagine ears, eyes, race and form in Me when I am without any. Though I am Unmanifestable, desireless and self-satiated they assign manifestability, desire and satiety to Me; I am without clothes or ornaments but they put them on Me; and I am the creator of this universe and they look for My origin. When I am in fact self-born, they make My idol and install it with ritualistic breathing of life into it. They invoke My presence and revoke it. They assign childhood, youth and old age to Me; when I am immortal they imagine death for Me and grieve imagining that I died; when I am present equally in all beings, they assign feelings of friendship and animosity to Me. Though I do not belong to any family or race they describe it so. Though I am the storehouse of bliss they describe Me as desirous of various pleasures. Though I am the soul of the entire universe, they slander Me saying I am partial to some and that I destroy others out of anger. Thus they attach human attributes to Me and consider these to be the real Me. If they see an idol they say it is God and if it breaks then they throw it saying there is no God in it. Thus the state of their knowledge is opposed to the real one and comes in the way of their gaining real knowledge. (9:155-171) In short, one who has such ideas about Me lives in vain. (9:172). Shame to the life of such fools and their actions! Their learning of Scriptures is as useless as weapons in the hands of a girl or a *mantra* told to an unclean person. (9:175-177).

Dangers From Worldly Entanglement

Similarly, all the knowledge and behaviour of those who have no control on their mind, becomes useless. They are caught in the grips of *Prakriti* thus getting entangled in worldly affairs and their mind gets afflicted by the *Tama* attribute affecting their reason and discrimination. Desire and violence generate dissatisfaction in them leading to unrighteous behaviour. Knowledge is destroyed by hate. Persons with materialistic thinking are specially victims of *Prakriti* and are affected by delusion. Affected by *Tama* attribute they cannot be saved by righteous thinking and are lost. (9:178-185).

I Am Where The Saints Are

Now listen to the description of saintly persons which gives pleasure to the tongue. (9:187).

I remain confined like a hermit in the clear conscience of such saintly persons whose detachment does not leave them even in their dream. Their benevolent concern is governed by righteousness and their intellect has the touch of discrimination. By bathing in the river of Knowledge, they have experienced the perfect Brahman and attained peace. Their devotion has reached such a peak that they do not desire liberation. Even in their normal behaviour ethics is apparent. They are full of peace and their consciousness has spread so much as to pervade even Me the pervader of all. Thus, these great souls, by knowing My true nature, become devoted to Me with increasing love without the slightest thought that they are different from Me. Thus they serve Me even after they become Me, but there is an interesting aspect to it. (9:188-196).

Such devotees, by dancing freely during *Kirtans* (discourses) have made the process of atonement obsolete because in their case there is no sin left. They are personifications of self-restraint, self-suppression and are verily to be considered places of pilgrimage. Thus they destroy the sorrows in the world by My name alone. (9:197-200). They brighten the world with their effulgence and by singing My name everywhere. (9:203-204). You may search for Me all over the universe, but one place you can always find Me is the place where these devotees sing My name under the spell of which they forget everything and remain happy. Continuously uttering My names: Krishna, Vishnu, Hari, Govinda and discussing spiritual matters they sing My praises and move about everywhere. (9:205-211).

And Arjuna, they keep their body and mind in complete control and sitting in *vajrasana* position and practising *pranayama* they go in the *samadhi* state and experience complete Self-realisation in the light flashes of *Kundalini* helped by the mind and the life-force. Thus the path of devotion is deep and mysterious and those who follow it realise that I completely pervade everything living and nonliving. From Brahmadeo to the tiny gnat and the creatures between these two extremes are all My forms. They thus identify everything with My form and respect it. To be humble and polite to every living being becomes their nature. Thus I have explained to you the nature of the great devotion. Now I shall tell you about those who worship Me through performance of *yajna* or sacrifice of Knowledge (i.e. through the path of Knowledge) though I have already told you about this earlier (Chapter IV) (9:212-229)

YAJNA OF KNOWLEDGE

This *yajna* of knowledge is as follows: The original thought that "I am one but I desire to be many," is the pole for tying the sacrificial animal and dualism is that animal. The five elements are the *pandal* (temporary enclosed shelter), the special attributes of the five elements namely the five organs and the five types of vital breaths *(Pranas)* are the material to be used in the *yajna* and ignorance is the *ghee* (clarified butter) to be burnt in it. In this *yajna*, the mind and the intellect are the two pits in which the fire of Knowledge is ignited. The feeling of equanimity towards pleasure and pain is the altar. The dexterity of the intellect to discriminate is the *Mantras* in the *yajna*. Peace is the pair of vessels *sruk* and *sruva* used in the *yajna*. The seeker is the host who performs the *yajna*. Using the vessels of experience, the *mantra* of discrimination and rituals of Knowledge, he sacrifices the dualism and destroys the ignorance and then what remains is only the host and the rituals. And when the seeker gets the purifying bath by the water of Self-realisation then he does not find the elements, organs and their objects to be separate from each but considers all of them to be one. When he experiences Brahman in the entire universe, the talk of his being an individual living being ends and he believes that from Brahmadeo downwards the Supreme Soul has pervaded everything. Thus some people worship Me by attaining Brahman through the *yajna* of Knowledge. (9:239- 248)

Some others believe that the material world is varied right from the beginning and it has different names too but that basically they are same, like the different organs belonging to the same body. (9:250). They believe that even if people are different and their nature different too, I am in all of them.[3] Thus they behave with the knowledge that everything in the world is Brahman and this also is a *yajna* of Knowledge but of a different kind in which they do not allow ideas of duality to touch their minds which are full of knowledge of the Brahman, by which they see Me in everything they perceive. (9:252-254). My expanse is same as the expanse of their knowledge of the Brahman and this itself is their worship *(upasana)* which they achieve without doing anything. But people who do not understand this are not able to attain Me. (9:261). Actions of all persons done by various means ultimately reach Me, but fools do not understand this and therefore do not attain Me. (9:264).

When that knowledge is obtained it becomes clear that basically I am the Vedas and the *Kratu* (sacred rite) to be performed according to the rituals given in them is also Me. The *yajna*, which emerges from it in all its main and secondary aspects, is also Me. The uttering *"swaaha"*, with which offering to gods is made, is also Me. Different herbs like *Soma* are also Me. Offerings in fire like *ghee*, firewood, the *mantra* with which the offering is made, the priest who offers it in My form as fire – are all Me. (9:265-268).

I AM THE FATHER AND THE MOTHER OF UNIVERSE

I am also the father of this universe created by the eight types of *Prakriti* by association with Me. Just as in the half-male-half-female form of the Supreme Dancer (Lord Shiva as *Nataraja*) both the male and female parts are present, I am also the mother of this entire living and non-living universe. He with whose support this

---

3 *Though it says here "people believe I am in all of them", elsewhere Shri Krishna asserts that "He is them".*

living universe survives and grows is none other than Me. I am also the grandfather of the universe because it is through My mindless state that the pair *Prakriti* and *Purusha* which gave birth to the universe was created. (9:269-272)

The place where all paths of Knowledge meet, where all Vedas came together, that which is the subject of knowledge, that about which different streams of thought merge to agree unanimously, that which is known as `holy', all these are only Me. (9:273-274).

I am the *AUM* sound, which is the source of the primary sound that sprouted from the seed of the Brahman. The letters *A, U* and *Ma* contained in the *AUM* gave birth to the three Vedas namely Rig-Veda, Yajur-veda and Sama-veda. Therefore these Vedas and the family of the subsequent literature is also Me. (9:275-277).

The highest place where *Prakriti* (in which this entire living and non-living universe is contained) takes rest when tired is also Me. I am the husband of that *Prakriti* who lives with My support and gives birth to the universe. I am the one who enjoys her attributes in her association. I am also the master of the entire universe. (9:278-280)

It is My command that sky (space or ether) should be everywhere, that wind should not be quiet even for a moment, that fire should burn, clouds should rain, mountains should not move, oceans should not cross the limits and earth should bear the burden of all living things. Vedas speak only if I make them speak, Sun moves only if I move it, *Prana* (life-force) the driving force of the universe moves only if I move it; it is by My command that living things die. Thus I am the master of this universe under whose instructions they perform their tasks and it is I who am the witness to all this. (9:281-285).

Arjuna, I fill this world with name and form and I am the support of the name and the form. The universe is in Me and I am in the universe. I liberate from the birth and death cycles, those who surrender single-mindedly to Me hence I am the only proper shelter for such a person. (9:286-288). I become many and by means of the different attributes of *Prakriti* perform actions through the living universe. I am the one who exists with equal affection in all creatures from Brahmadeo to the lowest form of life. (9:289-290). I am the support of this entire universe and the cause for its creation, sustenance, destruction and re-creation. The universe is rooted in the original thought and finally dissolves in it. The place to which that thought returns to rest at the end of a *Kalpa* (see *footnote* in Ch 8) until the thought to recreate occurs again, is also Me. (9:291-295)

When I take the form of the sun and radiate heat, the water bodies become dry and when I take the form of Indra[4] and make rain they fill up. Wood burnt by fire itself becomes fire; similarly creatures who die as well as those who kill them are both My form. Therefore I am both the perishable and the imperishable. Is there a place where I am not present? But it is their misfortune that people do not see Me. It is a surprising thing that those who are My own forms do not recognise Me. Their Karma comes in the way of their believing in My existence. (9:296-302). Therefore Knowledge is essential without which one cannot do what one ought to do and the good deeds are wasted. (9:305-306).

SIN AND MERIT

Those who are of model behaviour based on the rules of the caste system and who perform *yajnas*, attain the fruits of their performance in heaven. But what they have gained by all this is not merit but sin under the name of merit, because they have forgotten the very One to whom the *yajnas* reach and instead opted for the heaven where their stay would be limited only to a period appropriate for the quantity of merit. (9:307-310). People think that there is happiness in heaven because they compare it with the tortures of hell. Actually oneness with Me is the only perfect and

---

4 *Indra the king of gods is supposed to control rain.*

permanent bliss. Heaven and hell are the two diversions from the path towards Me. The rule is that sin in the form of merit leads one to heaven and pure sin leads to hell while pure merit leads to Me. (9:314-316).

I serve those who have completely surrendered to Me, who think there is nothing better than Me, consider that their whole life belongs to Me and thus, with extreme faith meditate on Me and worship Me. **The responsibility of taking their care in all respects fell on Me once they accepted the path of My worship, and I was compelled to do what they should have done for themselves.** Just as mother bird takes complete care of her babies who have not yet developed wings and lives only for them, I also take care of My devotees who have kept complete faith in Me. If they want *moksha* (liberation) leading to oneness with Me, I take them towards it and if they like to serve Me then I offer them My love. I give them whatever they want and having given, I guard it also for them. I provide maintenance to all those who give themselves to Me completely. (9:335-343).

Now, there are people who follow other paths who, not realising My all-encompassing quality, perform *yajnas* to propitiate deities like Agni, Indra, Sun, Moon etc., but all the *yajnas* reach Me because I am everything. This type of worship is indirect. Just as, even though roots, branches, flowers etc. have their origin in the same seed, the task of absorbing water is done only by the roots and it is proper to give water at the roots alone and not to other parts of the tree, in the same way, any worship done without knowing Me is fruitless. (9:344-346). Actions must be backed by Knowledge and this Knowledge must be pure. (9:349-350) By performing such *yajnas* therefore, they do not attain Me after they die but only those deities for whose propitiation they performed the *yajnas*. Those who performed rituals for propitiating the deceased ancestors reach the world of *Manes*[5] and those who propitiate *Vetal*[6] and other ghost

---

5 Pitruloka or the plane of the deceased ancestors.
6 Vetal is said to be the king of the ghosts/spirits. He is worshipped as a deity in some places, especially in rural India.

deities for evil ends attain the ghost state when they die. Thus, the fruits of the actions are as per their desires. (9:354-358). But those who worship Me only for My sake attain Me even while they live, therefore how can they go anywhere else after death? (9:359-365)

MY REAL DEVOTEES

Those seekers who worship Me with whatever rituals and have surrendered themselves to Me, attain Me. Arjuna, no other method will make a seeker attain Me unless he totally surrenders to Me. (9:366-367). He who claims to know Me does not really know Me. He who boasts about his achievements is imperfect and immature. Similarly the *Yajnas*, penance and other rituals, which people perform and boast about, are not even worth a blade of grass for attaining Me. Vedas stumble while describing My nature and describe Me as "Not this and not that" making Sanaka[7] and other sages confused about Me. (9:370-371). One can attain Me only when he gives up all thoughts about how great and scholarly he is and becomes humble. (9:378). Therefore one must give up the love of the material body, consciousness about his qualities and pride about his possessions and surrender himself completely to Me. (9:381).

Then, when the devotee offers Me a fruit from a tree with boundless love I anxiously spread My palms to receive it and eat it without even waiting to remove the stem. If he offers Me a flower, I should really smell it but overcome by his love I put it in My mouth and taste it. But why talk of flower? Even if he offers a leaf I do not bother to see whether it is fresh or dry and eat and savour it. And maybe even that leaf is not available, but there is no dearth of water which is available free. But when that devotee offers that water with complete devotion, then even if it was free, I feel as if he

---

7 *The sages Sanak, Sanatkumar, Sanandan and Sanaatan were the first four mind-sons of Brahmadeo.*

has built immense temples for Me, given Me jewels more valuable than *Kaustubha*[8] and served Me delicacies better than manna. You are aware how I devoured the fistful of rice brought by Sudama.[9] *(See notes)*. I only look at the devotion and accept the offering without differentiating between rich and poor, big and small. Really speaking, fruit, flower, leaf etc. are only a means of manifesting the devotion and are useless unless offered with the feeling of devotion. Therefore I am telling you an easy way. ***Do not permit yourself to forget Me.*** (9:382-397)

Whatever work you do, whatever things you enjoy, whatever *yajnas* of various types and other rituals you perform, whatever donations you give to worthy persons and pay your servants or whatever penance or observances you do, do them for the sake of love for Me. And after they are done make an offering of them to Me with such pure and desireless attitude that you should not even remember having performed them. (9:398-401). Then, just as a roasted seed does not germinate, the actions offered to Me do not bear fruit. Arjuna, it is only when *Karma* remains that it gives rise to fruits of happiness and sorrow and leads to rebirth in order to go through them. On the other hand, if the action is offered to Me then immediately the rebirth is avoided and one is saved from the pains accompanying it. Therefore Arjuna, avoid getting trapped into the bonds of the body and thus getting drowned in the ocean of happiness and sorrow and so by following this easy path become one with Me. (9:402-406).

MY NATURE

If you ask Me "What is your nature?" then the answer is, "I am present in all creatures equally without making distinction among

8 *Kaustubha is a precious stone worn by Vishnu.*

9 *Sudama was a co-disciple of Shri Krishna when they were studying under their Guru Sandipani..*

them." Those persons who know this nature of mine, who abandon their ego and are devoted to Me with their heart and actions are really in Me even if they are actually in their body; and in turn, I too am fully in their hearts. The difference between Me and My devotee is in name only. Though they are in their body they are unattached to it. Whatever ego is left in them takes My form and therefore is merged in Me. Those who are thus devoted to Me with love are not reborn whatever may be their nature. (9:407-415).

DEVOTION NULLIFIES PAST SINS

If you consider such a person's behaviour then you should note that even if he has committed sins in his earlier life, his final span of life has been spent in devotion. Whatever a person contemplates on at the time of death is what he gets in his next birth. Therefore he who has spent the final part of his life in devotion to Me should be considered as the finest among people even though he might have been a crooked person during the earlier part of his life. The sins committed in the earlier part of one's life get washed by the devotion in the later part. Therefore even a crooked person can become one with Me if he washes his sins with sincerity in the waters of repentance. And he becomes noble and pure. Then there is fulfilment in his life. He has the same merit as those who have studied Vedas and Yoga. Why say anything further? He who has unshakeable faith in Me alone is beyond the effects of all actions. He who has enclosed the affairs of mind and intellect in the box of faith and entrusted it to Me thus becomes free from the bonds of his actions. (9:416-424).

You may think that he may reach My state only after death but how can a person who is ever immersed in nectar die? Is not an action done without devotion to Me a sin? Therefore Arjuna, as soon as his consciousness reaches Me he really attains Me. He who is devoted to Me remains in My form. Then he attains My permanent qualities of peace and effulgence. He who wants to attain Me should not forget devotion to Me. All greatness about wealth, nobility and caste are in vain in the absence of devotion. A devotionless person accumulates only sins and his life is an invitation to sorrow. Therefore one may not belong to a noble family, one may be a low caste person or be an animal, what matters is his devotion. When the king of the elephants[10] prayed to Me when he was caught by the crocodile, did I not rush to his aid? And as soon as I helped him he was free of his elephant body. (9:425- 442).

Arjuna, some may be born in such unspeakably low type of species that even uttering its name may be considered a sin and are not different from a stone as far as Knowledge is concerned. But if they have a steady feeling about Me, always utter My name, see My form, think of nothing else but Me, listen to nothing except My praise, whose organs are proud to be of service to Me, whose intellect is unaware of sense objects and thus know Me alone, and if not so would rather prefer death and keep all their feelings in Me, then such persons are not less than Me. Remember that Prahlada,[11]

---

10 *Gajendramoksha means liberation of the elephant king. King Indradyumna was born as an elephant being cursed by Rishi Agastya. At the same time a gandharva (one of the demi-gods known for music) named Hoohoo also was born as a crocodile due to the curse from another Rishi. One day while the elephant had gone to a lake to drink water, the crocodile caught his leg and tried to kill him. The elephant in the throes of death prayed to lord Vishnu offering Him a lotus he had picked by his trunk. Hearing the prayers lord Vishnu rushed to save His devotee and killed the crocodile thereby liberating both the king and the gandharva.*

11 *Prahlada was the son of the powerful Daitya king Hiranyakashipu who had received a boon from Brahmadeo that he would die neither on land nor on water, neither in the open nor in a house, neither by man nor by animal, neither during day nor at night, neither by weapon nor by mantra etc. On the strength of this boon Hiranyakashipu conquered the Devas and started an oppressive rule prohibiting worship of Lord Vishnu whom he hated. Unfortunately for him, Prahlada became, through his mother Kayadhu a devotee of Vishnu. Hiranyakashipu made many unsuccessful attempts to kill Prahlada . Once when confronted and asked where Vishnu was Prahlada said that he was everywhere. Hiranyakashipu asked angrily if he was in the palace pillar nearby. When Prahlada said yes, Hiranyakashipu kicked the pillar hard which shattered and through it emerged the ferocious Narasimha, a man with*

though born to a demon father, was tortured because of his devotion to Me and I had to take *avatar* of Narasimha to save him What I gave him was what he asked for on the strength of his devotion, which even Indra could not surpass. The moral is, what matters is the devotion and not the antecedents of a being. (9:443-452)

Once a seeker's mind is filled with devotion to Me then his earlier life history is erased. As long as a person does not attain Me there are differences like Kshatriya, Vaishya, woman, Shudra, untouchable etc. But once they attain Me completely, all these differences of caste and gender vanish. (9:456-461)

Whatever may be the motive, it is enough that a person's mind is attracted towards Me. Such a person, in the course of time, reaches My form. (9:463). *Gopis*[12] attained Me through love, Kamsa through fear, Shishupal through hate, Yadavas through relationship of race, Vasudeva and Devaki through parental love, and Narada, Dhruva, Akrur, Sanatkumar through devotion. I am the ultimate destination of all paths be it devotion, dispassion or even enmity.

---

lion's face.. Narasimha caught hold of Hiranyakashipu, and sitting on the threshold of the palace held him on his lap and killed him by tearing open his intestines with bare hands. Thus Lord Vishnu saved his devotee Prahlada by killing Hiranyakashipu while still honouring the conditions of the boon because this happened at sunset when it was neither day nor night, his killer was neither man nor beast, he was killed neither outside nor inside but on the threshold and not by weapon because his intestines were torn by nails. Narasimha is considered as the fourth avatar of Lord Vishnu.

12 Gopis etc. These are persons from the early life of Shri Krishna. Gopis were the cowherd women who loved and played with Krishna in Gokul village where he grew up. Kamsa was his maternal uncle who had forcibly occupied the Mathura throne after imprisoning Krisha's parents Vasudeva and Devaki. Kamsa feared Krishna because it was predicted that Krishna would kill him. Akrur was Kamsa's official but was devoted to Krishna. Shishupal was Krishna's nephew but hated Krishna. He was also destined to die at Krishna's hands. Dhruva was the grandson of Swayambhuva Manu and a devotee of Vishnu. The pole star is named after him. Narada was a rishi devoted to Vishnu.
The lesson to be learnt is that a person's mind should be attracted towards God, does not matter whether through love or hate and you will realise Him because your mind is full of Him.

Arjuna, there is no dearth of methods to reach Me. One may be born in any species, be devoted or inimical to Me but he should be devotee or enemy of Me alone. Through either relation he will attain My form. Therefore those who are born in the species of sin, or Vaishya, *Shudra* or women, if they carry devotion for Me, then they reach Me. (9:465-474).

DEVOTION SAVES

I am the existence and liberation of royal Rishis and Brahmins who consider Me as their place of pilgrimage, contemplation and shelter. (9:489).

Arjuna, having been born on this earth full of pain and unhappiness, how can anyone stay away from worshipping Me? Or do they believe that they will get happiness from learning and youth, without worshipping Me? It is true that all the material things are for the enjoyment of the body but that body itself is in the jaws of death. (9:492-495). Who has heard of real happiness in this world? (9:501). The lack of concern of the people who have taken birth in this impermanent world is really surprising. People do not spend even a paisa[13] on things which would help them (spiritually) in this or the after-world. But they spend huge sums of money on harmful things. They consider a person engrossed in sense pleasures as a happy person and consider a person who is burdened by lust and desire, as a man of wisdom. They make obeisance to elders whose strength and intellect are weakened and whose death is approaching. As a child grows the parents are full of joy and celebrate birthdays not realising that as it grows its life is getting shorter. People cannot tolerate the word "death" and cry when a person dies. But they do not think about the fact that their own life is also getting shortened day by day. (9:507-513). How topsy-turvy are the ways of this world! (9:515). Arjuna, you have taken birth in this world by virtue of your Karmas. Free yourself of

---

13 *Smallest denomination coin of Indian currency.*

this burden by following the path of devotion, which will beget you the pure permanent position in Me. Concentrate your mind in Me, develop love for devotion to Me and offer obeisance to everything, knowing that I am in everything. He who gets rid of all thoughts and desires by concentrating in Me is known as My devotee. When you succeed in this then you will reach Me. I have told this secret of mine to you. You will reach perfection by knowing this secret, which I have hidden from everybody. (9:515-520).

10

Divine Manifestations

༺❧

✳ EARLIER CHAPTERS SUMMARISED

Dnyaneshwar Maharaj praises his Guru Nivruttinath and says, "By your grace I have this ability to compose in verse this commentary on *Bhagavad-Gita* which is supreme among all branches of spiritual knowledge and in which all *Shastras* are harmoniously included. By your grace I have completed the commentary on the first part of the *Bhagavad-Gita*. The first Chapter describes the despondency felt by Arjuna because of the thought of the annihilation of his friends and relatives in the war. In the second chapter *Karmayoga,* the yoga of action is explained and at the same time the difference between *Karmayoga* and *Jnyanayoga,* the yoga of knowledge of the *Sankhyas* is also shown. In the third chapter *Karmayoga* is recommended while in the fourth the explanation of the same in combination with knowledge is given. In the fifth chapter, the principle of Yoga is extolled while in the sixth the same principle is explained further describing the method of practice starting from the initial posture to the state of union with the Brahman. Similarly, what the yoga state is and the fate yogis reach, when they deviate from the path, are also explained.

In the seventh chapter are described the four types of devotees who worship God by destroying the effect of *Maya*. Then in the eighth chapter, seven questions (about *Brahman, Karma and Adhyatma, Adhibhuta, Adhidaivata and Adhiyajna*) are answered and till the end of the chapter the topic of the state of the mind at the time of death is discussed. Whatever philosophy is stated in the fathomless realm of the Vedas is contained in the hundred thousand *shlokas* of Mahabharata and whatever is contained in the Mahabharata may be found in the dialogue between Shri Krishna and Arjuna which is the *Gita* and the substance of its seven hundred *shlokas* is concentrated in the ninth chapter alone. (10:19-31). The greatness of the ninth chapter cannot be stated in words.[1] Oh Guru, if I could present it, it is because of your powers alone. (10: 35). (See note at the end of the chapter). I have thus explained the first nine chapters of *Bhagavad-Gita* to the best of My ability. Now listen to the second part. (10: 40).

ARJUNA IS NOW FIT TO KNOW TRUTH

Shri Krishna said, "Arjuna, your mind is now fit to listen to the complete explanation about knowledge of the Self. What I told you so far was to test how attentive you were and you were quite attentive. It is like testing a vessel for leakage by pouring a little water into it first. (10:49-51). Arjuna, I am not doing this as a favour to you but because of My own self-interest. (10:57). Arjuna, I really like you; therefore however much I chat with you, I remain unsatisfied. I am telling you the same thing again and again. Listen to My profound secret, which is actually as if the Universe has come to embrace you through words. You have still not understood the

---

1 *Regarding ninth chapter (10:19-31) and (10:135-140): Different commentators have stressed on different philosophies stated in the Gita. It is clear that Dnyaneshwar Maharaj has preferred to stress on the Path of Devotion, which is the subject matter of the ninth chapter. This is also clear from the paragraph ref. (10:135-140). Second point is that Dnyaneshwar Maharaj himself divides the Gita into two parts: first part comprising of the first nine chapters and the rest belonging to the second part.*

truth about Me. *What you are seeing as Me is really the Universe.*" (10:60-63).

I Am Difficult To Know

Vedas became silent while trying to describe Me. Just as the foetus in the womb cannot see its mother's age, in the same way no god can know Me. The knowledge of the great *rishis* cannot recognise Me because the questions such as who I am, how big I am, where and to whom I was born, are the ones which have taken aeons to decide on the answer. Since I am the root of gods, great *rishis* and other creatures, they find it difficult to know Me. (10:64-68).

Give Up Pleasures And Ego To Know Me

Though I am difficult to realise, he who gives up the worldly life with ease turning his back to the sense organs, and even if he leads a worldly life goes beyond the realm of the five elements by giving up the ego and I-am-the-body attitude and by remaining steady in this condition of mind, sees My beginningless form in the light of Self-realisation, and understands that I am the original power behind the universe, is among all men, a part of Me. (10:72-76). Even though he may appear outwardly to be an ordinary person, he is not affected by gross things and his sins get automatically nullified. He who knows Me becomes freed of all desires. (10:79-80)

If you are thinking about how to realise Me then listen first to what My nature is and what are My different aspects. These aspects of Mine occur in different beings according to their nature and are spread throughout the universe. (10:81-82)

My Nature And Aspects

Shri Krishna now details his aspects:

"Among these My aspects, intellect is the first. Then come the infinite knowledge, the freedom from delusion, tolerance, forgiveness and truthfulness. Then come both self-control and victory over the senses as also happiness and sorrow in the world and birth-death. Fear and fearlessness, non-violence and even-mindedness, contentment and austerity are also My aspects. Charity, success and fame, which are seen everywhere, are generated in creatures, from Me. Just as there are different creatures, there are also different aspects. But out of these, some aspects enable knowing Me; and some not. Knowing Me or not knowing Me, depends upon one's destiny hence different creatures acquire different aspects. Thus this earth is completely entwined in My aspects. (10:83-90)

Now listen about eleven more aspects which are the guardians of this universe and who influence the behaviour of all people. These consist of the seven great *rishis* Kashyap etc.[2] with excellent qualities and most knowledgeable among all great *rishis*, and the four main *Manus* like Swayambhuva, from among the fourteen *Manus*).[3] These eleven aspects were born out of My mind for creation of the universe. Prior to this when the three worlds were not yet created, the five elements were quiet and idle. After they came into being,

2 According to Mahabharata, the seven rishis (Saptarshi) are Marichi, Atri, Pulaha, Pulastya, Kratu, Vasishta, Kashyapa. However Puranas give the list as: Marichi, Atri, Angiras, Pulastya, Pulahak, Kratu, and Vasishta who are mind sons of Brahmadeo. Shatapatha Brahmana gives the list as Atri, Bharadvaja, Gautama, Jamadagni, Kashyapa, Vasishta, Vishwamitra. These personages are actually seven wise persons of ancient times but who lived in different time periods. Pulastya was the grandfather of Ravana. Kashyapa was the son of Marichi. Puranas credit Kashyapa as the progenitor of almost all higher species from man down to snakes. (See FN No 4)

3 It is not clear which out of the fourteen Manus Krishna implies. Most probably these are: Swayambhuva, Vaivaswat, Chakshusha and Savarni. Of these Puranas consider Swayambhuva Manu with his wife Shatarupa to be the first couple to create progeny through conjugal process. Vaivaswat saved his people from floods (probably in the Hindukush region) and settled them on the banks of the river Saraswati. The implication and principle seems to be that these are some aspects of Vishnu (whose avatar is Krishna), whose task is sustenance of the universe through various means e.g. continuing progeny, providing for their sustenance and protecting them from dangers. These Manus and Prajapatis have just done that. (See the next footnote also).

the eleven aspects – the seven *rishis* and the four *Manus* – created the three worlds, and appointed eight chiefs or *prajapatis.*[4] Thus these eleven are like kings and all the people are their subjects. But keep in mind that all the expanse of this universe has sprung from Me. (10:91-97)

DIVINE MANIFESTATIONS OF THE CREATOR

Shri Krishna continues:

In the beginning I was alone. Then mind was created from Me. From that mind the seven *rishis* and the four *Manus* were born. They created the eight *Prajapatis* (governors) who in turn created various types of creatures who have generated all the living population in the universe. Thus I have created this entire expanse, but only those who have faith that this is so will understand it. (10:101-103)

I am in everything: Therefore Arjuna, these eleven aspects are My Divine manifestations with which this universe is filled. Therefore from Brahmadeo down to an ant there is nothing in this universe which is not occupied by Me. One who understands this, wakes up to the state of Self-realisation and he and is free from the thoughts

---

4 *Most famous of the Prajapatis (praja=people, pati=chief) is Daksha who had many daughters. He married 17 of them to rishi Kashyapa who fathered most of the species on the earth from them; e.g., 12 Adityas (gods) from Aditi; Daityas from Diti (most famous was Hiranyakashipu, father of Prahlada, killed by Vishnu in the Narasimha avatar); Danavas (e.g Puloma and Vrishaparva) from Danu; aquatic animals from Timi; ferocious animals from Sarama; animals with cleft hooves e.g. cows and buffaloes from Surabhi; animals with uncleft hooves from Kashthha; eagles, vultures etc. from Tamra; Apsaras from Muni; Gandharvas from Arishtha; reptiles from Krodhavasha; creepers and trees from Ila; evil beings from Surasa; different species of birds from Patangi; Garuda (Vishnu's vehicle) and Aruna (sun's Charioteer) from Vinata; locusts from Yamini; Serpents from Kadru. (**Ref Canto 6, CH 6 of Bhagwat Purana, See Bibliograhy (AAP-SB)**)*
Sati, one of Daksha's daughters married Shiva with whom Daksha was inimical. This ultimately led to Sati's committing suicide by jumping in the Daksha's yajna fire.

of differences among creatures like big and small, good and bad. He who experiences through yoga that I, My Divine manifestations and creatures showing these manifestations – are all not different from Me, undoubtedly becomes one with Me. I surrender myself to the devotee who worships Me with the feeling of oneness with Me. Thus, the Yoga of devotion with the feeling of oneness with Me never gets interrupted; as I have explained in the sixth chapter, even if a seeker dies while leading his life with such devotion, he will reach me. Now I shall explain to you the nature of the devotion with oneness with Me. (10:104-111).

Arjuna, just as waves are generated in water, remain in water and are dissipated also in water so is the creation and sustenance of this universe done by Me. Just as the waves cannot occur without water there is nothing in this universe without Me. Those Self-realised persons who, knowing My all pervading nature are devoted to Me with true love, and remaining aware of the fact that place, time and the current circumstances are not different from Me, live happily in these three worlds while keeping their minds occupied with Me, feeling that every creature they meet is God. Such persons are the followers of the real path of *Bhakti* (devotion). (10:112-118).

ONLY PATH TO KNOW ME IS DEDICATED LOVE

When people whose minds satiated by being unified with Me and who are free from life-death cycles (by virtue of their Self-realisation) and who therefore dance in the bliss of non-duality under its increasing spell – meet each other, they mutually exchange only the bliss of Self-realisation. Their state is like two lakes whose waters mix after flooding. With the rising emotions of their devotion, they forget themselves and having been fully satisfied by gaining Me, they loudly sing My praise and utter even the secret *mantras* told by their Guru. Finally having been overcome by the joy they get by the loud singings, they forget the consciousness of the body and suddenly become quiet and dissolve themselves in that forgetfulness. Due to this excessive emotion of love for Me, they are not aware of whether it is day or night. (10:119-129)

Thus, these devotees have already taken possession of the very gift that I wanted to give them. In comparison to the road they have taken to attain Me the paths that lead to heaven and liberation[5] are mere side-lanes. The love and devotion they have for Me is the gift I wish to give them but it must be said that they have already obtained it. Only thing that now remains to be done is to see that this love grows and does not decrease later. (10:130-133)

I AM THE SERVANT OF MY DEVOTEES

It is My desire and duty to see that the spiritual efforts by means of which My devotees will attain Me, are encouraged and supported. Because the devotees are attracted towards Me with their dedicated devotion I also feel love for them. But there is a dearth of such loving devotees in My house. For the superficially devoted persons, I have created the two paths of heaven and liberation, and have put myself bodily along with My consort Laxmi, in their hands. But I have reserved the bliss that is beyond the consciousness of the body only for the devotees who worship Me with devotional love. (See note at the end of the chapter). Such is the closeness I have with them *but these things are not to be talked about.*[6] (10:135-140)

Because such knowers of the principle of the Self[7] sheltered

---

5 *A very important and peculiar aspect of the Path of Devotion is that while in other paths liberation through Self-realization is the main goal, here the devotee aims not for liberation but for unity with Him and in spite of the unity he also wants to be different from Him so that he can worship Him. His joy is in worshipping Him and not losing him by unification, because in that case he will have to worship himself.*

6 *Ovis (10:135-140) clearly show that Dnyaneshwar Maharaj has preferred to stress on the Path of Devotion. Different commentators have stressed on different philosophies stated in the Gita.*

7 *Dnyaneshwar Maharaj uses the term 'Tatwadnya' literally meaning either philosopher or knower of the principle (Tatwa). The latter version is chosen here.*

themselves throughout their life under My Divine Self looking at nothing other than Me, I am their vanguard holding the torch, destroying the darkness of ignorance and creating the permanent illumination of knowledge. (10:141-143).

ARJUNA WANTS TO KNOW ABOUT DIVINE MANIFESTATIONS

Arjuna then asked, "Oh Master, I am now fully satiated. You have removed the dirt of the material world from My mind. I have realised the real meaning of life and now am free from the fire of birth and death. I feel there is a fulfilment in My life now. (10:144-146).

"It is you who are the ultimate Brahman and the place where the universe rests. You are holiest of the holies and the deity whom Brahmadeo, Vishnu and Shiva worship. You are the twenty-fifth principle, the birthless One beyond the bounds of *Maya*. You are the one who controls the strings of the past, the present and the future; you are the master of the Soul and the universe. (10:149-152). *Rishis* also have described you thus, (10:153-155) but because My mind was clouded by the sensual pleasures I could not understand it and instead, the sweet nature of spirituality tasted bitter. (10:158-159). But now, having heard it from you, the mind has cleared and I am beginning to understand what the Rishis have said. I have now realised that one who has not heard your advice and tries to understand you on the strength of his intellect will be disappointed.[8] (10:163, 175).

Oh master, please reveal to me those of your Divine manifestations (modes or aspects) which are apparent throughout the universe by their power. Please show me the principal Divine manifestations by which you pervade throughout the universe. (10:184-186). I am puzzled about how to know you and how to meditate on you. You have just now briefly described your aspects.

---

8 *This is again a reminder (ref Ch 2) that one cannot realize Brahman through intellect. Whereas earlier it was mentioned that one can realize it through meditation, here the prescribed path is that of devotion.*

Now elaborate on them and explain to me those by which I shall be able to easily meditate on you." (10:187-189).

INNUMERABLE DIVINE MANIFESTATIONS

Shri Krishna said, "Arjuna, listen. The Divine manifestations which you asked about are innumerable. And though they are My manifestations, I myself am not able to understand them. Even otherwise I myself am not able to understand My nature and My magnitude. Therefore listen to those manifestations which are well-known. (10:208-211). When you understand them you will understand the minor manifestations also and actually the whole world. (10:212-213).

"Arjuna, I exist in every living being as the Soul. I am present in their inner self and in the outer shell or body. I am their beginning, their existence and their end. (10:215-216). Now I shall tell you about My principal manifestations as promised. (10:220).

Shri Krishna now enumerates His Divine manifestations which are the best ones among the various aspects of the universe.

DIVINE MANIFESTATIONS ENUMERATED

"Arjuna, I am Vishnu among the twelve *Adityas*[9] and the Sun among all the shining bodies. Among the forty-nine *Maruts* I am Marichi,[10] and the Moon among the stars. I am the Samaveda

---

9 *12 Adityas, 11 Rudras and 8 Vasus and 2 Ashwinikumars constitute the 33 Vedic deities. Maruts are another group of 21 deities. Out of these the twelve Adityas, supposedly sons of Aditi are more important. Rig-Veda mentions only 8 Adityas: Varuna, Indra, Surya, Savitra, Mitra, Aryaman, Daksha and Amsha. Later, four more Adityas were added: Vishnu, Tvashtra, Pusan, Vivaswat. Varuna was initially the most important Aditya; his place was taken by Indra whose place was again taken by Vishnu as the Aryan community stabilized from war to farming. In Krishna's time Vishnu was the most important Aditya hence he is named as a Divine manifestation. (See Bibiography PB-VA)*

10 *This Marichi is not one of the Saptarshi Marichi.*

among the Vedas and Indra among the gods. Among the organs I am the eleventh, i.e. the mind and the natural consciousness in the creatures is also Me. I am Shankar *(Shiva)* among all the eleven *Rudras*. Among the *Yakshas* and demi-gods I am Kuber,[11] the guardian of wealth and friend of Shankar. I am Agni among the eight *Vasus* and Meru,[12] the tallest among all the mountains. Among all the priests I am Brihaspati[13] the priestly support of gods and source of knowledge. Among the generals I am the most intelligent Skanda, son of Shankar. Among the lakes I am the ocean with immense storage of water and among the great Rishis I am Bhrigu. Among all the syllables I am the *AUM* the abode of eternal Truth. I am the *Japayajna*,[14] (i.e. *yajna* of silent repetition of *mantras*) which is the best among all the *yajnas*. *Namajapa* with syllables *AUM* etc. leads to liberation from all the Karmas and its performance does not need external rituals like taking bath etc. Both proper and improper deeds get sanctified by it. According to Vedas it is the path that leads to the realisation of the Brahman. Among all the stationary mountains I am the Himalaya. (10:221-234)

Among all the trees My principal manifestation is the *Ashwattha* (Peepul or *Ficus Religiosa*) tree. I am Narada[15] among the Divine

11 *Kuber: Puranas mention demigods like gandharvas, Kinnaras (both demigods of music), Vidyadhars and Yakshas (guardians) etc. Kuber is the king of the Yakshas and keeper of the wealth of gods. Kuber was the son of Rishi Vishrava and the elder brother of Ravana the villain of Ramayana. Brahmadeo had awarded the kingdom of Lanka to Kuber. Ravana wrested it from him and became the king.*

12 *It is fictitious mountain around which the sun was supposed to revolve according to ancient ideas.*

13 *The priest and Guru of the gods. He belonged to Angirasa lineage and lived in the 19th generation after Vaivaswat Manu in 28h century BCE. But as Guru of the gods Puranas depict him as immortal. (See Bibiography PB-VA)*

14 *Continuous repetition of a mantra or the name of a god (e.g. Rama). Aum generally precedes it. This is free from restrictions like place, posture or requirement of taking bath etc, as is needed in conventional worship or yajna.*

15 *Narada is a famous Puranic character who is a Divine rishi, devotee of Vishnu who moves in the three worlds carrying his string instrument veena uttering the name "Narayana", carrying information from one place to another and thereby causing quarrels among gods. Historically he is a real person from Angirasa lineage who lived 38th generation after Vaivaswat*

Rishis and Chitraratha among the *Gandharvas*.[16] I am Kapilacharya[17] among the great *Siddhas* and Ucchaisrava[18] among the horses. I am Airavat[19] among the elephants and *Amrit* (immortalising nectar) among the objects obtained when the ocean was churned.[20] Among men I am the king whom all people obey and serve. (10:235-239).

Also among My principal manifestations are *Vajra*[21] among all the weapons, *Kamdhenu*[22] the wishing cow among the cows and Madan[23] the god of love among the creative entities. Among the snakes I am the King Vasuki and among the cobras I am the Cobra Ananta. Among all the aquatic creatures I am Varuna the master of the Westerly direction. Among all the Manes I am Aryama.[24] Yama is My principal manifestation among the controllers who takes note of all the good and bad deeds of creatures, examines their conscience and gives reward or retribution according to their *karmas*. (10:240-246).

Among the *daityas*, Prahlada is My principal manifestation and it is because of this that he was not affected by their qualities. I am the lion among predators and forest animals. Garuda is My principal

---

Manu and a contemporary of the famous king Harischandra. He is credited with invention of Veena and is said to be author of Narada Bhaktisutras.

16 Chitraratha is the king of the Gandharvas

17 The author of Sankhya Philosophy.

18 Indra's horse.

19 Indra's elephant

20 According to Purana legend Asuras and Devas churned the ocean to get immortalising nectar Amrit. But before Amrit appeared 13 other entities came out of the churning which different gods took away. The first outcome was the poison Halahala which Shiva drank to save the gods and Asuras from its effects. Rishis took away Surabhi the celestial cow, Vishnu took away Laxmi the goddess of fortune, Kaustubha the jewel and the conch, Indra took away apsaras , Ucchaishravas the horse and Airavat the elephant and the Parijat tree while Asuras took the Varuni or Sura the wine. Dhanwantari became the physician of the gods.(See Canto 8, Ch 6-8 of Bhagwat Purana (AAP-SB) Bibliography)

21 The weapon of Indra.

22 The wish-cow that gives whatever you wish for.

23 The god of love.

24 Aryama is the master of pitruloka or the plane of the ancestors.

manifestation among birds and therefore he is able to carry Me on his back. Among the speedy entities, which can go at one stretch round the seven seas on the vast expanse of this earth in less than a *Ghatika* (24 minutes), I am the wind. I am Shri Rama among all the weapon wielders because it was he who succeeded by means of his bow alone in saving *Dharma*, which had come in great danger from Ravana during the *Tretayuga*. He saved the honour of the gods and revived the *Dharma* and became the sun of the Solar dynasty. Among the aquatic animals having tails I am the crocodile. River Ganges is My principal manifestation among the rivers. But Arjuna, if I start enumerating every manifestation even hundreds of births will not be sufficient to cover even half of them. If one has to know all of them that one must first realise Me. (10:247-260).

Therefore understand once for all that I am everything. (10:263). And if one knows My all-pervasiveness then what is the point in knowing My different manifestations? But you are not fit to know My all-pervasiveness therefore let Me stop this discussion.(10:264-265) However, since you have asked about My manifestations let Me tell you that Knowledge of the Self is My principal manifestation among all branches of knowledge.

Shri Krishna however continues:

Among debates I am the debate that does not end but creates more and more interest among listeners and sweetness in the speech of the speakers. Among the alphabets I am the first letter "A" and among the compound words I am the *Dwandwa* mode of compounding (double syllables). I am the destroyer who swallows everything from an ant to Brahmadeo the god of creation, the earth along with all the mountains, the ocean which floods the entire universe during the deluge and which accommodates the entire space. I am also He who creates the universe again. It is I who creates all creatures, sustain them and finally destroy them therefore I am also the Death.[25] (10:266-274).

---

25 *Thus Shri Krishna as Bhagwan asserts that He is the one who creates, sustains and destroys the universe.*

Among the manifestations of feminine qualities there are seven principal ones: I am the fame that never fades, and I am the fortune that is accompanied by generosity. And I am the speech that uses discrimination and is supported by justice. I am the memory that comes as soon as one sees a thing. I am also the intellect that is beneficial to one's well-being. Courage and forgiveness are also My principal manifestations. Thus these seven powers expressed as feminine qualities are Me alone. (10:275-279).

I am *Brihatsam* within the *Samaveda* and *Gayatri* metre among all the metres. Among the months I am *Margashirsha*[26] and *Vasant* (Spring) among the six seasons. (10:280- 283).

Among all games of deception, I am gambling (reference being to the game of dice) – therefore nobody can help a person who is looted even in public by gambling.[27] (10:284).

I am the brightness of all the shining objects and success among the determined intents. Among all professions I am that which brings out justice. I am the goodness among the good people and I am the most prosperous among all the Yadavas. I took birth for the sake of Vasudeva and Devaki and went to Gokul in exchange for Yashoda's daughter.[28] There, I eliminated many *daityas* even while a child, reduced Indra's importance by lifting the Govardhan mountain, got rid of the poison in the Kalindi river by killing the the serpent Kalia and left Brahmadeo puzzled by creating new calves when he smuggled away those from Gokul. In childhood itself I killed big fighters like Kamsa and Chanur. You yourself have heard many of these stories and seen them happen. Therefore

---

26 *The ninth lunar month that falls in December. It is said that in ancient days the year started with Margashirsha (probably because uttarayana (northward passage of the sun). Hence it has been specified as a Divine manifestation.*
27 *Thus, Divine manifestation includes even unsavoury aspects like gambling.*
28 *Krishna briefly narrates his activities of his childhood in Gokul where he was smuggled immediately after birth to save him from his maternal uncle Kamsa who wished to kill him. These activities are quite well known and legendary.*

I am the Divine manifestation among the Yadavas. And understand that I am also the Arjuna from the Pandavas of the Lunar dynasty. Therefore the love between you and Me has been uninterrupted. I did not feel inimical towards you even though you eloped with My sister Subhadra pretending to be *sanyasi* because you and Me are one. I am Vyasa among all the sages and Ushanacharya among poets. (10:285-295).

Among all administrators, I am the sceptre that administers control over everybody from an ant to Brahmadeo. I am the moral science among all the sciences that examine with discrimination all aspects of *Dharma* and knowledge. I am the Silence among all the secrets because even Brahmadeo cannot do anything to a person who observes silence. I am the knowledge that occurs in the learned. But how long one should go on like this? There is no limit to My manifestations. (10:296-299). Therefore I shall tell you the secret once for all. (10:304).

Recognise *Avatar* In A Leader

I am the seed that causes the propagation of life therefore one should never qualify anything as big or small and should not differentiate between high and low and realise that all the beings are My forms. (10:304-305).

Arjuna, I shall tell you a broad characteristic by which you will recognise My manifestation. **Wherever you see abundance and kindness occurring together, know that that is My manifestation.** (10:306-307).

He who is obeyed by all should not be considered as lonely or poor. Actually the splendour of the universe is within him. The signs by which one can recognise such a person is that the whole world bows to him and obeys him. Persons with these signs are My *Avatars*, and to say that a particular *Avatar* is better than the other is committing a sin because I am the entire universe. (10:308-312).

Knowing Manifestations Not Enough

Therefore Arjuna, how are you going to measure the extent of My limitless form by considering My manifestations one at a time? Enough of such efforts towards realising Me. Just a fraction of Me has amply covered the entire universe therefore abandon the idea of duality and be devoted to Me with an attitude of equality. (10:316-317)

Universe As Shri Krishna's Form

To this Arjuna replied, "The feeling of duality between you and me has gone after You told this secret of yours. (10:319). You are the supreme Brahman which has come within our reach by our good fortune." (10:322) Shri Krishna then commended Arjuna for thoroughly understanding his different manifestations. Arjuna humbly said that Shri Krishna was a better judge of that and as far as he was concerned he considered the entire universe to be Shri Krishna's form. (10:326-327).

11

Vision of Universal Form

⟨⟨⟨⟩⟩⟩

The previous chapter ended with Arjuna expressing his conviction that the entire universe to be Shri Krishna's form. Now he request Shri Krishna to reveal him this universal Cosmic form.[1] The description of that universal form is beautiful and unique in the history of spiritual literature. Now to the dialogue.

Arjuna Requests To See The Cosmic Form

Arjuna said, "Oh Ocean of kindness, you have made clear that which cannot be told in words. The form you assume at the time when the five elements merge in the Brahman and when no sign of life or *Maya* remains, is your place of rest. You had kept this form in your heart hidden even from the Vedas and now you have revealed this secret to me. You gave this spiritual knowledge to me in an instant. I should not speak as a separate entity after realising You. There is nothing in this universe without You, but it is my misfortune that I speak as if I am somebody different from you. (11:44-50)

---

1 *In vernacular or Sanskrit this is commonly referred to Vishwarupa.*

I was carrying the ego that I am an individual named Arjuna and was considering the Kauravas as my relations. Not only that, I was also having a bad dream about the retribution I would face after death from the sin of killing them, when suddenly you woke me up from that dream. I considered myself 'somebody' when in reality I am nobody and considered those other people as my people who I find are, in reality, not related to me at all. You saved me from this extreme madness. But your efforts were not wasted and you succeeded in getting rid of my ignorance. (11:51-64).

You explained to me the nature of *Maya* from which all creatures are created and to which they return. (11:70). And after explaining *Maya*, you showed me the root place of the Supreme Soul. By brushing aside *Maya* which was obscuring Knowledge, you introduced me into Brahman the Ultimate Principle. Now I am convinced of all this, but now one more thought has come to my mind and to whom else can I ask about it, other than you? (11:76-77)

By experiencing whatever you told me, my mind has become calm. I am eager to see that incomprehensible Divine Cosmic form, by whose thought the expanse of this universe comes into existence and then disappears, which you call your original form and from which you get yourself to take birth for some Divine purpose by taking two or four armed forms; and after that purpose is fulfilled, you return to the original form, the form that the Upanishads sing about and sages treasure in their hearts. I am eager to see this Cosmic form with my own eyes. (11:81-88).

I do not know whether I am worthy of seeing your Cosmic form, therefore first consider my capacity and only then start showing me your Cosmic form, and if I am not worthy then refuse to do so. (11:89). But I am sure you will show it to me because you do assume different forms both for the sake of knowledgeable and ignorant persons. Secondly, you are so large-hearted that once you think of giving something you do not think about whether the person is fit or not. You have granted a holy thing like liberation even to your enemies. (11:97-99); You are benevolent to even those who do disservice to you and are charitable even to the unworthy. (11:106). Please do satisfy my craving to see your form if you are sure I am capable of seeing it with my eyes. (11:111).

SHRI KRISHNA SHOWS HIS COSMIC FORM

And at this point, Shri Krishna, by His Yogic power revealed His cosmic form to Arjuna without even reflecting on whether he would be able to bear it or not. (11:121,122).

Shri Krishna said, "Arjuna, you asked Me to show My Cosmic form and if I showed you only that then what is so big about it? Now you will see that the entire universe is contained in My form. (11:123).

Different forms within the Cosmic form: Look at these forms of Mine: some lean and some fat, some short and some tall, some spread out and some straight, some limitless; some uncontrollable and some tame, some active some inactive, some impersonal and some loving, some very strict, some alert and some negligent, some shallow and some deep, some generous and some miserly, some angry and some calm, some arrogant some quiet, some happy, some noisy, some silent, some sociable, some greedy, some detached, some awake and some sleepy; some satisfied and some in difficulties, some pleased, some armed and some unarmed, some very fearful and some very sociable, some frightening, some strange, some in trance, some busy in social work and some busy sustaining them lovingly, some decimating people in anger, and some merely witnessing everything. Like this there are countless forms in it. (11:124-130).[2]

"Besides these, there are some shining with different colours by their effulgence. Some are like red-hot gold, some are brown, some are bright like the orange sky, some are beautiful like the universe

---

[2] *Dnyaneshwar Maharaj has beautifully detailed and included all the varieties of forms in the Cosmic form.*

studded with rubies, some are red like the rising sun. Some are like pure crystal and some blue like sapphire, some black and some red, some yellow like gold and some dark like rain clouds, some fair like *Champa* flower and some very green, some white like the moon. Watch these forms of Mine with various colours. As with colours they are shaped also differently. Some are so beautiful that they will defeat even Madan.[3] Some are well-formed, some bright and attractive like a treasure of decorative beauty unveiled. (11:131-138). Arjuna, there is no end to the shapes and you will see the whole universe on each of these shapes. (11:140).

Activities of the forms: "When even one of these forms opens its eyes, the twelve *Adityas*[4] (suns) are created and when the eyes close they merge together and vanish. Flames spread out from the hot breath from the mouth of the form from which are born the eight *Vasus (Pavaka, etc.)* and when the eyebrows meet together in anger, the eleven *Rudras* are born. But when the forms become soft, countless life-givers like Ashwinikumars[5] are formed and through the ears various *Vayus* are generated. Thus, by the simple play of the same form, gods and *siddhas*[6] are created. And there are countless number of forms in My Cosmic form which even Vedas find it difficult to describe and which even Brahmadeo could not fathom. Now you may see many of these forms in reality and enjoy thoroughly the wonderful experience (through this Cosmic form that I am displaying for you). (11:141-147).

"There are seeds of the world in each of the pores of the forms. Like dust particles in a light beam one may see many universes flying around in the joints of the organs of the forms. In the region of every organ can be seen the expanse of the universe. Now, if you also desire to see what lies beyond the universe, then that is also not very difficult because you will be able to see whatever you wish

---

3 *God of love, Cupid.*
4 *Sometimes the 12 Adityas are considered as aspects of the Sun in the 12 months.*
5 *Physicians of the gods.*
6 *Yogis who have reached perfection and have gained occult powers.*

in this form of Mine." (11:148-151).

Arjuna Cannot See Cosmic Form

Shri Krishna noticed that Arjuna was silent and unresponsive but with the eagerness still displayed on his face. He remarked to Arjuna, "I demonstrated to you the Cosmic form but you are not seeing it." Arjuna replied, "How can I, with My ordinary eyes, see the Cosmic form you are showing me, which according to the *Shastras* is invisible to senses and can be seen only with the vision of Knowledge?" (11:152-159).

Arjuna Bestowed With Divine Vision

Shri Krishna said, "You are right. I should have first bestowed on you the power to see the Cosmic form but I was overcome by the emotional surge of love for you and forgot to do so. (11:161). I am now giving you the power of Divine vision to enable you to see My real form. Use that power to enjoy the glory of My expanse encompassing the universe." As soon as Shri Krishna said this, Arjuna's darkness of ignorance melted. (11:176-177). Thus Shri Krishna showed Arjuna the glory of the Cosmic form. (11:179)

Visible World Vanishes

Once Shri Krishna blessed Arjuna, *Maya* (illusion) vanished. In the light of that glory he saw miracles everywhere. Engrossed in the appreciation of the Cosmic form Arjuna said,

"Oh! Who took away the wide sky which was here just now? Also where did the living and non-living world go? Directions have vanished. It is not possible to know where the sky and the nether has gone! The visible world also has disappeared. At the time when the mind-ness of mind got lost, intellect became uncontrollable and the tendencies of the senses recessed themselves together into the heart, the quiet and concentration reached the peak as if all thoughts are under the spell of delusion."

Surprised, he began looking in all directions and immediately he saw the four-armed form of Shri Krishna[7] before him but it had grown and spread itself everywhere in various forms. *(See notes.)* Now it was only Shri Krishna that remained. At first Arjuna felt happy seeing Shri Krishna's form but as soon as he opened his eyes he saw the Cosmic form. Thus Shri Krishna fulfilled his desire of seeing the Cosmic form with his own eyes. (11:185-196)

Cosmic Form - Beautiful And Frightening

Then Arjuna observed the many faces of Lord Vishnu wherein beauty and magnificence prevailed everywhere. He also saw there mysterious and frightening faces. Similarly, he also saw heavenly, ornamented and soft faces. Actually his Divine sight could not see where the faces ended. Then he began to observe with curiosity the eyes of that form and noticed rows and rows of eyes like opened lotus flowers of various colours shining like the sun. Seeing various such wonders in a single Cosmic form he realised that there are innumerable such scenes in it. Then he was more eager to see where the feet, the crown and arms were located. (11:197-206). Thus Arjuna saw all the organs of that limitless Cosmic form. He saw the greatness of that Cosmic form bedecked with the ornaments of diverse types of jewels. *How can I describe you the ornaments that the Supreme Brahman itself had turned itself into in order to bedeck its own body?* Who has the capacity to understand that the expanse of the Divine effulgence, which lights the auras of the Sun and the Moon and illuminates this universe is the ornamentation of the Cosmic form? Arjuna saw that Shri Krishna had decorated

---

7*Actually Vishnu is depicted in four-armed form. Shri Krishna being an avatar of Lord Vishnu is also thus depicted here in four armed form. Some Puranas imply that contemporary people as well Krishna himself knew that he was an avatar. This is apparently due to piousness, which overrides rational facts, logic or internal consistency.*

himself with ornaments that were also Himself. (11:208-213).

Weapon wielding arms: Then with his Divine sight, he began to observe the hands of the Cosmic form. He noticed that they were straight and holding weapons shining like the deluge of fire. He saw that Shri Krishna had filled the whole universe by becoming Himself the organs, Himself the ornaments, himself the arms and himself the weapons held in them, himself the individual soul and himself the body. The stars were bursting like popcorn due to the rays from the weapons held in the innumerable hands; and fire itself was getting scorched by it and trying to take shelter in the ocean. (11:214-217).

Cosmic form everywhere: Frightened, Arjuna looked away and turned his eyes to the neck and the crown. There were bouquets of flowers on the crown, strings of flowers on the body and bright garlands in the neck. Round the waist was wrapped the shining yellow cloth. His whole body was covered with sandal paste. Arjuna was so bewildered by the various decorations that he could not understand whether Shri Krishna was sitting or standing or lying down. Then he opened his eyes and what he saw was the Cosmic form everywhere. Then he closed his eyes and sat quietly but he saw the same Cosmic form inside too. Because he was seeing innumerable faces, out of fright he turned his back, and saw the same faces, hands and feet there too. See the effect of God's blessing! Arjuna's seeing and not seeing were both covered by Shri Krishna. (11:218-230).

Brilliance of the Cosmic form: How can one describe the brilliance of that Cosmic form? The combined brilliance of the twelve suns at the time of the great deluge was nothing compared to it. (11:237-238). The entire expanse of the universe could be seen on the Cosmic form. When Arjuna saw all this on the body of Shri Krishna, the Supreme God, whatever feeling he had about the universe being different from himself, vanished and his mind easily dissolved. He was flooded internally with joy and his external organs became loose. From head to foot his hair stood erect and his body was covered with sweat, His body was shaking due to waves of internal bliss. His eyes were flooded with tears of happiness and mind was filled by emotions. But even in that bliss of the Brahman there still remained some degree of non-identity between Shri Krishna and Arjuna because of which Arjuna looked around sighing. (11:244-254). Then, folding his hands he spoke.

Cosmic form encompasses everybody and everything: "Oh Master, you have done a great favour on this ordinary person because of which I could see this Cosmic form. I have personally seen that you are the actual support of this universe and I felt very happy by it. Oh object of my worship, innumerable worlds are visible on your body. Heaven along with the gods, are visible in your Cosmic form. I am seeing the five elements and all the living beings created from them on your body. The *Satyaloka*[8] with Brahmadeo living in it, is present in your form. Another place I can see is Kailas with Mahadeo (Shiva) and Parvati. What more! I am seeing even you in this Cosmic form. The families of Kashyapa and other *Rishis* and the nether place along with the *Nagas* are also seen in your Cosmic form. It is as if the fourteen worlds[9] are depicted on each of your organs and the innumerable people in these worlds are also in those pictures. Thus I am seeing your unworldly greatness. (11:255-265).

"When I watch with the Divine sight, I see that all your hands are in action at the same time. Your limitless bellies appear to me like treasures of cosmic eggs thrown open. Your heads, which number in thousands, look like fruits hanging on the tree that is Brahman. Similarly there are rows and rows of countless mouths and eyes. The heaven, the nether world, the earth, the directions

---

8 *Abodes of various deities: Satyaloka is the plane on which Brahmadeo is said to live. Kailas is the abode of Lord Shiva (Mahadeo) and his consort Parvati. Lord Vishnu's abode is Vaikuntha where he is depicted as lying on the great thousand-headed snake Shesha as bed in Kshirasagar the ocean of milk. Shesha is supposed to be holding and supporting the earth on his head. Indra lives in Heaven while Asuras, demons live in Patal the nether world. Nagas (serpents) are also supposed to live in the Nether place.*
9 *See footnote No 8 Re: lokas in Ch 8.*

and the space have lost their differentiating identities and the entire universe appears on your Cosmic body. Not an iota of space may be found to be without you. This is the extent you have occupied everything. It is apparent that you have pervaded all the different kinds of creatures in this universe. (11:266-273)

You are your own support: "When I began to search for the place where have you come from, what supports you, I realised that you are your own support. You are not born of anybody but you are without origin and self-born. You are neither standing nor sitting, you are neither tall nor short; above you and below you there is only yourself. If one asked what your age is and how you look, the answer is both are *"Only like yourself"*. Your back, belly are all yourself and I find that whatever I see is all you alone. But I find one thing lacking in your Cosmic form and that is you do not have a beginning, the middle and the end. Thus I have observed your Cosmic form. (11:274-280).

Your usual form is a favour for devotees: This great Cosmic form of yours is marked with countless forms. The forms from each of which the three worlds get created and dissolved are spread like hair on your body. When I began pondering over who you really are – you who have created such an expanse of the universe – and whom you belong to, then I realised that you are the driver of My chariot. Oh Shri Krishna! Even after being all-pervading you assume this loving human form only to shower favours on your devotees. The mind and eyes get satiated seeing your dark form with four arms and if one desires to embrace it, it can be easily embraced by the span of two arms. You assume this beautiful form to favour the devotee but we think of it as ordinary, because our sight is limited. Now because of the Divine sight that you have bestowed upon me, this defect is gone and I could see your true greatness. (11:281-294).

But I realise that this vast form belongs to you who are now sitting in My chariot. (11:295).

Unbearable brightness: I am not worthy of even getting amazed by your form, the brightness of which fills everything. Its brightness is so unearthly that even the sun appears pale in comparison. It is getting increasingly intense and scorching and even My Divine sight cannot bear looking at the brightness. It appears as if the fire that consumes everything at the time of deluge, which is dormant in the third eye of Lord Shiva, has come out. Similarly the Cosmic egg engulfed in the five fires ignited by the brightness of your Cosmic form, is turning into cinders. There is no end to the extensive unearthly brightness of your form, which I have witnessed in my lifetime. (11:296-306).

YOU ARE THE BRAHMAN

Shri Krishna, you are the immutable Supreme Brahman, which the Upanishads search for and are beyond the sound *AUM* of three and half syllables. You are the root of all forms and the one and only place of dissolution of the universe. You are inexhaustible, fathomless and imperishable. You are the life of *Dharma* and though birthless you are constantly new. You are the master of this universe and lying beyond the thirty-six principles you are the thirty-seventh principle *Purusha*. (11:307-309). *(See Ch 13 for thirty-six principles.)*

You have no beginning, middle or the end and your power is boundless. You have limbs all over. Moon and sun are your eyes and they exhibit the play of pleasure and displeasure, punishing some and supporting others with benevolence. (11:310-311).

YOUR COMIC FORM IS FRIGHTENING

Your mouth spits fire and your tongue, like the flames dancing during a forest fire is moving among the teeth and the jaws. The universe is getting scorched by the heat of the fire from your mouth and from the brilliance of your Cosmic form. (11:312-314).

And I am seeing that the heaven and the nether world, earth and the sky, the ten directions and all horizons are all pervaded by only you. How can I understand this amazing form of yours? I cannot even imagine this gigantic and all-pervading form of yours and neither can I bear the brilliance of your ferocious form. Instead of feeling the pleasure of watching your Cosmic form I find even surviving to be difficult. I was enjoying the pleasures of the worldly life until I saw your Cosmic form but now I am disgusted with them and am actually feeling frightened. Oh! How the desire to see your Cosmic form has been fulfilled! (11:315- 325).

SAGES, GODS ALL SURRENDER TO YOU

Now look at those sages. Some of them are dissolving into your form in good spirit after burning the seeds of their karmas by the brightness of your body. While some are frightened and praying before you, "Oh God, we have fallen in the ocean of ignorance and are entangled in the web of sense-objects. We are caught between the heavenly pleasures and the worldly life. Who else, except you, can save us from this calamity? Therefore we have surrendered to you in all respects." There are also sages, *Siddhas* and assemblies of *Vidyadharas*[10] who are praising you with holy words. (11:326- 331).

The eleven *Rudras*, twelve *Adityas*, eight *Vasus*, all *Sadhyas*, Ashwinikumars, *Vishwedeo* and Vayu with all their splendour as also the *Mane-s*, *Gandharva-s*, *Yaksha-s*, demons, Indra and other gods and all *siddhas* are observing eagerly your Divine form from their respective planes, and wonder struck, they are bowing to you.[11] Your

---

10 *A type of class of inferior but benevolent deities inhabiting the regions between the earth and sky. Ref: Vidyadhara in (EP); see Bibliography.*
11 *Sadhyas are a group of 12 inferior deities; Ashwinikumars are twins deities who are physicians to gods; Vishwedeo are a group of 9 or 10 Vedic inferior deities; Gandharvas are type of demigods who sing in Indra's court in heaven; Yakshas are supernatural beings who are servants of Kubera the keeper of wealth. Manes are deceased ancestors or Pitaras. (See various entries in (EP), in Bibliography*

form itself is the reward for their humble obeisance. (11:332-337)

EVEN GODS ARE FRIGHTENED

Even the gods became frightened after observing your form occupying the three worlds because from whatever direction one looks it is always facing you. Even if the form is only one, it has strange, frightening mouths and eyes and countless hands bearing weapons. This form has countless beautiful arms, legs and stomachs and various hues and each mouth appears to be eager to swallow. (11:338-341).These huge mouths of yours appear frightening because they are not able to hide the teeth. (11:344). You have reduced me, a person of *whom even Rudra in his most destructive mood is afraid and from whom Yama the god of death hides* to a shivering state inside and out, due to fright.[12] It is really surprising that this plague, when its frightfulness defeats very fear itself, is called Cosmic form. (11:338-352)

Your angry mouths appear as if they are at war with the lord of death and even the sky appears to be dwarfed in comparison with their expanse. These mouths are not identical but each differs from the rest in colour and form. The three worlds are turning to ashes by their brilliance. Even the brilliance has mouths and they contain teeth and jaws. (11:353-356)

I do not understand what you wish to achieve by creating this frightening show but I have started feeling the fear of death. Oh Master, my desire to see your Cosmic form is now fulfilled and I am now satisfied. Who cares if this material body is destroyed? But now I have doubts whether the consciousness will survive. I am

---

12 *This baffling statement ascribed to Arjuna by Dnyaneshwar Maharaj is not supported by Mahabharata text. Arjuna did battle once with Shiva who wanted to test his mettle. Probably what Dnyaneshwar Maharaj wants to convey is that Arjuna is so skilled in battle that his capability of destructing the enemy is superior to even Rudra at the time of the destruction of the world at the end of the eon and for the same reason, even Yama the god of death is frightened of him. This is obviously the figure of speech "exaggeration".*

shivering with fear across my body, mind, intellect and the soul. I became obsessed with wanting to seeing your Cosmic form but after seeing it, all my discrimination and comprehension are lost. Now I am wondering whether our relation of Guru and disciple will survive. (11:365-370)

ARJUNA REQUESTS TO WIND UP THE SHOW

Now please wind up this colossal form of yours. If I knew beforehand that you would do something like this I would not have even mentioned it to you. Now please control this *Maya* of yours and release me from this great fear. (11:383-385)

These Kaurava warriors and the sons of Dhritarashtra have gone into your mouth along with their families. Also the kings of various nations who have come to help them have not survived. You are swallowing the death-like weapons and the four-pronged army and the chariots along with their horses without even your teeth touching them. You have swallowed the truthful and valiant Bhishmacharya and the Brahmin Dronacharya. The great fighter Karna the son of Surya, also entered your jaws. And I also saw that you swiped the warriors on our side too. Oh God! What strange situation has arisen out of the favour I begged for? By my prayers I have brought death to the world. Nobody can avoid what is written in one's destiny!" (11:392-402).

Arjuna was thus wailing in distress, feeling unhappy. He really did not understand the intention of Shri Krishna in showing him the Cosmic form. Arjuna was in the grips of the delusion that he was the slayer and the Kauravas were the slain. Shri Krishna showed the Cosmic form to him to remove his misunderstanding and to show him that nobody kills anybody but it is He, Shri Krishna who destroys everybody. But Arjuna still could not understand it and he was feeling distressed by the fright. He then repeated the description of the destruction he was observing in the Cosmic form. (11:410-443)

He added, "Oh Shri Krishna, You are understood only through the Vedas, venerable to the whole universe and the root cause of the three worlds. It is because of this that I requested you to show the Cosmic form but you immediately became eager to swallow the three worlds. Therefore I am wondering as to who you really are and why you have acquired so many horrible mouths. Also why you are holding so many weapons in your hands? And why you are frightening us in frequent anger, by growing taller than the sky and with dreadful eyes? Why are you competing with death? (11:444-449).

Sʜʀɪ Kʀɪsʜɴᴀ Tᴇʟʟs Wʜᴏ Hᴇ Is

To this Shri Krishna replied, "You are asking Me who I am and why I have assumed this ferocious form. Then listen. I am really *Kaala*[13] and am expanding My form to destroy the universe. My mouths are extended everywhere and I am going to swallow all people." (11:450-451). Then, by the way of consolation, He added. "Arjuna, all of you Pandavas are safely outside the range of the calamity of destruction. The Pandavas are dear to me, but I am swallowing all others".[14] (11:456).

You are only instrumental: You have seen this universe enter My mouth and surely nothing out of it will survive. The boasts of this army are meaningless. (11:457-458). Their utterances may appear to be sharper than weapons, more scorching and dangerous than fire but these warriors are no more better than fruits in a painting. This is not an army but toys arranged for decoration. The strength on which their bodies do actions has already been destroyed by Me. Now these warriors are as lifeless as the statues in a potter's house. (11:463-466). Therefore Arjuna, come to your senses and get up. (11:468). This army, which has expediently come to the battlefield,

---

13 *Kaala means Time but is also used colloquially to mean Death, implying that with time death is inevitable.*

14 *This is suggestive of his earlier promise that he takes care of his true devotees who are dear to him. By implication this also implies these devotees are followers of dharma.*

has already died. So Arjuna, it is merely for namesake that you are to be an instrument in destroying it. (11:470-471).

The gathering of the army is only an illusion. When you saw them falling into My mouth, then itself they had died. I have already killed (destroyed) them. You are merely an instrument to aid their killing. So be victorious and let the world say that those relatives who had become oppressive by their arrogance and were unconquerable by their strength were destroyed effortlessly by Arjuna." (11:475- 481).

ARJUNA HAS A DOUBT

Arjuna said, "Oh Shri Krishna, I agree when you say that you are the Death and swallowing the universe is your play. But it does not stand to reason that when it is not yet the time for the destruction of the universe you should assume the role of death and destroy the universe. (11:490-492).

"It is true that you are ceaseless and you assume your three states of creation, sustenance and destruction which are active at their appropriate times. At the time of creation the states of sustenance and destruction are not present. At the time of sustenance the states of creation and destruction are not active and later at the time of destruction, the states of creation and sustenance vanish. Today the universe is in the state of sustenance and at its height of enjoying it, therefore I do not find it proper that you should destroy it." (11:494-498).

Shri Krishna gestured his agreement with this and said, "I demonstrated to you that the life span of this army is over. Other persons will die in their own time." (11:499).

FEROCIOUSNESS IS WITHDRAWN

By the time these words where uttered Arjuna saw that everything was as it was before. He said, "Shri Krishna, you hold the strings of this universe. It is because of you that the universe has regained its original state. "Oh Shri Krishna, you are well known for pulling people out of sorrow. I am experiencing the great bliss by thinking of it again and again. Because this world is alive it is feeling great love for you, but the demons from these three worlds fear you because you destroy those who are evil and they are running away from you in all directions. But others, like gods, human beings, *Siddhas, Yakshas* and all the living and nonliving are bowing to you out of joy. I know why these demons are running away from you instead of surrendering to you. You are the source of inner light and have appeared in person therefore the demons are blown away like dust. I had not understood this until now, but now I saw this unworldly greatness of yours. (11:500-510).

You are the Creator: You are the eternal limitless Principle. You are full of countless attributes. You are the state of continuous balance. You are the chief of all gods. You are the life of these three worlds. You are inexhaustible with ever-auspicious form. You are the Principle beyond the truth and untruth. (11:512-513)

You are the origin of both *Prakriti* and *Purusha* and are beyond *Maya*. You are eternal and nobody is older than you. You are the life and support of this world and you alone know the past and the future. Oh incomparable God, the *Shrutis* find happiness in your form. *Maya*, which supports the three worlds itself, has your support therefore you are called the highest place in which the Brahman rests after the end of the universe. In short it is you who have created this expanse of the universe therefore, Oh the Infinite, who can describe you? (11:514-518).

Is there any object or place not pervaded by you? Oh Infinite One, you are the Vayu (wind), you are also the Yama who punishes, you are Varuna, Chandra (moon), Brahmadeo the creator and his parent. And whatever other forms you have are your manifestations with or without form. I offer my obeisance to all of them." (11:519-522).

YOU ARE THE WORLD

Then Arjuna intently looked at Shri Krishna and was satisfied after observing each part of his body. Then he said, bowing at every sentence, "Oh Master, I bow to you. I really experienced that you are not separate from the world but you are everything in it. (11:523-536). But in ignorance I made the most improper error of behaving with you as one behaves with one's relatives. (11:537). You are a living deity and we used you for ordinary tasks for worldly gains. I have been a fool not to realise that you are the inner bliss of the yogis in *samadhi* and talked to you in anger. (11:542-543). Therefore Oh Master! Forgive me as a mother would if I have directly or indirectly committed indiscretion. (11:556). You are unique in these three worlds. There is none equal or superior to you. I do not know how to express this unworldly greatness of yours." (11:566).

ARJUNA REQUESTS FOR RETURN TO MATERIAL FORM

Speaking in this fashion, Arjuna, full of pure emotions, prostrated before Shri Krishna (11:567) and said, "I am feeling frightened of this Cosmic form therefore please restrain it and show me again your usual four-armed form which is more relaxing and which is experienced after practising all types of *yogas* or by studying the *Shastras* or by performing *yajnas* or after getting by charity. I am eager to see it again. (11:593-597). These eyes do not like to see any form other than the material form. Nothing else other than that beautiful form is capable of giving us pleasure and liberation. Therefore, Oh God, please restrain this Cosmic form and go back to your material form." (11:605-608).

SHRI KRISHNA REBUKES ARJUNA

On hearing this Shri Krishna, the form of the universe was

surprised. He said, "I have not seen another thoughtless person like you. You are not feeling happy about the so unprecedented a show you had the good fortune to watch. Instead, you are speaking like a persistent frightened coward. When I grace anybody I give him only worldly things. But as regards My inner secrets whom should I reveal them except to My really dear devotee? It is only for you that have I arranged today this demonstration of the Cosmic form. The extent to which I am impressed by your devotion is something beyond My understanding and therefore I have exhibited this most secret form to you.[15] This most secret form of mine is beyond *Maya* and beyond the most limitless objects. The *Avatars* like Krishna etc. are born from here only. This form of Mine is formed of only the effulgence of Knowledge and pervades the entire universe. There is endless, steady and is the root of the entire world. Nobody has seen or heard of this Cosmic form because it cannot be gained by any external means. (11:609-616)

NO EXTERNAL MEANS CAN LEAD TO THE FORM

Elaborating further on this point, Shri Krishna continues, "The Vedas maintained silence as soon as they reached up to this Cosmic form and *Yajnas* did not reach beyond the Heaven.[16] The seekers gave up the practice of yoga because it was laborious and students of *Shastras* did not develop liking for it. The perfectly performed actions raced to gain it but could reach only up to the *Satyaloka* level after great difficulty. Penance *(Tapas)* saw its splendour and its ferociousness vanished and thus it remained unattainably far from the path of austerity. The Cosmic form, which you could see without effort, has not been seen by any human being in this world. Even Brahmadeo has not been fortunate enough to see this form

---

15 *This is one more instance where Dnyaneshwar Maharaj brings out the extreme love of God for his dearest true devotee.*

16 *That is, Yajnas were being performed only with the aim of getting either worldly gains while living or for gaining heaven after death, as the concept used to be in the ancient days.*

which you just did.[17] (11:617-622)

Therefore consider yourself fortunate for the vision of the Cosmic form and do not at all get frightened by it. Do not think that there is anything superior to this Cosmic form. (11:623)

What you are really doing is you are trying to embrace the shadow rather than the real body. This four-armed form is, not My real form. It is not proper that you love it eagerly. At least now you leave the desire for the four-armed form and do not ignore the Cosmic form. Even if it is frightening and vast, concentrate steadily on it.[18] (11:629-633).

SHRI KRISHNA RESUMES MATERIAL FORM

You may meditate on My four-armed form for your external satisfaction but do not let your faith deviate from My Cosmic form. Save your love for it. Now you may gladly see My earlier form." So saying, Shri Krishna resumed His human form. (11:636-640)

Arjuna said, "Now I can breathe a sigh of relief." (11:663)

ONLY DEVOTION CAN LEAD TO MY FORM

Shri Krishna asked, "Have you forgotten My instruction to first love the Cosmic form and then only come in person to meet My four-armed form?" (11:673-674). There are no worldly means of reaching My Cosmic form. (11:682). Remember that it can be found by only one means and that is by filling your mind with devotion. (11:685)

But that devotion must be like a river flowing towards sea and does not stop until it meets it. Thus the devotee must be ceaselessly

17 *We may of course remind the loving incidence of Krishna's childhood in which his foster mother Yashoda saw it in his mouth when he opened it to show he had not eaten mud.*
18 *Shri Krishna impresses on Arjuna that the visible universe is really Maya.*

devoted to Me with all his feelings in order to reach Me and become one with Me. (11:686-688). Real devotion is that which sees My presence everywhere right from a small ant onwards and in all living and non-living things. And when he sees thus, then he will experience My form and with that, naturally see Me. (11:690-691). As soon as one experiences My form his ego is destroyed and duality vanishes. Then he realises the natural oneness between Me, himself and the entire universe. What is more, by becoming one with Me, he gets absorbed in Me. (11:694-695)

All actions of such a devotee are for My sake and there is nothing in this world he loves apart from Me. He considers Me alone as the fruit of his actions in this world and the next and considers Me as his goal in life. He forgets the word "creatures" because he sees Me in everything and thus with an attitude of equality and without enmity he worships everything. Such a devotee, when he leaves his material body, reaches Me and remains unified with Me." (11:696-699).

12

Yoga Of Devotion

~∞∞~

In this Chapter Dnyaneshwar Maharaj elaborates on the qualities of a true devotee and reiterates the superiority of the path of devotion.

Who Is Better - Sage Or Devotee

Arjuna asked, "Shri Krishna, The Cosmic form you showed me was unworldly and therefore I was frightened. You doubtless exist in both the material form and the attributeless non-material form. One gains your material form by the devotional path, while the path of yoga leads to the non-material form. These are the two paths to attain you which lead to the threshold of the respective forms. But I know both paths are equally important. (12:21-25).

Shri Krishna, now I ask you whether the Cosmic form you showed me was your real form or just your play.[1] (12:28).

Arjuna now expresses his dilemma and asks, "Everything that your devotees do is for your sake because for them, nothing else is superior to You. They have surrendered all their desires and thoughts only towards devotion to you. *(Another type of devotees)* the *jnani*

---

1 *Generally the word "leela" is used for the playful activities of deities in vernacular religious literature.*

(men of Knowledge) devotees also serve you while treasuring your image in their hearts. With the feeling "I am Brahman" in their minds they meditate on the Entity which is beyond the syllable *AUM*, is indescribable, incomparable, indestructible, not felt by the senses, cannot be shown and is not bound by space or time. Please tell me who out of these two, the *jnani* and the devotee really attains Knowledge? (12:29-33).

DEVOTEE IS A SUPERIOR *YOGI*

Shri Krishna replied, "The devotees whose faith increases steadily with devotion, in whose heart love upsurges, who concentrate their attention on Me day and night and offer themselves completely to Me are the ones I consider as superior yogis. (12:36-39).

YOGA PATH INVOLVES MORE LABOURS

"Arjuna, many (other) seekers endeavour to realise the formless and indestructible Brahman with the I-am-Brahman attitude (12:40). With courage and detachment they restrain the organs eliminating the sense-pleasures and then, by means of yogic postures they make the *Kundalini* force reach the *Brahmarandhra (Sahasrara)* and experience the Brahman. Thus, they gain the indescribable Brahman after adopting a balanced attitude towards everything and everybody and following the difficult path of yoga and sacrificing their ego. (12:47-48, 50-57). But what they attain after all these efforts is only Me. Thus they do not gain anything special from yoga other than incurring more labours. (12:58-59).[2]

Such of the people who hope to attain the indescribable Brahman without devotion are impeded in their path by the lure of positions in heaven and the lure of *Riddhis* and *Siddhis* (occult powers) and have to face the disturbances from desire, anger etc.

2 *Thus once more Dnyaneshwar Maharaj shows his favour towards the Bhakti path.*

They have to seek happiness in restraint and austerities, suppress hunger and thirst, face the elements like the wind and sun, to endure the elements like heat, wind and rain and the chill. (12:60-66). Only thing the followers of this path of yoga gain is a share of sufferings. (12:69). Such a person cannot attain the Formless (Brahman) while they live. Those who strive in spite of all these difficulties for the attributeless Brahman with intense desire suffer great pains. But Arjuna, those who follow the path of devotion do not have to undergo these sufferings. (12:73-75).

A DEVOTEE OFFERS EVERYTHING TO ME

Such devotees perform happily the duties that have come to their lot by their position and stature in society. They perform their actions in a prescribed manner avoiding prohibited actions, and burn the actions by offering the fruits of those actions to Me. Their mental and physical tendencies do not go anywhere except towards Me. By such ceaseless worship they have become My place of abode through the medium of meditation. They lovingly indulge with Me alone, forsaking pleasures and even the need for liberation. They sacrifice their body, mind and life at My feet with unexceptionable devotion. (That being so,) is it possible for Me to describe these devotees with mere words? Arjuna, I am obliged to satisfy all their wishes. (12:76-82).[3]

I LOVE MY DEVOTEES

My devotees are dear to Me the way they are, like a child is to its mother. And I have undertaken to take care of their problems of strife and life. And why should My devotees worry about the worldly problems? These devotees are like My family members, therefore, I am not ashamed to do anything for them to save them

---

3 As in the earlier Chapters, (8:124-134) Shri Krishna once more expresses the reciprocal obligations of God towards his true devotees.

from difficulties? When I see that this world is in the throes of life and death I say "Who would not get frightened by this ocean of earthly life one has to cross?" Thus, I take *Avatar* and rush to My devotees lest they get frightened. I became a saviour to them through the means of the raft of My thousand names.[4] I set those who are single and unencumbered for the paths of meditation while I set those who have a family on the boat of My names.[5] I tie the lifebelt of love to some devotees and bring them to the shore of liberation. But those who call themselves My devotees, even if they be animals, I make them worthy of occupying a place in My kingdom in *Vaikuntha*. Therefore My devotees have no reason whatever to worry, because I am ever ready to save them. I become obsessed with My devotees as soon as they surrender their mind and consciousness to Me. Therefore Arjuna, you should follow this singular *Bhakti* path to become a superior devotee. (12:86-96).

VARIOUS WAYS OF ATTAINING DEVOTION

Arjuna, concentrate your mind and intellect determinedly on Me. Once you enter inside Me with love then you will attain Me. Because, if your mind and intellect remain steady in Me, then what difference can remain between you and Me? (12:97-99). Ego automatically accompanies mind and intellect therefore let mind and body be concentrated in My form and let it be steady there. You will thus attain My all-pervading form.[6] I am swearing by this unexceptionable statement. (12:101-103).

Abhyasayoga (yoga of practice):[7] And if you are not able to give

---

4 *Vishnusahasranama or list of thousand names of Vishnu e.g. Keshava, Madhava, Narayana etc. is a standard text for daily recitation used by many devotees as part of worship. (There are similar lists of Shiva and Devi names also.)*
5 *To cross this river of worldly life to the shore beyond of liberation.*
6 *There is no place for ego in Brahman (God). Thus when mind and intellect are concentrated on His form and enter it then ego is left out and you are in a position to attain Him.*
7 *Krishna now gives a practical advice to overcome the usual obstacles for*

your undivided attention along with your mind and intellect to Me, then do thus: During the entire day, turn your mind to Me for a moment at least once. At the very instant your mind enjoys the bliss of the experience of My contact, at that moment a dislike for the sense pleasures will be created in your mind and it will slowly come out of worldly matters. (12:104-107). Then slowly and steadily it will enter in Me until it becomes one with Me. This is what is called *Abhyasayoga* or *Yoga of practice*. There is nothing that cannot be obtained by it. Nothing is difficult if one adopts this *yoga of practice*. Therefore be one with Me by adopting this yoga. (12:108-113).

Offering actions to God: If you do not have the strength to adopt this *Yoga of practice* then remain as you are. Do not control your sense organs, do not leave your pleasures and do not give up your pride also. Obey the family traditions and the rules of law. You are thus free to behave in this manner but see that, whatever you may do or decide to do or say, do not claim "I did it". Because only the almighty God knows whether something may or may not be done. Without bringing into the mind the thought that the action is complete or incomplete be one with the Self. *Giving up the pride of being the doer, avoid loading your mind with thoughts of worldly actions or spiritual actions.* Always steady your concentration on Me and make an offering of it to Me whatever happens.[8] And if your attitude becomes like this then you will be liberated after your death. (12:114-124).

Become desireless: And Arjuna, if you are not able to perform actions for My sake then just be devoted to Me. If you find it difficult to offer Me your action before or after resolving to do it, before or

---

spiritual path allowing a broad tolerance.
8 Often one wonders how to offer actions to God. This is how you can do it. One must understand that every action starts as a thought in the mind, while its success depends upon His grace. What one has to do is to develop an attitude that "Whatever has happened, from the thought of doing the action to its execution with or without success was all due to the will of God and I am only an instrument in the process." Thus one sacrifices the actions and their fruits to God and becomes free of the associated Karmas.

after completing it, then do not bother about it and you need not even long for Me. But with awareness restrain the sense organs and even as the actions take place, abandon the desire for the fruits of those actions. Just as trees and creepers shed their (ripe) fruits you too should renounce the fruits of completed actions. Let there not be even a feeling that I should be remembered or the actions should be performed for Me. Let these feelings along with the fruits of action vanish into nothingness. (12:125-130). Arjuna, you must become desireless regarding all your actions. *This sacrifice of the actions may appear to be easy but it is the greatest among all the Yogas.*[9] The actions, so nullified by surrender, do not accumulate and one does not have to take rebirth after death. (12:132-136).

ATTAINING PEACE

By practice one can get Knowledge, by Knowledge one gains success in meditation, and once one is engrossed in meditation, actions *(karmas)* go away. Once actions (thus) go away, then the fruits are automatically surrendered and one gets uninterrupted peace. Thus this step-by-step method of practice is the method to achieve peace. (12:137-140).

Arjuna, Knowledge is superior to practice and meditation is superior to Knowledge and renouncing the fruits of actions is superior to meditation and the bliss and peace of the mind is even more superior to renunciation of fruits of actions. These are the successive steps in this path that lead to peace or bliss of the Brahman. (12:141-143)

WHAT A DEVOTEE IS LIKE

Just as Consciousness does not differentiate between "mine" and "yours" My true devotee does not possess the feeling of hatred

9 *I-am-the-doer ego makes it difficult for a person to offer actions to God. To be desireless requires great courage and hence a great yoga by itself.*

for any creature. (12:144). He is equally friendly to all and like a loving nursemaid he takes care of them. Egotistic or possessive feelings do not occur in his mind and he is not even conscious of the feelings of pleasure or sorrow. He is forgiving like mother earth and bliss is always apparent in him. (12:148-150).

Just as ocean is always full whether it rains or not, he is happy without external aids. He restrains his mind with staunch and true determination. In his heart he and the supreme Soul have become one. He who is thus enriched by the wealth of yoga surrenders his mind and intellect in Me and having been purified internally and externally by it, is devoted to Me with love, is *THE* devotee, *THE* liberated one, *THE* yogi and I like him as a husband likes his wife. (12:151-156). I love him like My own life but even this simile is inadequate. The love for a person is like an enchanting *mantra*. It is not something that can be expressed in words but I am compelled to tell you because of your faith. And that is why I gave the simile of husband and wife; otherwise how else is it possible to express this love? (12:157-159).

THE DEVOTEE I LOVE

Now listen to the characteristics of the devotee for whom I keep a place in My heart. (12:164)

He is not offended if this world is rude to him and others also do not feel embarrassed by him. He feels that he is one among all the creatures therefore he is not fed up with them. He thinks of the world as his own body and therefore thoughts of likes and dislikes do not enter his mind. Thus, *dwaita* i.e. duality or the sense of being different from the universe does not exist in his mind and feelings of glee and anger vanish. Oh! How I love the person who, having been thus liberated from feelings of happiness and pain, fear and sorrow, worships me! He is fully satiated with the bliss of the Self and has reached perfection. He is free of all desires and his happiness ever increases. (12:166-172)

Liberated while living: One can easily attain liberation in Kashi but it is necessary to die there.[10] One's sins are atoned by a visit to the Himalaya Mountains but one's life is in danger there. On the other hand the holiness of saints is not so dangerous. Ganges water is holy and washes the conscience-pricking sins but one is likely to get drowned there. The knowledge of the saints is deep like the Ganges and is difficult to fathom but a devotee does not get drowned in his company. On the contrary he gets liberated while still living. How holy must be the company of a saint by whose touch even Ganges gets rid of her sins. By his holiness such a saint becomes the shelter of even holy places and causes the bad thoughts from a person's mind to vanish. He is pure like the sun from inside out and experiences the principle of the Brahman. His mind is all-pervading but unconcerned about everything. He is always happy and nothing bothers him. He never carries an ego when he does any action. Just as fire gets extinguished without fuel he becomes possessed of peace and is marked for liberation. Thus such person filled with the feeling of "I am Brahman" goes beyond dualism. But for the sake of the bliss that he gets from devotion, he splits himself into two, calling one the devotee and the other as God and thus sets an example of the right path of devotion to non-devotees. I am obsessed with only such devotee who becomes for Me the object to meditate upon. I feel happy when I meet him. I take birth as an *Avatar* for him and come into this world. I like him so much that he becomes My life-force. (12:173-189).

He likes nothing as much as Self-realisation and therefore he does not get pleasure from any kind of physical enjoyment. Having realised that he himself is the universe, the feeling of duality has gone from his mind and so has the hatred. Firmly believing that his real self will never get destroyed, he never rues death. And since he himself has become Brahman beyond which nothing exists, he does not desire anything. He does not have feelings like "This is good"

---

10 *Hindus strongly believe that a person who dies in Kashi (Varanasi) is liberated from the birth-death cycles.*

and "That is bad." Thus even after having attained the ceaseless Brahman he continues to remain My devotee. I state on oath that no one is closer to Me than such a person. (12:190-196).

Arjuna, he does not carry an iota of feeling of differentiation between people and he treats an enemy and a friend on equal footing. Honour and insult, hot and cold are same to him. He remains undisturbed by happiness or sorrow. He treats all creatures alike. He is liked by people in all the three worlds. Such a devotee leaves the sense pleasures and desires totally and by remaining in seclusion lives by steadying his consciousness in the Self. He does not feel discouraged by slander or elated by praise. He behaves with an attitude of equability towards both. Neither uttering truth nor untruth he observes silence enjoying the mindless Brahmic state from which he does not return. He never takes shelter anywhere and considers the whole world as his place of rest. He is certain that the entire universe is his home. Furthermore, even after becoming the entire universe himself, he is eager to be devoted to Me. Therefore I hold him on My head like a crown. Anybody would bow before a superior person but before such a devotee the whole world prostrates. Only a true Guru like Lord Shiva can explain this respect towards devotion, but praising Lord Shiva is like praising Myself.[11] (12:207-216).

Even after reaching the goal of the fourth duty[12] i.e. the liberation, My devotee continues to follow the path of devotion and sets an example to the world. He is entitled to the liberation and (by his example) decides who should be or should not be accorded the liberation and even then he is very humble. And it is because

---

11 *It has always been advised (unfortunately in vain) in religious literature not to differentiate between Vishnu and Shiva. This sentence is to that effect.*

12 *Every man is supposed to fulfill four duties in his lifetime. These are: Dharma or behaving as per the righteous code; Artha or earning livelihood for himself and his family; Kama or fulfilling sexual duties towards his wife and Moksha or pursuit of liberation. These are called the four Purusharthas. Of these the first three are to be done with the co-operation of his wife but the fourth i.e. striving for liberation has to be pursued alone.*

of this that I bow to him and wear his footmark on My chest.[13] In order to gain the bliss of his companionship I who am formless, had to take *avatar*. There is no comparison with the extent to which I like him. I also like extremely those who listen to the life story of such a great devotee and praise him. Arjuna, What I have told you is the yoga of devotion. Its greatness is such that I personally love such a devotee and hold him in My mind and carry him on My head. (12:219-229).

I Also Like Those Who Glorify Other Devotees

Arjuna, in this world, I consider those as my devotees and yogis, who, after listening to the interesting narrative (about this yoga), which is like a shower of immortalising nectar, experience it themselves and in whom it grows by virtue of their faith and by becoming firm in the heart makes them practice it, and who, even when they get beneficial fruits due to their minds being in proper state as explained earlier (like seeds sown in a fertile field), love Me and consider that I alone am their ultimate goal and their all in all. Therefore Arjuna, I am always concerned about them.

Those who have a liking for the stories of God are themselves the holy places and holy persons. I meditate on them. They are my deity to be worshipped and I do not like any other persons. I am obsessed by them; they are my treasure and I feel satisfied only by meeting them. But Arjuna, I consider those who narrate the stories about my loving devotees as the highest deity. (12:230-239).

---

13 *According to a Purana legend Rishi Bhrigu sent to find out who among Brahmaa, Vishnu and Shiva was the fittest to receive offerings, found Vishnu asleep when he reached him. In anger he kicked Vishnu on the chest to wake him. Instead of being offended Vishnu held the feet on his chest and said that he was honoured. Vishnu proudly carries this mark on his chest which is known as 'Srivatsa'.*

13

The Field And The Knower
Of The Field

～⚭～

So far Gita/Dnyaneshwari dealt with topics of emotional nature
like the relationship between devotee and God. Now we enter
discussions of theoretical nature based on the Sankhya philosophy
but again leading to the goal of Self-realization.

DEFINITIONS

Shri Krishna said, "Arjuna, this body is called the Field and one
who knows this is called the Knower of the field. And understand
properly that it is I who am the Knower of the Fields and the one
who sustains all the Fields. I consider Knowledge as that which
makes one properly understand the Field and the Knower of the
Fields. Now I shall tell you why the name Field has been given to
the body. (13:7-10)

Why it should be called Field, where and how it is created, which
processes make it grow, whether it is exactly three and half cubits
long or not and whether it is a wasteland or a fertile land and to

whom does it belong and all its qualities are the matters which will now be fully told. Listen to them carefully. (13:11-13)

IGNORANCE ABOUT THE FIELD BY VEDAS, SHASTRAS ETC.

Vedas: Vedas continue to talk about this Field and even the science of logic began to talk about it endlessly. The six *Darshanas¹* became tired discussing it and they have not come to any conclusion. Because of it, the relations between the various *Shastras* have broken and debate is going on throughout the world for their coming to an agreement. So far nobody has been able to say whom this Field belongs. But the power of ego is such that this field continues to be

---

1 *Darshanas are schools of philosophy. There are six Darshanas: Nyaya, Vaisheshic, Sankhya, Yoga, Purvamimamsa and Uttarmimamsa. They are the hypotheses about the structure of the universe and also give guidance about the path to liberation. These are: Nyaya postulates that valid knowledge is the only way to gain release from suffering. This knowledge is to be obtained from logical analysis of information gained from the four sources of knowledge: perception, inference, comparison, and testimony. (Proponent: Gotama). Vaisheshic is supplementary to the Nyaya; together it is called the Atomic School, because it teaches the existence of a transient world composed of aggregations of eternal atoms. Brahman is regarded as the fundamental force that causes consciousness in these atoms. (Proponent: Kanada). Sankhya is a dualistic and atheistic philosophy that proposes that Purusha, the Supreme Being and uses his power Prakriti to create the material universe. Ignorance (similar to I-am-the-body ignorance.) lies in identifying Purusha with Prakriti and leads to binding liberation from which is obtained when this ignorance is removed and one realises that they are different. (Proponent: Kapila). Yoga founded by Patanjali accepts Sankhya principles except that it is theistic and assumes Brahman to be Supreme and higher than Purusha. Purva-mimamsa asserts the authority of the Vedas placing great emphasis on dharma, which consisted of the performance of Vedic rituals like yajna in the prescribed manner. It believes in the power of the mantras and yajnas to sustain all the activity of the universe. Later it adopted the principle of Brahman and liberation (Moksha). Uttara-mimamsa or Vedanta: Vedanta came to be the dominant current of Hinduism in the post-medieval period. Based on Upanishad teachings that state Brahman as the Supreme Entity it recommends meditation etc. in order to attain Self-realization and moksha. (WK-SD) Wikipedia Article on Hindu Philosophy.*

debated and discussed everywhere. (13:14-18).

Atheists: Seeing that the Vedas have tried to elaborate on it in order to face the atheists, the hypocrites started arguing differently. They tell the Vedas that their arguments are false and without base. Some of the hypocrites shed their clothes and move around naked while some shave their heads but the arguments they offer do not carry any weight.[2] (13:19-21).

Yogis: Yogis opted for secluded life and practised *Yama* and *Niyama*[3] (control of behaviour and tendencies) because this body or Field will be wasted by death. Because the ego associated with this Field comes in the way of yoga, Lord Shiva gave up the kingdom and went to live on the cremation ground. With strong resolve he remained unencumbered by clothes and burnt Kama the god of Love to ashes, because he lures people with pleasure of sex. Brahmadeo acquired four mouths to gain additional strength but even he could not understand anything about it. (13:22-26).

Karmayogi: Some (people who follow the path of action) say that the field belongs completely to the Individual Soul and *Prana* (the life force) is its tenant. In this house of *Prana* his four brothers *(Apana, Vyana, Samana and Udana,* (see footnote on *Pranas* at 6: 186-191) toil, and Mind is their supervisor. Mind is the owner of bullock pairs in the form of the ten organs (five sense organs and five action organs) and he labours day and night in the farm of sense pleasures. Avoiding the bed of righteous duties, planting the seeds of injustice and using the fertiliser of sinful deeds he gets accordingly the harvest of sins because of which he is reborn millions of times

2 *This appears to be a comment in reference to Buddhist and Jain customs.*

3 *Practitioners of yoga are enjoined to practice control of their behaviour and tendencies in order to purify mind and body. These require observing certain restrictions which are called Yama and Niyama each having five types of restrictions. Yama: Ahimsa (non-violence), Satya (truthfulness), Asteya (non-stealing), Bramacharya (celibacy) and Aparigraha (Non-receiving or non-accumulation of property). Niyama: Shoucha (internal and external purification), Santosha (contentment), Tapa (austerity), Swadhyaya (study), Ishwarpranidhana (Worship of God).*

and undergoes suffering. On the other hand, if he uses the bed of righteous duties and plants the seeds of righteous deeds then he enjoys happiness for hundreds of rebirths. (13:27-32)

Sankhyas: On this the followers of the *Sankyha* philosophy say that this Field does not belong to the Individual soul. He is only a wayfarer in this Field and his residence is temporary. *Prana* is an entitled labourer who guards it day and night. The Field is leased to the beginningless *Prakriti* described by the *Sankhyas*. Since she has domestic labourers it is she who carries out the farming. The three attributes which farm the Field have been born of her. Of these three, the attribute *Rajas* sows, the *Sattva* attribute sustains it and the *Tama* attribute harvests it. Then *Prakriti* prepares the trampling enclosure out of the *Mahat* principle and gets the harvest trampled by the bull, which is Time, to separate the grains. The evening of the *Unmanifestable* (Brahman) then approaches. (13:33-39)

The intellectuals: The intellectuals did not like these arguments of the *Sankhyas*. They said, "*Prakriti* stands nowhere in comparison with the Supreme Brahman. The Will was sleeping in the bedroom of the Formless Brahman on the mattress of dissolution. He suddenly woke up and being always of active disposition he discovered the treasure of the three worlds as per his wish. Then the three worlds, which had dissolved, took form again in the garden of the formless Brahman. Then he brought together the barren plots of the five principles (Air, Water, Earth, Fire and Sky) and built the four kinds of life, i. e. those who are born from sweat, those born from eggs, those through mating and those born from seeds. Then he created the material world by taking fractions of each of the five principles. Then using the rubble of actions and non-actions he built walls on two sides and converted the barren land in their middle into forests. In order to sustain the comings and goings in the forest, he created the two tunnels of birth and death arranging by means of the Divine will that the tunnels should extend from the material world to Brahman. Then the Divine will in collaboration with the ego and with the intellect as intermediary, arranged to cultivate the living and nonliving world throughout life. Thus the Divine will which branched out of Brahman is the root of the world." (13:40-50)

Naturalists: When the intellectuals said this, the Naturalists *(Swabhavavadi)* asked, "If one has to imagine the bedroom of the Divine will in the village of the Brahman then what is wrong with believing in the *Prakriti* aspect of the Brahman as propounded by the *Sankhyas*? But forget about these things and listen to the real facts. Who filled the sky with the clouds? Who supports the stars in space? Who stretched the ceiling of the sky and when? Who decided that wind should always flow? Who planted the hair? Who filled the oceans? Who makes the rain pour? Just as these things occur because they are natural the Field is also natural. No particular person has proprietary right over it. Whoever carries its burden and works gets its benefits; nobody else gains by it." (13:51-57)

Fatalists: On this the Fatalists said, "If this were true then how does Death always rule over the body? The tentacles of Death extend even beyond the time of the great *Kalpa* (Time at which world is destroyed by deluge) when it devours even *Satyaloka,* (Brahmadeo's abode). He kills the eight ever-renewed Guardians and the keepers of the eight directions and the residents of heaven. And other weaker lives die and fall in the ravine of birth-death just by the breath of Death. (**Note:** this part was a free translation). Just look at the jaws of death that are big enough to swallow the entire universe. Therefore we hypothesise that it is Death that rules the Field." (13:58-65)

Debate by Rishis: Thus there are various opinions about this Field. The Rishis in the *Naimisha* Forest[4] debated on it extensively as recorded in the Puranas. In Vedas, the *Brihatsama Sutra*[5] is very holy from the point of view of Knowledge. But it has also not been able to fathom it. Many great poets also have used their intelligence to analyse this question of the Field. But this Field is of such a nature

---

4 *A forest on the banks of the Gomati River in Uttar Pradesh region mentioned in the Puranas where traditionally Rishis meditated or gathered for mass rituals like discussions, Yajna etc.*

5 *A poetic composition from the Samaveda.*

and so extensive that nobody has ever found out whom exactly it belongs. Now I shall explain to you completely the nature of this Field. (13:66-71)

CONSTITUTION OF THE FIELD

This Field is made up of thirty-six principles which are: the five elements (earth, water etc.), the ego, intellect, the *Unmanifestable*, the ten organs (five sense organs and five organs of action), the mind which is the eleventh organ, the ten objects of the senses, pleasure-pain, desire-aversion and the aggregate of all these *(sanghat)*, the consciousness and fortitude. Now I shall tell you about which the five principles are, which the sense objects are, what the nature of the organs etc. one by one. (13:72-75).

The Five elements and ego: The five elements are the earth, water, fire, air and sky. (13:76). The ego is hidden and is latent within *Prakriti*. When the five elements come together to form the body, it is this ego that makes this body dance around. (13:79, 81). *The surprising thing about this ego is that it does not affect the ignorant persons but gets its hold on the learned ones putting them into all sorts of difficulties.*[6] (13: 82).

Intellect: Now listen to the characteristics of intellect. When desire (lust) becomes strong the sense-organs, if they are favourable, help to bring in their objects and expose the individual to a variety of pleasures and pains. The intellect decides how much is the pleasure and how much is the pain. It decides where the pleasure lies and where pain occurs; which is a meritorious deed and which is sinful; which is pure and which is impure. The quality by which an individual is able to tell between good and bad, small and big etc. and judge the sense-objects, that which is the basic means of gaining knowledge and due to which the *Sattva* attribute in a person grows and which is the meeting place of the individual and the Soul

---

6 *Once again Dnyaneshwar Maharaj asserts that book knowledge is useless for spiritual progress.*

is to be recognised as the intellect. (13:83-89)

Unmanifestable: Now I shall tell you the characteristics of the *Unmanifest.* The *Prakriti* of the *Sankhya* philosophy is the *Unmanifestable.* Two different aspects of *Prakriti, A-Para* and *Para,* was described when the *Sankhya* philosophy was discussed in Chapter 7. Of those, *Para* which is the Life (or life-force) is also called *Unmanifestable.* (13:90-92). Just as after death of the material body all the impressions of actions done throughout the lifetime, merge with the Karmas associated with the subtle body of desires, (13:94) the five principles (elements) and the creatures / things created by them shed their gross qualities. The place where they merge is known as *Unmanifestable.* (13:96-97).

The Ten Organs: Now listen to the different types of organs. Ears, nose, eyes, skin and tongue are the five sense organs. Once these five senses come to an accord then the intellect starts thinking about pleasures and pains. The organs of speech, hands, feet, anus and the sex organs are the five organs of action through which the power of action which accompanies life and is present in a living being, makes its body perform actions. (13:98-102).

Mind: Now I shall explain to you what mind is. That which lies at the joining place of the organs and the intellect, playing around by its fickle nature and with the help of the *Rajas* attribute, which gives deceptive appearances like the blue colour of the sky or like the waves in a mirage, is mind. When the body takes shape out of the five principles (elements) through the union of the sperm and the ovum the air principle (for example), gets divided into ten parts with ten different aspects, which get themselves established in ten different parts according to the individual properties and functions of each. Due to its purely fickle nature it gains its strength from the *Rajas* attribute and implants itself firmly outside the intellect and above the ego i.e., in between them. It has been named as "mind" for no particular reason but actually it is only a concept. Because of it the Soul gets to be associated with the body. It is the root cause of the inclination for action. It strengthens the lust and always incites the ego. It increases desire, strengthens hope and nurtures fear. Because of it, duality (disunity) is created, ignorance prevails and it pushes the organs into sense-pleasures. It creates a conceptual world and immediately destroys it too. It assembles stacks of ambitions and disassembles them. It is a storehouse of delusion and is the inner core of the air principle. It has closed the doors of the intellect. This then without doubt is the mind. (13:103-116).

Sense-objects: Now listen to the various types of sense-objects and their names. Touch, sound, form, taste and smell are the objects of the five sense organs through which knowledge reaches out. (13:117-118).

Action-objects: The pronunciation of vowels and consonants, the action of taking or throwing, walking, passing of faeces and urine are the objects of the five organs of action through which the body functions. These are then the ten objects present in the body. (13:119-120).

Desire: Now I shall describe desire. That which excites the emotions after remembering or hearing about past events, that which generates craving when the senses encounter sense objects, causes the mind to run helter-skelter and the organs to step in where they should not go, that which makes the intellect crazy and that which has a liking for the sense objects is called desire. (13:121-125)

Hatred: The feeling in the mind when the organs do not get the desired pleasures of sense objects is called hatred. (13:126)

Bliss: Now, bliss or happiness is to be understood as that due to which an individual, because activities of the body and mind have ceased, forgets all other things including one's body. The state of mind which causes the life force to be inactivated but makes goodness grow, which causes the tendencies of the sense organs to be lulled into sleep and in which the individual meets the soul, that state is called bliss. And the state of mind where these things are not gained is called sorrow. One does not gain happiness when desires and ambitions are present but it comes automatically when they are absent. Therefore presence or absence of desire and ambitions are the causes of sorrow and happiness respectively. (13:127-133).

Chetana: The aloof and unattached power of the consciousness is called the vital power or life-principle (*Chetana*). It functions throughout the body right from the toe-nail to the hair on the head and remains unchanged during the three states of the body viz., waking, dream and deep sleep. It brings freshness to the mind, intellect etc. and keeps the nature lovely and cheerful. It is present in some measure or other in all the animate and inanimate objects. (13:134-137). By association with the Soul this vital power or life-principle puts life into the inanimate body. (13: 141).

Fortitude: Now listen to the description of fortitude or courage. The five principles are natural enemies of each other. Water destroys the earth and is itself dried away by fire. Wind fights with fire and is itself devoured by the sky (space). These five principles come together in the body and abandoning the mutual conflict they help each other through their individual characteristics. The quality, which causes this rare unity to occur and sustains it, is called fortitude or courage. (13:142-148).

Sanghat: And the assembly of all these thirty-six principles including the life principle is called the aggregate or *Sanghat*. (13:149).

Thus I have explained to you the characteristics of the thirty-six principles that constitute the Field. When these thirty-six principles come together, that aggregate is called the Field. Figuratively also it is called the Field because the crop of meritorious and sinful deeds is harvested in this aggregate. Some also call it the body and is also known by many other names. But whatever is created and destroyed, between the material up to this side of the Brahman, is all Field.[7] (13:150, 155-158).

Attributes influence birth: Creatures are born in various species such as deities, humans, reptiles etc. They are born so, according

7 *What is created and destroyed is the material world. For Self-realization one has to experience Brahman or Self which is non-material. For this one has to cross the boundary of the material world or Field over into the non-material world, metaphorically speaking.*

to the influence of the three attributes (*Sattva, Rajas* and *Tamas*) and the *Karma*. The details about these attributes will be discussed later (Chapter fourteen). Thus I have told you all the characteristics and attributes of the Field. (13:159-161).

Knowledge

Now I shall tell you about the generous Knowledge. For the sake of this Knowledge yogis adopt the difficult path of yoga avoiding the attractions of a place in heaven and of the *Siddhis*. People perform difficult penance, *yajnas* and other worship rituals or jump wholeheartedly into devotion or follow the path of *Kundalini* yoga and in the hope of attaining this Knowledge some day, spend hundreds of lifetimes in the service of their Guru. This Knowledge, which destroys ignorance and unifies the individual with Brahman, closes the doors of the senses, cripples the tendency for materialistic actions and removes the unhappiness from the mind. Because of it, duality becomes scarce and the sense of equality prevails. It removes arrogance and destroys delusion and does not permit the language of "I" and "others". It uproots the worldly attitude and cleans the mire of desire and embraces the difficult-to-know ultimate principle of Brahman with ease. When it manifests itself, the vital force which drives the world, loses its power. Intellect opens its eyes by its light and the individual rolls in bliss. The pure and holy Knowledge purifies the mind laden with all sorts of impure notions. By attaining it the disease of I-am-the-body feeling with which an individual is afflicted is cured. I am explaining that Knowledge though really it is not explainable. It has to be heard and understood through intellect because it is not visible to the eyes. But once it is understood by intellect it becomes visible to the eyes through the actions of the organs. (13:162-179)

Body Signs On Man Of Knowledge

Just as the presence of underground water discovered by the

deep roots becomes apparent through the foliage, in the same way the presence of this Knowledge in the heart of a person is indicated through certain characteristic signs on that person's body about which I shall now tell you. (13:180-184)

Humility: Because he lacks pride a man of Knowledge does not like to be equated with anybody and he feels awkward if burdened with greatness and honour. He feels nervous by praise or honour or if one openly applauds his worthiness. He does not let greatness to be showered upon him. He feels distressed even by obeisance from others. Lest his greatness increase in public eyes he pretends to be a simpleton hiding his wisdom. Ignoring his own greatness he deliberately goes around as if he is a mad person. (13:185-192).

Being prideless he avoids attention: He detests fame and does not like discussing *Shastras*. He prefers to sit quietly and he strongly wishes that people should ignore him and relatives should not worry about him. His actions are generally such that they will instil humility in him and gives the appearance of being insignificant. He prefers to live in such a way that people ignore his existence. He moves around in such a light-footed manner that people wonder whether he is really walking or is being carried around by wind. He prays that his existence should be ignored; that nobody should remember his name or looks or feel frightened of him. He always prefers to live in solitude and feels happy in deserted places. He is in sympathy with the wind, converses with the sky and is friendly with the trees. He who has these characteristics of pridelessness may be considered as having attained Knowledge. (13:193-202).

Unpretentiousness: Now listen to the characteristic of unpretentiousness *(inostensibility)* and how to identify it. (13:202). An unpretentious person does not speak about his meritorious actions. (13:204). He keeps his charitable and benevolent deeds secret. He does not talk about the favours he has done to others. He does not boast about his learning and does not sell his knowledge for public applause. He behaves like a miser when it comes to expenditure on his own person but he spends generously on religious work. At home he may be wanting in everything but when it comes to charity he competes with the wishing tree. In short, he is wise in religious duties, generous in charity and clever in spiritual discussions but behaves like a simpleton in other matters. Though he knows the path to liberation perfectly well, he is inept in worldly matters. (13:207-212). Therefore Arjuna, he who has these characteristics may be considered to be having Knowledge in his grasp. (13:216).

Non-violence: Now I shall tell you about the characteristics of non-violence. Many people have defined non-violence in different ways according to their own school of thought. (13:217-218).

Nonviolence according to Purvamimamsa: It has been told rather oddly in *Purvamimamsa*[8] that some types violence, such as cutting the branches of a tree to fence its trunk or satisfying one's hunger by cutting one's hand, cooking and eating it are not violence but non-violence. People perform *Yajnas* for preventing drought. The very base of the *Yajnas* is the killing of animals. Under this situation how can one achieve non-violence? How can one harvest non-violence where only violence is sown? But the greed of the performers of the *Yajnas* is strange. (13:219-224).

Non-violence according to Ayurveda: In Ayurveda also the same approach, i.e. that of taking a life to save another has been recommended. For preparing the medicines the Ayurveda experts dig the roots of the trees, some trees are uprooted with the roots and leaves, some are cut in the middle, the bark of some is peeled away and the cores of some are boiled. They bleed the trees dry, trees that have no enmity with anyone at all, by making cuts all over them to extract their essence. Diseased people are thus cured by killing the trees. They cut the stomach of live animals to remove the biles in order to save sick people. (13:225-230). It is like looting the poor to distribute free food in charity or like burning one's blanket to warm oneself. One does not know whether one should

---

8 *See the footnote on Darshanas in the beginning of the chapter.*

laugh or cry. (13:231-234).

Non-violence according to Jain Religion: In one religion (Jain) they drink water after filtering it. But because of the filtering many living organisms die. Some people, afraid of committing violence, eat the grains raw without cooking. But this indigestible food causes agony to the person and brings him on the verge of death, which is nothing but violence. (13:235-236).

Non-violence according to Shri Krishna: Thus, understand that according to the ritualistic approach, permitted violence is equivalent to non-violence. When I first mentioned non-violence, I did not want to omit mentioning these opinions. I therefore mentioned them first so that you also would know about them. When one puts forth one's opinions other opinions also should be considered and that is the reason I discussed them so far. (13:237-240).

Now listen to the characteristics of non-violence according to my opinion. If these characteristics are found in any person then it will be found that he has attained Knowledge. Whether non-violence is ingrained in a person or not may be found from his behaviour. Similarly, the impression of non-violence on mind after one attains Knowledge is as follows (13:241-245).

Characteristics of non-violence: Such person treads very carefully due to compassion for the minute living beings which he knows are present even in atoms. His path is filled with friendly feelings and he is extremely careful about treading on the insects and other living beings under his feet. His sense of non-violence cannot be expressed in words. (13:249-251). He treads on the ground so delicately that if by mistake his feet touch any living thing then the creature actually gets comfort from it. (13:254). He feels that if he were to walk stamping his feet then the sleep of the all-pervading Lord would get disturbed and His health would get affected. With these thoughts he returns without treading on any creature. (13:257-258).

You will notice kindness even in his speech. When he speaks, love oozes from his mouth first and then the words follow. As far as possible he does not speak to anybody and if an occasion for speaking arises then fearing that his words may hurt somebody he observes silence. If perhaps someone requests, then he speaks with love and it appears as if the listener's own parents are talking. (13:263-268).

His talk, true but soft, limited but straightforward is like the flow of nectar. Contradiction, arguments, irritating harsh words, ridicule, torture, maliciousness, obstruction, irritation, nastiness, showing false hope, doubt, falsehood are completely absent in his talk. (13:270-272).

Also, his gaze is such that his eyebrows are never raised. The reason is that he believes every living creature has a soul and is afraid that his gaze might hurt it. He therefore generally does not look at anybody and if at all he looks out of the inner kindness then the creature that he looks at feels a sense of satisfaction. (13:273-276).

Just as his eyes are kind to the living creatures so are his hands. Yogis are not left with any desires because of their fulfilment. In the same way his hands are inactive because nothing more remains to be done. He does not like to take even a staff or stick in his hand; then why talk of a weapon? He does not stroke his body lest the hair on his body get disturbed. And he feels that cutting his nails is like committing violence, therefore he grows them. He feels reluctance even while raising his hands in reassurance or giving a supporting hand to a falling person or gently stroking a suffering person. But even the moon's rays do not have that love with which he helps to remove the suffering by his touch. The movements of his hands have the character and nature of a good person. (13:277-292).

Now regarding his mind, understand that the behaviour of the organs I told so far are not different from the behaviour of the mind. (13:293). Mind expresses itself through the organs. (13:296). If there is no place for non-violence in the mind itself then how can it be seen outside? Anything is created in the mind first and is then expressed through speech, looks or hands. How can anything be expressed in words if it is not there in the mind? When the mind-ness of mind vanishes then the organs stop functioning. (13:297-301). Mind is the root of actions of the organs and functions through the organs. The desires in the mind are manifested through the organs. If non-violence is well ingrained in the mind, then the organs function on its strength. The mind imparts the kindness in it to the limbs and makes them behave in a non-violent manner. Thus, he who has abandoned all violence from his mind, body and speech is the beautiful temple of Knowledge. Not only that, he is the Knowledge personified. If you wish to see non-violence, the greatness of which we hear and read about, then you see that person and your wish will be fulfilled. (13:303-313).

Tolerance and Forbearance: Now that your outlook has become clear, I shall introduce you properly to Knowledge. Knowledge is present where there is forbearance (forgiveness) without regret. (13:339-340). Forbearance gets nurtured within a man of Knowledge. I shall now tell you the signs by which one may judge a person with forbearance. (13:342).

He is tolerant to all good and bad situations. He does not feel perturbed by any of the three kinds of difficulties – personal, external and elemental. He gets the same sense of contentment with the expected gains as with the unexpected losses. He accepts honour and insult, pleasure and pain with the same calmness. Praise and slander do not disturb his balance. He does not feel uneasy by the heat of the sun nor does he shiver by cold and he does not feel frightened in any situation. (13:343-347). There is nothing which he cannot tolerate and he is not even aware that he is tolerating. He considers that all the sufferings and enjoyments that his body has to undergo are a part of his self, therefore he does not feel that he is doing something out of the ordinary. He who possesses such forbearance without regret imparts greatness to Knowledge. Such persons are really the essence of Knowledge. (13:351-353).

Uprightness: Now I shall tell you about the nature of uprightness.

An upright person is impartial to everybody like the vital force *(Prana)* which supports both good and bad people with equal favour. (13:354-355). His mental attitude and behaviour does not change from person to person. He knows the nature of the world thoroughly and behaves as if he has known it since old times and therefore he does not know the meaning of "mine" and "yours". He can mix with anybody and he does not have prejudice against anybody. His nature is straightforward. There are no desires or doubts in his mind. He does not hesitate to express his mind before people. He cannot hide anything in the corners of his mind. His mind being pure his actions are also pure. Since he is fully satisfied due to Self- realisation, he does not spend his time in thoughts. He neither reins in his mind nor does he let it go adrift. He does not have either deceit in his mind or vagueness in his words and he never harbours ill-will towards anybody. All his actions are straightforward, without deceit and pure and his five vital airs *(Pranas)* also are always free. A person having these qualities is to be understood as uprightness personified and Knowledge resides in him. (13:357-368).

Devotion to Guru: Now I shall tell you about the method of devotion to one's Guru. This service of the Guru is the birthplace of all fortunes and makes an individual attain Brahman even when in sorrowful state. Listen with complete attention. (13:369- 371).

He who has dedicated his mind and body to the Guru-tradition is the storehouse of Guru-devotion. His thoughts are about the place of abode of his Guru. He rushes to welcome even the wind blowing from that region and requests it to visit his home. Out of the mad love he has for his Guru he likes to talk only about the direction in which his Guru lives. He considers Guru's home as his own but being bound by Guru's orders he has to live in his own place. Then he longs for the release from Guru's orders and an opportunity to meet him and in this mood a moment feels like a thousand years to him. If somebody arrives from Guru's village or Guru himself sends someone then he feels like a person revived from death. (13:374-380). He feels elated even by the name of his Guru's tradition. If you find anybody with this kind of love for the Guru tradition then understand that Knowledge is always at his service. (13:382-383).

Then, with great love in his heart he meditates on the form of his Guru. By installing that form in his pure heart he himself becomes the articles of worship; or he installs his Guru like a *Shivalinga* in the temple of bliss situated in the premises of Knowledge and bathes it with the nectar of meditation. Then, when the sun of Self-realisation rises he fills the basket of intellect with flowers of pure (*sattvic*) feelings and offers them to Lord Shiva in the form of his Guru. He considers all the three times i.e. morning, noon and evening as auspicious for this worship and burns the myrrh (*dhoopa*) of ego and ever waves *Arati*[9] with the lamp of knowledge. He offers his Guru the food of non-duality, and taking him to be *Shivalinga* serves as its priest. (13:385-390).

Sometimes his intellect imagines his Guru to be the husband lying on the bed of life and experiences his loving admiration. Sometimes, there is such strong wave of love in his mind that he calls the love as *Kshirasagara*,[10] the ocean of milk where the limitless bliss of meditation is the bed formed by *Shesha* the Great Serpent on which his Guru is relaxing in the form of Lord Vishnu; and he himself becomes His consort *Laxmi* serving Him. He stands before Him becoming *Garuda* as well and becomes Brahmadeo too, created from His navel; and with the love for his Guru he experiences the bliss of meditation within his mind. (13:391-395).

---

9 *Arati is a ritual performed during a worship rite wherein a lamp (or smoking myrrh) is waved in clockwise fashion before the deity, singing a song of prayer also called Arati.*

10 *In the Puranic depiction of Vishnu he is showing as relaxing in recumbent position on the thousand headed snake Shesha as his bed floating on Kshirasagara the ocean of milk. He is accompanied by his consort Laxmi the goddess of wealth and servants like his vehicle Garuda. Sometimes he is also depicted with a lotus stemming from his navel, with Brahmadeo sitting in the lotus.*

Sometimes on the strength of devotion he fancies his Guru as his mother and lying on her lap enjoys the breast milk. Or imagining his Guru to be a cow under the tree of Knowledge becomes its calf. Sometimes an idea that he is a fish in the waters of his Guru's benevolence flashes in his mind. He imagines the Guru's benevolence to be a shower of nectar watering the plant of attitude of service. (13:396-399).

See how limitless his love is! Sometimes he considers himself to be just a hatched chick without eyes or wings belonging to his Guru and imagining him to be the mother bird, gets fed by her beak. Thus, just as waves arise one after other at high tide, he goes from one state of meditation to the next, overcome by the love for his Guru. (13:400-402).

Now I shall tell you how he serves the Guru externally. He resolves, "I will serve my Guru in the best possible way and Guru will become pleased by it and tell me affectionately to ask for something. Once my master is pleased with my service I shall pray to him thus: 'Oh Master, Let me be your entire entourage. I shall be all the articles you need. And you will see the wonder of my service.' Guru is a mother to many but he will be mother to me alone and I shall make him say so on oath. (13:403-410). I shall arrange such that the Guru will be obsessed with me and will be dedicated only to me and will shower his love only on me." (13: 411)

Thus runs his mind in fanciful thoughts. He says, "I shall be the place of abode of my Guru and serve him by becoming his servant. I shall be the threshold which my Guru crosses and I shall also be the doors of the house as well as the doorkeeper. I shall be his sandals and I myself shall make him wear them. I shall be his umbrella too and I myself shall hold it over him. I shall be his vanguard and warn him of the ups and downs of the ground before him. I shall be the fly sweep (a brush like device to drive away flies), the valet, the server of water-jug for washing hands and mouth and I shall be the clean basin to receive the mouthwash. I shall be the server of the betel leaf and also the residue which is spitted out. And I shall be the one to serve him in preparing his bath. (13:412-420).

"I shall be the seat, ornaments, clothes, applications like sandal paste etc. of my Guru. I shall become the cook and serve him food and wave the lamp round him in worship (*Arati*, a ritual of worship in which a lamp is waved around the object of worship). When the Guru sits for his meals I shall sit with him and later I shall come forward to offer him the betel leaf. I shall remove his dish, spread his bed and massage his legs. I shall be his throne and the Guru will sit on it. Thus I shall fulfil my vow to serve him. (13:421-425).

"There will be a miracle by which I shall be whatever the Guru's mind turns to. I shall be the countless words that enter the Guru's ears and I shall become everything that touches his body too. I shall be the forms and shapes which my Guru's affectionate eyes see. I shall be the eatables which his tongue will savour and shall serve his nose by becoming a fragrance." (13:426-429).

Thus he feels that he should pervade all things to serve his Guru from outside as long as he lives. But he feels that even after death he should serve his Guru. Listen to how he thinks. (13:430-431).

He thinks, "Wherever the feet of my Guru touch, I shall mix the Earth principle of my body into that earth and where he touches water, I shall mix the Water principle of my body into it. I shall mingle the Fire principle from my body into the light of the lamps used for waving around the Guru and those lighted in his temple. I shall merge the Air principle into both, the fly-swap and the fan of my Guru, and be the breeze that comforts his body. Whichever space my Guru goes with his entourage I shall introduce the part of my Sky (space) principle in it. But on no account I shall allow the service of my Guru to be interrupted whether during my life or after death and neither shall I let other people to serve my Guru. Eons will pass while I serve my Guru thus." (13:432-437).

He who holds such courage and serves his Guru with limitless devotion does not keep count of days or nights nor of the extent of burden; on the other hand he feels happier if the Guru asks him to do more. Even if the tasks the Guru tells him to do are bigger than the sky, he carries them out single-handed. In this respect his body competes with his mind and completes the task. Sometimes he stakes even his life in order to fulfil the Guru's commands, including those made in jest. He strains his body in the Guru's service, gets strength from Guru's love and becomes the mainstay of Guru's orders. He derives respectability from his Guru's tradition and is polite to his brother disciples and is addicted to the Guru's service. He considers the rules of his Guru's tradition as the prescribed duties for his caste, and devotional service to his Guru as his daily duty. To him, the Guru is the place of pilgrimage, Guru is the deity, mother and father and there is nothing other than the Guru's service.

The Guru's door is his everything and he has brotherly love for all those who serve his Guru. He always has the *mantra* given by his Guru, on his tongue and he does not touch any *shastras* except for his Guru's words. To him the water which his Guru's feet have touched are superior to all other holy waters from the three worlds. If by chance he gets leftover food from his Guru's plate, he prefers it to the bliss of *Samadhi*. Even a particle of dust raised when his Guru walks is like the bliss from liberation to him. There is no end to how much one can talk about his devotion to his Guru. (13:438-452).

Dnyaneshwar Maharaj says,

"I am saying all this because I am overcome by the feelings of devotion towards my Guru. One who likes this feeling of devotion does not find anything sweeter than to be of service to the Guru. Such a person is the abode of Self-realisation and because of him, Knowledge itself gets respectability and becomes his devotee considering him to be God. In such a person lies Knowledge, sufficient for the whole world and to spare. I am extremely anxious about service to the Guru and therefore I have described it extensively but I am handicapped in all respects in this regard. However the extreme love I have in my heart for my Guru compelled me to expand on this topic. I am praying him to accept it and give me an opportunity to serve him so that I shall be able to explain this book further in a better way." (13:453-460)

Purity: Shri Krishna continued, "Like camphor which is clean from outside as well as inside purity is seen in that sage, both externally and internally. (13:462). From outside he has become pure by his actions and from inside by his Knowledge. (13:464). Arjuna, to keep the body clean without the internal purity is nothing but mockery. (13:468). If there is Knowledge in the mind then one automatically attains external purity. How else can pure Knowledge and pure action be found together? Therefore Arjuna, he who has cleaned himself from the outside by actions and on the inside by Knowledge, is pure both from inside and outside. What more! Only purity remains in such a person. Pure feelings in the mind are reflected in the body. Passions do not touch him even if he comes in contact with sense-objects through the sense-organs. (13:473-479). When the heart is pure, desires and doubts do not survive; but one knows what is proper and improper. The mind of such a person is not affected by doubts. Arjuna, this is called Purity and in whomsoever you see it, know for sure that Knowledge also occurs in him. (13:482-484).

Steadfastness: A person in whom steadfastness occurs is the life-force *(Prana)* of Knowledge. Even though the natural actions of his body go on outwardly, his mind remains undisturbed internally. (13:485-486). His mind does not get discouraged by calamities. He is not tortured by poverty or pain nor does he tremble from fear and sorrow. And he is not frightened even by the approach of death. His straightforward mind does not waver even under pressure from hope or pain or by the rumblings of various diseases. (13:492-494). His mind does not waver when he has to face slander, insult, punishment, desire, and greed. (13:495-496). Arjuna, this state is what is called steadfastness and whosoever has it ingrained in him is the treasure trove of Knowledge. (13:501).

Self-restraint: Such a sage takes care of his mind and does not allow it to go near the sense-objects. (13:504). He keeps a stern watch on the tendencies of his mind and deliberately controls his organs by self-restraint. Then by steadying himself in the three *Bandhas* (see chapter 6), he fixes his consciousness in the central nerve *Sushumna* and steadies his state of meditation into *Samadhi*. His consciousness then unites with the Divine energy and merges in it. This is what is called controlled state of mind. Knowledge is manifested where it occurs. He whose commands are respected by the mind, is Knowledge personified. (13:508-512).

Dispassion: And he is ever dispassionate in his mind regarding the sense-pleasures. (13:513). He does not even like the topic of sense-pleasures mentioned and does not permit the senses to come in contact with the sense-pleasures. His mind is apathetic to sense-pleasures and his body also becomes lean. Even then he likes *Shama* (control of the mind) and *Dama* (restraint of the senses). He constantly performs penance and austerities and to live among people is like a calamity to him. He likes to practice yoga and live in isolation, and he cannot stand crowds. (13:517-520).

He finds worldly pleasures and heavenly enjoyment distasteful. This kind of detachment from the sense-pleasures is a sign of Self-realisation. Understand that Knowledge resides in a person who has developed such dislike for worldly and heavenly pleasures.

Absence of pride: Like a man of desires, he performs *yajnas*, builds lakes, prepares gardens etc. for public but he does not carry the sense of pride of having done these things. (13:521-525).

He spares no efforts in performing his daily and incidental duties appropriate to his status/position in life. But ego about having done them or the feeling that the action was successful because he did it, does not touch his mind. (13:526-527). This characteristic of his mind is called egoless-ness. There is no doubt that Knowledge occurs where this is fully evident. (13:534-535).

Awareness about evil of birth, death etc.: He observes caution even when birth, death, old age, pain, disease and sin are far away (13:536) and is careful to ensure that he is not reborn because he does not forget the pains of the previous births. The sense of shame of having been born does not leave his mind. Even if death is very far away in the future, he is alert about it right from birth. (13:544-545). He lives with a dejected mind thinking of death. Having received the warning of the old age while in youth itself he listens to things worth hearing, visits places of pilgrimage, commits good quotations to memory and gives away wealth in charity before the organs become weak and useless. Because the mind may not remain pure after reaching such a situation, he ponders in detail on Self-realisation. (13:576-581). He who remembers that he is going to become old someday and takes steps by doing righteous actions while in youth itself, before getting disabled by old age, is to be considered as having Knowledge. (13:587).

Detachment: Now I shall tell you about one more strange characteristic of a man of Knowledge. He is very detached towards his body. He does not have any affinity for his home and feels detachment towards his wealth. He lives in the world respecting the precepts of Vedas. Such a person who does not keep desire towards his wife, son and property is where Knowledge takes shelter. His mind does not waver by pain or pleasure and his sense of balance does not change. Understand that Knowledge actually exists in such a person. (13:594-603).

Devotion to God: He is resolved in his mind that there is nothing good in this world except Me. He has decided that there is no goal in this world other than Me and he has developed so much love for Me that both of us have become one. Even after becoming one with Me he keeps on worshipping Me with devotion in all sorts of ways. He who becomes one with Me with dedication and worships Me is Knowledge personified.

Liking for seclusion: He who likes to live at places of pilgrimage, holy river banks, excellent forests and caves, he who prefers to live in a cave in the mountains or on the shores of a lake and does not like living in cities, he who likes seclusion and dislikes living in villages is Knowledge in the guise of a person. I shall tell some more characteristics of Knowledge to explain its nature further.

(13:604-615).

Certain that Knowledge leads to Self-realisation: He has decided with certainty that except for the Knowledge by which the entity called Supreme Soul may be experienced, all other types through which one gains knowledge of the worldly life and heaven etc. only are all ignorance. He gives up the desire to gain a place in heaven, ignores the worldly matters and keeping his attention in Self-realisation becomes engrossed in it. He directs his mind and intellect only towards Self-realisation. His intellect becomes steady with the definite understanding *that Knowledge of the Self alone is real and knowledge of any other kind only leads to delusion.* There is no doubt at all that Knowledge occurs in such a person. And once the Knowledge thus *gets completely ingrained in his mind* then he becomes one with Me. But just as a person who has just sat down cannot be said to have been sitting around, so too, unless Knowledge becomes fixed in a person, he cannot be called a person of Knowledge. Then he steadies his sights on Brahman, the Object-to-be-known, which is the fruit of gaining pure Knowledge. If after gaining Knowledge one does not experience Brahman then it is as good as not gaining the Knowledge.[11] (13:616- 626).

Dedication to Knowledge: If the intellect cannot reach the Supreme Brahman in the light of Knowledge then it must be considered as

---

11 *Since Knowledge is synonymous to Brahman it looks strange that a situation suggested in which after gaining Knowledge one does not experience Brahman. However the following clarifies it. There are two things involved: one is the intellect and the second is the mind. In ovi (12:97) it has already been advised that both mind and intellect should be directed towards God in order to be one with Him. It is the mind that gets an experience or information via senses but mind tries to close its doors to intellect (13:115). It is the intellect that analyses the information received in the mind and tells what is what and whether it is good or bad etc and judges the sense objects. According to (13:83-89) intellect is the basic means of gaining knowledge and due to which the Sattva attribute in a person grows; it is the meeting place of the individual and the Soul. If his intellect alone reaches the Brahman then it is not experience but kind of book knowledge and effectively he is blind to its presence. And if the mind experiences Brahman but if does not realise what it is experiencing is Brahman then the individual merely remains in bliss until intellect tells him that what he is experiencing is Brahman.*

blind. Therefore he gets the right desire for gaining that Knowledge by which he can see the Supreme Brahman wherever he casts his eyes and he finally gains that Knowledge. His intellect has developed as much as his Knowledge therefore no words are needed to tell that he is the Knowledge personified. Therefore one need not wonder at my saying that he whose intellect has met the Supreme Brahman in the light of Knowledge has become Knowledge. (13:627-633).

Thus Shri Krishna explained the eighteen characteristics of a person of Knowledge. He then said, "Now I shall also reveal to you what is known as ignorance along with its characteristics. (13:653).

IGNORANCE

Understand that what is not Knowledge automatically becomes ignorance. I shall tell you some of its main signs. An ignorant person lives for status. He eagerly awaits honour and is pleased by felicitations. He who is stiff with pride and does not bend should be considered as the abode of ignorance. He brags about his religious actions and makes a big noise about his learning. He makes public announcements of his good deeds and all his actions are for getting prominence and greatness. He deceives his followers by external appearances by applying ash, sandal-paste etc on the body. Understand that such a person is a mine of ignorance. (13:656-661).

Cruelty: He whose actions make the whole world suffer, even casual words from whom prick like a spear and whose all plans are more dangerous than poison may be considered as possessing a lot of ignorance. His life is the home of violence. (13:662-664).

Slave to emotions: He becomes elated by meeting his loved ones and depressed when they depart. He feels pleased by hearing his own praise and if he hears even slight criticism he becomes unhappy. He who cannot bear the onslaughts of mental emotions, may be considered as completely ignorant. (13:665-668).

Secretive: His talk appears to be frank outwardly but actually he is very secretive. He shows friendship towards one but helps another. He somehow or other maintains good relations with straightforward type of persons and wins the minds of good people but with an ultimate aim of harming them. It is a fact that such a person has ignorance. (13:669-672).

Disrespect for Guru: He is ashamed of his Guru tradition and does not like to serve his Guru. He learns from his Guru but is disrespectful to him. To even utter the name of such a person is like using the tongue to eat prohibited food but I had to do it while telling you the characteristics of ignorance. Such a sin can be atoned by uttering the name of a Guru's devotee. (13:673-676).

Impure mind and Greed: An ignorant person who neglects his duties, has his mind full of doubts is impure from inside and outside. Due to greed of wealth he does not care about whether it belongs to him or others. He has very loose morals regarding women. He does not feel shame if he misses the usual time for performing his prescribed actions or his incidental duties. He has no shame in doing sinful deeds and no liking for righteous deeds. His mind is always full of doubts and he always has his eyes on money. Understand that such a person is like a statue of ignorance. (13:678-684).

Fickle-minded: He deviates from his resolves for the sake of personal gains. He gets shaken by frightful situations. He gets engrossed in flights of imagination. His mind gets totally lost by unpleasant news. He cannot remain steady in one place, and goes on wandering, unless he falls down flat. Such a person is full of ignorance. He is as fickle-minded as a monkey and he does not have the strength of determination in him. He is not afraid of doing prohibited actions. He abandons penance halfway, kicks away righteousness and does not bother about the rules of the rituals. He does not shun sinful actions and does not have liking for righteous actions. He tramples on the taboos about doing shameful actions. He does not bother about family traditions and about what is proper or improper. His mind wanders unrestrained in thoughts of sense-pleasures. (13: 685-699). Such a person is rich in ignorance. (13:702).

Passion-lover: He does not give up the desire for sense pleasures not only while he lives but even after death. While he lives he makes preparations in order to attain heaven after death for the sake of pleasures there. He struggles incessantly for bodily pleasures. He prefers actions where he can fulfil his desire of enjoying the fruits thereof. He thinks it is inauspicious to meet a dispassionate person and takes bath to clean himself. The sense pleasures may get tired of him but he does not get tired of them. (13:703-705). For their sake he will even jump into fire and he goes around exhibiting this nature like an ornament. From birth until his death he incessantly toils for the pleasures and not minding the troubles they give him, he likes them more and more. (13:707- 709).

Infatuation with family: He is infatuated with parents during childhood. When that is over he gets attracted to female body during his youth and while he is busy enjoying the marital life, old age approaches, when he directs that same love towards his children. Like a congenital blind person he spends all his time with his children but he never gets tired of the sense-pleasures until his death. There is no limit to ignorance in such a person. Now listen to some more characteristics of ignorance. (13:710-713).

False pride and jealousy: He performs his duties sticking to the I-am-the-body impression and feels disturbed if there are any shortcomings in his performance. Proud of his youth and learning, he goes around with stiff posture and says, "I alone am great and rich. Who else is there with behaviour as good as mine?" He becomes stiff with the ego that there is none as great as himself, that he knows everything and that he is popular. (13:714-717).

He is jealous of virtuous persons, proud of his own learning and of the strength he has gained from penance and of his knowledge. You will see him swollen by pride. He does not bend nor does he feel kindness. Even virtuous persons cannot bring him to his senses. I definitely tell you that such a person's ignorance is on the increase. (13:724-727).

Forgets birth-death cycles: Arjuna, the ignorant person bothers about his household, body and wealth but not about his past and future births. (13:728). Even when the body is infected and cannot even control excreta, he does not regret the reasons why he has reached that state.[12] He forgets the pain of birth and the fact that he has just finished his last lifetime and the next lifetime is approaching.[13] Not only that he does not worry about death while the life progresses rapidly; he is so sure that he will continue to live that he refuses to accept the existence of death. (13:732-738).

While he is engrossed in sense-pleasures, he does not realise that death is approaching as he continues to remain alive. He considers only the growth of his body and the sense-pleasures as real. But the poor fellow does not realise that when a prostitute offers him everything, therein lies his destruction. (13:743-745). Engrossed in eating and sleeping, he does not realise that his destruction lies in those very same things. As time passes the body grows, so does the indulgence in sense-pleasures and the shadow of death falls

12 *Here the effect of his karmas which led to his rebirth and this unhealthy state is implied.*
13 *A brief statement made by Dnyaneshwar Maharaj has been removed because scientifically it is no longer true. It is customary even today for many conservative religious writers and speakers to make statements about the birth process which are outdated and scientifically wrong; they also make statements about the female sex which are derogatory and in bad taste. As regards the birth process, these conservatives state that the baby foetus has to lie and suffer in urine and spit whereas in reality God (nature) has provided a beautiful cushioned, aseptic place in the womb for the baby and also provided for its nourishment through umbilical cord until birth. The real sin is to call the birth process filthy instead of thanking God for this beautiful arrangement. Such an arrangement is an essential part of the process of conception and birth towards perpetuation of the human species without which mankind will vanish in no time. Regarding denigration of women, on one hand she is praised as a mother, for her love and sacrifice for the family and she is even worshipped (only if she is not a widow) by offerings of coconut, flowers and dress, on certain occasions while on the other hand she is denigrated as a mine of sin and a lure causing downfall of man. Unfortunately even if man is responsible for immoral acts including rape, it is the woman who has to suffer socially and otherwise and bear the burden of pregnancy etc., but man generally escapes the punishment. People forget that conjugality as per God's plan is for perpetuation of species and not for pleasure alone.*

increasingly on life but he does not see it approaching. He who cannot see the approaching death because of his getting engrossed in sense-pleasures is the king of the land of ignorance. (13:747-753).

Intoxicated by life he remains without care about the approaching old age. During youth he does not understand what would be his condition when he becomes old. (13:754).

Such a person is really ignorant. When he sees a lame or a bent person he mocks him but he does not realise that he too will be bent in old age. And even when he attains old age, which is the sign of the approaching death, delusion about his own youth does not leave him. Understand that such a person is undoubtedly an abode of ignorance. (13:760-763).

He who remains carefree when the enemy sleeps thinking that the enmity is now over, perishes along with his family. In the same way he does not worry about falling ill in future, as long as his appetite and sleep are good and he is not ill at present. And in the company of his wife and children and growing affluence which intoxicates him, he does not see that he is going to be separated one day from his sons etc. and his wealth. He who cannot see this future sorrow is ignorant. (13:767-770).

Indulgences and Excesses: And he who lets the sense-organs go astray unrestrained is also ignorant. In the prime of his youth, supported by wealth, he indulges in all sorts of pleasures whether proper or improper. He does what should not be done, longs for the impossible, and thinks about things he should not think of. He enters where he should not, asks for what he should not take, touches things which he should not touch and does all the things one should not even think about. He goes to places where he should not go, sees what he should not see, eats what he should not eat and instead feels satisfied in it. He keeps the company of those he should not, maintains relationships with those he should not and behaves in a manner he should not behave. He listens to what he should not and blabbers about things which he should not speak, but does not realise that he will get the blame for it. He does things which please the body and the mind without thinking about their propriety. But the thought that it will result in his committing sin or he will have to suffer in hell does not enter his mind. Association with such a person leads to the spread of ignorance in the world to such an extent that even sages get affected. (13:771-780).

Attachment to wife at the cost of parents: Now listen to some more characteristics of an ignorant person. His attachment is totally towards his home and his wife and he cannot get his mind away from them. (13:781-783). He loves his home as parents love an only child born in old age and he does not know anything other than his wife whose body he worships without any thought about, "Who am I?" or "What should I do?" Just as the mind of a great sage gets totally engrossed in Brahman resulting in an abandonment of worldly actions, an ignorant person surrenders himself completely to his wife and does not care for his losses, public shame or slander. He keeps himself in her good books and dances to her tunes. Like a greedy person toils for money even by hurting his friends and relatives, he gives little to charity and does not do many righteous deeds. He cheats persons from his family and clan but gives his wife plenty fulfilling all her wants. He somehow manages to perform worship of his family deity and bluffs to his Guru. He tells his parents excuses that there is not enough money to give to them but brings for his wife various articles of pleasure and the best things he comes across. He serves his wife with unstinted dedication like one lovingly devoted to his family deity. He gives the best and costly articles to his wife but for other persons in the family he does not give enough even for their bare survival. If somebody gives improper looks to his wife or behaves with her improperly he feels as if the end of the world has come. He satisfies her every command. His wife is everything to him and he feels special love for children born of her. Whatever things she possesses and her wealth are more valuable to him than his own life. Such a person is the root of ignorance and it gains strength from him. He is ignorance personified. (13:788-804).

Slave to pleasure and sorrows: He reaches the height of happiness when he gets the thing he likes and he sinks into sorrow when what he gets he does not like. However highly intelligent one may be, if he worries because of favourable and unfavourable circumstances, then in reality he is an ignorant person. (13:805-806). He may be devoted to Me but that devotion is with a material objective in mind. He makes a show of being devoted to Me, but keeps his sights on pleasures. If he does not get them after being devoted to Me, then he gives up the devotion saying that the talk of God etc. is all lies. Like an ignorant peasant he sets up different deities and after failing with one he goes to the next. He joins that Guru tradition where there is a great pomp and show, receives Guru-*mantra* from him and considers others as ordinary. He behaves cruelly with living creatures but showers special love on a stone idol. But his love is not steady in one single place. He makes my idol and installs it in one corner of the house and he himself goes on pilgrimage to places of other deities. He offers devotion towards his family deity and on auspicious occasions he worships other deities. After installing Me in the house he makes vows to other deities.[14] On the day of

---

14 *This is an interesting and realistic description of what people do to propitiate different gods for material gains. It is evident that the custom was prevalent in Dnyaneshwar Maharaj's days also as it is now. Explanation of various rituals: Shraddha, Nagpanchami, Ekadashi, Chaturthi, Chaturdashi, Navaratri etc.:*
 In the Hindu religious calendar, each day of the week and each tithi have significance with respect to various deities. Shraddha is an annual ritual performed to propitiate the dead forefathers. Nagpanchami is the day cobras are worshipped. It falls on the fifth day of the bright fortnight of the lunar month Shravana. Chaturthi or Ganesha Chaturthi is observed as the birthday of Lord Ganesha; it falls on the fourth of the bright fortnight of the lunar month Bhadrapada. Chaturdashi is the fourteenth day of a fortnight by lunar calendar when some devotees worship Mother Durga. Similarly Ekadashi is the eleventh day when some devotees (especially the devotees of Vishnu) observe fast. Navaratri (nine nights) is the first nine nights in the bright fortnight of the lunar month Ashwin observed all over India in honour of Mother Durga. Navachandi is a religious text in her praise. Bahiroba is a corrupted form of Bhairava, a member of the entourage of Lord Shiva. Of the weekdays Monday is known as Lord Shiva's day. Linga is His symbol which is worshipped by offering of Bel leaves and white flowers. Bel is a tree having three pronged leaves.

Shraaddha, he belongs to his forefathers; he worships cobras on *Nagpanchami* day as much as he worships Me on *Ekadashi* day; Then on *Chaturthi* day he becomes a devotee of Ganapati and on *Chaturdashi* day he avers, "Oh Mother Durga, I am a devotee of only you." He leaves the daily rituals and incidental actions during *Navaratri* and sits for the reading of *Navachandi* and on Sunday gives an offering of *Khichadi* to the deity Bahiroba. Then on Monday he rushes to Shivalinga for offering *Bel* leaves and thus he somehow manages to perform the worship ritual of all deities. That devotee performs the worship ritual of all deities without taking rest for a moment, just like a prostitute who demonstrates her love for all the people in the town. Such a devotee who rushes every now and then to different deities is ignorance reincarnated. (13:810-823).

Dislikes quiet and holy places: And he also is ignorant who feels disgusted at the sight of quiet forests meant for penance, and places of pilgrimage. He who feels happy living in the town, likes to sit in a crowd and likes to gossip is nothing but ignorant. (13:824- 825).

Prefers black arts to holy knowledge: A person, who has only book-knowledge, ridicules the real knowledge that leads to Self-realisation. He does not look at Upanishads. He does not like the science of yoga and his mind does not turn towards spiritual science. Breaking the interest created by the intellect towards thoughts of the Soul, his mind wanders here and there like wayward cattle. He is clever in the ritualistic techniques, knows the Puranas by heart and is such an expert astrologer that whatever he predicts does happen. He is skilled in sculpture and in architecture, an expert in culinary art. And he knows the *mantras* from *Atharvaveda* (Black magic, charm etc.). There is nothing more left for him to learn in the science of love. He gives discourses on Mahabharata and other branches of knowledge stand attentively before him in person. He is skilled in medicine and there is none who is more well-versed than him. He discusses *Smritis*. He knows the secret of snake-charming and he has mastery on the vocabulary of Vedas. He is expert in grammar and learned in the science of justice. But it is only regarding the knowledge of the Self that he is a congenital blind. He may be considered as an authority on the principles of every branch of knowledge. But like a child born at an inauspicious time (unlucky for his father) all that is in vain. Ignore him. (13:826-835).

Except for the spiritual science, all other branches of knowledge are meaningless. Therefore Arjuna, remember that a person with only book-knowledge is a fool who has not realised the Self. His body has grown out of the seed of ignorance and his learning is a creeper of this ignorance. Whatever he speaks is the flower of ignorance and whatever righteous path he practices is the fruit of the ignorance too. Is there any need to tell that one who does not believe in Knowledge of the Self has not understood its meaning? (13:839-843). How can a person, who is not acquainted with Knowledge of the Self, find its subject matter that is the Soul? One need not work out complicated arithmetic to tell that such a person does not understand the principles of Knowledge. (13:846-847).

Turn your back to ignorance: The characteristics of ignorance are contained in the eighteen characteristics of knowledge which I had explained to you earlier. The characteristics of Knowledge when applied in reverse become the characteristics of ignorance. (13:849-851).

Arjuna, turn your back to the characteristics of ignorance that I have just told you about and make a good and firm resolve regarding Knowledge. By means of that pure Knowledge you will realise its objective, namely Brahman. (13:862-863).

OBJECT OF KNOWLEDGE

Now I shall tell you about the object of Knowledge. Brahman is called the object of Knowledge because it cannot be achieved by any means other than Knowledge itself; and after it is attained there is nothing more left for the sage to do, because the Knowledge unifies him with itself. After its attainment the seeker gives up worldly matters and remains immersed in the bliss of Brahman. That Object of Knowledge is such that it has no beginning and naturally it is called Supreme Brahman. If one goes to deny Its (i.e. of Supreme Brahman's) existence then one can see It in the form of the universe; and if one goes to say that universe itself is the Supreme Brahman then it is only an illusion *(Maya)* because it (Supreme Brahman) does not have form, colour or shape. Also it is not visible nor can it see. Then how can one say that it exists? And if its existence is denied then where from have the principles like *Mahat* etc. sprung? Speech becomes dumb because one cannot at all affirm or deny its existence and even the thought about it cannot proceed further. Just as earth is seen in the form of a pot similarly Brahman has taken the form of the universe and has pervaded it throughout. (13:865-873).

It fills all spaces all the time and is not different from space and time. The very actions performed by gross and subtle things are its hands. Therefore Brahman has been called *Vishwa-Bahu* or *hands of the universe* because it inspires actions everywhere, all the time and in all ways. And it is present everywhere at the same time therefore it is called *Vishwataspat* (or *Vishwandhri*) i.e. *having feet everywhere*. Like the sun it observes all forms by its light therefore even if it does not have eyes, Vedas have cleverly called it *Vishwachakshu* or *eyes of the universe*. It is present always and everywhere on everyone's head therefore it is called *Vishwamurdha* or *intellect of the universe*. The form of fire is its mouth because it accepts all things through the fire (of a *yajna*) therefore Vedas have called Brahman as *Vishwatomukh* or *mouth of the universe*. And its ears engulf all sounds just as space engulfs all objects and it is because of this that we call Brahman as "one which listens everywhere". It is because of its all-pervasiveness that this simile has been used otherwise how can one speak in terms of hands, feet, eyes etc. about something which is the essence of void or nothingness?. How can there be the sense of pervader and pervaded in Brahman that is everywhere? But this differentiation had to be made for the purpose of explaining what Brahman is. Just as for indicating zero or nothing one writes a small dot[15] similarly to explain monism one has to use dualism. If this is not done then all dialogue between Guru and disciple will stop. It is for this reason that it has been customary to explain non-dualism using the language of dualism. (13:874-890).

HOW BRAHMAN PERVADES OBJECTS

Now listen to how Brahman pervades objects that are visible to the eyes. That Brahman appears to be in all objects in various forms (like for example the water or liquid principle which occurs in water or brightness that resides in a lamp in the form of a lamp, or odour that resides in camphor on the form of camphor or action in the form of the body). (13: 891-895).

Because of the shape of the pot is round, the sky appears to be round when one sees it reflected in the water in the pot; or because a window of a hut is rectangular, the sky also looks rectangular but the sky does not have any shape, round or rectangular. Similarly though objects have attributes, Brahman that pervades them is superimposed with those attributes, whereas Brahman itself is attributeless. That Brahman appears to be like the mind and other organs or like the three attributes (*Sattva*, *Rajas* and *Tamas*) but just as sweetness of jaggery (solidified raw sugar) does not lie in the shape of its block, the mind and attributes are not Brahman. (13:898-901). In plain words, it is different from the mind and the attributes. The relations between name and form, and the differences in duties for different castes are applicable to the form and not to the indwelling Brahman. Brahman is not the same as attributes and it is not related to attributes but there is an illusion of these *gunas* appearing in Brahman. (13:904-907). Therefore the ignorant think that the attributes belong to Brahman. The attributeless Brahman holds the attributes without any relation to

---

15 *Now-a-days we write zero with a circle. But it used to be written as a dot which Arabs still use.*

them, but that is not real but only an illusion, just as the reflection seems to belong to the mirror. Therefore one should not mention attributes in relation to Brahman. (13:910-912).

Same Brahman pervades all: Though Brahman exists in all moving and non-moving objects it is the same entity in all things and beings. That entity is indestructible and pervades the entire universe and is the Object-to-be-known. That same entity which is inside the body as well as outside, is near as well as far and is unique without duality, pervades everything completely. (13:913-915). Brahman's pervasion is as a single, unbroken entity in all four types of beings: those born out of the womb, from eggs, from body sweat and from the earth or seeds. It is also the cause of the creation of the universe. (13:917,920). Therefore just as the waves are supported by the sea, so is the universe supported by the Brahman. At the time of creation we call it Brahmadeo, during sustenance we properly call it Vishnu and when the universe dissolves we call it Rudra. And when all the three attributes or *gunas* vanish, what remains is called cipher (zero) or the Void. And that which swallows the nothingness of space and destroys the three attributes is this great cipher (*mahashoonya*) as declared by the Upanishads. (13:921-926).

Brahman - the basic principle in all principles: That Brahman is the igniting principle in the fire, the nectar of life that the moon provides the plants and the power of sight by which the sun oversees the affairs of the world. The galaxies of stars brighten by its light and light from the sun easily spreads in the universe by its brightness. It is the 'root' of the origin, the 'growing' of growth, the 'intelligence' of the intellect and the 'life-force' of life. It is 'mental power' of the mind, vision of the eyes, hearing of the ears, the power of speech of the tongue, vitality of life-force, the 'feet' of motion, and the activity of action. Formation, growth and destruction occur by its power. The five principles: earth, water, air, fire and space (or sky) derive their characteristics from it. In short, all objects appear in the universe because of it and actually everything is Brahman and no duality exists. Once it is experienced, the seer and the seen, the means and the end become one and the difference between Knowledge, the Knower and the object of Knowledge, vanishes. One cannot speak of duality in the context of that (Brahman) which exists in the heart of all. (13:927-939)

Thus, Arjuna, I have first made clear to you what Field is. Then I also explained to you what Knowledge is. Then I discussed the characteristics of ignorance and now I have explained to you what Object-to-be-known is by analytical reasoning. (13:940-943).

Easiest method to attain me: Arjuna, after thinking about all these things my devotees come to Me longing to attain Me. By giving up the attachment to the body they concentrate their mind and feelings on me. These devotees, after they know Me, take me in exchange for their ego and thus become one with Me. I have thus planned the easiest method for their being one with Me. (13:944-947).

PURUSHA AND PRAKRITI (SANKHYA)

Arjuna, if I had merely told you that Soul is everywhere then you would not have believed it. I explained to you the same Brahman in four parts to enable your intellect comprehend this easily. Considering your ability to concentrate I divided the Brahman into four parts namely the Field, Knowledge, Object-to-be-known and Ignorance. If even after this you have not understood my explanation then I shall explain the same thing to you in another way. Instead of dividing into four parts I shall divide into only two parts namely Soul and Non-soul (*Purusha* and *Prakriti*). Listen to it. (13:949-955).

I shall tell you about the two parts: *Prakriti* and *Purusha*. Yogis call this path *"Sankhya"*. To explain it I have incarnated as Kapila.[16] Listen to its pros and cons. (13:957- 959). *Purusha* is without beginning and so is *Prakriti* and they are both stuck to each other like day and night or like a shadow to a form. What

16 *Kapila Muni was the proponent of the Sankhya philosophy.*

I explained to you as Field must be understood here as *Prakriti* and the Knower of the Field is the same as *Purusha*. Even if the names are different the principles to which they refer are the same. (13:960-964). *Purusha* is the power and *Prakriti* is the one which causes all actions to take place. Intellect, organs, mind etc. which are responsible for feelings and passions and the three attributes *Sattva*, *Rajas* and *Tamas*, all arise from *Prakriti* and are the cause of *Karma* (action). (13:966-968).

Creation of Ego: Desire and intellect first create ego in *Prakriti* and make the individual get involved in some cause. The procedure used for achieving a desired object is called action. When desire becomes strong it activates the mind and makes it get the tasks done through the organs and that is what is called the effectiveness of the *Prakriti*. Therefore *Prakriti* is the root of action, the cause of action and the agent or doer of action. When the triad come together, *Prakriti* becomes active but the quality of the actions is determined by the three attributes which are born of *Prakriti*. The action in which the *Sattva* attribute predominates is a good righteous action. That which takes place due to *Rajas* attribute is a medium or mixed type of action while that which takes place due to *Tamas* attribute, is a prohibited and unrighteous action. The good and bad actions thus occur due to *Prakriti* and give rise to pleasure and pain respectively. The *Purusha* experiences this pleasure and pain. As long as this pleasure and pain is produced, the *Prakriti* remains busy creating them and the *Purusha* in experiencing them. The affairs of this couple *Prakriti* and *Purusha* are strange. Whatever the wife earns the husband enjoys without himself making any efforts. This couple does not come together and yet *Prakriti* the wife gives birth to this universe. (13:969-980).

Actionless Purusha and Gunamayi Prakriti: He who is without form (body) and cripple, poor and lonely and older than the oldest of the objects is called *Purusha*. Nothing can be said about gender – whether he is female or a neuter. He does not have eyes, ears, hands, feet, form, colour and name. He has no organs. Such is the husband of *Prakriti* who has to experience pain and pleasure. Though he is actionless, unattached and non-indulgent, the *Prakriti* makes him experience the pain and pleasure. This *Prakriti* uses her form and attributes to create a strange drama, hence *Prakriti* is called *Gunamayi* or one having attributes. She ever takes a new form every moment and her vitality makes even the passive objects active. Names are assigned, love is felt and sense-organs are able to sense because of her. She makes the mind, even though it is neuter, wander in the three worlds. Such is her capability. (13:981-990).

Play of Prakriti: This *Prakriti* which is like a big island of illusion and which extends everywhere creates emotions. Passions are fostered with her support. Delusion blooms because of her. She is known as Divine *Maya*. (13:991-992).

She makes language grow, creates this material world, and ceaselessly invades it with a materialistic way of life. All arts, skills are born of her. Desires, knowledge and actions are created from her. All the tunes and sounds are minted out by her. She is the home of miracles. In fact everything that happens in the world is her play. The creation of the world and its dissolution are her morning and evening respectively. She is thus the wonderful illusionist. (13:993-996).

She is the mate of the lonely *Purusha*, companion of the unattached Brahman and she resides in the void. Her capability is so high that she keeps the uncontrollable *Purusha* under control. Actually the *Purusha* is not attached to anything but this *Prakriti* becomes everything for him. She becomes the creation of the self-born, form of the formless *Purusha* and his very existence and base. (13:997-1000).

Illusion of attributes: Thus, by her strength *Prakriti* creates passions in that dispassionate *Purusha* and his effulgence wanes like that of the moon on the new moon day. (13:1005-1008). *Purusha's* brightness vanishes and he has to experience the effect of the attributes once he surrenders to the *Prakriti*. By association with her *Purusha* has to suffer the impact of birth and death. When moonlight is reflected in moving water, people see many reflections and feel that there are many moons. Similarly by association with attributes it appears as if the birthless *Purusha* has taken birth but that is not true. Just as a *Sanyasi* sees in his dream that he is born in a Shudra caste[17] similarly the *Purusha* feels that he has taken birth in a low or high caste but that is not true and therefore the *Purusha* does not have to experience the effects of Karmas. It only appears to him so because of the association with the attributes. (13:1014-1021).

Purusha is beyond Prakriti: *Prakriti* has the support of the *Purusha* but there is a vast difference between the two. This *Purusha* is on the bank of the river that is *Prakriti* and though his reflection is in the river it is not carried away by the current. *Prakriti* is created and is dissolved but *Purusha* is eternal. Therefore he controls everything right from Brahmadeo downwards. *Prakriti* exists because of him and by his power alone she creates the world, therefore he is the Lord of *Prakriti*. The world, which has been going on since the beginningless past, dissolves in him at the end of the eon. He is the Lord of the realm of *Mahat* that is the *Prakriti*. He controls the whole universe and envelops it entirely by his expanse. Really speaking he is the Supreme Soul, which is said to exist in the body. (13:1022-1029).

One who understands that this *Purusha* is one and the only one and all the actions and attributes belong to the *Prakriti*, that *Purusha* and *Prakriti* are like the form and the shadow or like water and mirage, may be considered as having understood the difference between *Purusha* and *Prakriti*. Even if he performs actions by virtue of possessing a body, he does not get tainted by them. He does not feel attachment to his body while he lives and when he dies he is not reborn. In this unworldly way the understanding of the difference between *Purusha* and *Prakriti* becomes favourable to

17 *A sanyasi has no caste having given up worldly matters and surrendered to spiritual path.*

him. There are many ways by which this understanding will arise in your heart. Listen. (13:1030-1036).

PURIFICATION OF THE INDIVIDUAL

Some people purify gold that is the Soul (which is tainted by attributes) in the fire of thought by coating it with layers of listening, pondering and longing for it, and burning away the impurity of the worldly attributes.[18] By burning the thirty-six impure principles they separate away the pure Soul and see it within themselves by the eyes of meditation. Some meditate on it using the principles of *Sankhya* philosophy or by the philosophy of action and attain liberation. (13:1037-1040).

Looking up to Guru: Thus people adopt different ways to get safely out of this whirlpool of life and death. But there are others who, by ridding themselves of pride, keep faith in Guru's words. They listen attentively and respectfully to whatever the Guru says and offer themselves and all their possessions to him. Guru cares about what is good and bad for them, feels for their miseries and mitigates them, makes them feel relaxed and happy by inquiring after them. They keep aside all their work in order to be able to hear his words and are prepared to sacrifice their life for him. Such people also finally cross the ocean of the birth-death cycles. Thus in this world of mortals there are many ways to experience the Supreme Soul (*Paramatma*). I shall present you with the cream of the philosophy of these methods. (13:1041-1050).

INTERACTION OF THE FIELD AND THE KNOWER

The entire world is created from the mutual interaction of the "Field" and the "Knower of the Field" both of which I explained to you. (13:1051-1052). All the movable and immovable things and the entity which we call *"Jiva"* or "life" are created out of the union

---

18 That is by listening to saints, contemplation and desire for liberation.

of these two. Therefore materials or persons are not different from *Purusha*. (13:1055-1056).

Even though cloth is not same as thread, it is made of it. In the same way one should see by insight the sameness between *Purusha* and the material world i.e. *Prakriti*. You should experience the fact that all creatures are different forms of the same entity and they are basically the same. Their names are different, their behaviour also is different and they appear different outwardly but if by these considerations you sustain in your mind the idea that they are all different then you will not escape from this birth and death cycles in a million years. Individuals may have crooked shapes but the Soul is straight. Even though there are piles of lives the soul inside all of them is same. The physical appearance of individuals is illusive and destructible but the souls inside all of them are indestructible. Thus, he who understands that soul is not different from the individual but does not possess the attributes of the individual, is the man of vision among all men of Knowledge and the most fortunate of men. (13:1057-1068).

MAN OF KNOWLEDGE IS LIBERATED WHILE IN BODY

This body made up of the five principles and full of wind, biles and phlegm (*Vata*, *Pitta* and *Kapha*) is like a horrible bag full of the three attributes and the organs.[19] It is plainly a scorpion with five sting-tails. It is burning in five types of fire. The lion that is the individual Self is entrapped in the snare of this body. Who would not free himself from this impermanent body by stabbing it with the knife of eternality? Arjuna, only a man of Knowledge does not harm himself even though he lives in the body and ultimately he reaches the state of Brahman. To attain that state, yogis, by the power of

19 *These are three Doshas or humors in the body according to Ayurveda, defining the basic health structure of a person. Just like attributes they are present in various proportions in each person. Their balance is an indication of good health. (Here Dosha does not mean defect).*

their knowledge of yoga, cross millions of births and leave their body resolving that they will not be reborn. The Supreme Brahman, which is beyond name and form and is in the realm of vibrations (sound), is the final resting-place of all destinations including that of liberation. He who does not entertain ideas of differences between individuals, due to their external differences, experiences the bliss of Brahman while he is still alive in his body. Just as the same light emanates from different lamps, the Soul pervades everything right from the beginning. Arjuna, he who has this outlook of equality is not caught in the throes of birth-death cycles. He is very fortunate and I sing his praises often because he looks at everything with eyes of equality. (13:1069-1079).

And he fully knows that it is *Prakriti* that causes actions through the mind, the intellect, the five sense-organs and the five organs of action. (13:1080). That *Prakriti* aided by the three attributes, sets up different kinds of acts in the light of the Soul (meaning, in the presence of *Purusha*) but the Soul itself remains steady and unaffected by it. He who has decided that this is so has realised the Soul. (13:1082-1083).

Even otherwise, Arjuna, you may consider one who sees unity in the diverse shapes of living beings, as having attained Brahman. (13:1084). When one is certain in his mind that all creatures are created from the same Soul, then it can be said that he has found the boat that is the wealth of Brahman (for crossing the ocean of birth and death cycles). Everywhere he casts his eyes he sees that all is full of Brahman. He attains endless bliss. Thus you should completely know by experience the arrangement of *Prakriti* and *Purusha*. The benefit you have gained is similar to an opportunity to gargle with nectar. (13:1087-1090). Now I am going to tell you one or two more profound ideas. (13:1092)

SOUL LIVES IN BODY AS A PROJECTION

What is known by the name Supreme Soul, always remains in its pure state, even though it exists in the body. (13:1094). In fact, it is not correct to say that Soul resides in the body. The soul is said to be in the body in the same way as when one looks at one's face in the mirror and says it is his face. It is totally meaningless to say that the soul is related to the body. (13:1096- 1098). Body is strung in the thread of the five principles and it rotates in the wheel of birth and death. This body is like a ball of butter inserted in the mouth of the fire that is Time. It vanishes in the short span of time that it takes a fly to flutter its wings. If it falls in fire, it turns to ashes and if it falls prey to a dog then it turns to faecal matter. If it escapes these two then a bunch of worms is created in it. Thus the body comes to a disgusting end. Though the body reaches this fate the soul is eternal, self-illuminating, self-sufficient and beginningless. (13:1103-1107).

Soul is neither this nor that: Because it is without attributes, it is neither without phases nor can it be said that it has phases; it is neither active nor inactive, neither fat nor thin. Because it is without form, it is neither visible nor invisible, neither bright nor dull, neither less nor much. Because it is a void it is neither full nor empty; it is in no way without company nor does it have company; it is neither shapeless nor does it have shape. Since it is the Self, it has neither bliss nor sorrow; it is neither one nor many; it is neither free nor bound. It is without characteristics, it is neither this much nor that much, neither ready-made nor prepared, neither able to speak nor dumb. It is not born along with the creation of the universe and does not get destroyed when it is destroyed. It is the place of dissolution of both being and not-being. It is dimensionless therefore it cannot be measured or described. It does not grow nor does it diminish, fade or get exhausted. Such is the nature of the Soul. It is unbroken (i.e., without parts), therefore it neither takes the form/shape of the body nor rejects it, but remains as it was. Just as days and nights occur in the sky, so are bodies acquired and given up by this Soul. Therefore the Soul does not do anything in the body nor cause it to be done nor does it get involved in any of the affairs of the body. Nothing happens to its nature. Not only that, even though it is in the body it is unattached to it. Though Soul is in all bodies, it does not get tainted by the characteristics of the bodies. I am telling you again and again to take into consideration the characteristic of the Soul – that the Knower of the Field is different from the Field. (13:1108-1119, 1121-1122).

A magnet by its proximity moves iron but iron is not the same as magnet. The same principle is applicable to the Soul and the body. There is fire hidden inside wood but wood is not fire; in just the same way, the Soul has to be viewed. Just as the sun is alone in the sky but illuminates the whole world, the Soul illuminates in the same way all the living bodies. (13:1123-1128)

Intellect with real sight: The intellect that understands the difference between the Field and the Knower of the Field is the intellect with the right vision. It alone can assimilate the essence of the meaning of the words. It is for understanding the difference between the Field and the Knower of the field that the wise persons frequent the abodes of sages. It is for that alone that the wise pursue the valuable peace and nurture the study of *Shastras*. It is for that knowledge that men practice yoga with high aspirations. And some people, by taking the body and other worldly matters to be insignificant respectfully serve the saints. Thus they shed their worries by following different paths of knowledge. *I surrender my knowledge to the knowledge of those who understand the difference between the Field and Knower of the Field.*[20] (13:1129-1135)

And they know the real nature of this *Prakriti* or *Maya*, which is spread everywhere in different forms and manifestations like the five principles. (13:1136). Those who are convinced in their heart that *Prakriti* is different from the *Purusha* have attained Brahman. (13:1140). The Brahman is more extensive than sky, it is the outer border of *Prakriti* and after attaining it the feelings of similarity or dissimilarity vanish. Shape, feeling of being alive and duality vanish in It and It remains as one and only one Supreme Principle. This Supreme Principle is attained by those who understand the difference between *Purusha* and *Prakriti*. (13:1140-1143).

---

20 *Note that this is coming from Shri Krishna, the Brahman Himself who shows His highest regard for a man of Knowledge who understands the difference between Field and the Knower of the Field meaning a person who has experienced Brahman.*

14

The Three Attributes

About How Soul Gets Attached And Experiences Pain Etc.

In the thirteenth chapter Shri Krishna told Arjuna that the universe is created through the union of the Field and the Knower of the Field (i.e. *Prakriti* and *Purusha*), and by association with the three attributes the soul becomes involved in the worldly affairs. When the soul comes in the grips of *Prakriti*, it experiences pleasure and pain; but if it gets rid of the three attributes then it is liberated. (14:32-34).

Now, how does the non-attached soul get attached to *Prakriti*? What is the meaning of the union of the soul and *Prakriti* (Knower of the field and the Field)? How does the soul experience pleasure and pain? What are these attributes and how many are they? How can these attributes be wound up? What are the characteristics of a person who is beyond the attributes? The discussion of these points forms the subject matter of the fourteenth chapter. (14:35-37)

The Meaning Of *Para*

Shri Krishna said, "Arjuna, I explained to you in many different ways what Knowledge is, but you do not seem to have experienced it so far. Therefore I shall once again explain to you the meaning of the word *Para* [pronounced as *paraa*] which is well-known in the *Shrutis*." (14:39-41).

Para the supreme Knowledge: Other branches of knowledge do not extend their scope beyond the world and the heaven. But the Knowledge of the Self goes beyond that, therefore the term *Para* has been used in its context. It is because of this that I call the Knowledge of the Self as the best Knowledge. Compared to it the rest of the knowledge is like grass in the presence of fire. The knowledge which recognises only the world and the heaven, which considers only *Yajnas* and rituals as the best and which is not acquainted with anything other than duality, appears entirely like a dream in front of this Knowledge of the Self. (14:42-45). Once the Knowledge of the Self rises all other types of knowledge vanish, therefore Arjuna, I call it the best. The liberation, which is within us right from the beginning, comes into our reach due to this Knowledge. Once it is experienced, the brave thinkers do not let worldly thoughts enter their minds anymore. Those who have controlled their minds with the help of the mind itself and have become relaxed and at peace go beyond the bodily affairs while still in the body. They cross the bounds of the body and become one with Me. (14:47-51).

Arjuna, they are eternal like Me and have reached perfection. Just as I am infinite, blissful and ultimate truth, they also become so. (14:52-54). The feeling of "you" and "I", that is the feeling of duality, vanishes and everybody exists at the same level. Therefore whenever the entire universe gets reborn, these Self-realised persons are not reborn. How can those who do not get caught in the fetters of the body at the time of creation of the universe, die at the time of its dissolution? Therefore Arjuna those who have attained Me with the help of Knowledge of the Self, go beyond the birth-death cycles. (14:56-59).

HOW THREE ATTRIBUTES TRAP ME

Now I shall tell you how the trappers in the form of the three attributes entangle Me, despite My being one and the only one, in the traps of different bodies and how I create this universe with the help of *Prakriti.* (14:64-65).

Prakriti: Prakriti is called the Field because it gives rise to the harvest of living creatures by the seed of the union with Me. (14:64-66). Since it is the place where *Mahat* and other principles reside it is also called *Mahatbrahma* (Universe of *Mahat* etc.). It strengthens passions therefore it is *Mahatbrahma.* Those who believe that the universe is not expressible, call it "Unmanifest" while the *Sankhyas* call it *Prakriti. Vedantins* call it *Maya.* But why talk more about it? It is the same as what is called Ignorance. This Ignorance is the very entity due to which we forget our real Self. It vanishes once we start thinking about the nature of our Self. (14:67-72). Sometimes a person cannot make up his mind about whether what he is seeing in front of him is a pole or man but he is aware he is seeing something, similarly he is not sure whether what he realises is Soul (Brahman) or not. Just as at the time of twilight in the evening it is neither day nor night, similarly Ignorance is neither true knowledge nor contrary knowledge, but the middle stage of doubt about the Soul. *And the Soul entangled in Ignorance is called the Knower of the Field* (individual). Forgetting the real Self and increasing the ignorance is the characteristic of the Knower of the Field. Understand properly that this is the yoga or union of the Field and Knower of the Field. This union is the basic nature of the Self. Thus, by union with the Field, the Knower of the Field (or individual) forgets his original form due to ignorance and takes different forms. (14:76- 82).

What is world: Whatever one observes after the eyes shift away from the form of the Self is called the world and that world is created out of Me. A person, though alone, sees several things in his dream by delusion and what happens when an individual forgets his Self, is similar. I shall explain the same principle in another way. (14:83-86).

Outcome of Ignorance: This ignorance of the Self is My wife and she is young, beginningless and with indescribable qualities. She does not possess a specific form. Her expanse is very large. She is found near ignorant persons and far away from persons of Knowledge. It is she who is awake when I am asleep[1] and becomes pregnant through the union with the power of the Self. In her womb grow the foetuses of the eight types of *vikaras* (passions).[2] (14:87-90).

Birth of the universe: From the union of the Self and the *Prakriti* the intellect is born first and mind is born from the intellect. The young wife of the mind namely the affection gives birth to the ego. From ego are born the five principles. The sense-objects and the sense organs being naturally parts of the five principles are also created along with them. When passions develop, the three attributes also raise their head and start spreading through the seed of desires. Just as a seed coming in contact with water sprouts and becomes a tree, similarly as soon as *Maya* becomes united with Me it sprouts shoots of various types of the universe. Listen to how that foetus takes shape. From it are formed the four types of creatures namely oviparous i.e. those born through eggs, those born from sweat e.g. lice etc., those born through seeds i.e. plants and those born through the womb. The foetus having more of the sky and wind principle is called the oviparous foetus. Foetus possessing *Tamas* and *Rajas* attributes and with more of the water and fire principle is the foetus that is created through sweat. Foetus having more of the water and earth principle and which is created from the inferior *Tamas* attribute is the non-moving foetus born of seed. The foetus that is aided by the five sense organs and five organs of action, with further support from mind and intellect is the foetus born in the womb. (14:91-102).

Thus *Maya* gave birth to a child (i.e. the entire universe) whose

1 *God cannot be asleep hence this is metaphorical meaning "when an individual is not awake to Me and indulges in material pleasures subjects."*
2 *Main vikaras are the six enemies: Kama (lust or desire), Krodha (anger), Lobha (greed), Moha (delusion), Mada (arrogance) and Matsarya (envy). The Tamil religious text Ayyavazhi lists the following eight vikaras: Lust, Wrath, Envy, Arrogance, Penuriousness (lack of generosity), ungovernable lust, ostentation, recklessness. Ref: (WK-TAT) Wikipedia Article on Tatvas (see Bibliography)*

arms and legs are the four types of foetuses, the eight-fold *Prakriti* its head, activism its protruding belly, renunciation its straight back, the eight species of the deities the parts of the body above the navel, the blissful heaven its throat, the mortal world the trunk and netherworld the part below the waist. The expanse of the three worlds is the baby's plumpness. The 8.4 million species are the joints of the bones. The child began to grow steadily. Many bodies are the various parts of its body. *Maya* started decorating it with ornaments of different names every day and fostering it on the milk of delusion. Different worlds are its fingers, which she adorned with rings of different bodies. Thus the delusive beautiful *Prakriti* became swollen with pride having given birth to the only child that is the living and non-living universe. Brahmadeo, Vishnu and Mahesh (Shiva) are respectively the morning, noon and evening of this child. By setting up this play of the universe the child sleeps on the bed of the delusion and when the new eon/age starts, it wakes up again with the ignorance of the Self. Thus this child steps around happily in the house of ignorance of the Self, according to the passage of the different eras. Will is its friend and ego its playmate. This child dies only due to Knowledge of the Self. *Maya* gave birth to the universe with the help of My power therefore I am the father, *Maya* is the mother and this huge world is our child. (14:103-116)

Diversity: Though you see diverse types of bodies ignore the differences between them because mind, intellect etc. are the same among them. Just as the same body has different organs similarly the diverse kind of universe has arisen from a single entity. The world and I have a mutual relation similar to a tree, which though grown out of a single seed has different types of branches, some short, some long and some bent. (14:117-119). Just as fire and flames are the two forms of the same fire, in the same way the world and I are the same. Therefore to imagine a relation between us two is not correct. If one says that creation of the world shadows my form, then the question is who appears in the form of the world? (14:122-123). If you try to see Me by moving aside the world then it is not possible because it is I who am in the form of the universe. Arjuna let this principle be fixed in your mind. Now even if I show my forms in different bodies consider that it is I who am bound in them by different attributes. Is one who is afraid of his own shadow, different from it? Therefore consider the binding by which I became many by assuming innumerable bodies. This binding does not remain after one experiences Me but this is not realised because of one's ignorance. Therefore Arjuna, listen to which attributes lead to which type of bindings, how many attributes are there, what their properties, their nature and names are and how they came into existence. (14:135-137).

THE THREE ATTRIBUTES

Sattva, *Rajas* and *Tamas* are the names of the three attributes and they arise from *Prakriti*. Out of these the *Sattva* attribute is superior, the *Tamas* attribute is inferior and the *Rajas* attribute is mid-way between these two. These three attributes may be seen as coexisting in the same entity. (14:138-140). The nature that develops when ignorance is embraced gets not only the *Sattva* and *Rajas* attributes but the *Tamas* attribute as well. Arjuna, I will tell you how these attributes bind a person. (14:143-144).

The time when a soul (Knower of the Field) reaches the status of an individual (i.e. is born) by adopting the I-am-the-body attitude is an inauspicious moment. From birth until death this Knower of the Field identifies with the Field, imagining the functions of the body to be his own. (14:145-146).

Sattva attribute: The *Sattva* attribute traps the individual by the strings of pleasure and learning. A learned individual roars due to vanity and kicks around due to conceit and misses the bliss of the Self-realisation. He feels elated when people honour him for his learning. He feels happy by small gains and he goes around bragging that very little satisfies him. He says how fortunate he is to have none as happy as himself. He is flooded with the eight righteous *Sattva*-attributed emotions.[3] As if this is not enough, another binding – the pride of his being learned – trails him. He does not feel sorry that he has lost the realisation of his being the Soul. On the contrary he swells with the pride of his worldly knowledge. (14:147-153).

The soul in the body, because of the worldly knowledge considers itself as the body. He knows the art of handling worldly affairs and becomes expert in the rituals of *yajnas*. His knowledge can take him up to heaven and he thinks that currently there is none as knowledgeable as he is and that he alone is clever. In this way the *Sattva* attribute pulls this lame individual-like bull with the reins of pleasure of learning. (14:154-158).

Rajas attribute: Now I shall tell you about how the *Rajas* attribute also binds the individual. It always keeps him amused and his passions remain ever alive, therefore it is called *Rajas* attribute. If it enters even slightly in an individual, it keeps him infatuated with passions and that individual rides on lust. Just as fire flares up when ghee (clarified butter) is poured into it, burning things big and small, similarly his desire becomes wild because of which painful things appear to him as pleasure giving. He feels dissatisfied even with the wealth of the gods. After desires for sense-objects have thus grown, even if a mountain as large as Meru comes in his possession he feels that he should get something still bigger. He is prepared to sacrifice his life even for a penny. He considers himself lucky if he gains even a piece of straw. Worried by what would happen to him if the wealth he possesses gets squandered, he starts big industries. Then worried that he may not be able to get anything to eat in heaven he performs *Yajnas* and practices vows, He builds wells and lakes for the public. He does not do any penance except with the aim of getting some desire fulfilled. Thus he keeps himself busy day and night in such activities. (14:159-168).

---

3 *These are together called Ashta-sattvic bhava. These are what your body experiences when you are in devotional state of mind: inability to speak, perspiration, standing of the hair on end, stuttered words, shivering, pale face and flow of tears and fainting.*

A fish or the glances of a pretty woman are quick and fickle and the lightning is still more so, but that is nothing compared with the speed and fickleness of the *Rajas* attribute. He jumps with that speed into the fire of actions hoping for gains in this world and to gain heaven. Thus, the individual soul, although separate from the body, being in the body, shackles itself and gets its neck in the noose of the struggle for actions. Thus the individual who resides in the body has a strong binding of the *Rajas* attribute. (14:170-173)

Tamas attribute: Now listen to the characteristics of *Tamas* attribute. *Tamas* attribute is that which veils the practical/rational view of a person by the dark clouds of delusion. It grows by ignorance and makes the whole world dance with delusion. Thoughtlessness is its password and it is the pot of honey of ignorance which keeps individuals in delusion. This *Tamas* attribute chains those who consider the body itself to be the soul. Once it starts growing in the living and non-living world it does not leave there scope for anything else. It brings heaviness to all organs and makes the mind dull and gives shelter to laziness. The body becomes shaky because of it. A person loses all desire to work and starts yawning again and again. He cannot see anything even with eyes open and even when nobody has called him he gets up like a demented person and responds. Once he lies down and sleeps he does not even turn over. He has no desire to get up even if heavens fall. Once he sits quietly he forgets what is proper or improper because his tendency is to stay as he is, without moving. He sits in the hopeless pose either with his hands on the forehead or his head in between his knees. He likes sleep so much that when he is sleepy even heaven is bothersome to him. He does not have any vice other than wishing that he should be accorded the long life of Brahmadeo which he should like to spend entirely in sleep. If he slips and falls down while walking he sleeps there itself in that state and once he is asleep he refuses even nectar. Similarly if he is forced to work he becomes blind with anger. He does not think about how he should behave with others or talk with them or if he is likely to gain anything or not. He sometimes ventures to commit some bravery but his tendency is to do things that should not be done. He likes making mistakes. Thus the *Tamas* attribute binds the free individual with the three tentacles of sleep, lethargy and mistakes. The individual is thus caught in the tentacles of these attributes and thinks that their characteristics belong to him. (14:174-193).

EFFECT OF PREDOMINANCE OF AN ATTRIBUTE

When *Sattva* attribute grows more than the *Rajas* and *Tamas* attributes the individual thinks he is happy. When *Sattva* and *Rajas* attributes wane and the strength of *Tamas* increases, the individual is easily prone to committing mistakes. Similarly when *Rajas* predominates over *Sattva* and *Tamas*, that individual, the king of the body, thinks that there is nothing better than action (14:199- 202).

Predominance of Sattva: Now listen to how the attributes grow. The signs, which are apparent when the *Sattva* attribute grows in the body after conquering the *Rajas* and *Tamas*, are as follows:

He is full of knowledge which can be seen from outside by his external appearance itself. All his organs are able to discriminate and in fact even limbs are able to see. The organs themselves discern what is good or bad and are in control. The ears do not hear what should not be heard, eyes do not see what should not be seen and his tongue avoids speaking what should not be spoken. Just as the darkness recedes from the lamp, the prohibited actions do not venture near the organs. His intellect becomes active in all the branches of knowledge and Knowledge pervades his mind. All his desires vanish, tendency towards actions reduces and he feels disgust for sense-pleasures. If he dies while these characteristics of growing *Sattva* attribute become apparent in him, then it is an occasion of happiness similar to the arrival of heavenly guests after a good harvest.[4] If a person is he wealthy as well as generous and courageous, then why should he not benefit in this as well as the next world? What other fate can such an incomparable person full of *Sattva* attribute have? Being full of *Sattva* attribute he becomes the very image of *Sattva* when he abandons the body, the means of enjoying worldly pleasures and he becomes the very image of *Sattva* and he is reborn among the men of Knowledge. When the *Sattva* attribute gets thus purified, knowledge grows and the intellect floats on it. Then, by thinking about the order in which the *Mahat* and other principles were created, he dissolves in the Self along with that thought. He attains the principle of the Self which is the thirty-seventh principle beyond the thirty-six principles proposed by the *Vedantins*[5] or the twenty-fifth principle beyond the twenty-four principles of the *Sankhya* philosophy. He takes rebirth in the highest class of family of those who brush aside the trio of three attributes, the three stages of life (Childhood, youth and old age), the three types of body (the material, causal and subtle) and easily attain the fourth, that is, the Self. (14:203-225).

Predominance of Rajas: Similarly, when *Rajas* attribute grows suppressing the *Sattva* and *Tamas* and plays havoc in the body then the apparent signs are as follows:

The organs play around freely among the sense-pleasures. They forget that looking at other peoples wives is against the righteous code (*dharma*) hence this individual's sense organs graze around everywhere like a goat. His greed grows freely to such an extent that

---

4 *It may appear strange that anyone should be happy by a person's death even if he were full of Sattva attribute. This is not very clear but probably it means that a person's gain of Sattva attribute is like a good harvest with which he is able to entertain even heavenly guests and in the same way able to enter the spotless world of the jnanis (men of Knowledge) which should make even the people left behind happy. This also implies that when that person's Shraddha ceremony is performed in future and pitris are invocated to come to be fed this person of Sattvic attribute will be their heavenly guest. Though he is full of Sattva attribute, he has not yet realized Brahman so he has to be reborn but that also will be in a family of men of Knowledge.*
5 *See Chapter 13 (13:72-75).*

only those things, which escape his attention, survive. He does not hesitate to do any kind of work. He goes after hobbies like building a temple or performing an *Ashwamedha* (Horse sacrifice) yajna. He takes up unusual tasks like establishing towns, building lakes or develops large forests. In spite of all this his desires related to gains in this world as well as the next remain unfulfilled. His desires grow tremendously. His hopes and ambitions gallop forward and he is not satisfied with roaming over the whole world. Such signs are seen when the *Rajas* attribute grows in a person. If he dies under these conditions then he is reborn as a human being in another body having the same characteristics. (14:226-238). He joins the rank of persons who do not have any rest during the day or night from the worldly business. He who dies drowning in the pond of *Rajas* attribute is reborn in the family of persons of ritualistic tendencies. (14:241-242).

Predominance of Tamas: Now listen carefully to the external signs when the *Tamas* attribute grows after defeating the *Sattva* and *Rajas* attributes. His mind is like the sky on the new moon night without the sun or the moon. Full of darkness of ignorance he does not even talk about thought. The subtleness of his intellect dips to such an extent that it will surpass even a stone in the hardness. His memory appears lost and his body appears to be filled inside out with thoughtless arrogance and his transactions are of foolish nature. Improper behaviour is in his bones. His evil actions cease only after his death. He likes doing bad deeds. He is very fond of doing prohibited deeds and his natural tendency is also similar. He becomes intoxicated without drinking liquor and he babbles as if in delirium even without fever and is deluded like a madman even without any sign of infatuation. He is in ecstasy but that is not the same as the *samadhi* of meditation because he is possessed by infatuation. These signs are apparent when the *Tamas* attribute grows with all the accompanying assistance and if he dies in that state then he is reborn in the *Tamas* attribute. The rebirth that one gets after death with the *Tamas* wrapped up in the desires, is as an animal or a bird or a tree or a worm. (14:243-259).

Fruits of attributes: Therefore what one gets from *Sattva* attribute is the fruits of righteous deeds as told in the Vedas. Therefore *Sattva* attribute leads to the incomparable fruits of natural happiness and Knowledge, which are called *Sattvic* fruits. The actions caused by *Rajas* attribute are outwardly sweet but bitter from inside like the fruits of a Vrindavan tree.[6] Just as a poisonous root when planted gives rise to a poisonous offshoot similarly the fruits of an action due to *Tamas* attribute gives rise to fruits of ignorance. (14:260-264).

Therefore Arjuna, the *Sattva* attribute is the causal agent for Knowledge. Just as forgetting the Self is the cause for the non-dual Supreme Soul to take birth as an individual, similarly the *Rajas* attribute is the cause for greed. It is only the *Tamas* attribute that is responsible for the three defects, namely delusion, ignorance and mistakes. Thus I explained to you the three attributes individually, in order to clear your thoughts. Out of these the *Rajas* and the *Tamas* cause one's downfall while without the *Sattva* attribute one does not attain Knowledge. Therefore just as some people renounce everything to adopt the fourth type of life (that is that of *sanyasi*), a *Sadhak* (aspirant) should give up everything and live throughout his life with the *Sattva* attribute. (14:265-270).

Fate after death: Those who dance with joy adopting the *Sattva* attribute and finally die, live in heaven. Similarly, those who live with the *Rajas* attribute and die are reborn on earth as human beings. They have to undergo a mixture of pleasure and pains but cannot avoid death. Similarly those who live with the *Tamas* attribute are allotted hell after death. Thus I have explained to you the three attributes and their workings which develop by the power of Brahman. Here the Soul follows the workings of the attributes due to their influence, but itself does not undergo any change (14:271-276). Heaven, earth and hell are variations of the natures of the attributes. If we try to see beyond the workings of the attributes then what we see is the form of the Self. Keep in mind

6 *In one place name of the tree is given as Indrayani but it is not clear which tree it is except that its fruits appears sweet from outside but has bitter seeds.*

that there is nothing other that the Self. (14:278).

By the strength of the Soul these three attributes appear in the form of the body just as we see the earth and water appear in the form of a tree. (14:280-281). These three attributes become the body inclusive of the mind, therefore they become the cause of the binding. Arjuna, it is a miracle that such a complex intertwining of the attributes and the body does not hinder the path of liberation. These three attributes do make the body move towards progress or regress according to their nature but that does not hinder anybody from going beyond them (towards liberation). I shall now tell you how one can achieve the liberation. (14:283-286).

Effect of Self-realisation: I have already [7]told you that Consciousness, though it pervades the attributes, it does not become like them. Arjuna, one understands this once the individual attains Self-realisation through Knowledge. (14:287-288). The individual *(seeker)* does not consider anymore that he is full of the attributes and only watches them. (14:290). Thus the individual who is full of the attributes but is also beyond them realises that "I am Brahman" and with this attitude says 'I am not the doer but only a witness to the action and it is the attributes that control the actions.' All actions occur through the differences in the nature of the three attributes *Sattva*, *Rajas* and *Tamas*, therefore action is the affliction of the attributes. (14:292-294). Among these three attributes I stand like the spring season which is the cause for the splendour of the woods. (14:295). Even though actions take place by my power, I remain the non-doer in the body. The attributes are apparent because I pervade them and I nurture their characteristics; and what remains when they are destroyed is also Me. In this way the person in whom knowledge has arisen is obviously beyond the attributes.[8] (14:297-299).

Now, the seeker accurately knows the Principle that is without

---

7 *Chapter 13 Gita Shloka 24*
8 *When the attributes are destroyed what remains is Brahman which is the seeker himself after Self-realization.*

the attributes because the stamp of Knowledge has been imprinted on his mind. Just as a river ultimately meets the sea he also meets only My regime. That person who is beyond the attributes knows that I am the Brahman. (14:300-301). He who was asleep and snoring in the slumber of ignorance wakes up to find himself in the form of the Self. Because the mirror of confusion fell down and has broken, he cannot see his image in it once the wind of I-am-the-body ego subsides. Then the individual and the Soul become one like the waves and the sea, and when that happens that person who has gone beyond attributes becomes one with Me. And once he becomes one with Me then even if he remains in the body he does not get in the clutches of the attributes. (14:303-307). Attributes may come and go, but his Knowledge does not get unclean and though he may be in the body he remains unattached to it. The three attributes play with their strength in his body but he does not let his ego look at them. He is so steady inside that he is not aware of the affairs of his body. (14:309-311). Just as the departed fragrance of a lotus does not return to it but merges in the sky, similarly once he attains unity with the Self he is not aware of the body and its affairs. Therefore the six qualities like birth, old age, death etc., that are associated with the body are absent in a man of knowledge. (14:313-315). Once the awareness vanishes one recognises the original Self and then he no longer remains aware of anything else but the Self. Therefore I call a person who has realised the Self as a person beyond the attributes even though he may be in the body. (14:317-318).

Arjuna asked, "Please explain how he goes beyond the attributes and how he behaves." (14:321-322).

GOING BEYOND ATTRIBUTES

Shri Krishna replied, "When he is drawn into performing actions due to strengthening of the *Rajas* attribute, he does not get afflicted by the egoistic thought that it is he who is doing the actions nor does he feel sorry if he is not able to perform them. When the *Sattva* attribute increases and the light of Knowledge pervades all organs, he does not get elated by the joy of his learning. He is not engulfed in delusion if the *Tamas* attribute increases, nor is he ashamed of ignorance. When he is under the spell of delusion he does not aspire for Knowledge. Similarly, when he achieves Knowledge, he does not avoid actions and is not sorry for it. He does not pay attention to the attributes. Does such a person of Knowledge need any other knowledge? Will he feel proud by the thought that he is the doer? Will he miss Knowledge when he is under delusion? (14:327-335).

Thus, since he himself is the attributes as well as their tasks/actions, he is not separated from them. He remains in the body like a traveller temporarily occupying a rest-house. And similarly he does not do actions or get them done through others by coming under the influence of the attributes. He neither conquers the attributes nor does he get conquered by them. (14:336-338). He is not disturbed by the comings and goings of the attributes. (14:340)

A person of Knowledge does not get bound by the attributes. Without being influenced by them he watches their play from a distance. When the *Sattva* tendency bends one towards righteous deeds, the *Rajas* tendency to enjoyment of pleasures and the *Tamas* tendency towards delusion, he considers that all these actions are taking place by the power of the attributes. (14:342-345). He is not disturbed by the stir made by the attributes. A person beyond the attributes may thus be recognised by these qualities. Now listen to the behaviour of such a person. (14:347-348).

Once he attains My form, he sees only My form in all the living and non-living things. Therefore whether happiness or sorrow falls to his lot his mind is balanced like a pair of scales. Now he has left the I-am-the-body attitude and has attained the Self. The seed, which was planted, has resulted in the harvest of grains. Once he has merged into the Self he is not affected by pleasure or pain even though he remains in the body. Just as day and night are the same to a pole and do not make any difference so are the pleasure and pain to a soul in the body

Whether the heavens come to him or a tiger rushes to him his attitude of the Self does not get disturbed. Nothing disturbs his equanimity. He does not get angered by slander or pleased by praise. (14:349- 361).

Whether he is considered by people to be God and worshipped or a thief and beaten, it is all the same to him. (14:362). There is no feeling of inequality in his mind. Another quality he possesses is that he does not do any kind of transactions. He does not commence any work. He loses his tendency to actions gets interrupted. The fruits of his actions burn away in the fire of his Knowledge. He does not at all think about the enjoyments and sufferings in this world or the next. He enjoys whatever falls to his lot. He is not elated by pleasures nor gets discouraged by sorrows. Similarly he neither accepts nor forgoes anything in his mind. He whose behaviour is thus developed should be considered as a person beyond the attributes. Now I shall tell you the methods by which one can be beyond the attributes. (14:364-370).

I AM NOT SEPARATE FROM UNIVERSE

He who is devoted to Me with unwavering mind can get rid of these attributes. Therefore I must explain to you as to who I am, how to be devoted to Me and what the signs of dedication are. (14:371-372). Just as fluidity and water or space and sky, sweetness and sugar are the same likewise what is called universe is all only Me. (14:374,377). It is not true that I can be attained only after the universe is dissolved, but on the contrary, I must be realised along with the universe. Realising Me with this attitude of oneness is actually the unadulterated devotion. If one imagines a difference between Me and the universe then it is adulterated devotion. (14:380-382). Therefore one should not have any thought of any such difference. (14:383). The dust particles in the soil on the earth or the snow particles in the Himalayas are not different (i.e. they are all matter); similarly I am in Me (i.e. the universe).

(14:385). When the outlook of equality that one is not different from God is developed I call it devotion. This outlook is the best form of Knowledge and the essence of yoga.[9] (14:387-388). Because of it the attitude that "I am Brahman" comes to the surface. That Knowledge (of being one with Him) also dissolves with this attitude. (14:391-392). When the difference vanishes the knowledge also vanishes. (14:394). The illusion that the devotee is on this shore and I am across on the other shore, disappears and what remains is only the oneness between the two. Then the question of conquering the attributes does not remain because with the entwinement of oneness they also disappear. Arjuna, this state is called the state of oneness with the Brahman. He who is devoted to Me is the one who attains it. Brahman weds him who carries devotion towards Me in this manner. (14:395-398). He who serves Me with the outlook of knowledge is the crown jewel in the state of oneness with the Brahman. Attaining this state of oneness is called 'liberation while still in the body' or the fourth achievement[10] Devotion to Me is the ladder for reaching this oneness with the Brahman. But if you are thinking that the means of attaining Me is different from Me, do not do so. (14:400-403). What is meant by Brahman is only Me. There is no difference between Brahman and Me. That Brahman is the incomparable entity that is constant, steady and open, having the form of the code of righteous living and which gives infinite bliss. I am the ultimate form and the place where Knowledge dissolves after its task is over. (14:404-407).

～∞～

---

9 Remember that Yoga means union (with Him)

10 Every man is supposed to fulfil four duties (Purusharthas) in his lifetime viz. Dharma or behaving as per the righteous code; Artha or earning livelihood for himself and his family; Kama or fulfilling sexual duties towards his wife and Moksha or pursuit of liberation. Here the fourth goal means Moksha or liberation.

15

The Supreme Person

∽◊∽

COMMENTS BY DNYANESHWAR MAHARAJ

Dnyaneshwar Maharaj says, "There is no doubt that Knowledge leads to liberation. But in order that the Knowledge steadies itself in a person the mind must be very pure and Knowledge cannot be steady without detachment. This principle has been very thoughtfully stated by Shri Krishna. He has also discussed how the mind can get completely detached. Just as a person taking his meal runs away leaving the dish when he knows that it contains poison, similarly once the idea of the impermanence of this world gets stamped on the mind, one runs away from attachment. The detachment thus gained does not leave you even if you try to get rid of it. In this fifteenth chapter Shri Krishna is explaining how the world is impermanent using the simile of a tree." (15:35-40).

THE TREE IS IMPEDIMENT TO LIBERATION

Shri Krishna said, "Arjuna, The illusion of the visible universe which comes in the way of the path towards Self-realisation, is not the expanse of the universe but the giant tree of the worldly set-up. But it is not like the other trees that have roots below and branches above and therefore its expanse cannot be measured by anybody. Even if one sets fire to its roots or axes them, instead of getting destroyed it proliferates. When cut at the roots other trees fall down along with their branches but that is not the case with this tree which not an ordinary tree. (15:46-50).

UNIVERSE COMPARED WITH THE TREE

Arjuna it is an unusual thing that this tree which is extraordinary and unusual grows from below. (15:51). This tree in the form of the world is strange. Whichever objects occur in this world are all occupied by it. (15:53). It does not have fruits to be tasted or flowers to be smelt. What occurs is only the tree itself. Though it is upside down it has not been uprooted therefore it is always green. Even though one may say that it has roots above, it has countless roots below too. This tree has proliferated on all sides and its tuft roots also have grown branches like the *banyan* or *pipul*[1] tree. It is not that this world-tree has branches only below. Bunches of innumerable branches have spread out on the upper side also. Looking at it gives the impression that the sky itself has sprouted with green leaves or as if the wind itself has taken the shape of the tree or as if the three states of creation, sustenance and destruction have assumed this form. Thus, the dense tree with roots above is born in the shape of this universe. (15:55-62).

MORE EXPLANATION ABOUT THE TREE

Now I shall explain to you, in a way that you will clearly understand, who is above this tree, who is at its roots, what its characteristics are, why it spreads downwards, which are its branches or which are the branches which have grown the upward

---

1 *It is also known as ashwattha. Its Botanical name is ficus religiosa.*

branches and how they are created and how it received the name *Ashwattha* and what the Self-realised persons concluded from it. (15:63-65).

Brahman becomes the universe when tainted by limiting qualifications: Arjuna, this tree has his roots above because of the Brahman above it. Otherwise this Brahman does not have a middle, top or bottom; It is one and unique. (15:72-73). This Brahman which sees here, there, front, back and everywhere without sight but is itself invisible becomes the universe with name and shape when it comes in contact with limiting qualifications.[2] It is pure Knowledge free of either the knower or the object to be known and is pure bliss pervading the space. It is neither the cause nor its effect (i.e. action). There is neither a sense of duality nor a sense of uniqueness in it but something that can be understood by an individual through Self-realisation. In this way this pure Brahman is the upward root of the world-tree. And the shoots of the root are as follows. (15:75-78).

PROPERTIES OF *MAYA*

The entity known as *Maya* does not exist. Actually it is like the child born to a barren woman and is named *Maya*. It cannot be said that *Maya* is real nor can it be said that it is unreal. It cannot survive in the presence of Knowledge and yet it is called beginningless. It is the holder of many principles and just as clouds are formed in the sky the universe is formed in her. All sorts of forms and shapes are folded into the folds of her fabric. She is the root of the world-tree, source of the worldly affairs illuminated by the dim light of improper unrighteous knowledge. Such an entity as *Maya* is, takes shelter in Brahman and appears through its power. (15:79-84). *Maya* which is created from Brahman makes it forget its

---

2 *The* **Gunas** *viz.* **Sattva, Rajas** *and* **Tamas** *are translated as Attributes. They are a component of the nature of a person or thing.* **Upadhi** *is translated as limiting qualification. Qualifications are not same as attributes; in this case they are kind of restrict the scope of action of the qualified entity..*

own nature. This is the first root of the world-tree. Non-realisation of the Self as Brahman is the main root-bulb of the tree at its top. It is called by *Vedantins* as *"Beejabhaava"* or "the root principle" in the form of *Maya*. The sleep state of deep ignorance is called its *"Bijankurabhaava"* or "seed-sprout principle" while the dream and wakeful states are its *"Phalabhaava"* or "fruit principle". This is how Vedantis express these aspects of *Maya* but understand in all this that the basic root is ignorance. (15:87-90).

EVOLUTION OF THE UNIVERSE

Roots sprout upwards and downwards from the pure soul, which is at the top, and they become strong in the base-soil of *Maya*. Then shoots sprout in all directions from the centre of that root. Thus the world tree gets its strength from Brahman. Then it develops bunches of shoots from below. Among those, the first to sprout is the delicate green leaf of *Mahat* principle in the form of consciousness *(Chit)*. Next sprouts the three-leaf shoot of the ego with the three attributes *Sattva, Rajas* and *Tamas* on the lower side. Later it sprouts another shoot, the shoot of intellect which fosters the growth of the feeling of differentiation which in turn gives rise to the twig that is the mind and keeps it fresh. Thus the root gaining strength from the sap of ignorance, sprouts four types of young twigs namely mind, intellect, ego and consciousness. (15:91-97).

From these the branches of the five principles: sky, air, fire, water and earth rise straight. From these branches the tender soft leaves of the five sense organs and their sense objects grow. Out of these when the shoot of the sound grows, the hearing organ grows twice as much and gives rise to the branches of desires. Then the creeper of the body and the leaves of skin give rise to the sprout of touch leading to an abundance of novel passions. Then the leaves of form grow and the eyes rush to that branch leading to growing delusion. Then the leaves of taste grow and the tongue develops endless cravings. Similarly the leaves of smell give rise to increasing desire by the nose that leads to greed. In this way the *Mahat* principle, ego, mind and the five principles (elements) cause the world to grow. It grows only by means of these eight parts (namely *Mahat* principle, ego, mind and the five principles or elements). The world-tree grows more and more branches and just as a sea shell appears like silver due to illusion the Brahman, by showing itself in the form of the world-tree, becomes the root of ignorance. (15:98-107).

WHY THE TREE IS CALLED *ASHWATTHA*

I shall also tell you why knowledgeable people call this tree as *Ashwattha*. "*Shwa*" means morning or tomorrow. This world-tree does not remain like this even up to tomorrow. (15:110-111). It gets destroyed every moment therefore it is called *Ashwattha*. Shri Krishna does not imply this *Ashwattha* to be the ordinary Peepul *(Ficus Religiosa)* tree. (15:114-115). This tree is well-known to be indestructible but its hidden meaning is that just as ocean is depleted by the clouds on one hand and filled by the rivers on the other therefore it neither gets depleted nor does it grow. As long as the action of the clouds and the rivers does not cease it is always filled. Likewise, the destruction and reformation of this tree occurs so fast that it cannot be guessed. Therefore people call it indestructible. (15:118-122). With the passage of time, the branch which represents the animal kingdom dries and falls down but it grows millions of shoots but one cannot understand when the first branch fell down and when the millions of other branches sprouted. At the time of the deluge the branches of this world-tree fall down and at the time of creation they sprout into a veritable forest. The stormy winds at the time of deluge cause the barks of the tree to drop and in the beginning of the new eon they grow again. Then one Manu period follows another, then dynasties like the *Solar* dynasty, *Lunar* dynasty[3] follow and expansion occurs. At the end

---

3 *Two lineages of kings started from Vaivaswat Manu (ca. 3100 BCE). The dynasty that started through his son Ikshwaku is called in the Puranas as Surya Vansh or Solar dynasty. This name is derived from Manu's father*

of the *Kali-Yuga* the barks of the trees in all the four *yugas* are shed and the tree dries but when the *Krita-Yuga* starts again the barks grow many times faster.[4] One cannot understand how many branches grow and how many fall. (15:125-129).

APPARENT INDESTRUCTIBLE NATURE OF THE TREE

No sooner does a twig of this world tree (i.e. a body) fall hundreds of others sprout because of which this world-tree appears to be indestructible. With whatever speed river water may flow, the water behind meets it with the same speed, so that the water looks perennial. In the same way this world appears perpetual even though it is destructible. People foolishly consider this world tree to be indestructible because it grows even as it breaks. But knowing its speed, he who realises that this world-tree is momentary and is created millions of times during the batting of an eyelid and knows fully well that there is no cause for all this other than ignorance and its existence is unreal, is the person who knows everything. He is the one who knows the principles of Vedanta and whom I adore. He alone gets fruits of yoga. Who can describe the person who realises this world tree to be impermanent? (15:132-143).

Then, branches grow on the lower side of the world-tree, which after reaching the ground grow upward branches too. In turn they also grow roots. Creepers growing from them sprout new leaves. The root of this tree is ignorance and with the help of the eight

---

Vivaswat which is also another name of the Sun. The second dynasty the Chandra Vansh, Soma Vansh or Lunar dynasty started from Manu's daughter Ila who married a rishi Budha who was the son of Rishi Atri's son Soma from Brihaspati's wife Tara. Pururava or Aila, son of Ila and Budha is considered as the founder of this dynasty. The name Lunar is rooted in the fact that Soma is also another name of the moon. Except for this the names have nothing to do with real Sun or Moon.

4 Four yugas viz. Krita-, Treta- Dwapara-, and Kali-Yuga make one Mahayuga. The cycle of the four yugas gets repeated. Kaliyuga is 1200 Divine years or 432000 solar years long. Krita, Treta and Dwapara are respectively 4, 3 and 2 times the length of Kaliyuga. This time scale of the Puranas is obviously unrealistic. (See similar footnote in Ch 8)

constituents of *Prakriti viz., Mahat* etc. a forest of Vedas is created. (15:144-147)

FOUR KINDS OF LIFE

Then sprout four large branch-shoots of four types of life namely – those born from eggs or oviparous, those born from sweat, those born through seeds and lastly, those born in the womb. From each branch are created 8.4 million branches of species of life. The criss-cross branches growing from these straight branches are the different species. Individuals are divided into male, female and neuter, which clash with one another due to the pressure of passions. Like clouds form one after another during the rainy season, similarly different types of creatures are born through the cause of ignorance. The branches bend under their own weight and get entangled in one another and then the attributes create a storm and with its force the world tree with upward roots gets split in three places. (15:148-154).

INFLUENCE OF THE THREE ATTRIBUTES

Effect of Rajas attribute: "When the winds of *Rajas* attribute are strong, the branch of human race grows rapidly. Instead of the upper side or lower side on this branch, shoots grow abundantly in the middle part that is on the mortal earth plane and these shoots are those of the four castes. These branches constantly grow leaves of codes for deciding proper and improper actions according to the Vedas. Of the four dutiful actions, the two – namely earning and sex, spread and shoots of passing pleasures sprout. Countless shoots of good and bad actions grow with the intention of increasing the action tendency. Similarly, by the time the past Karmas are annulled by suffering or pleasure and the dry branches of the bodies of past life drop off, branches of new bodies sprout in another place. And then new foliage of words and similar subjects, which decorate by their natural hues, grows constantly. Thus, when the winds of *Rajas* attribute blow, bunches of the branches of human beings proliferate and the human race gets established on the earth. (15:155-162).

Effects of Tamas attribute: Similarly when the winds of *Rajas* attribute subside, the strong winds of *Tamas* attribute start blowing. Then the same branches of human beings grow foliage of low passions and twigs of evil deeds sprout below. Then twigs of wicked tendencies grow and from them emerge transgressions. Young leaves of the prescribed rules and injunctions laid down by the three Vedas – *Rigveda, Yajurveda* and *Samaveda,* grow at the end of these branches. Leaves of *Agamas*[5] in which *mantras* and techniques of black magic for giving trouble to others are given, emerge and the creeper of passions spreads. Later, the many branches of rebirth sprout as and when the roots of evil actions grow big. Then the large branch of *Chandalas*[6] and other very low caste persons emerges from the tree and evil doers who have been attracted by evil deeds have to be reborn in those castes. Many horizontal branches of animals, birds, pigs, tigers, scorpions, snakes shoot out. Thus new branches continue growing and remain fresh

---

5 *Agamas are non-Vedic religious texts in Sanskrit and Tamil which are post-Vedic in origin but some may be pre-Vedic compositions. They deal with topics related to temple construction and idol making, methods of worship, philosophical doctrines, meditative practices, mind control, yoga etc. Various sects use different kind of agamas. Some popular agama-based religions are those of Shaiva, Vaishnava, Shakta, Ganapatya, Kaumara, Soura, Bhairava and Yaksha-bhutadi-sadhana. Often the word Tantric is used in reference to Shakti Tantra related to worship of Shakti (Devi) according to Shakta Agama (more commonly the Vama or left handed Tantra which is not considered pure). Agama traditions have been the sources of Yoga (including Kundalini Yoga) and Self Realization concepts in the Hindu spiritual community. Tantrism includes within its fold Buddhist and Jain tantras suggesting that Hindu, Jain and Buddhist tantrism developed separately after arising from common sources of Tantric elements. Each Agama consists of four parts: Kriya pada (temple and idol construction, initiation), Charya pada (rules for daily worship, religious rotes, rules for atonement of sins), Yoga pada (yoga and the mental discipline) and Jnana pada (philosophical and spiritual knowledge, liberation). Ref Wikipedia Article on Agamas See Bibliography (WK-AG). Agamas are downgraded here because some Agamas are related to left-handed tantra*
6 *Chandala is an untouchable sub-caste in the four-caste system.*

on the tree and they give fruits of suffering in hell. The branches of the violence and wickedness grow for many lifetimes. In this way shoots of trees, grass, iron, soil and stones are formed and they also give similar fruits. Arjuna, the branches consisting of human beings to non-living things are thus on the lower part of the tree. Therefore the branch of human beings may be considered as the root of other living being and non-living things and the world tree grows from it.[7] Arjuna, if one looks for the roots of the upward branches it will be found that this very same branch occurs midway between the upward and downward going branches. The branches of evil actions and good actions corresponding to the *Tamas* attribute and *Sattva* attribute respectively go from this middle branch downwards and upwards respectively. (15:163-177).

The code of Vedas applicable only to human beings: The code of the Vedas are not applicable to anybody else other than human beings therefore though the branches corresponding to human beings have grown from upper side roots, the accumulation of actions grows from this branch. Other trees also behave similarly that is when branches grow, the roots go deeper and when roots go deeper the branches grow more. Body also behaves similarly, i.e. as long as there is the accumulation of *karmas* (actions) one is compelled to acquire the body in this world and as long as one is in the body actions cannot be avoided. *Therefore human body is the root of the branches of actions and there is no getting away from it.* (15:178-182).

Effect of Sattva attribute: After the storm of the *Tamas* attribute subsides, the storm of *Sattva* attribute starts with great force. When this happens the same branches of human beings sprout good desires from which shoots of knowledge grow. After these shoots of knowledge develop, shoots of sharp intellect grow from them, which expand within moments. After the shoots of intellect

---

7 *The gist of this is that man is the root of evil, especially a man of Tamas tendencies. Such person's actions (Karmas) lead him first to a place in hell after which he is reborn in a low caste family or as an animal or even a tree and even may turn into inert objects.*

expand they gain the strength from inspiration and the intellect gains discrimination. From there the beautiful foliage of devotion filled with the essence of intellect grows and from it straight shoots of good tendency come out. From there many shoots of good actions come out leading to loud singing of Vedas. Then leaves of proper social behaviour, behaviour as prescribed in the Vedas and different types of *Yajna* rituals grow one after another. In this way, the branches of austerity *(vratas),* with bunches of regular self-controlled behaviour and young twigs of detachment grow. Shoots of some specific austerities *(vratas)* arise from the sharp sprouts of courage and go up rapidly. As long as the storm of *Sattva* attribute blows the twigs of Knowledge grow with force from the thick foliage of Vedas. And then a straight twig of wealth arises and grows and gives rise to a cross branch of fruits like heaven etc. The second red branch of detachment also grows which grows by continuously getting new foliage of liberation. (15:183-194).

Next come the cross branches of the planets Sun, moon etc., the manes, *rishis, Vidyadhars* etc. Branches come out even higher than these and they get fruits like *Indraloka (Indra's abode).* To these branches sprout other high level branches of rishis like Marichi, Kashyapa[8] etc. who excel in austerity and knowledge. Thus the rows of branches grew and expanded more and more on the upper side and therefore though the tree is small at the base it has become big due to being full of fruits. The branches, which come even above these, get shoots like *Brahmaloka (Brahmadeo's* abode) and Kailas (*Shiva's* abode) and due to weight of these fruits the upper branches get bent down up to the roots. In other trees also when branches become heavy with fruits they bend towards the root. Similarly due to attainment of deep knowledge the branches of this world tree bend towards the root (i.e. towards Brahman) from which the tree sprouted in the first place. Therefore Arjuna, an individual cannot go above the level of *Brahmaloka* or Kailas. If he goes above that he himself becomes Brahman. But the branches

---

8 *These are members of the famous Saptarshi (Seven rishis) group.*

of *Brahmaloka* etc. are nowhere in comparison with the root Brahman. The branches of renunciates like Sanak, Sanandan (The mind-children of Brahmadeo) etc., do not get fruits or roots and they are like Brahman itself. Thus the branches of *Brahmaloka* etc., which are above those of human beings, have gone very high up. They have grown out of the branches of human beings therefore the latter which are at the lower side, are their roots. Thus I have described to you this unworldly world-tree which has the roots on the upper side and branches on both the upper and lower sides. I also discussed in detail the roots on the lower side of this tree. Now listen to how this tree can be uprooted. (15:195-209).

How To Uproot The Tree

Arjuna, you may get a doubt as to what can uproot this giant tree. Because it is such a vast and strong tree, the uppermost branches of which have reached *Brahmaloka,* its root in the formless Brahman, its downward branches spread in non-living undergrowth and the mortal world spread in its middle part. If you are going to bring ordinary thoughts like who will be able to destroy the tree, then look here, what difficulty can there be in uprooting this tree? (15:210-214).

Arjuna this world-tree is not real. What courage is required to uproot it? The description I made of this tree about its roots and branches is meaningless like describing the many children of a barren woman. (15:216-217). If the tree were really having strong roots and spread like I described, then who on earth would have been capable of uprooting it? Arjuna the description of the world I made metaphorically by comparing it to the tree, is all *Maya*. (15:219-220). Where ignorance itself is an illusion then how can the actions arising from it be otherwise? Therefore really speaking this world-tree is unreal. (15:223).

When it is said that it has no end, it is true in a way. (15:224). Arjuna, so long as discrimination is not generated in a person there is no end to this tree. (15:226). Ignorance, which is the root of this tree, does not vanish unless knowledge arises. Similarly the talk that this tree is beginningless is not a rumour but is appropriate to its characteristics. Because if the tree is not real, how can it have a beginning? Who is the mother of a person who is not even born? (15:229-233). Therefore it has been called beginningless because it has no existence. Arjuna, this tree has neither beginning nor end and its intermediate state is also unreal. (15:236-237). But what a wonder! This tree is unreal but at the same time real also. This world-tree appears beautiful to an ignorant person. It creates an illusion that deludes an ignorant person. (15:239-241). But this illusion of the universe is momentary and hollow. It appears real but when one tries to grasp it slips away. (15:243-244). Therefore what efforts are required to uproot a tree which has neither beginning, nor end nor existence nor a form? Arjuna, has not the tree proliferated because of the ignorance about ourselves? *It has to be felled by the axe of Self-realisation.* But other than that of knowledge, whatever other methods you may use will get you more and more entangled in this tree. And how many branches will you climb up and get down from? Therefore you destroy ignorance, the root of this tree by appropriate Knowledge. (15:247-250).

Persons engrossed in methods miss liberation: Arjuna, a person who is worried about the methods to be used for destroying the unreal world misses Self-realisation and therefore the impression he has gained of the world being real actually strengthens. Only the sword of knowledge can destroy the world created from ignorance but to use that sword of knowledge with ease, the intellect needs constant support of detachment. Once the detachment becomes firm only then the binding to the religious code, to the need for earning livelihood and passions, vanish. Arjuna, the detachment becomes strong only when one gets disgusted with every worldly object. One should then take the sword from the sheath of ego in the hands of inward looking intellect and sharpen it on the stone of discrimination until it attains the sharpness of "I am the Brahman" and then clean it with knowledge of the Self. Then holding it in the grip of determination, one should try it once or twice and balance it with mind. Then once the sword becomes one with oneself by continued contemplation, nothing can stand before it. That sword of Self- realisation shining with the brightness of non-duality will not let any part of the world-tree survive. Just as all darkness vanishes as soon as the sun rises, similarly the sharp edge of the sword of knowledge does its task and the upper and lower roots of the world tree or the expanse of the branches grown on the lower side vanishes. Thus Arjuna, you cut the tree with the upward roots, by the sword of Self-realisation. (15:253-266).

Once this is done then one should observe the Self, which is something that cannot be pointed at as "it is this" and by attaining which the ego goes away. But do not do like fools who look in the mirror and think they have two faces. (15:267-268). The proper way of observing the Self is similar to the fire which merges into its original latent form when fuel is over or like tasting its own taste or eye seeing its own pupil that is one should observe it with the feeling of non-duality. (15:271- 272, 274).

Realisation of the Self: The primeval place which is seen without seeing and known without knowing is called the Primeval Man *(Adya Purusha).* But even he is described by the *Shrutis* by taking help of attributes and making meaningless noise that it has a name and form. But people who are disgusted with heaven and worldly life swear that they will not be reborn and turn to yoga and Knowledge. Then they become detached and turn their back to worldly life; and crossing the *Brahmaloka,* which is the highest stage attainable by the path of action, they march ahead. Then those men of Knowledge, shaking off the feelings of ego etc., take the entry pass to enter the abode of the Self. In the absence of the knowledge of the Self one is subjected to the experience of the expanse of this universe and the feeling of the duality of "I and you"; this Self is something which must be experienced by oneself. There is one more sign of recognising it and that is once realisation of this Self is attained one does not return from it to be reborn. People who are full of Knowledge only can reach this state. (15:275-284).

Losing Duality: Delusion and pride leave such persons. They do not come in the clutches of passions. Just as a banana tree falls after bearing fruit, their actions gradually cease because of Self-realisation. All doubts leave them. They are not capable of seeing duality between themselves and others. The consciousness and pride about their body vanishes along with ignorance. The sense of duality that can cause delusion leaves them and they lack in it. They do not face the duel between pain and pleasure experienced by a body. The duel between pain and pleasure, which causes sinful and meritorious actions, does not affect them. These thoughtful persons are the swans who separate the water of material objects from the milk of the Self and drink the latter. (15:285-296). Because of ignorance they were seeing the Brahman in its manifested form in things scattered here and there but once they attained the sight of Knowledge they come to see Brahman as one continuous entity in all objects. Their thoughts merge steadily in Brahman. Because they see Brahman in everything desires do not touch them. No emotions enter their mind nor is it agitated by feelings of lust. They are not troubled by hope. They do not like the topic of sense pleasures even to be mentioned before them. In this way those who have burnt all sense pleasures in the fire of Knowledge, go and get merged "there". If you ask where is this "there", then it is that place which never gets destroyed and which is not something that can be seen if you try to see it or know if you want to know it, or can be described as similar to or with reference to another object. (15:297-307).

That place cannot be seen even when everything is visible in the light of a lamp, the moon or the sun. *The world is apparent only when the Self is hidden.* (15:308-309). It is only when the light from the entity of Self is shielded that the sun, moon etc. shine by their intense brightness. That entity is extremely bright and all encompassing and illuminates even the sun and the moon. The light of the sun and the moon originates from this light therefore giving brightness to all shining objects is the basic aspect of this entity of Self. (15:311-313).

The radiance of Brahman: Just as the moon and the stars disappear when the sun rises, similarly in the Light of this entity, the entire universe along with sun and moon vanishes. (15:314). The entity in which no material object appears is my highest abode. Those who reach there do not come back. (15:316-317). Those who become one with Me by means of pure Knowledge are not reborn. (15:320).

Arjuna's doubt: Hearing this Arjuna expressed a doubt. He said, "Your statements are contradictory. If an individual is different from you then he will not become one with You and if he is one with You then the question of his returning does not arise." (15:321-328).

Some devotees do not prefer liberation: Shri Krishna said, "There are two types of devotees who do not return after reaching unity with Me: those who are *separate* from Me and those who are one with Me. If you think superficially, they appear separate from Me but if you think deeply then you will find they are one with Me. (15:330-331). If one sees with the eyes of Knowledge, they are one with Me, but they appear separate due to ignorance. If you really consider the Self, then how can there be two types of behaviours – of being one with Me and another being different from Me? (15:334-335).

Even though I am pure, the influence of *Maya* creates a doubt in the mind of the individual about "Who am I?" and ignorance leads to the reply "I am the body". When Knowledge of the Self gets limited to the body, it is seen as part of Me because of its smallness. Just as waves on the sea appear to be part of the ocean to a person of limited understanding, I, the giver of vitality to the material body and creator of the I-am-the-body ego, become known as an individual. (15:341-345).

The activity that is seen by the intellect of the individual is called the living world. Where birth and death are considered real, I call that place as the living world or world. The moon is different from water but we can see its reflection in water. This is how I exist in this living world too. (15:346-348). The status of my being beginningless and a non-doer does not change or get affected, but the appearance that I am the doer and the experiencer is an illusion. (15:350).

Prakriti: By mixing with *Prakriti,* the pure soul appropriates its *(Prakriti's)* properties to itself and then assuming that *Prakriti,* the mind and the five sense organs are his, the pure individual Soul gets engrossed in worldly activities. (15:351-352). Forgetting himself the soul considers himself to be similar to *Prakriti* and gets involved with it. Then he rides on the chariot of the mind, gets out through the ears and enters the woods of the words. He enters the deep forest of touch holding the apron strings of *Prakriti.* Sometimes the soul gets out through the eyes and roams freely on the hill of form. He goes out through the tongue and enters the valley of taste. This individual soul who is my fraction, gets out of the nose and enters the thick forest of odours and wanders there. Thus with the help of mind, the master of the body and the organs, this individual experiences the sense objects like sound etc. (15:354-360).

When that individual soul enters a body he gives the impression that he is the doer and experiencer. (15:361). His ego increases and the sense-objects and sense organs play havoc. (15:363). When he abandons the body he takes with him the five sense organs and the mind. (15:367). When the individual again attains a body in this world or in heaven the mind and the group of sense-organs accompany him. To an ignorant person the behaviour of an individual appears like a lamp, which disappears along with its brightness when extinguished and reappears along with the brightness when lighted again. People think that it is the soul which entered the body and it is he who experienced the sense-objects and it was also he who went away with the body. However, taking birth and dying, or doing and experiencing, are the properties (actions) of *Prakriti,* but it is thought that these are the actions of the soul. (15:368-370).

When the little (infant) body starts making movements due to vital force, people say the individual is born. Similarly, when the organs (in the individual) experience their respective sense objects, then that is called "experiencing". Then when the body becomes weak due to experiences and gets destroyed, people cry that the individual has gone. Are we to suppose that wind is blowing only where there is a tree making movements and there is no wind where there is no tree? (15:373-376). In the same way, people blinded by delusion determine that the birth and death of a body are actually those of the soul. It is a different class of people who know that the soul is in its own place in the body and merely witnesses the body's activities. Those who, through the eyes of Knowledge, consider the body to be merely a cover for the soul and do not get involved in its affairs, and those whose sense of discrimination has grown and as a result they have been inspired towards realisation of the soul are the ones who know the soul. (15:380- 383). When we see the reflection of the star-studded sky in water we know that it has not fallen down in it, but remains where it was and what we see in the water is merely an illusion. Similarly the individual (soul) though covered in the body, is actually the soul. (15:384-385). Body may come and go but I remain unaffected and persons of knowledge know Me as I always am. They know that the soul continues to be uninterrupted while bodies are imagined due to ignorance as being created and destroyed. They understand Me with proper knowledge of the Self, that the soul does not grow or diminish, does not do actions nor cause them to be done. (15:389-390).

Knowledge must be accompanied by detachment: A person may attain this Knowledge, his intellect may become subtle as to penetrate even an atom and he may become learned in all branches of knowledge; but unless this learning is accompanied by detachment, he will not encounter Me even though I am all-pervasive. He may talk mouthfuls about discrimination but if he harbours sense-objects in his mind then definitely he will not find Me. (15:391-393) Even if all branches of knowledge are on the tip of his tongue, as long as ego exists in the mind he will not attain Me even after millions of births. Now I shall explain to you how I encompass all beings. (15:396-397).

I support the Universe: The radiance with the help of which the affairs of this world are seen, including the radiance of the sun, is mine. Understand that this radiance existed in the beginning as well as at the time of the end of the world. The moonlight, which gives moisture to the world after the sun has made it dry, is also mine. And the strong radiance, which does the functions of burning and cooking, also belongs to Me. (15:398-400).

The earth does not get dissolved in the limitless ocean because I enter the earth and give it support. And this earth, which supports the countless creatures, does so because I support them (the creatures) by entering them. Arjuna, I have become a moving lake of nectar in the sky in the form of the moon. I nurture the entire plant kingdom by forming canals of nectar of the rays, which originate there and spread below. Thus I give life to all creatures in the form of food, by means of growing and nurturing grains etc. And even if food is grown, how do the individual creatures digest it and feel satisfied? (15:401-406).

For this I set the fires burning at the navel in the stomach and I Myself am that fire. And by working the blowers of the *Prana* and *Apana* airs day in and day out, I consume food in quantities that just cannot be measured. It is I who digests the four types of food: dry, fatty, cooked and raw. Thus I am all creatures, I am their life (that is, the food) and I am the digestive fire that burns and digests this food that sustains life. What more can I tell you about my all-encompassing nature? There is nothing in this world other than Me. I pervade everywhere. But then you will ask Me why one sees some creatures happy and others unhappy? (15:407-412). If you are harbouring doubts like this then I shall remove them completely. (15:414).

Now look, it is I alone who pervade everything and everywhere. Nothing is different from Me. But I appear to individual creatures according to individual intellect. Sound is the property of space but different musical instruments give different sounds. In the same way my appearance results differently in different creatures. (15:415-

416). If an ignorant person and a wise person both see a sapphire string then the ignorant person may think it is a snake but the wise person will know it as a sapphire string. (15:419). Similarly persons of knowledge gain happiness from Me but the ignorant ones feel unhappy. (15:420).

Actually the ego in the hearts of all creatures that asserts, "I am so and so" is also Me. But by keeping company of saints, by practice of yoga and knowledge, serving one's Guru with detachment and by good behaviour this ignorance disappears and the ego dissolves into the Self and when this happens the individual knows Me and with the realisation of the Self he becomes happy. (15:421-424).

On the other hand, those whose ego is involved only with the body by serving it and by bragging about the worldly affairs, follow the path of desires, acting to fulfil them, keeping in mind the goal of worldly pleasures and *attainment of heaven after death*.[9] Because of this the choicest parts of sorrow come to their lot. Just as what we see while awake becomes the base for what we see in dreams similarly I am the base for the illusion due to their ignorance. (15:425-428). It is an established fact that I alone am the root of Knowledge as well as of ignorance. Therefore Arjuna, when the Vedas did not understand my real nature, they attempted to understand Me and that resulted their splitting into branches.[10] But even though the branches are different they all lead to the understanding of my real nature. Even *Shrutis* (Upanishads) stumble when they reach the great Principle ('*Aham Brahmasmi*' or 'I am the Brahman') and where the Shrutis are unable to express my real nature, it is I who reveals it. And I alone am the knower of that pure Knowledge of the Self where everything including the *Shrutis* dissolves. (15:431-436). I know my unique form free of the limiting qualifications[11]

9 *Even after the deep influence of the Upanishads, common man still thinks of attainment of heaven after death. This is partly due to the influence of the Puranas who have perpetuated the myth of heaven of the Vedic times.*
10 *It is not clear whether this means Vedas split into three Vedas: Rig-, Yajur- and Sama- or into the components of the Vedas viz. Samhita, Brahmana, Aranyaka and Upanishads.*
11 *As explained in the footnote 2 in the beginning of this chapter, Shri Krishna*

of worldly affairs and I am the cause of its realisation. (15:438). When the Knowledge that swallows this ignorance itself dissolves, it is not possible to state whether it exists or it does not. (15:440). Thus, while explaining to Arjuna how he pervades both the living and non-living universe Shri Krishna ultimately described the pure form without limiting qualifications. (15:442).

On this Arjuna remarked, "What a wonder that the more one knows about the Self, the more interesting it becomes! Oh Shri Krishna, please tell me again about the unqualified or attributeless form which you described while telling me about your all-pervasiveness." (15:445-447)

LIMITING QUALIFICATIONS

On this, Shri Krishna expressed his happiness at Arjuna's question and went on to describe His two types of forms. (15:461-462). When it comes to describing the pure form, words and spoken texts (Vedas) are unable to do so and are silent. In order to explain why the attributeless form is indescribable, Shri Krishna now first tells about qualifications because it is necessary to discuss about qualifications itself, first. (15:467-469)

Shri Krishna said, "Arjuna, this world is like a town with very small population consisting of only two individuals. There is a third individual also but he cannot bear to hear even the mention of the name of either of the two. But let us talk about him later. First let Me tell about the two who have come to live in this town. (15:471-474)

Of these two, one is blind, foolish and crippled while the other has all his organs in good shape. Because they are living in the same town they happened to give company to each other. One of them is named *Kshara*[12] and the other as *Akshara*. This world is completely filled by the two. Now Arjuna, I shall explain to you

(as Bhagwan) though attributeless is still restricted due to limiting qualification of the universe.
12 Kshara means perishable and Akshara means unpeprishable.

who is *Kshara* and who is *Akshara* and what their characteristics are. (15:475-477).

A *KSHARA* PERSON

From the *Mahat* principle to a blade of grass, be it small or big, moving or stationary; all that is intelligible to both mind and intellect; all that is produced from the five principles that acquire name and form and moulded into the cast of the three attributes (*Sattva, Rajas* and *Tamas*); the substance from which living beings are cast; the dice with which Time gambles; that which can be known or understood through improper knowledge; that which is created and destroyed every moment; that which enters the woods of delusion and creates the world, and why go far, is known as the universe, has already been explained earlier as the Field formed out of eightfold *Prakriti* and thirty six principles. But why repeat all that? I have already told you about it a short while ago through the analogy of the *Ashwattha* tree. (15:478-485). The conscious Self, having imagined this world to be its place of residence, has become like it. Like a lion that sees its reflection in the well water and jumps into it in anger, the non-dual Self assumes duality. In this way, the Soul, imagining the world to be its residence, slumbers in it, disregarding its primary form. Under the influence of sleep he snores that "I am happy" or "I am unhappy" and talks incoherently using words like "I" and "mine". Dreaming that "This is my father", "This is my mother", "I am fair skinned or dark or perfect", "Are not this son, this wealth, this woman, mine?" The soul wandering in the forest that is this world and the heaven is known as *Kshara Purusha* or person. (15:486-493).

When the Knower of the field *(Kshetrajnya)*, in the state which is known as the individual *(jiva)*, forgets his essential nature as the Self and becomes like all creatures, then he is known as *Kshara* Person. (15:494-495). But his state of being the Self is completely intact disturbed even when in the body therefore he is called *Purusha* and also because he resides in the body – albeit in a somnolent state – he is again called *Purusha*[13] And because he has been tainted by the limiting qualifications he has been falsely accused as being a *Kshara* or perishable. He becomes freed of the qualifications once they are destroyed. The qualifications make him impermanent and thus by virtue of the impermanence of the qualifications, he has been called *Kshara*. *Thus all living creatures should be called Ksharas.* (15:496-501).

AKSHARA AND SUPERIOR PERSONS

Akshara Person: Arjuna, now let Me explain what *Akshara* is. The second aspect of the individual which is *Akshara* is an intermediary i.e. one behaving like a disinterested witness. He does not get involved with knowledge or with ignorance. He does not assume non-dualistic nature by proper or true knowledge nor does he assume dualistic nature by means of improper knowledge. Detached non-awareness is its natural form. When earth is mixed with water and made into a lump of mud for making a pot, it no longer remains the original earth, it has yet to take a form and become a pot. The state of the *Akshara Purusha* is similar to this in between state. (15:502-505). It may be compared with the sleep state that occurs between the state of wakefulness and the dreaming state. *The state of ignorance, which lies between the stage when delusion of the world has vanished, but Knowledge of the Self has not yet occurred is the state known as Akshara.* (15:507-508).

Manifest and Unmanifest: The place where the individual soul dissolves after all qualifications vanish, where qualifications and the qualified individual remain in a state of dissolution is called the **Unmanifest**. Complete ignorance occurs during the state of deep sleep[14] therefore it is called the *seed aspect* of the **Unmanifest**

---

13 *Puri means town; body is likened to a town in which the Soul resides as stated earlier.*
14 *A normal person is in one of the three states: Wakefulness (Jagriti), Dream (Swapna) and Sleep (Sushupti). When we observe objects we see them (in our*

in Vedanta Philosophy while the dream state and the state of wakefulness are its seed-*fruit aspects*. This seed aspect is the place of the *Akshara* Person. From this place originates the false knowledge that makes the states of wake fulness and dream to spread and journey through the thought-forests of the intellect. Arjuna, the place from where the individual raises the world and where the Manifest and the Unmanifest meet is the state called the *Akshara* Person. (15:510-515).

The states of wakefulness and dream that the *Kshara* person experiences, by taking on a body, arise from this abode of the *Akshara* Person. These two states arise from the sleep state well-known as the state of ignorance and is one step lower than the state of attainment of Brahman. Really speaking, if the individual had not reached the wakeful or dream states from the state of sleep then he would have reached the state of the Brahman. But instead it goes to dream state with the vision of *Field (Kshetra)* and the *Knower of the Field (Kshetrajnya)* due to the influence of *Prakriti* and *Purusha*. This *Akshara Purusha* is the root of the inverted world tree. The reason why he is called a *Purusha* or individual when he is really a Soul is that he takes a slumber in the town of *Maya*. Also, the state in which the comings and goings of passions – which is a type of ignorance – is not felt, is verily the sleep state. Therefore this *Akshara Purusha* does not get destroyed by itself and nothing except Knowledge can destroy it[15] and hence he is well-known as Akshara in the great principle of the Vedanta philosophy. *Thus,*

---

mind's eye) by the illumination from the Consciousness, Chitta or Self. After the mind sees the object, it deliberates on the object seen referring to memory for its definition. The sleep state is that of ignorance without this illumination, while the other two are states in which knowledge, not the spiritual kind but false or non-spiritual or worldly kind exists through mind and memory. Sleep state is like a dormant seed hence these is a beeja or seed aspect. In the other two states thoughts emerge and in the wakeful state there also actions. This is the seed-fruit aspect. But even all this occurs under the power of Self that occupies the body.
15 Akshara Purusha is not Self but just short of it as will be seen from the last sentence which says he is the Consciousness qualified by Maya. Knowledge destroys Maya and turns Akshara into self. Kshara is the Individual.

Akshara Purusha is actually the Consciousness which, due its being qualified by Maya, assumes the form of an individual (Jiva). (15:516-525)

Superior Person (Purushottama): From the false knowledge arise the two states namely that of wakefulness and of dream, which dissolve themselves into deep ignorance. When that ignorance disappears and one faces Knowledge, the latter destroys the ignorance and after giving you an experience of the Brahman destroys itself, similar to the fire which consumes itself after burning wood. Thus, after Knowledge has destroyed ignorance and destroyed itself, the state of experience of the Self, which remains without Knowledge itself, should be considered the **Superior Being or Purushottama.** This third type of person is different from the two *(Kshara* and *Akshara)* discussed earlier. Just as the state of wakefulness is different from the two other states, namely the sleep and the dream states in that the experiences differ, (15:526-530), similarly the Superior Being is different from the *Kshara* and *Akshara* (15:531). He is different from them in the manner that fire, though intrinsically existing in wood is different from it. (15:532). No trace of the three states of dream, sleep and wakefulness remains there and because all the three states have been nullified, neither monistic nor dualistic state is experienced nor is experienced 'being' and 'not being'. Such a state is called the *Superior Being,* which those in the state of *jiva-hood,* call Supreme Soul *(Paramatma).* But calling him by such a name is possible only by those who have not yet dissolved themselves in Him and who are thus still individual souls. Arjuna, only a person standing on the shore can speak about a person drowning in the river similarly, the Vedas are able to speak about superior and inferior only by staying on the border of discrimination. Therefore they consider *Kshara* and *Akshara* as inferior as compared with the Superior Being and identify Him with the form of the Supreme Soul. Understand therefore that the term "Supreme Soul" thus signifies the Superior Being. (15:534-540).

Otherwise, the supreme Soul is such that He is spoken about without actually speaking, about whom knowing nothing is actually same as knowing Him, who occurs without any happening. There, even the aspect of "I am that" vanishes, the speaker becomes the spoken and view disappears along with the viewer. (15:541-542).

When the seer and the seen both vanish, can anybody say that something has survived behind? Whatever one experiences in this situation should be considered as His form. The light other than that which illuminates an object, the controller who is other than the controlled, exist in His own form. He who is the realm of sound that gives the power to hear, the realm of the taste that gives the power to taste, the cosmic bliss that creates the bliss, the pinnacle of perfection, Supreme Person among all persons, the resting place of the repose, bliss of the bliss, brilliance of the brilliance and the place of dissolution of the zero of the big naught, who is beyond growth and dissolution, who is larger than the largest, it is He that bears the universe without becoming it. (15:545-550).

I AM BEYOND ALL

The universe and the Supreme Soul are not different. (15:552). He is the one responsible for the expansion and contraction of the universe. He does not change even if He takes the form of the universe or does not go anywhere even when the universe dissolves. He does not get destroyed by anything under any circumstances. He can be compared only with Himself. I am that unique Entity who illumines Himself, in whom no duality occurs, he who is beyond form and superior to *Kshara* and *Akshara* and therefore the Vedas and the people call Him, (i.e. Me), as Supreme Person. Dawn of Knowledge has arrived for one who understands Me as such. After the onset of Knowledge the whole universe appears to be meaningless to him. Once he attains My Knowledge, he no longer gets deceived by the illusion that is this world. Knowing my real form he gives up the sense of distinction and says, "I myself am the self-created, true bliss, existing everywhere" and he knows Me as not being different from himself. It is difficult to state that he has known everything because no sense of duality exists within him. Therefore Arjuna he alone is worthy of My devotion just as sky alone is fit to embrace sky. (15:554-565). Only he who becomes one with Me can be devoted to Me. Otherwise, how can the devotional relation develop?. (15:567-568). The relation between Me and the devotion of My devotee with the sense of oneness with Me, can be compared only with the Sun and its brilliance which are not different from each other. (15:570).

IN PRAISE OF THE GITA

Thus, the fragrance of the *Gita*, which can be obtained only through the *Shastras*, spread from the lotus of the *Upanishads* right from the beginning of this chapter. The *Gita* is the essence extracted by churning the Vedas, using the intellect of the sage Vyasa. It is the river of the nectar of Knowledge, the seventeenth phase of the moon of bliss; or another goddess Laxmi rising from the Ocean of Milk of contemplation, therefore there is no one other than Me who can know this from the heart in his own words and letters. When *Kshara* and *Akshara* persons confronted it (the *Gita*), it avoided them and surrendered to Me completely. Therefore the *Gita*, which you are now listening to, is my faithful spouse. Really speaking, this *Gita* is not a *shastra*, which can be told through words. It is the science of conquering this world. The letters of this *Gita* are *mantras* that can lead you to attaining the Self. Arjuna, by telling you this *Gita* I have brought forth my secret treasure. And if my conscious Self is compared to Lord Shiva then you who have managed to bring out the Ganga of the *Gita* from his head are like the Sage Gautama.[16] (15:571-579). Arjuna, because the impurity

---

16 *According Puranic legend kings Sagara and Bhagiratha brought the River Ganga from heavens to earth and because her force would be unbearable for the earth, Shiva let it first fall on his head before letting it out on the earth. The above reference however refers to River Godavari near Nasik which flows through Maharashtra and Andhra Pradesh. The story is that Rishis wanted a river similar to Ganga in the south to help them in their spiritual path. At that*

of the three attributes has left you, you have become My residence along with the *Gita*. The Gita is my creeper of knowledge and he who understands it becomes free of all delusions. (15:582-583). But what is there to wonder if after delusion vanishes one understands the *Gita* perfectly? That Knowledge of the Self leads him to the form of the Self. After this Knowledge of the Self is attained *Karma* also dissolves realising that its life work is over. When the pinnacle of Knowledge is installed over the temple of *Karma, Karma* ceases automatically. Therefore a person who has attained Knowledge has no reason to perform duties. Thus said the Saviour of the destitute. (15:585-588).

~∞~

time Rishi Gautama who had his hermitage there, was doing penance and had enough spiritual power to bring Ganga down (many rivers are commonly called Ganga). The rishis played a trick by making a straw cow and showing as if she was eating the grain crop in the nearby field belonging to Gautama. To drive the cow away from his field Gautama charged a darbha grass with a mantra and threw it in her direction. The cow "died" and the rishis insisted that Gautama perform atonement which would consist of brining Ganga down in that region. After a long penance God was pleased and granted Gautama's wish for the river. The river is often called Gautami for this reason.

16

Divine And Demoniacal Endowments

THE TWO ENDOWMENTS[1]

A subject for which one develops a liking penetrates the mind deeper and deeper and that is called "love". It is natural that curious persons, who have not experienced this love, should feel worried about whether they would gain Knowledge and having gained it how it would last. Therefore it is necessary to first ponder over the questions: "How that pure Knowledge may be attained and how it will last after it is attained?" Or "Why am I not attaining that Knowledge? Or "Which is that powerful anti-Knowledge entity that would set one on the wrong path?"

Shri Krishna will now speak in this chapter in order to satisfy the wishes of the curious seekers so that they would get rid of those things that are impediments in the path of knowledge and concentrate on those things that increase it. He will sing the praises

---

1 The term endowment is used here to mean natural quality or property.

of the Divine endowment that gives rise to Knowledge and increases peace. Similarly, the terrible nature of the demoniacal endowment, which supports the evil emotions like anger and enmity due to knowledge related to sense objects, will also be described. During the discussions in the ninth chapter it was mentioned in passing that these two natures cause good and bad effects and thus the topic has already been introduced. This topic should have been discussed in detail there but other topics came up, therefore Shri Krishna is explaining it now. This sixteenth chapter may therefore be considered as an extension of the earlier chapter. But enough of this introduction! The present topic concerns the fact that the power of these two endowments causes a good or a bad form to be imparted to Knowledge. (16:53-64).

Now listen first to the nature of the Divine endowment, which guides the seekers like a flame, illuminating the path through the darkness of delusion. Collection (or accumulation) of several objects, which support one another, is called wealth in this world. Divine wealth creates happiness and one gets it as a Divine gift and therefore it is called *Divine endowment*. (16:65-67).

THE TWENTY-SIX DIVINE ENDOWMENTS

Fearlessness: Shri Krishna says, "The best among the qualities of this Divine endowment is fearlessness. (16:68). He who does not allow ego to develop while he is working or while at rest is not afraid of this world. When non-duality pervades the mind he realises that the whole universe is filled with Brahman and he abandons even mentioning the word fear. Spirit of non-duality destroys fear. These are the indications of the quality called *fearlessness* and it is part of the path towards true Knowledge. (16:70-73).

Purity: Now the quality called *purity of the mind* is to be recognised by the following indications. (16:74). After one gives up the tendency towards desires and doubts and after casting off of the burden of *Rajas* and *Tamas* attributes, the intellect is attracted towards contemplation about the Self. The intellect does not waver at all even when enticed by sense objects. Intellect becomes dedicated having developed a liking for the form of the Self. (16:77-78). This is what is called purity of the mind. (16:80).

Steadiness: Concentrating and involving oneself completely in one of the two paths, i.e. the path of Knowledge or the path of yoga, whichever is suitable for attaining Self while abandoning other tendencies of the mind and ridding one's mind of all doubts, is the third quality called *steadiness* in Knowledge and Yoga. (16:81-82, 84).

Charity: Practising *charity* by helping a distressed person in every possible way and in all sincerity even if he were an enemy, giving whatever one can and not sending him away empty handed is a quality which shows the path to real Knowledge. (16:85, 87-88).

Self-restraint: Now listen to the indications of *self-restraint.* A *yogi* dissociates the organs from the sense objects. Also he does not permit the breath of sense objects via the sense organs, to touch the mind. For this purpose he binds the organs in the chains of discipline and controls them. By lighting the fires of detachment in the organs, he expels from hidden in the corners of the mind the tendencies for sense objects. He ceaselessly observes routines stricter than those of breath control *(pranayama).* These are the indications of what is called *self-restraint.* (16:89-93).

Yajna or sacrifice: Now I shall briefly tell about the indications of *Yajna or sacrifice.* Everyone, from a Brahmin to a woman should do religious actions according to the rightful code of conduct appropriate to him or her, in the manner prescribed in the *Shastras.* For example, a Brahmin observing the six rituals and a *Shudra* making obeisance to him, both lead to a like sacrifice from each of them. Thus, everyone should perform the sacrifice as per his entitlement but let it not be contaminated by the poison of the desire of fruits. And let one not think out of ego that, "Oh! I have performed the sacrifice", for the code set by the Vedas must in any case be obeyed. Arjuna, this is what is called "appropriately conducted sacrifice". Such a sacrifice should be considered as a knowledgeable guide in the path of liberation. (16:93-99).

Personal study of the Vedas: God is the subject of discussion in the Vedas which one should constantly study in order to understand Him. For attaining Self, Brahmins should contemplate over the writings about Brahman in the Vedas. Others should frequently sing the songs praising God or utter His name. This is what is called the *personal study of the Vedas.* (16:103-105).

Austerity: Now I shall tell you the meaning of austerity *(Tapas).* To give away one's all possessions is to put them to best use and that is the real austerity. (16:106). Straining one's body, organs and life force for experiencing the Self is called austerity. All other types of austerities which people talk about must be critically examined. Austerity keeps alive in a person the sense of discrimination which separates *"I am the living soul"* feeling, from the *"I am the body"* feeling. While contemplating on the Self, the intellect turns inwards. Just as both sleep and dreams vanish when one wakes up, similarly that which makes a person turn to contemplating about the Self is the real nature of *austerity.* (16:108-112).

Uprightness: Life may be of diverse type but all have similar life-force; similarly to show gentleness to all is called *uprightness.* (16:113).

Non-injury: To behave by words, actions and feelings with the intention of making the world happy is the indication of non-injury. (16:114).

Truthfulness: Truthfulness is pointed but soft and bright but comfortable. Just as one cannot find a medicine that can cure a disease but is not bitter, similarly a simile cannot be found for truthfulness. Water sprinkled on the eyes does not hurt the eyeballs but the same water is capable of breaking stones. Similarly truthfulness is hard like iron in crushing doubts but is sweet to the ears. With its strength it penetrates the principle of the Brahman.

In short, that which is sweet but not deceptive like the song of a trapper, (16:115-121) and which does not hurt and proves to be true and which is without evil aspects, is to be considered as *truthfulness*. (16:124).

Absence of wrath: The state of mind in which a person does not get angry even by words that would normally make even a boy angry is called *absence of wrath*. (16:128-130).

Relinquishment: Freeing themselves of the "I am the body" attitude, intelligent people give up worldly affairs. This is called *relinquishment*. (16:134-135).

Tranquillity: After knowing the knowable (i.e. experiencing the Brahman), the state in which both the knower and the knowledge dissolve is called *tranquillity*. (16:137).

Non-calumny: When one sees somebody drowning, he does not bother whether that person is a Brahmin or a untouchable but thinks that saving him is his first duty. (16:143). Such a person, instead of bothering about the failings of another, tries to overcome those by his own good qualities and does not taunt him about them. (16:149-150). Not taunting people for their failings by comparing them with perfect persons is the indication of *non-calumny* and there is no doubt that this is one of the resting stages on the path to liberation. (16:152-153).

Compassion: Compassion is that which, while helping to remove the miseries of the unfortunate, does not let one distinguish between high and low. (16:155). When he sees the sorrows of others he thinks nothing of sacrificing everything he possesses in order to mitigate them. If he encounters a destitute, he does not go a step further without satisfying him. (16:157-158). His life is spent in helping the miserable. Such a person is compassion personified and I am indebted to him from birth. (16:162).

Lack of greed: The state of mind when one is averse to enjoying the pleasures of this world or the world beyond even if they are available to him at his mere wish, and what more, when one has no desire of any kind for sense-pleasures is the indication of *lack of greed*. (16:166-167).

Gentleness: A tender, loving behaviour towards all creatures (16:170) and a life devoted to welfare of the world is the indication of *gentleness*. (16:174)

Humility: When a person feels ashamed of being imprisoned in this body of three and a half hand-span length,[2] of taking birth and dying again and again, of remaining constricted in the womb before being born as a human being, that feeling is the sign of *humility*. Only persons without blemish feel so ashamed, but others take pleasure in it. (16:179-182)

Absence of fickleness: When the life-force is controlled the organs of action become slow. Similarly, just as sunrays do not come out after sunset, the sense-organs become dim after the mind is controlled. Thus all the ten organs become less active, by the control of the mind and the life force. This condition is called *absence of fickleness*. (16:183-185)

Spiritual vigour: When the determination to follow the path of Knowledge for attaining God is very strong then there is no dearth of strength. (16:186). The individual, anxious to realise his master, the Soul, follows the difficult path towards the formless Brahman treating the sense objects like poison. In this path he is not hindered by the ritualistic rules nor is he attracted by the great *Siddhis*. This quality of mind, which automatically goes towards God, is called *spiritual vigour*. (16:188-190).

Forgiveness: Now, forgiveness is the quality by which even though one is the most tolerant among others is not proud about being so. (16:191).

Fortitude: Even when flooded with calamities, one faces them with

---

2 *This refers to the soul; the rest of the paragraph refers to the painful and humiliating stage of being constricted in the womb before being born in a child's body.*

courage as Rishi Agastya did.[3] He tolerates all distresses of spiritual, Divine and earthly origin. The quality which keeps a person from feeling distressed in mind by maintaining one's courage is called *fortitude*. (16:193-196).

Cleanliness: Cleanliness is like the purity of the Ganges water filled in a clean gold pot. Doing actions without desire of fruits and maintaining discretion in the mind is the indication of cleanliness from inside and outside. (16:197-198).

Absence of envy: And just as Ganges water removes a bather's sins and troubles and at the same time also supports the trees on the bank while flowing to meet the ocean, (16:199), similarly a person without envy liberates those who are bound to this world and removes the difficulties of the afflicted. In fact, he gains his goal by helping others be happy. Not only that the idea of hurting anybody for his own success never touches his mind. These are signs of *absence of envy*. (16:200-204).

Lack of pride: And just as Ganga felt shy when Shiva bore her on His head, similarly feeling shy after one gets recognition is the quality called *lack of pride*.

These are the twenty-six qualities of Divine endowment and are the gift of the great emperor of Liberation. (16:207). How much can I describe it to you? It has to be experienced by itself. (16:212).

THE SIX DEMONIACAL ENDOWMENTS

Now, the demoniacal endowment is the creeper of sorrow in the heart and it is full of thorns of failings. Understand it thoroughly because even if an object is fit only to be rejected and is of no use to us, yet one should understand its nature properly before rejecting it. The set of serious defects, which are brought together in order to

---

3 *This refers to a Puranic myth in which Rishi Agastya drank the ocean because it had offended him. Another version is that he drank the ocean to expose Daityas who had hidden in the ocean during a war with Gods.*

subject beings to horrible tortures of hell, is actually the demoniacal endowment. It is the storehouse of all failings. (16:213-216).

Hypocrisy: The principal among the failings of the demoniacal endowment is hypocrisy. (16:217). If one publicises his practising of *Dharma* (the code of righteous behaviour) which is the companion and friend in this world and the next, then instead of helping to take him towards liberation, it actually becomes a hindrance. The righteous behaviour becomes in effect, unrighteous behaviour *(Adharma)* and this must be considered as *hypocrisy*. (16:222-223).

Arrogance: Like a beggar who feels himself to be great just by receiving a single alms, a person becomes haughty due to possession of women, wealth and learning, and due to listening to praise and honour bestowed upon him. (16:227). Swelling by pride of being rich is what is called *arrogance*. (16:229).

Conceit: God is venerable to the whole world because the world believes in the Vedas. People enthusiastically praise the Vedas and God because they desire to gain a high position and immortality. But sometimes a person burns with jealousy and says that he is going to swallow God, poison the Vedas and destroy their power by his strength. Overcome by pride, he is unable to tolerate people uttering God's name. His nature is such that he gives step-motherly treatment to his own father for the fear that he will be a claimant to his wealth. Such a person is said to possess *conceit* and is arrogant. Such conceit is a certain path to hell. (16:230-236).

Wrath: A person gets angry by seeing the happiness in others. (16:237). He is annoyed at seeing the learning, development, wealth and fortune of others. This is what is called *wrath* (resentment). (16:242).

Harshness: He whose mind is like a snake-hill (ant-hill), eyes like the throw of an arrow, speech like a shower of cinders and whose other actions also are like a sharp saw and whose all external and internal behaviour is troublesome to others is a very contemptible person and an icon of *harshness*. (16:243-245).

Ignorance: Now I shall tell you the sign of ignorance. (16:245). The condition of being blind to the differences between good and evil deeds, (16:249) and lack of understanding of what is good and what is bad is called *ignorance.* (16:251-252).

Thus I have told you about the signs of all the six failings. (16:252). The demoniacal endowment has become strong because of these six failings. That it is founded only on six failings does not mean that it is unimportant. (16:255-256). On the other hand the coming together of these six can create horrible consequences to a person. He, who, ignoring his inclination towards the path of liberation, immerses himself in the worldly affairs, descends down the ladder of rebirth to states even below that of the non-moving species (trees etc.). Thus I have explained to you the two types of endowments. (16:259-264).

WARNINGS ABOUT DEMONIACL ENDOWMENTS

Of these two endowments, the first i.e. the Divine endowment is like the dawn before the sunrise of liberation *(moksha)* while the second, the demoniacal endowment is really like iron shackles in the form of delusion. (16:265-266). There are well-established modes of behaviour of people possessing these two types of endowments. (16:271). Out of these the Divine endowment has been discussed earlier in detail. Now listen carefully to what I am going to tell about the demoniacal endowment. (16:275). The demoniacal endowment does not become evident unless it has taken shelter in the body. (16:277). After taking shelter in the body it takes possession of it and grows. Arjuna, I shall now tell you the signs of a person who is afflicted by the demoniacal endowments. (16:279-280).

Signs in afflicted Persons: His mind is dark about the desirability of performing meritorious actions and/or the non-desirability of performing sinful actions. (16:281). People afflicted with demonical endowment do not understand what is action and what is non-action and they do not even dream about what is purity. (16:284). They do not bother about prescribed actions, do not follow the path of their elders and do not even know the language of proper behaviour (16:287). Their behaviour is without inhibitions and they are always averse to truth. (16:289). They are evil by nature even though they may not have done anything. Now I shall tell you about the strange things they talk. (16:292).

Defiance of the Vedas: This universe has been going on from time immemorial and is controlled and ruled by God. Vedas clearly and openly decide about what is moral and what is immoral. People considered as immoral by the Vedas are punished by being placed in hell. Those who are considered as moral go to heaven where they remain happily.[4] Now, these people (afflicted with demoniacal endowment) say that "This arrangement, which has been going on since time immemorial, is all false. They further say that people obsessed with *yajnas* perform them and get cheated. Those who love God worship idols; and those who become yogis by wearing ochre coloured clothes get deceived by the illusion of *Samadhi*. One should enjoy whatever one can get by one's own capability. There is no merit other than this. Real sin is not being able to enjoy sensual pleasures due to physical weakness. Though it is a sin to kill the rich, the wealth one gets from it is the result of merit. If it is objectionable for the strong to destroy the weak then how is it that big fish that eat small fish do not become extinct? Marriages are arranged on auspicious time between boys and girls of good families with the intention of producing progeny but who arranges the marriages of birds and animals that produce abundant progeny? Has anybody ever been poisoned by stolen wealth? Or, has anybody ever been afflicted by leprosy because he had loved and had sexual relations with another man's wife? Vedas say that God is the ruler of this universe and He rewards or punishes people according to their righteous or unrighteous behaviour and that the fruits of the deeds in this world are obtained in the next. But one can neither see God nor the other world therefore it is all untrue. If a person

---

4 *It is understood that this is after death.*

who does meritorious or sinful deeds himself dies then who is there left to enjoy or suffer for them? Just as Indra lives happily with Urvashi in heaven, the worm in the mud also lives contentedly in it. Therefore heaven and hell are not the consequences of meritorious or sinful deeds because the lust is satisfied in both places. The world is created when man and woman come together inspired by lust; therefore whatever is beneficial to the world is all supported by the lust. And because of the mutual enmity it is the lust that destroys the world."

Thus the people afflicted with demoniacal endowment say that there is no reason for the creation of the world other than the sensual pleasure. Now let us not discuss these evil things further because they cause strain to the tongue. (16:295-313).

Evil Nature: They despise God and spend time in meaningless talk. They even have already decided that God does not exist and they openly profess that they are atheists. Atheism is well entrenched in them. Belief in the existence of heaven or fear of hell has completely disappeared from their minds. They are then caught in the trap of the body and like a bubble of gas in dirty waters they get immersed in the mire of sensual desires. (16:314-317). Persons with demoniacal endowment are born for destruction of people. They are like living victory towers of sin. Like fire that does not bother about what it burns, they destroy everybody who comes near them. I shall describe the enthusiasm with which they do all this destruction. (16:319-322).

They sustain insatiable lust, the foremost among the insatiable desires and add to it hypocrisy and pride. As they grow in age these persons with demoniacal endowment become arrogant. To the obstinacy is added foolishness too. And then who can say what they decide to do? Right from birth their tendency is to do things that create misery for others or destroy their life. They treat rest of the world as trivial and brag about their own deeds. They spread the net of their desires in all directions. The persons with demoniacal endowment increase enthusiastically their load of sins. (16:322-329).

All their actions are thus governed by this approach while they live and they worry in the same way about their future after death. (16:330). The boundless worry does not leave them even at the time of death. Pining for futile sense-objects the persons with demoniacal endowment endlessly worry about attaining them. The idea that there is nothing better than enjoyment of sex is fixed in their minds. They are then ready to go to heaven or hell or to the four corners of the world. (16:333-336).

***The Trap of Desire and Anger:** Like a fish swallowing bait, desire for sense objects makes them heedless. If they do not get what they desire then they trap themselves within the cocoon of dry hope that they will someday get it and if the desire is still not fulfilled, then hatred is immediately born. And then they feel that there is no valour other than desire and anger. (16:337-339). The individuals who are pushed away from the precipice of desire crash on the rocks of anger below but even then their love for desire and anger does not diminish. Now, even if the desire arises in the mind, how can it be satisfied without money? Therefore they raid the world for earning enough money to satisfy the desires. They waylay a person and kill him or loot somebody. They scheme and plot to destroy somebody. (16:340-344). They kill others and loot their wealth and feel happy only when they get it. (16:347).

The person with demoniacal endowment says, "I have taken away the wealth of many. I am happy and satisfied." And immediately, greedy thoughts of looting more people arise in his mind. He decides to use his gains to earn more estate and own ultimately everything in this world by possessing everything that he sets his eyes on. He says, "I shall kill bigger enemies than what I have destroyed so far and I alone shall enjoy the wealth. Then they would become my servants. Besides, I shall destroy others and will be the master of all living and non-living things in the universe. I shall be the king of this mortal world and gain all happiness. Even Indra will be put to shame when he sees my splendour. How can anything fail when I apply my mind to it? Who is there more powerful than I to issue orders? Time may brag about its power as long as it has not seen the powerful me. I am really the bundle of all happiness. No doubt Kuber is wealthy but he is nothing compared to me; and even Vishnu, husband of the Goddess of wealth Lakshmi is not as wealthy as me. The greatness of my family, my friends and relatives is such that even Brahmadeo will be lower in comparison. Therefore none of those who consider themselves superior in the name of God can be compared with me. Now I shall revive the now-forgotten techniques of black magic and perform *yajnas* that will cause distress to people. As for people who sing my praises and entertain me through dances and dramas, I shall give them whatever they ask. I shall enjoy the pleasure of intoxicating food and drinks and of embracing women in these three worlds." (16:348-363).

Arjuna, the crazy persons of demoniacal endowment thus hope to smell the celestial flowers and babble away their thoughts like a person in delirium. Whirlwinds of hope are raised in the dust of their ignorance and spin through the sky of their daydreams. They desire endless sensual pleasures and then their daydreams get shattered. As delusions grow in their minds, their desire for sensual pleasures also grows. That gives shelter to sins. When sins become strong and numerous, he has to suffer like hell even while he is alive. Therefore the persons with demoniacal endowment reach (after death) a place where trees have leaves like sharpened swords, where there are mounds of embers and oceans of boiling oil rage. They reach hell where agonies are lined up and Yama the Lord of Death imposes fresh kinds of suffering every day. Even those who reach some better parts of hell spend their time in performing *yajnas*. Now, the *yajna* rituals are beneficial but these people, like those in show business, make a show of their performance and make the rituals fruitless. (16:364-376). Their *yajna* need not have proper arrangements like *kunda, vedi* or a *pandal,*[5] nor the usual materials. They are averse to following the prescribed rituals. They

---

5 *The platform for performing the yagna fire is known as vedi. The pit into which the oblations are offered is known as kunda. Pandal (Mandapa) is a temporary shed generally using cloth.*

cannot tolerate the names of deities and Brahmins uttered in their presence. (16:384-385).

Now who will attend *yajnas* such as theirs? But just as cunning people stuff a dead calf to make it look real and show it to the cow in order to get her milk to flow, these persons invite people for the *yajna* rituals and loot them by accepting presents from them. Thus they perform *yajna* for their own benefit and desire that others should lose everything. Then they make a fanfare and pretend that they have been initiated in the learning. With this false status these crafty people become all the more conceited and their ego and excesses double. Then they use their power to see that no name other than theirs is mentioned around. The ocean of arrogance overflows once their ego increases. Once arrogance gets unleashed then lust also rises and in the combination of the two, anger also flares up. (16:386-394). When ego intensifies and arrogance gets entangled in lust and anger and the two come together, will they not kill any creature they feel like killing? (16:396-397). These so-called initiated persons waste their own blood and flesh by getting obsessed with black magic. When they do this, the exertion they cause to their body really harasses Me who is the soul occupying the body. And when they harass other people by black magic, since I am in their bodies also, it is I who am really harassed. And whoever manages to escapes their attack by black magic, is bombarded by nasty talk. Saintly women, saints, donors, performers of *yajnas*, great *tapaswis*, *sanyasis*, or devotees and great souls which are My favourite abodes of residence, which have been rendered pure by fire-sacrifices, are the targets of their sharp poisonous talk. And now listen to what I do to these sinners who try to hold Me in enmity. (16:398-405).

HOW I PUNISH THEM

I punish the fools who bear human body but hate the world, by snatching their humanness and keeping them in the species of *Tama* attribute, of the type that has to suffer the worst kind of filth and tortures. They are made to be born as tigers, scorpions etc. in places where not even a blade of grass grows for them to eat. They bite their own flesh to feed their hunger and after death they are reborn in the same species. Or, I make them be born as snakes that burn their own skin by their own poison and confine them to holes. I do not permit these evil souls even a breathing time for taking rest. And I do not take them out of this situation even after millennia pass. But this is only the first stage of their journey towards the final destination. Then imagine the extent of tortures they would suffer when they reach there. Thus they reach this low state due to their demoniacal nature. Then I snatch whatever little rest they get in species like tiger. Then I put them in pitch darkness. Thus, these vile people reach this lowest state after suffering through all the species of *Tama* attribute. Even the tongue weeps when describing this *Tama* attribute and its very thought causes the mind to shudder. Alas! How these fools have earned hell! Why do they nurture the demoniacal endowment that leads to such a downfall! Therefore Arjuna, do not go anywhere near the place where persons with demoniacal endowment live and I advise you to give up the company of those who possess all the six aspects of it. (16:406-424). Wherever desire, anger and greed prevail is the place where inauspicious things grow. It is as if these three have been appointed as guides by all the sorrows in order that people experience them. Or it is as if all the sins have gathered together to push the sinners into hell. As long as these three failings do not arise in the mind there is no occasion for the *Rourava*[6] type of hell mentioned in the Puranas. These three cause misfortunes with ease, and pains become cheap. What is known as detriment in the world is not really detriment. Real detriment is these three. These three lowest types of failings are the gateway to hell. One who heartily embraces desire, anger and greed is fit to be honoured in the assembly in hell. Therefore I am telling you repeatedly to totally give up this harmful trio of desire, anger and greed. (16:425-432).

---

6 *It is one of the 21 kinds of hell to which sinners are supposed to be sent for different types of sins.*

One should bother about the four obligations (*Dharma* or righteous conduct, *Artha* or earning, *Kama* or conjugal life and *Moksha* or liberation) only after having got rid of the three failings. If anybody tells Me that a person can profit with these three emotions present in the mind, I am not going to listen to it. He, who is interested in personal welfare or fears self-destruction, should be alert and never give shelter to these three. (16:433-435).

He who has abandoned these three failings becomes happy as a body feels happy when it is rid of phlegm, wind and bile, or as a town becomes happy when freed from thefts, betrayal and gossip or like one's conscience when it is free from worldly, Divine and spiritual sufferings. (16:439). He gains the company of saints and gets set on the path of liberation. Then he crosses the wasteland of births and deaths with the power of the company of saints and help of prescribed code of conduct. Then he reaches the beautiful place of Guru's benevolence where bliss of the Self exists forever. There he meets mother Soul, the ultimate form of love and in her embrace the sounds of the world are not heard. One who rids himself of desire, anger and greed is only able to attain the Self. (16:441-444)

But he who is not inclined towards Self-realisation and keeps himself engrossed in passions commits self-destruction. He does not heed Vedas, which are like a father benevolent equally to all and a guiding lamp showing what is good and what is bad.

He does not bother about the do's and don'ts given in the *Shastras* and pampers the sense organs without considering the consequences. He does not leave the company of desire, anger and greed and obeys their dictate and leaving the straight path to liberation he goes by the side lanes of uncontrolled behaviour. He is not able to free himself even for a moment from these failings and he does not think about it even in his dreams. He misses the enjoyments of not only the world beyond but of this world as well. (16:445-450). Having got in the clutches of death while obsessed with sensual pleasures he misses them in this world and having become ineligible for the world beyond, forfeits them there too. How can then there be any scope for liberation? (16:452-453). Therefore Arjuna, he who is keen about self-advancement should refrain from showing disrespect to the edicts in the Vedas. (16:455). The disciple who listens sincerely to the advice given by the True Guru *(Sadguru)* gains Self-realisation. (16:457). Similarly Arjuna, he who desires to achieve success in the four obligations should be reverent to the *Shrutis* (Vedas) and *Smritis* (Codes of conduct). Whatever the *Shastras* advise to be avoided, those should be considered as insignificant as a grass blade even if it were a kingdom and whatever the *Shastras* advise to be accepted, should not be opposed even if it were a poison. How can anybody having such unshaken faith in the Vedas encounter anything harmful? There is no mother like *Shrutis,* which can free one from harmful influences and which enhances the benefits; therefore one should never forsake *Shrutis,* which take you towards unification with Brahman. Arjuna, you too should remain steadily devoted to them. Because you behaved according to *Dharma* in the past lives you have been reborn to bring the good *Shastras* into action and therefore you have consequently gained the name of "The Follower of *Dharma*". Therefore do not behave contrary to the Vedas. Actions should be planned as prescribed in the *Shastras.* Evil actions should be avoided. And whichever may really be your dutiful action it should be sincerely performed successfully. Today you are wearing the ring which bears the seal which the whole world recognises. Therefore, if you behave properly then people will also follow you, such is your worth. Thus Shri Krishna explained to Arjuna the signs of demoniacal endowment and their effects. (16:459- 469).

17

THREE KINDS OF FAITH

SCOPE OF THIS CHAPTER

In the last *Shloka* of the sixteenth chapter Shri Krishna came to a definite conclusion that one's behaviour whether good or bad must be guided by what is laid down in the *Shastras*. (17:21). At this, Arjuna said to himself, "What is this? How is it that there is no freedom of action without the rules set by the *Shastras*? (17:23). Who will bring the different *Shastras* together and come to a common conclusion from them? And even if one did come to a common conclusion, who would have time to act according to it? Who would live that long? And how can everybody find conditions relating to the *Shastras*, money, place and time, all to be favourable at the same time? Therefore it is not always possible to act according to the *Shastras* and in that case what should the ignorant seekers do?" The subject that Arjuna raised to get the advice of Shri Krishna is given in this seventeenth chapter. (17:26-30).

Arjuna said, "Why do you say that an individual cannot attain liberation without the *Shastras*? It can happen that the time

and the place are not favourable for the study of the *Shastras* or
a teacher is not available or the paraphernalia required for the
study are not available and also, one is not adequately endowed
with the intelligence due to unfavourable past *karmas*. In spite of
this, individuals would like to follow the example of those who
have performed actions as prescribed in the *Shastras* and enjoyed
happiness in the next world. (17:35-41). Considering the behaviour
of persons learned in all the *Shastras* to be ideal and, like a blind
person following the man in the front, they worship Shiva and other
deities, donate land etc., in charity, perform *yajnas* etc. Please tell
me what kind of fate out of the three: *Sattva, Rajas* and *Tamas* is
in their destiny? (17:42-45).

NATURE OF FAITH DEPENDS UPON ATTRIBUTES

Shri Krishna replied, "Arjuna, you find the study of *Shastras* as
a means of liberation, to be very difficult but it is not easy either to
attain liberation through faith alone. *Do not believe that on mere
faith will be enough.* Just as gold when mixed with other metals
loses its purity (17:49-51), similarly, though faith is basically pure,
it does not remain so when creatures have it since creatures are
naturally constituted from the three attributes *(gunas)* due to the
power of the timeless *Maya*. When two attributes become weak and
the third becomes strong, the natural tendencies of an individual
are moulded according to that dominant attribute. Then, the mind
gets moulded according to these natural tendencies; actions of
this individual follow the moulded mind, and the individual takes
rebirth according to the consequent karmas, the accumulated effect
of actions. (17:55-58).

Just as a seed disappears to create a tree and tree gets
incorporated later in the seed and the species of the tree does not
disappear even after millions of aeons of this cycle, similarly even
when a creature is reborn countless number of times, there occurs
no change in the three attributes. The faith, which has come to

the lot of a creature, is therefore according to these attributes. If *Sattva* attribute increases it leads to acquiring of knowledge but it is opposed by the other two attributes.

Pure faith based on *Sattva* attribute fructifies into liberation, but how will the *Rajas* and *Tamas* attributes remain quiet? When *Rajas* attribute overrides the Sattva attribute then the faith (now tainted by the *Rajas* attribute) sweeps the karmas together. And when the *Tamas* attribute becomes strong the faith gets tainted by *Tamas* and entangles the creatures in all sorts of sense-pleasures. Thus Arjuna, faith cannot be separated from the three attributes; faith is qualified by the three attributes *Sattva, Rajas* and *Tamas*. (17:62-67).

Water is the essence of life but it becomes fatal if mixed with poison, pungent if mixed with pepper and sweet if mixed with sugarcane juice. Similarly, when *Tamas* attribute increases, the creature is reborn each time with a faith that is *Tamasic* i.e. tainted by the *Tamas* attribute. Thus the faith of a creature dominated by *Tamas,* is also *Tamasic in nature.* Similarly the faith of a *Rajasic* (i.e. one tainted by *Rajas* attribute) creature is *Rajasic* and a *Sattvic* creature *Sattvic* (i.e. one tainted by *Sattva* attribute). Thus is this structure of the universe constituted from faith. But you should understand the impressions of the three attributes on it. Just as one can recognise the nature of the past karmas of a person from his condition in this life, similarly there are signs that can indicate the three forms of faith. I shall now describe these signs to you. (17:68-75).

Three types of faith: Those, whose constitution is made of *Sattvic* faith, have their thoughts inclined towards heaven. They acquire all knowledge and choosing proper types of *yajnas* they reach the abode of Gods. Those whose constitution is made of *Rajas* faith, worship the *Yakshas*[1] and demons who travel in the sky; but those who are constituted from *Tamas* attribute are like mountains of

---

1 *Type of demi-gods.*

sins and are extremely hard-hearted and cruel. They make sacrifice of animals in cremation grounds to propitiate spirits and ghouls. These persons who are made from the essence of *Tamas* attribute are the storehouse of *Tamasic* faith.

There are thus three types of faith which I am describing to you only because one should see that the *Sattvic* faith must be preserved and the remaining two types of faith namely *Rajasic* and *Tamasic* should be rejected. (17:76-83). He who nurtures this *Sattvic* faith does not find it cumbersome to the attain liberation. Even though he has not studied *Brahma-sutras*[2] or independently understood the principles of the Vedas, if he only follows the footsteps of those who have become venerable to the world by keeping their conduct according to the meaning of *Shrutis* and *Smritis* and lives with *Sattvic* faith, he gets same fruits as them. (17:84-87). He who emulates those who carefully perform actions as per the *Shastras* is saved even if he were a fool. (17:92).

Those who are not inclined towards the study of the *Shastras* from their heart and do not permit persons learned in the *Shastras* even to enter the town, those who tease their elders doing worship and mock during the discourses by the learned, behave like an atheist driven by the pride of their high status and arrogance due to wealth. They fill the *yajna* vessels with their own and others' blood and pour it in the burning *yajna* fire as sacrifice to inferior deities and further sacrifice young children to fulfil vows. To obtain boons from inferior deities they obstinately observe seven-day fasts and perform other rituals. Thus they plant the seeds of self-torture and torture of others in the *Tamasic* heart and reap the harvest. (17:93-99). They leave the path of the *Shastras* and rush hither and thither in the woods of delusion. They act under the influence of desires and consumed by anger, beat others. Otherwise they bury even Me in the ditches. The pain they cause to themselves and others are actually the pains caused to Me that is the Soul. One should not even utter the name of such a sinner but I had to mention all this in order that

---

2 *A composition giving collective teachings of the Upanishads.*

he is cast out. (17:103-106). Arjuna, if you see such persons then remember Me because there is no other atonement for it. Therefore one should always maintain *Sattvic* faith. (17:109-110).

Three types of diet: Secondly, one should keep in touch with those things that increase *Sattvic* faith and adopt a diet that increases the *Sattvic* nature. Even otherwise, there are no means more effective than diet for moulding one's nature. (17:111-112). A person gets afflicted by wind, phlegm or bile according to the food he eats. (17:114). Different chemicals are produced in the body according to what one eats, and these chemicals support the feelings in the mind. The state of the mind depends upon the chemicals therefore a *Sattvic* diet makes the *Sattvic* quality grow. Any other diet would lead to growth of the *Rajasic* and *Tamasic* natures. Listen carefully now to what a *Sattvic* diet is and what the indications of *Rajasic* and *Tamasic* diets are. (17:116-119).

I shall first explain to you how the same diet assumes three qualities. The cook has to prepare food according to the taste of the eater because the eater is a slave to the three attributes. He behaves with three different types of mental attitude naturally depending upon the three attributes. Therefore diet as well as actions like *yajna*, charity and austerity (penance or *tapas*) are of three types. But first I shall explain to you about diet. (17:120-124).

Sattvic food: If by good fortune an individual is inclined towards *Sattvic* attribute then his tendency is to eat sweet food. *Sattvic* food items are by nature juicy, sweet, oily[3] and properly cooked. They are not big in size and are soft to touch. They feel tasty and melt on the tongue. They are juicy and soft and the liquid part in

---

3 *The original word even in Gita is snigdha which means oily. It also means affectionate and tender as applied to feelings. In Dnyaneshwari the word used is "sneham" which means "friendship" as well as "oily". In the diet-conscious environment of today it may look strange that oily food is Sattvic. But this is in the days before fast food and overindulgence. It has been mentioned in Gurucharitra that fried food does not become stale and can be used over days, unlike food cooked in water. Of course any food will be harmful with over-indulgence.*

it is well absorbed within by the heat of the fire. Just as the words from Guru's lips are few but have great effect, similarly one feels satiated by eating even a little quantity of these items. Also, the *Sattvic* food not only tastes good while eating, its effects are also sweet. A *Sattvic* person has a special liking for such food. Such are the indications and qualities of a *Sattvic* diet. It increases the life-force of the eater. (17:125-132). This is the most appropriate diet for increasing the *Sattva* attribute. Growth of physical and mental strength is achieved by this diet. Then how can disease enter there? One who eats *Sattvic* food enjoys the fortune of good health. His actions bring happiness not only to himself but to others as well. Thus the effect of this *Sattvic* diet is great and is useful to the body from inside and outside. (17:134-137).

Rajasic food: Since we are on the topic of diet, I shall tell you about the kind of diet a *Rajasic* person loves. A *Rajasic* person loves food items that may not be digestible but are bitter like poison, burning like lime but sour, with large quantities of salt and salty materials added to it. The food he eats is so hot that it is as if he swallows fire itself. He asks for food that is so hot that one can even light a flame on the vapours coming from it. He eats sharp food items that hurt without wounding. Similarly he likes food that is dry like hot ashes but which will scald the tongue. He takes pleasure in eating hard food that needs grinding the teeth. What a *Rajasic* person likes more than life are items that are already hot and pungent, with mustard added on top causing the mouth and nose to burn, putting even fire to shame. Not satisfied with such food, the *Rajas* person who has madly surrendered himself to the taste-buds puts actually fire in the form of food in his stomach. He rolls on the ground after eating cloves and ginger and once he puts a glass of water to the mouth he does not put it away until empty. What he eats is not really food but it is like putting in the stomach items which will awaken the diseases in the body. As soon as they get this food, the diseases wake up and compete with each other. In this way, the *Rajas* type of food leads only to sorrow. (17:139-151).

Tamasic food: Now I shall also tell you about the food a *Tamasic* person likes but you will feel disgusted by it. Just as a buffalo eats the leftover soured food, a *Tamasic* person eats rotten and leftover food and does not even think that it will be harmful to him. Similarly, he eats the food cooked in the morning in the afternoon or the next day. A *Tamasic* person does not at all like well-cooked and fresh food. Instead, he prefers food that is half cooked or burnt. If perchance an occasion comes for him to eat good food, he keeps it aside like a tiger until it starts smelling. He eats in a common dish, with his wife and children, tasteless food which has been kept for a long time, has become dry or rotten, infested with worms and which has become like slime having been handled by children. He feels happy when he eats such dirty food but is not quite satisfied by this. The wonder is that he gets a strong desire for eating or drinking those things that have been prohibited by the *Shastras.* Arjuna, he has a liking for eating such desecrated food and he is immediately penalised for it, for when he consumes such food, he becomes liable for sin because what he eats is not food but an affliction which fills the stomach. He gets some experience of what it feels like to be beheaded or to enter a fire, but he bears all that and therefore one need not tell further about the effects of *Tamasic* food. (17:153-168).

THREE TYPES OF YAJNAS

Similar to diet, *yajnas* are also of three types. Out of these I shall tell you the characteristics of the *Sattvic yajna* first. (17:169-170).

Sattvic yajna: Persons who perform *Sattvic yajna* use all their inner tendencies for gaining spiritual benefits without bothering about selfish material gains (17:173). They get totally engrossed with body and mind in the *yajna* rituals without any personal desires or expectations, and being detached about everything except *Swadharma* (17:175-176), they perform the *yajna* systematically according to all its aspects prescribed by the Vedas, arranging for the *Kunda* (fire-pit), *pandal,* platform etc. in a way that would make it appear that the very *Shastras* have personified to make the preparations themselves. All the *yajna* materials are neatly arranged. If one sees the *yajna* pandal, one would feel that the very science of the *yajna* has come there for the sake of the *yajna*. The *yajna* thus performed systematically without any desire for self-importance (17:179-182), or without desire of fruits should be considered as *Sattvic yajna*. (17:184).

Rajasic yajna: Rajasic yajna is also performed in the same systematic manner, (17:185), but it is performed purely with the desire of benefits in mind, like attaining heaven after death or getting honoured in public as an initiated person. The *yajnas* performed for gaining fame and with desires are *Rajasic yajnas*. (17:187-188).

Tamasic yajna: Just as marriage among birds and animals does not require a priest other than the mating instinct similarly *Tamasic yajna* needs only a compulsion or insistence. (17:189). *Tamasic yajna* is not bound by any rules therefore a *Tamasic* person is a libertine. He is not bothered about the rules governing the rituals and he does not find *mantras* to be necessary. He is inimical to Brahmins so there is no thought of *Dakshina* (honorarium) to them. Even a fly does not get any food there. Money is wasted unnecessarily but there is no trace of faith in all this. Thus, the *yajna*, which superficially looks like one, is a *Tamasic yajna* – accompanied by faithlessness and waste. (17:191-195).

THREE TYPES OF *TAPAS*

Tapas (penance or austerity) also is of three types according to the three attributes. One of them leads to sin and another leads to emancipation. Now you may be anxious to know how *tapas* can be of three types therefore I shall tell you about *tapas* which may be corporal, vocal or mental. Now listen to what corporal *tapas* is. (17:197-200).

Corporal Tapas: The feet of a person doing corporal *tapas* are always engaged in going to the temple or going on a pilgrimage to the places of his favourite deity, Shiva or Vishnu. His hands are ever ready for decorating the front yard of the temple, for supplying materials for performing worship rituals and for serving God. (17:201-203). He prostrates as soon as he sees a *Shivalinga* or an idol of Vishnu. He serves Brahmins who are venerable due to their learning and humility. Or brings succour to people who are tired by travel or tortured by calamities. He sacrifices even his body for serving parents who, for him, are the best among all the holy locations. He serves his Guru who is so kind as to impart Knowledge and who brings succour in this difficult world. He offers the practice of yoga in the fire of *Swadharma* to remove the impurity of the ego. He makes obeisance to all creatures realising that the same Soul exists in all of them. He is always ready to help others. From time to time he controls his desire to have sex. His mother's body was the only contact he had with a female body at the time of his birth and he does not want to have any more contact with any female body and towards this end he remains chaste all his life. Realising that there is life in every creature he does not tread on even a blade of grass and does not break anything. When the affairs of the body are thus purified, understand that the corporal *tapas* has reached perfection. I call it corporal *tapas* because it is performed mainly with the body, with practice of austerities using the body. (17:204-214).

Vocal tapas: Now I shall tell you about the pure vocal *tapas.* (17:215). The speech of a person who performs this *tapas* is straightforward and pleases the listener without hurting him. He speaks to one but it is beneficial to all. His words make one shed bad thoughts and lead to realisation of the Self. Like nectar, one does not get tired of them even after listening for a long time. He speaks only when somebody asks him something otherwise he keeps himself busy studying Vedas or repeating the name of God. He has installed the three Vedas in the temple of his speech and converted it into a school of Vedas. The name of Shiva, Vishnu or some other deity always occurs in his speech. This should be understood as vocal *tapas*. (17:217-223).

Mental tapas: Now I shall also tell you the characteristics of a (person doing) mental *tapas*. (17:224). Free of entanglement with doubts, his mind is engrossed in the Self. He sees the Self as light without heat or space without vacuum. Just as limbs numbed by cold no longer feel sensation, his mind, having got rid of its fickle nature, does not exist anymore. In this state he is not troubled by the strains of detachment and becomes free of greed and fear. Only thing that remains is the realisation of the Self. Lips that are capable of giving advice on the *Shastras* remain silent. Having attained Self-realisation, his mind loses its mind-ness. In such a state, how can feelings occur in the mind? And how will the mind rush to sense pleasures through the organs? Therefore the mind is always free from any feelings. Arjuna, when the mind reaches this state it is fit to be called *mental tapas*. (17: 227-237).

Thus I have told you about the three kinds of *tapas* divided according to the aspects of body, speech and mind. Now I shall tell you about the three types of *tapas* classified according to the three attributes. Understand it with an alert mind. (17: 238-239).

Tapas According To Three Attributes

Sattvic Tapas: Arjuna, perform these three types of *tapas* which I explained to you, with total faith and without nursing any desire for the fruits from them. When *tapas* is performed with faith and a pure mind, sages call it *Sattvic tapas*. (17:240-241).

Rajasic Tapas: When a person, in the name of *tapas,* creates duality with the intention of reaching the pinnacle of greatness, desiring for himself alone and nobody else the greatest honour in the three worlds, wanting that the place of honour in meetings or parties should be his, that everybody should praise only him, meet only him and venerate him with special preference, and all important pleasures should be only his, makes a show of *tapas* for increasing self-importance, for wealth and honour, that tapas is called *Rajasic tapas*. (17:242-247). The *tapas* done for earning fame does not bear fruit and is wasted, just as a young crop is eaten by cattle before it matures. Seeing it to be fruitless, he abandons it halfway and therefore that *tapas* does not have stability. (17:249-250). The *Rajasic tapas* is not only unproductive but remains incomplete too. (17:252).

Tamasic Tapas: Now, if the same *tapas* is of *Tamasic* type then one gains neither heaven nor fame. People perform such *tapas* due to foolishness treating their body like an enemy. They burn their body by inciting the five fires within. Some burn myrrh on their head, some pierce themselves with hooks on their backs, some light fire around themselves and cause burns on their body, some perform fast at the same time holding their breath, some hang themselves upside down in smoke, some people stand immersed neck-deep in ice-cold river water on rocky floor, and some cut off pieces of flesh from own body. The *tapas* thus performed by torturing the body with the intention of destroying others, is called *Tamasic tapas*. (17:253-259).

THREE TYPES OF CHARITY

Thus I have told you about the three types of *tapas* based on the three attributes. Since the occasion has arisen, I shall also tell you about the three types of charity based upon the three attributes. Now first listen to the characteristics of *Sattvic* charity. (17:263-265).

Sattvic charity: Wealth earned by behaving according to *Swadharma* donated respectfully to another (is *Sattvic* charity). Even when proper seed is available, land and water can be unsuitable; similar is the case with charity. (17:266-267). Charity takes place when *Sattva* attribute is coincident with favourable place, time, right beneficiary and wealth. Therefore one should make efforts to choose Kurukshetra, Varanasi or some other place of similar status. At the time of charity there should be solar or lunar eclipse or some such auspicious time. At such a place and time a person worthy of receiving charity, who is purity personified, should be found. He should be a Brahmin[4] who is the foundation of morality and abode of the Vedas, who should be given one's wealth in charity. (17:269-275). He should be donated land etc. with desireless attitude without expecting anything in return. The person should be chosen such that there will not be any return gift of that charity. (17:277-278). And there should be no feeling of differentiation that "I am the giver and he is the receiver." The charity that fulfils all these conditions is the *Sattvic* charity and is the best among charities. Such a charity that occurs with the concurrence of proper place, time and worthy beneficiary is faultless and just. (17:282-284).

Rajasic charity: Just as one feeds a cow for getting milk from her, or invites relatives on festive occasions for the sake of gifts they might bring, or lend money after deducting interest in advance, the charity made with the intention of gaining from its performance, is of *Rajasic* type. (17:285-289). Charity made with the desire of pleasures of the after-world and of so little an amount that it will not even suffice for a single meal and that too with a feeling that one has been totally robbed (i.e., as if one has had to sacrifice unfairly), is of *Rajasic* type. (17:290-293).

Tamasic charity: Some people visit in the evening or at night localities where foreigners live or to jungles or in camps or in public meeting places to give away very generously wealth that was stolen. This too they give to jugglers, prostitutes, gamblers or witches (those

---

4 *Until the British rule scriptures talk about Daana (donation) only to Brahmins with some justification because most Brahmins, whose only education was study of Vedas, Shastras and associated specializations like astrology were very poor. Daana, Dakshina were the main sources of income. Thus we find scriptures telling us that Daana to a Brahmin is a meritorious deed. After the British rule, with the Western influence in the lifestyle moralistic views also changed. Today, Brahmins are not poor any more. It is accepted that the poor and downtrodden should be the recipients of charity. Even though religion based Daana as during worship ceremonies and ceremonies like Shraaddha, is still given to Brahmins.*

practising black arts) having got attracted to them. They fall for the women among them due to their beauty and dancing skills and the false praises sung by the praise-singers reverberate in their ears. They fall under the spell of fragrance of the flowers and scents. Then they give away in charity what they have looted from others. I call this type of charity as *Tamasic charity*. (17:294-300).

There is another aspect of it. That *Tamasic* person, may sometimes visit a holy place. There he may, due to his wealth, encounter a worthy person and feeling swollen by self-pride may feel like giving him something in charity. But on account of lack of faith in him (the worthy person), he will not greet and offer water and do other formalities like offering him a seat etc., let alone do proper worship[5] (reference is to being respectful of him in ordinary conduct). Thus the *Tamasic* person behaves with him improperly and sends him away giving him a few coins without showing him any respect. He counts what he gives and sends him off with insults. The charity in which only money is utilised is called *Tamasic* charity in this world. Thus, I have told you about the three types of charity along with their characteristics. (17:301-308).

Thus I have told you about the three types of activities from faith to knowledge, which are all encompassed by the three attributes. (17:313). To explain to you the *Sattva* attribute, I had to tell you about the characteristics of *Raja* and *Tama* attributes also. Abandoning the latter two, you achieve success by means of the *Sattva* attribute. Perform *yajna* and other duties with this *Sattva* attribute and you will achieve Self-realisation. (17:317-318). Arjuna, *Sattva* attribute has the power to impart success but the thing that gives liberation is a different thing altogether. With its help alone can one enter the realm of liberation. (17:319-321). A river may be quite big but it is only when it joins the main river, that its waters can reach the ocean. Now I shall explain to you how *Sattva* attribute

---

5 We read in the Puranas the description of welcome of worthy guests in which the guest is offered a seat, offered flowers and water and food as if he is a god according to the maxim "Atithi Devo Bhava" that is "a guest is god". Even today it is customary to offer a chair and a cup of tea to guests.

can lead to liberation. (17:327).

AUM TAT SAT

The timeless Supreme Brahman, which is the resting-place of the entire universe, has a name made of three parts. Really speaking, that Brahman has neither name nor caste but Vedas have given that name in order that people immersed in the darkness of ignorance should understand it. The name to which the Supreme Brahman responds when people tortured by the worldly miseries cry for relief, is its symbolic name. (17:328-329). With the intention that it should be possible to have a link with the non-dual formless Brahman which appears to people in dual form, the Vedas were kind enough to find a *mantra*. When called by that *mantra* the formless Brahman assumed form and appeared before them. But only those people who understand Upanishads know this. What more, Brahmadeo got the power to create the universe only by reciting this *mantra* once. Before it was created, Brahmadeo was lonely and confused. He was not able to recognise Me the Supreme God, neither could he create the universe. But he got the power to create after he repeatedly recited that *mantra* of three syllables. He then created Brahmins and instructed them to obey the dictum of the Vedas and assigned to them performance of *yajnas* as the means of their earning. Next he created countless people and gave them the three worlds to live in.

Now listen to the characteristics of the *mantra* that brought greatness to Brahmadeo. The king of all syllables *Aum* is the first syllable, *Tat* is the second and *Sat* is the third. Thus, *AUM TAT SAT* is the threefold name of this Brahman which has blossomed. like a fragrant flower from the Upanishads. If a person adopts *Sattvic* behaviour by becoming one with this name then liberation is at his service. (17:331-344).

Even if good actions are performed and the name of Brahman is uttered, one should understand the importance of its deployment i.e. systematic performance as prescribed in the *Shastras* (17:346), otherwise those good deeds are wasted. (17:349). Therefore I shall tell you how to deploy the three-syllable name of the Brahman. (17:353).

Deployment of Aum: The three syllables of this name of Brahman should be deployed in the beginning, in the middle and at the end of a ritual (or action) respectively. It is by this method that Self-realised people attained Brahman. (17:354-355). Those who have studied *Shastras* do not give up performance of *yajnas* and other rituals. But in the beginning, they concentrate their mind on the syllable *Aum* and utter it. They start the ritual thus by first meditating on *Aum* and pronouncing it clearly. (17:358). These self-realised persons perform *yajnas* at the hands of Brahmins in order to propitiate the benevolent deities by offering a lot of materials earned in ways prescribed by *Dharma*. They perform *havan* (offering in fire) in prescribed ways into the three kinds of fire, (viz. *Ahavaniya, Garhapatya and Dakshin*). In other words they give up undesirable worldly attachments by performing various types of *yajnas*. They give away land and wealth in charity to holy Brahmins choosing proper time and place. By fasting on alternate days or by observing penance during alternate months they drain their body. Thus the rituals like *yajna*, charity and *tapas* which are known to be binding (non-liberating), facilitate the attainment of liberation when performed after pronouncing *Aum*. (17:360-365). This syllable which frees one from the binding nature of the Karmas like *Yajna*, learning, and *Tapas* is uttered in their beginning. Then, once it is seen that the actions are beginning to bear fruits, the syllable *Tat* is used. (17:367-368).

Deployment of Tat: The Supreme Brahman which is beyond the entire universe and which observes everything by itself is also known as *Tat*. It is pronounced clearly keeping in mind (and meditating on it) that it is the root cause of everything. Self-realised persons then say, "May this be an offering of all actions and their fruits to Brahman which is in the form of *Tat*; and may nothing be left of them for us to undergo their fruits". Thus, by offering the actions to Brahman in the form of *Tat,* and disclaiming their authorship they become disentangled. Now it may appear that the action that started with *Aum* and was executed by *Tat* has reached Brahman, but that is not the end of that action because duality still remains within the doer of the action. To assume that the action has reached Brahman itself is duality (seeing doer different Brahman) and this is what is stated by the supreme God through the Vedas. In order that this difference that the doer feels between himself and the Brahman goes and turns into Self-realisation, the word *Sat* has been reserved. When the action performed by uttering *Aum* and *Tat* reaches Brahman it has been praised as appropriate action. It is worth hearing about the deployment of *Sat* in the appropriate action. (17:369-379).

Deployment of Sat: The word *Sat* destroys the untruth and makes the true nature of Brahman appear clearly. That *Sat* does not, at any time or place, take any other form because it is ceaselessly the form of the Self. Since this visible universe is unreal it is not a part of the *Sat* principle. It is in the form of the Self that the *Sat* principle is realised. By that the appropriate action takes the form of Supreme Brahman and removes the duality in the doer to unify him with it. The action, which, due to *Aum* and *Tat* becomes apparent, dissolves into the form of *Sat* i.e. the Brahman. Thus should one understand the internal deployment of the word *Sat.* (17:380-385).

The word *Sat* is useful to *Sattvic* actions in another way. Even though these good actions, performed as per one's qualifications, go well, sometimes there exists some shortcoming in them. (17:387-388). Even if an action is good it becomes evil because it lacks some quality. At such time *Sat,* with the help of *Aum* and *Tat* elevates its status. With the strength of its *Sattvic* attribute it removes its evilness and raises it to the status of good. (17:390-392). Due to some error, the action crosses its limits and takes a forbidden path because sometimes a person loses his way or a discerning person becomes doubtful; what is not possible in day to day life? If the limits are crossed thoughtlessly and the action becomes fit to be described as evil then if the word *Sat* is used in preference to the other two *(Aum and Tat)*, it turns the evil action into a good one. Its use is like that of nectar on a dead person. When you utter the word *Sat* by understanding its essence then you will realise that it is nothing but Brahman. The words *Aum tat sat* lead a seeker to the place from where the visible objects (material world) come into being. *Aum tat sat* is the name that indicates the inner aspects of the pure and attributeless Brahman and it is also supported by Brahman. (17:393-402).Its utterance leads to attainment of the Brahman, therefore it is not a name containing mere letters but verily Brahman itself. For attaining it, whatever actions you do, be it a *yajna*, charity or *tapas,* whether they be complete or incomplete, if they are offered to Brahman then they take Its form. They can no longer be called complete or incomplete. Thus have I told you about the power of Brahman. I also told you nicely about the deployment of each letter of the name of Brahman. If faith in it grows in your mind then you will be liberated from the birth and death cycles. If the action is properly completed by deploying the word *Sat* in the best possible manner, then it will reach the status of the Vedas. (17:405-413). But if you leave this path and obstinately perform millions of *yajnas,* give the entire earth filled with precious stones in charity, and perform *tapas* by standing on one toe for thousands of years, then all those efforts are a waste. (17:414-416). By such actions one does not get happiness in this world; then why expect that one would get in the next? Therefore, whatever actions one does without keeping faith in the name of Brahman, is nothing but a tiresome exercise. (17:421-422).

18

Release Through Renunciation

~∞∞∞~

This Chapter Is The Pinnacle

Dnyaneshwar Maharaj says. "This eighteenth chapter is like the pinnacle of a temple. Once one sees it from a distance then he knows that the goal is near and it gives a feeling that one has actually met the deity inside. Similarly, the eighteenth chapter brings the whole essence of the *Gita* in view. (18:31-32). This eighteenth chapter reviews the entire *Gita* from beginning to end." (18:43).

Arjuna Thinks Renunciation Is Better Than Action

At the end of the seventeenth chapter Shri Krishna told Arjuna that actions done without any faith in *Aum Tat Sat,* the name of Brahman, are evil and wrong. Hearing this, Arjuna thought, "Shri Krishna is faulting persons involved in the ritualistic path. But the individual doer of actions is really blinded by ignorance and basically does not understand the nature of God. How should he then know anything about *Aum Tat Sat,* the name of the Brahman?

Besides, as long as *Rajas* and *Tamas* have not gone from within him, his faith also would remain impure, then how would he have faith in the name of the Brahman? (18:60-64). These *karmas* (actions) are very mischievous. Terrible calamities like birth and death are incorporated in them. If by good fortune the actions are successfully completed then the doer acquires the worthiness for attaining Knowledge otherwise the same action would cause his downfall. Many impediments are faced by the time an action is completed; then when would a follower of the path of action get his turn to be liberated? Therefore it is better to break away from this trap of the path of actions, to give up all actions and adopt the path of renunciation (*sanyas*) that has no shortcomings. Renunciation and abandonment are two things with the help of which Self-realisation can be attained without being affected by the *karmas*. With their help the relation with the material world breaks. Therefore it would be better to ask Shri Krishna to explain the nature of renunciation and abandonment. (18:66-72). This eighteenth chapter contains the reply given by Shri Krishna to Arjuna's question on this subject. (18:74).

Arjuna asked, "Shri Krishna, *Sanyas* (renunciation) and abandonment seem to have the same meaning. Please explain to me if there is any difference between the two." (18:87-89).

ABANDONMENT AND RENUNCIATION

Shri Krishna said, "The two words are really different but they appear to you as having the same meaning which I agree is also correct in a way. It is true that both words signify abandonment but the reason why their meanings are different is that if all (ritualistic) actions are abandoned altogether, then it is called *Sanyas* but if only the *fruits* of the actions are abandoned then it is called abandonment. Now I shall explain to you about actions, *the fruits of which* are to be abandoned and about actions which are to be abandoned altogether. (18:90-93).

The routine actions take place naturally but actions with desire behind them do not take place without the will. Actions with desire of fruits behind them such as Horse-sacrifice *yajna*, digging wells, gardens etc., gifting away lands, establishing new towns, performing rituals with a lot of formality etc., are rooted in personal desire and it binds the doer to the enjoyment of the fruits thereof. (18:97-100).

Arjuna, once you acquire a body you cannot say no to the birth and death phenomena (18:100), similarly one cannot avoid enjoying or suffering the fruits of one's actions. Just as one cannot avoid repaying a loan, once a desire-based action is done, the fruits thereof remain in waiting to make you enjoy or suffer for them. (18:103). Even if a desire-based action occurs inadvertently, (18:104) it has the power to make you enjoy or suffer the fruits. Therefore a seeker should be careful not to do such actions even in fun. They should be abandoned like poison. This abandonment (of desire-based actions) is called *Sanyas* or renunciation. Abandonment of desire-based actions means complete destruction of passions in one's mind. (18:106-109).

Routine and incidental actions: The ritualistic actions which one has to perform, such as at the time of an eclipse or when a guest comes are called incidental actions *(Naimittic karmas).* (18:111). These are actually part of the routine duties but performed whenever an occasion arises and hence it is called incidental. Whatever one does in the morning, afternoon and evening are the daily routine actions *(Nityakarma).* (18:114-115). This performance of routine actions is, like the fragrance within sandalwood, intrinsically virtuous and cannot be avoided. (18:117).

Abandonment: Some people consider these routine and incidental actions as useless because they must be done routinely anyway. But, just as food gives satisfaction (to the taste-buds) and also removes hunger, similarly these routine and incidental actions give all-round results. (18:119-120). Performance of these routine and incidental actions removes the blemishes from one's mind, raises one's worth and because of it one reaches a good state in the after-world. But even though one gains such fruits of the routine and incidental actions, one should abandon those fruits. (18:122-123). Thus, while one should attentively perform the routine and incidental duties, keeping oneself within the prescribed bounds, the fruits thereof should be abandoned totally. This abandoning of the fruits of actions is called abandonment. Thus I have explained to you abandonment and *Sanyas* (renunciation). (18:125-126).

Renunciation: When renunciation occurs the actions done with desire do not bother. Prohibited actions are not done because they are prohibited and the routine and incidental actions are automatically nullified because of the abandoning of their fruits.

Trick of abandonment: Once all account of all the actions is nullified, then Knowledge of the Self comes searching for you. By this trick those who abandon the fruits of the routine and incidental actions and renounce the actions with desire acquire the knowledge of the Self. (18:127-130). But those who do not adopt this trick and instead try to practice abandonment by guesswork, do not at all achieve abandonment but get into more complications. (18:131). The actions not fit to be abandoned should not be abandoned while those which should be abandoned should not be coveted. If one misses the trick of abandonment then that abandonment becomes a burden. But a truly detached person does not even think about the prohibited actions. (18:133-134).

People, who are unable to free themselves of the desire for fruits of their actions, charge that all actions are binding. Just as a person, who is slave to the taste-buds eats all sorts of food and blames the food if he cannot digest it, likewise, persons incapable of abandoning the fruits but having desire for them blame the actions themselves and decide that they should be abandoned. Some others say that rituals like *yajna* etc. must be performed because there are no other means of purifying the mind. If one has to succeed in purifying the mind quickly then there should not be any hesitation in performing actions capable of doing so. (18:135-139). Actions should not be abandoned saying that they are arduous. Many people turn their mind to ritualistic actions with such thoughts. Thus, abandonment has become a debatable topic. Now I shall explain to you properly the real nature of abandonment and remove any differences in opinion regarding it. (18:142-144).

THREE TYPES OF ABANDONMENT

Abandonment may be considered as of three types. I shall now explain them to you. But even if I explain to you the three types of abandonment, understand that what I have told you so far is just its essence. Listen to Me, who is all-knowing, for my definite opinion about what truth is. The seeker, who is ever alert towards liberation from the bindings of this world, should follow only that. (18:145-148).

Like a traveller who should not stop taking steps forward, one should not abandon the essential actions, namely *yajna*, charity and *tapas*. (18:149). As long as one is not sure about attaining Self-realisation one should not be nonchalant about these rituals. On the other hand one should observe them according to one's qualifications, with more attention. Performing more rituals is helpful for non-action. (18:152-154). The *Rajas* and *Tamas* attributes are destroyed completely when actions (rituals) are performed quickly and according to the prescribed rules. (18:156). Action performed with faith destroys *Rajas* and *Tamas* and brings out the importance of the purity of the *Sattva* attribute. Righteous actions are like places of pilgrimage when it comes to gaining this purity. The places of pilgrimage remove the external dirt while righteous deeds remove the internal dirt.[1] Therefore righteous deeds are the places of pilgrimage for attaining purity of the *Sattva* attribute. (18:158-160). Like a river itself coming to the rescue of

---

1 *People take bath in holy waters at places of pilgrimage which removes external dirt but a bath cannot remove the impurities of mind which can be removed by righteous deeds. There is a poem by Saint Kabir which says that Ganga water may clean the body but how can clean the mind?*

a drowning person, it is the actions that liberate a seeker from the bondage. There is a trick in doing actions, which, though basically binding in nature, makes them work as the main cause (or means) of liberation. Now I shall tell you about the trick that makes actions nullify themselves. (18:162-165).

He (who adopts the trick) does not swell by pride when the principle *yajnas* are being performed systematically. (18:166). He performs the rituals systematically at appropriate times without carrying the ego that he is the doer. He does not harbour any desire in his mind for the fruits of those rituals. Arjuna, one should first give up expectations about the fruits and then start the action. (18:170-172). He who does actions adopting this trick encounters the Self. Therefore one should do actions giving up the desire for fruits and the I-am-the-body consciousness. This is my message. I repeat again and again that he who is tired of the bindings of life should not disobey this My command. (18:175-177).

Tamasic abandonment: When one thinking that actions bind and abandons all actions in anger, I call that *Tamasic* abandonment. It is like cutting one's head because of a headache. (18:178-179). Because of his confusion, the *Tamasic* person does not understand the trick of eliminating the affliction of the actions by actions themselves. Therefore he abandons the duties that have come to his lot by his *Swadharma*. You should not even touch such a *Tamasic* person. (18:182-183).

Rajasic abandonment: Even while knowing fully what his entitlements and duties are, he is hesitant about them fearing the labour involved. (18:184). Or else, he begins an action knowing that it is so prescribed but as soon as it becomes laborious he abandons it in the middle. He says. "It is by great fortune that I have got an admirable thing like this body, then why should I make it toil like a sinner? If happiness is to be gained later by doing actions now, then I do not want it. Why not make best of the luxuries I have now?" Abandoning actions because they are laborious is called *Rajas* abandonment. It does not give the fruits of abandonment because he foregoes actions due to his attachment to the body. (18:189-193, 195).

With the rise of Knowledge, all actions vanish along with the ignorance and that is really an abandonment of actions leading to liberation. He who abandons actions out of ignorance does not gain this liberation. Therefore the *Rajas* abandonment should not be considered as abandonment. Now, while on the subject, listen also to which abandonment leads to liberation.(18:196-199).

Sattvic abandonment: Whatever actions naturally come to his lot as his entitlement, he performs them systematically as prescribed and with love. But he does not keep in mind that it is he who is performing them. Also he abandons the desire of the fruits of these actions. (18:200-201). Actually, ego about actions and desire for fruits are what cause the actions to bind. One who keeps away from these two while performing prescribed actions does not become unhappy. The most superior tree of abandonment begets the large fruits of liberation therefore this abandonment is known in the world as *Sattvic* abandonment. (18:205-207).

When actions are abandoned after abandoning the fruits, the *Rajas* and *Tamas* attributes get destroyed. Then the pure *Sattvic* attribute causes the light of Self-realisation to shine and removes the illusion of the reality of the world. (18:210-211).

The duties that fall to his lot due to the past karmas are, in his view, without blemish hence he does not bother about happiness or sorrow. He is not excited by the thought that a duty is auspicious or become unhappy by taking it to be inauspicious. He does not carry any doubts in his mind about whether a particular duty is auspicious or not. When the feelings of duality that "This is the duty" and "I am the doer of that duty" – which separate the duty and the doer – do not enter his mind, then it is an abandonment of *Sattvic* type. Actions are completely abandoned with this manner of abandonment. If they are abandoned in any other manner then they bind you more. (18:212-217).

Turning actions into non-actions: Those who are indolent about their duties after they acquire the body are rustic simpletons. (18:218). Is it not foolish to try to abandon actions as long as the impression that I am the body is sustained? One can erase the sandal-paste put on the forehead but how can the writing of one's future on it be erased?[2] One can stop the prescribed rituals after they are begun but how can the actions of the body be stopped? Because even if a person is asleep or sitting idle, his breathing action continues. The actions associated with the body cannot be abandoned while we live or even after death.[3] *It can be abandoned only by one trick: while doing the actions one should not be in the clutches of the desire for its fruits.* If the fruits of the actions are offered to God then one attains Self-realisation by His benevolence and that destroys all actions along with the ignorance. Abandoning actions in this manner is real abandonment. Therefore he who has abandoned actions in this way is a great abandoner. I am again telling you that he who has turned actions into non-actions by abandoning the fruits should alone be considered as true abandoner in these three worlds. (18:222-232).

Unfavourable, favourable and mixed actions: Arjuna, action is of three types and only those who do not give up the desire for the fruits of action have to enjoy or suffer for it. (18:233). Whether one does the action out of the ego of one's capability or after abandoning the desire for its fruits, the action *alone* cannot bind the doer in either case. Only he who desires the fruits gains them. But he who does not accept the fruits even after doing the action does not take rebirth anywhere in these three worlds because the worlds themselves are the result of the fruits of the actions. Deities,

2 *It is believed that a goddess comes at midnight and writes child's fate on its forehead on the sixth day after birth. What is written can never be erased. It was customary in olden times to keep the door of the delivery room open, stay awake and sing during this night to welcome her. Since this happens on the sixth day, the goddess is called Satwai or Chhathi. With urbanization this custom is observed only in rural areas.*
3 *This refers to the account of Karmas which one carries with him after death and are continued as Prarabdha karmas on rebirth.*

humans and immovable life constitute what is known as the world, and are themselves in three different types of fruits of actions. The same action is of three types, namely unfavourable, favourable and mixed. (18:236-240).

Those who are full of lust and who transgress in their behaviour by doing forbidden deeds are therefore reborn in low forms such as worms, insects, earth, stones etc. These are called unfavourable fruits of action. (18:241-242).

Those who respect *Swadharma* and do meritorious deeds according to one's qualifications as prescribed in the Vedas attain the bodies of deities like Indra etc.. These are favourable fruits of actions. (18:243-244).

When truth and untruth are mixed a third type of entity is created. Therefore when an action contains good and bad deeds its fruits lead to being reborn as a human being. This is what is called mixed fruits of actions. (18:245-247).

Nullifying the fruits of actions: These are the three types of fruits of action in this world. Those individuals who get entrapped in the desire for the fruits of actions are compelled to enjoy or suffer them. (18:248-249). People who continue doing actions while they are living may advance materially but they have to undergo the enjoyment or suffering of those actions after their death. (18:251). When a grain from an ear of corn falls on the ground, it sprouts and gives rise to another ear of corn. The grain from that ear again falls on the ground and again sprouts to give another ear and this cycle goes on. Similarly, while undergoing the fruits of actions, other fruits (of actions) are created. (18:253-254). The burden of the fruits increases in the order – goal and means, and those individuals who do not give up the desire of the fruits of action get entangled in the material world. On the other hand, those who nullify the actions even while doing them by giving up the desire of their fruits cause the effects of the fruits to cease. (18:256-258).

With the help of pure moral behaviour and the nectar of Guru's benevolence, Self-realisation comes to fruition and the distress caused by the attitude of duality ends. The three types of fruits of actions responsible for the creation of illusion about the reality of this universe vanish and in that state, the fruits and their enjoyer both dissolve. Those who have been successful in adopting renunciation (*sanyas*) of knowledgeable actions are liberated from the troubles of birth and death arising out of the fruits of actions. How can they, whose vision has reached the Self due to such renunciation, feel that the deeds are different from the doer? (18:259-262). Once the fruits of actions are abandoned, the material knowledge vanishes (and the seeker attains unity with Brahman); in this situation then who is going to enjoy the fruits and who is going to impart the enjoyment? Therefore in the case of a renunciate (*Sanyasi*) the talk of actions is not at all applicable. (18:266-267).

As long as ignorance remains within and an individual is induced to do actions, good or bad, by virtue of his capability and with dualistic attitude, there exists a separateness between the Soul and the action (18:269), but only the ignorance shows it as such. (18:275).

CAUSES OF ACTIONS

There are *five* causes for an individual's actions. I shall describe them to you. (18:277). But perhaps you already know them because *Shastras* have prominently described them. They are well known through the elucidation of *Sankhya* philosophy in the realm of the Vedas. These are the basic causes essential for success of the actions. But even so, do not relate them to the Soul who is the master. (18:278-280).

Arjuna, we were talking about how all actions are separate from the Soul. (18:296). It is verily a fact that all actions originate from these causes without the knowledge of the Soul and the five causes combine to give a shape to the actions. The very same five causes are the purpose of the actions. There, the Soul is detached (as a disinterested witness) and does not constitute a cause or an incidental motive for it. It neither does actions nor assists in leading the action to completion. Just as sky is different from the day and night (18:304-308), similarly though good and evil actions do take place in the individual, the Soul remains separate from them. (18:313).

First cause: Body is the first cause (of actions) and is the seat of action because the enjoyer, along with the objects to be enjoyed, resides in it. After toiling day and night using the ten organs, there is no other place for an individual to experience the pleasures and sorrows created by *Maya.* Hence the term "seat of action" is used with reference to the body. It is the residence of the twenty-four principles and the entanglement of the binding and the liberation is resolved here. It is this body that supports the three states viz. wakefulness, sleep and dream; therefore it has been named as the body. (18:315-320).

Second cause: Second cause of actions is the doer. This doer is the reflection of the Consciousness. (18:321). Forgetting its own nature, under the "I am the body" illusion, it appears in the form of the body. The Consciousness, which has forgotten its true nature of the Self, is known as an individual. That individual is pledged to live with the body in every way. Due to delusion he claims that all actions done by the body are actually done by him and therefore that individual is called the doer. (18:324-326).

Third cause: Even though the power of understanding of the intellect is same, it appears in different ways through different organs. This is called *manifold distinct functions (Prithagvidha Karan).* It is the third cause of actions. (18:330-331).

Fourth cause: The air has ceaseless power of action that manifests itself differently in different places. When it appears through the tongue, it is known as speech, and when it is expressed through hands it is called give-and-take transaction; when it is manifested through feet it is called walking and when it goes through urine and faeces it is called cleansing. It is called vital air *(Pranavayu)* when, while moving from navel to the heart, it gives rise to the *Aum* sound. The same vital air when it moves around in the upper parts is called *Udana,* when it comes out through the lower end it is called *Apana,* while when it occupies the whole body it is called *Vyana.* When it supplies the alimentary juices to all corners of the body and gets filled in all the joints then it is called *Samana.* And the actions like yawning, sneezing, burping etc. are the manifestations of the minor aspects of vital energy namely *Naga, Kurma, Krikal* etc. (See Ch 6). Thus the power of action of air, which has different names when it behaves differently, is the fourth cause of action. (18:333-343).

Fifth cause: The intellect alone is the best among all the inner properties of an individual. It excels by the strength of the organs which is supported by the group of the presiding deities. The presiding deities like Sun etc. give strength to respective organs like eyes etc. This group of presiding deities is the fifth cause of actions.[4] Thus I have explained to you the root causes of all actions.

Now, the same root causes lead to countless actions. I shall explain to you the purpose due to which this happens. (18:348-352).[5]

Mind, the cause for intent of actions: Arjuna, mind is the cause

4 Each organ has a presiding deity as follows: Eyes- Surya; Ears-Dik (directions); Nose-Ashwinikumars; Skin-Vayu; Tongue-Agni (Varuna?); Mind-Chandra; Hands-Indra; Feet-Vishnu; Intellect- Brahmadeo; Ego-Shankar. (From various sources). For successful action by any organ corresponding deity must be pleased. (see next footnote also in the same context).

5 Bhagvadgita (Shloka 14) uses the term Daivam which is interpreted by Shri Dnyaneshwar Maharaj as referring to deities presiding and controlling the various organs. Others e.g. Saint Mukteshwar and Dr S Radhakrishnan interpret it as (unforeseen) providence. In both interpretations a supernatural hand is indicated but in the latter case it is implied that there is always an element of providence and luck in all actions. Some actions are inspired by the past karmas and by the will of God. This is in conformity with the principle of desireless actions in which one is entitled only to do actions but not to its fruits as mentioned in Chapter 2.

for the intention behind actions; and once that intent is born it finds its expression through speech. In the light of the speech the path of action becomes clear and the doer begins the task of doing the action. Because of that the body itself becomes the purpose of the actions of body. (18:357-359). The actions of mind, speech and body become the purpose of mind, speech and body because they (mind, speech and body) are involved in the actions of the body etc. (18:361, 365).

Birth Of Actions

When body, speech and mind join the five causes (body etc.), actions are born. If the action is done as prescribed in the *Shastras* then it becomes a just action and also becomes the cause for just behaviour. (18:366-367). Action that takes place by coming together of the purpose and the cause, is a blind action. (18:370). But if the same is done consciously with the support of the *Shastras* then it become a just action. If the unrestrained action that takes place by the combination of purpose and cause is not done as per the *Shastras* then it is as good as not done. Such action is an unjust action and is the cause of immorality. (18:375-376). Thus the actions which take place due to the five causes also have five purposes and the soul is also involved in them due to its being in contact. (18:377). The soul makes the actions discernible without itself taking their form and without being the doer. (18:378). But a person whose intellect is restricted only to the body because of the I-am-the-body illusion, is in the dark about the Self. He who has considered the body itself as the Soul, God and Brahman is under the impression that it is the soul who is the doer but really speaking he is not definite even about that, for he considers that it is the body that is the doer. That he himself who is the Soul, is beyond actions and is only a witness to them, is something he has never heard of. Therefore it is no wonder that he gauges the immeasurable Soul with the measure of the body! (18:382-385). It must be said that he who does not even permit the name of *Shastras* or Guru to be uttered in his presence survives on the strength of his foolishness. With the understanding that body itself is the Soul he imprisons himself within the body with the strong walls of actions. (18:390-392). He who attributes the actions of *Maya* to the Soul continues accounting for the actions for millions of aeons. (18:394).

NON-ATTACHMENT TO ACTIONS

Now I shall tell you how to recognise a person who does not get attached to the actions even after doing them. (18:396).We ourselves become liberated while we think of such a liberated person (18:397). One regains the Self while thinking of the saints therefore one should sing and hear the praise of the saints. (18:400). Such a person does not get attached to the fruits of his actions, whether good or bad. I shall tell you through indirect arguments the characteristics of such a person who has gone beyond actions. (18:401-402).

He, who was experiencing the universe as a dream during the sleep state of ignorance for a long time, woke up to experience the bliss of the Brahman after hearing the great dictum *"Tatvamasi"* (You are that) with the power of Guru's grace, not just by having him keep his benevolent hands on his head, but having him to pat it.[6] (18:403-405). The feeling of "I" and "mine" vanishes from his mind just as a dream disappears after waking up. (18:408). When a person who has reached Self-realisation sees a visible object, that object and the seer both merge with the Self. (18:410). When, due to the misunderstanding that action is different from the doer, an imputation made about the Soul being the doer vanishes, only the state of the Self remains. Would he, who is the ruler of this state of the Self, maintain the I-am-the-body feeling? (18:412-413). How would a person who has the knowable and the knower united within him possess the I-am-the-body ego? (18:418). Whatever

---

6 *It is not very clear what Dnyaneshwar Maharaj wanted to say. But most probably it means that not just Guru's advice but a firm instruction from Guru or even Shaktipat by Guru's touch is meant here because a benevolent hand need not touch disciple's head but a patting does.*

he does becomes his own form (of the Self); then which actions should he claim as his? (18:420). One who feels that the ego as the doer is meaningless, continues doing actions too as long as he has his body. (18:422). Even though the I-am-the-body ego has gone, the nature which has created the body gets the actions performed by that body. (18:428). Because of the five causes (body etc.) the actions occur naturally without any movement on the part of the Soul. Because of the influence of the earlier lives these five causes and purposes induce many actions whether those actions destroy the entire universe or create a new universe. (18:431-433). Whatever be the case, he remains in the body without the I-am-the-body feeling. (18:435). He is oblivious to the affairs of the world but others who see him with the material eyes as a body consider him to be the doer. (18:436-437). He who has woken up and realized the nature of the Self and whose attitude that it is he who does the seeing has dissolved along with the scene, is not aware of the activities if his organs.[7] (18:441). Bodily movements of a person who is liberated from the birth and death cycles occur as per the *karmas* of earlier lives but because they do not understand it people call him the doer. Even if the three worlds are destroyed by his natural actions one should not charge him with it. A man of Knowledge does not possess feeling of duality therefore there is nothing else that he can destroy. (18:447-449).

Just as the Ganga does not get impure even after another river meets it similarly his intellect is not affected by the thoughts of sin and merit. (18:450). How can the intellect of a person who does not consider his actions different from himself be affected by them? Therefore he who himself has become the triad of the action, the doer and the cause does not get bound by the action done by his body etc. The individual, considering himself as the doer, works skilfully with the five types of intents doing innumerable righteous and unrighteous actions by means of the ten body organs but the Soul has no connection with this activity. You may say that the Soul

---

7 *This means that a Self realized person is oblivious to his bodily actions.*

helps in the preparedness for these actions but that is also not true because the Soul is Brahman and only a witness (*Chidrup* or form of *Chit* or Brahman) then how will he permit intent to act? The intent to action, which makes people toil, does not affect the Soul. Therefore, one who has attained Brahman cannot at all be trapped by actions. It is the triad[8] that is responsible for depicting improper type of knowledge in the light of ignorance. (18:450-460).

IMPROPER TYPE OF KNOWLEDGE

The triad of knowledge, knower and the knowable is the root of the universe. The inclination to act comes from it. Now I shall explain to you forms of each member of this triad. (18:461-462).

Knowledge is the name given to that, which makes an individual experience pleasure and pain and vanishes while in deep sleep. The individual is the knower. That which is experienced by the individual is what is called knowledge. This knowledge born of the ignorance of the Self, distributes itself in three parts as soon as it is created. It keeps the knowable in its front and knower at its back and connecting them creates interaction between the two. This knowledge, the reach of which is limited up to the boundary of the knowable and which gives different names to different things is without doubt ordinary knowledge. Now listen to the characteristics of the knowable. (18:465-471).

Sound, touch, form, smell and taste are the five ways through which knowable becomes known. Just as the same mango is known by taste, colour, smell and touch, similarly even though the knowable is one it is known through five organs. Therefore knowledge is of five types. (18:472-474). The place where knowledge obtained through organs ends, is the knowable or the sense object.[9] Thus

---

8 *Mind, speech and body.*
9 *What this means is that using the information about an object through sense organs (sight, smell, touch etc., the intellect decides after referring to memory, what the object is.*

I have explained to you the characteristics of knower, knowledge and the knowable. (18:475-477).

This knowable becomes the cause of three types of actions. (18:477). Though the knowable is of five types by virtue of the five senses viz. sound, touch, form, smell and taste, it is only of one type, either liked or disliked. When the knower knows even a little about a knowable object he tends to either accept it or reject it. (18:478-480). This knower rushes to the sense objects like a crane rushing to catch a fish as soon it sees it. (18:480, 484). Therefore Arjuna, all actions originate from the knowledge, the knowable and the knower. (18:485).

If the knower likes the knowable sense-object then he cannot tolerate a moment's delay in enjoying it. But if he dislikes it then every moment of delay in abandoning it seems to him like aeons. (18:486-487). Then he does actions in order to accept or reject it. (18:489). *Thus the knower becomes the doer of actions.* (18:491). He who, with the desire of sense pleasures, makes the organs work becomes the doer and then knowledge becomes the cause or in other words the means and consequently the knowable becomes the action. The basic nature of the knowledge changes in this manner. (18:493-495). By giving impetus to the organs, the knower is caught in the ego of being the doer.[10] Listen to the characteristics of the doer under these conditions. (18:497).

Intellect, mind, attentiveness and ego are the four internal elements of the body and skin, ears, eyes, tongue and nose are the five external sense organs. The doer takes a measure of the possible actions with the help of these inner elements and if he thinks that the action is going to give him pleasure then he makes the eyes etc., the ten external organs (five organs of sense and five of action) work until he gets the outcome. On the other hand if he thinks that the

---

10 *This is a very interesting logical sequential analysis of how vasana is generated through sense organs and which through a lack of discrimination or detachment or even a sense of duty causes an action and how ego creates the "I am the doer" syndrome leading to karma.*

action would result in pain or unhappiness then he inspires the ten organs to abandon it. Like a king making people toil day and night for unpaid revenue, he makes the organs work day and night until the pain or unhappiness is completely removed. When the knower thus engages the organs to accept or abandon the action he is called the doer. (18:498-505).

We call the organs 'means of action' because the doer engages them to do actions. That which encompasses the acts done using these means is what is meant by action in this chapter. (18:506-507). Just as the intellect of a goldsmith encompasses the ornament, similarly, without doubt, all that which encompass the acts of the doer[11] is the action. (18:508, 510). Thus I have told you about the characteristics of action, doer and the means of action. Here, the knower, knowledge and knowable are the provokers of actions while the doer, the means and the deed are the aggregation of actions. (18:511-512). The triad of the doer, means and the act of doing are the lifeline of action; therefore, wherever there is an ego – "I am the doer of this deed" – the Soul keeps away from such actions. Therefore there is no need to tell you separately that Soul is different from actions. You already know it. (18:514-516).

KNOWLEDGE, ACTION AND THE DOER

The knowledge, action and the doer, which I explained to you, become of three kinds, due to the three attributes (Sattva, Rajas and Tamas). You should not trust the triad of knowledge, the action and the doer because two of the attributes lead to binding and the Sattva attribute alone is capable of leading to liberation. I shall explain to you the features of Sattva attribute, which are clearly explained in the Sankhya doctrine. That Sankhya doctrine is an ocean of thoughts, it is the Sun, which makes the lotus of Self-realisation bloom and the best among the knowledge giving doctrines. It is the Sun that distinguishes between Prakriti and

11 Including likes, dislikes, acceptance, rejection or abandonment.

Purusha (Nature and the Supreme Self) who are enmeshed together like the day and the night. This doctrine gauges the immeasurable ignorance by means of twenty-four principles and leads you to the experience of the bliss of the Supreme Principle. Arjuna, the features of the three attributes described by the *Sankhya* doctrine are as follows: (18:517-523)

These three attributes are so great that they have turned all things in the world into three types by their power and consequently everything from Brahmadeo to a tiny insect has been transformed to the three types of attributes. But first I shall tell you about the principle by which this entire universe has come into the clutches of these three attributes. In order to see anything clearly the eyesight has to be clear first. Similarly if the knowledge is pure then it is possible to understand the real nature of things. Therefore I shall tell you about *Sattvic* knowledge. (18:524-528).

Sattvic knowledge: Arjuna, the knowledge into which the knowable merges with the knower is *Sattvic* knowledge. (18:529). This Knowledge sees no difference between anything from Shiva to a blade of grass. (18:531). When the knowable is seen by the light of this knowledge no difference is perceptible between the knower, knowledge and the knowable. (18:533). Knowledge, which does not notice visible things, is the *Sattvic* knowledge. Just as an observer sees his own reflection in a mirror similarly knower sees knowable as knowledge (which is also himself). His *Sattvic* knowledge is the temple of liberation. Now listen to the characteristics of *Rajasic* knowledge. (18:535-537).

Rajasic knowledge: That which goes by presupposing differences among creatures is *Rajasic* knowledge. That knowledge has splintered itself into pieces by assuming diversity among creatures and tricked the knower. That knowledge spreads the paraphernalia of *Maya* around the premises of Self-realisation and shows the individual the play of the three states of wakefulness, dream and sleep. (18:538-541). Awareness of the differences in the name and form of objects comes in the way of the sense of the non-duality.[12] (18:545). The observation that there are differences among creatures makes the feeling of one-ness vanish. The knowledge that considers things as different from each other in various ways, and distinguishes them as big and small, is the *Rajasic* knowledge. (18:547-548).

Tamasic knowledge: Now I shall tell you about the characteristics of *Tamasic* knowledge. That which is bare and not covered by the fabric of the rules of the *Shastras* is the *Tamasic* knowledge. Therefore, *Shrutis* (Vedas) turn their back to it. The *Shastras* which follow the Vedas have also charged this knowledge as despicable and relegated it to the realms of the *Mleccha* (non-Hindu) religion. Such knowledge does not get hindered by any rules in corporal relations, nor does it find any object objectionable. (18:549-552). In the heat of enjoyment of sense pleasures it does not think about avoiding objectionable actions and/or of doing those prescribed by the *Shastras*. It rushes to enjoy whatever sense pleasures it comes across. Without bothering about what should be eaten or be avoided, what is proper or improper, it thinks as sacred only what it likes. It only knows that women are for sexual enjoyment only and is eager to keep relations with them. It keeps friendship only with those whose contact is profitable to its selfish motives and not with those who are its relatives. *Tamasic* knowledge thinks that the whole world is meant for their benefit. It feels that the whole world is something that should be enjoyed. It thinks that all actions are for filling the belly. He is ignorant about what actions should be done and what should be avoided. His intellect does not go beyond the thinking that body is the soul and God is a stone idol. He thinks that after death the soul is destroyed along with actions and no one is left to experience the fruits of action. (18:557-568). That, if God is a witness to one's actions and makes him experience the fruits thereof, then one can simply sell away the idol of God and spend

---

12 *A Self realized person sees unity (non-duality) in all animate or inanimate objects all being manifestations of Brahman.*

the money. That, if one says that the village (local) deities hold control over the people, then why do the hills (stones from which are used for making idols) in the country keep quiet? And if at all the *Tamasic* knowledge believes in God then it considers only the stone idol as God and that the body itself as soul. It thinks that the concept of sin and merit is false and one should enjoy the sense pleasures voraciously. They are certain that what is seen and what pleases the sense organs is the only reality and this understanding of theirs grows day by day. (18:569-573). The *Tamasic* knowledge is meaningless and useless like the life of a eunuch.[13] We call it as knowle.dge in the same way as we call an undrinkable liquid as drink. Actually, instead of knowledge it should be considered as *Tamasic* attribute itself. (18:576-581).

Thus I have told you about the three kinds of knowledge along with their characteristics. Now, the doer does actions in the light of these three kinds of knowledge. The same action becomes of three kinds due to these different kinds of knowledge. Now listen first to the characteristics of *Sattvic* actions. (18:582-585).

Sattvic actions: Just as a faithful wife embraces her husband by herself similarly the action that comes to one's lot by one's entitlement, the action that gives decorum to the entitlement when regularly performed, is the proper routine action. If it is joined by incidental action then the combination is good like fragrance dabbed on a gold ornament. Action should be performed with all one's mind and heart, making an offering of it to God without keeping desire for fruits thereof or without feeling happy if the action is successful or sorry if it is not. Actions done in this skilful way may be called *Sattvic* actions. (18:586-594).

Rajasic actions: Now I shall tell you about *Rajasic* actions. A person doing *Rajasic* actions does not speak properly with his parents but

---

13 *Reader should note that these beliefs are more than seven centuries old. They are not valid today. Today every human being is considered productive and helpful to life and society. We see eunuchs even taking part in politics and they are not as despised as they used to be once.*

like a fool shows respect to everybody else in the world. (18:595). He does not get up from his seat to perform the essential routine and incidental actions but when it comes to actions of pleasure and lust he does not spare any efforts. (18:597-598). Such a person labours a lot keeping in view the future fruits of his efforts but feels that he has not laboured enough. With desire of fruits in mind he does many actions as prescribed and systematically and after he has done them announces it to the world, distributing tokens of gift to establish that he is religious.

Then his mind is filled with so much ego that he stops respecting his parents. Whatever actions he does with ego and desire of fruits in mind he does without sparing any efforts. (18:601-606). Such people like to labour. They labour with the attraction of the pleasures in heaven. The action, which is thus laborious and done with desire of fruits, is *Rajasic* action. (18:608-610).

Tamasic action: Now listen to the characteristics of *Tamasic* action. It is the dark dungeon of slander and is the place where prohibited actions and sin are born. (18:611). Just as drawing a line on water does not result in anything, similarly the fruits of such action cannot be seen and the action is wasted. (18:612, 615) The action done by toiling the valuable body and spending wealth destroys the happiness of the world. (18:616). *Tamasic* action not only destroys everything belonging to the doer and injuring his body but it injures others as well. (18:619). The *Tamasic* doer does actions without thinking about his own capability. While doing those actions, due to indiscretion and ego, he sets upon the work without bothering about his own capability, propriety of the occasion, and whether he will gain anything by it. (18:621-623). He proceeds without thinking of the past and the future, without distinguishing between right and wrong ways and does not distinguish between proper and improper or whether a particular thing belongs to himself or to others.

Thus, I have explained to you how action has become of three types due to the differences in the three attributes. (18:625-627).

Due to the three types of actions the doer also becomes of three types. Now I shall describe to you a *Sattvic* doer first. (18:628-630).

Sattvic doer: A *Sattvic* doer performs his routine and incidental acts but they should not be called fruitless. These acts never go waste because Arjuna, (actions themselves are fruits and) how can fruit itself beget fruits. He does many acts respectfully but does not keep ego of being the doer. In order to do acts worthy of offering to God, he selects proper time and place and decides, with the help of the *Shastras*, which acts should be done. Combining the organs and the inclination he binds himself with a set of rules without letting his mind waver towards the fruits. He takes care throughout his life to develop excellent courage in order to succeed in controlling the organs. And he does not bother about physical happiness while doing his duties, driven only by the love for Self-realisation. While doing these duties he loses sleep, does not feel hungry and his body is away from sense pleasures. His enthusiasm for doing his duties increases. Because of the intrinsic liking for the Self he treats even his life as insignificant. Will he, who is in love with his soul, feel sorry if his body has to labour? As the desire for sense-pleasures vanish and physical tendencies vane, his joy in performing duties doubles. Even if performance of his duties is interrupted he does not feel sorry nor does he feel he has won a victory if he has finished his duty successfully. He, in whom such qualities are found, should really be called a *Sattvic* doer. (18:632-648).

Rajasic doer: Now the sign by which a *Rajasic* doer may be recognised is that he is full of worldly desires. (18:649). He is the meeting place for all the desires and failings in the world. He starts with acts that give fruits easily, and he will not even leave a paisa (a small coin) from whatever profits he can get from them and for this he will sacrifice even is life. He is ready to swallow other people's property while guarding his own. (18:651-654). He uses all his faculties to give trouble to others. He works for his own gains without bothering about the welfare of others. He does not let thoughts of distaste arise in his mind for any type of work even if he has no ability to complete it. He is poor in keeping sanctity. If he succeeds in any task he mocks the world in the surge of happiness and if he is unsuccessful then, stricken with grief, he denounces it. A person who does actions thus is a *Rajasic* doer. (18:655-661).

Tamasic doer: After this I shall now tell about the *Tamasic* doer who is like a repository of evil deeds. (18:662). Just as strong poison does not know its own power of destruction, he is inclined to do evil deeds which can destroy others and while doing them he is not aware of what he is doing. There is no relation between his acts and his intentions. This *Tamasic* doer surpasses a madman. He lives by enjoying the pleasures of the organs. His behaviour is unrestrained and being controlled by nature he does not know what is proper or improper. He swells by the satisfaction of his own evil acts. And under the influence of pride he does not bow even before God. He is always deceitful about enjoying the sense pleasures. His behaviour is stealthy and his looks are like a prostitute taking away other man's possessions. In other words his whole body is made up of falsehoods and his life is like a gambler's den. His life should be considered as home of a selfish robber. Therefore nobody should get involved with him. He gets enraged when he sees good deeds of others (18:664-675) and tries to turn them into bad deeds. He considers good qualities of others as bad qualities and he turns nectar into poison. When some good deed that can make the worldly life bear good fruits and give a better position in the after-world comes to his lot it is most certain that he would be sleeping at that time. But when it comes to doing evil deeds the sleep goes away immediately. (18:677-681). When it is the time to do beneficial deeds he feels lethargic, and contrarily when evil deeds are to be done the lethargy is under his control. He burns with jealousy when he sees the advancement of others. He remains jealous throughout his life. He begins to labour for fulfilment of desires, which will last him for aeons (because he does not succeed). He does worry about matters beyond this world but is not able to gain even a blade of grass. Such a person who is definitely a pile of sin may be considered as a *Tamasic* doer. Thus I have explained to you three kinds of acts, doer and knowledge. (18:683-689).

THREE TYPES OF INTELLECT

Now the intellect, which is covered by delusion and embellished by doubt moves in the realm of improper knowledge and is the mirror through which an individual sees himself, is also of three types. Arjuna, is there anything in this world that has not been turned into three types by the three attributes? What is there in this visible world that is not of three types? Therefore the intellect has also become of three types due to the three attributes. Fortitude is also similarly divided. Out of these two I shall explain to you about the three divisions of intellect first. (18:690-695).

Superior, medium and inferior ways: There are three types of ways namely, superior, medium and inferior by which every creature is reborn in this world. These three ways are respectively known as: doing prescribed acts, doing fruit motivated acts, and doing forbidden acts. Because of these the creatures are subjected to worldly perils.

Superior way: The doing of prescribed routine acts according to one's right, is the superior way. The same should be practised keeping in view the attainment of Self-realisation. Thus practised, the performance of the prescribed routine acts frees one from the fear of this world and facilitates liberation. A wise person who acts in this manner becomes free from the fear of this world and by his behaviour sets himself on the path of liberation. The intellect that decides the behaviour of the individual through reinforcing his trust in the prescribed routine deeds guarantees liberation. Therefore why should one not base one's renunciation (of fruits) on the foundation of the inclination to act and engage oneself in actions? (18:696-704).

Sattvic intellect: Doing the prescribed routine deeds definitely leads to liberation. *Sattvic* intellect is that which has the inclination towards doing the prescribed routine deeds. It also knows which deeds are not proper. It does not turn towards fruit-motivated deeds that create fear of the world and towards forbidden deeds which should not be done and which entangle one in birth-death cycles (18:707-710). The *Sattvic* intellect is definitely afraid when it notices forbidden actions and actions binding one to birth and death cycles; fearing these, the *Sattvic* intellect keeps away from it. That intellect which understands which deed is good and which is evil – after carefully considering actions and non-actions and measuring them with the scale of inclination to action and renunciation – is the *Sattvic* intellect. (18:713-717).

Rajasic intellect: The *Rajasic* intellect does deeds without understanding which a good deed is and which is not. A good deed is one that conforms with the code of *Dharma* and a deed that goes against the tenets of *Dharma* is an evil deed (18:720). The *Rajasic* intellect misses the latter only by good luck; the intellect that considers both kinds of deeds as alike, the intellect that does not know how to choose between proper and improper deeds, is *Rajasic* intellect. (18:722-723).

Tamasic intellect: The intellect that considers all religious deeds as sinful and real things as false, interprets the meaning of the *Shastras* in reverse manner and considers good qualities as bad, and which considers matters agreeable to the *Shrutis* (Vedas) as perverse, should be called *Tamasic* intellect. How can such intellect, which is like a dark night, be proper for religious deeds? (18:726-729).

THREE TYPES OF FORTITUDE

Thus I have explained to you the three divisions of intellect. Now, when the intellect decides to perform a deed, then the fortitude supports it and that is also of three types. I shall tell you about the three types of fortitude also. (18:730-732).

Sattvic fortitude: *Sattvic* fortitude is that, by which the activities of the mind, the life-force and the sense organs are restrained. Then the association of the ten organs with the sense-objects breaks and withdraw into the womb of the mind (i.e. instead of turning towards sense objects the organs turn inwards towards the mind). Since both the upper and the lower pathways of the life force are blocked, it brings together its nine aspects and goes to the *Sushumna Nadi*. Since the mind is freed of will and doubt, the intellect rests quietly behind it. Thus, the peerless fortitude which, by stopping the activities of mind, life-force and the organs, imprisons them to the confines of meditation and keeps them so without getting lured by them until they are handed over to our emperor the Supreme Soul, is the *Sattvic* fortitude. (18:737-744).

Rajasic fortitude: The individual who gets engrossed in the affairs of the world and of heaven by means of righteous living, earning and a family life attains his ambitions on the strength of the *Rajasic* fortitude. That fortitude with which he puts in efforts making certain that they would give four times as many gains is called *Rajasic* fortitude. (18:745-748).

Tamasic fortitude: Now I shall tell you the characteristics of *Tamasic* fortitude. This fortitude is made up of all mean qualities. Why should it be called a quality when it is inferior and mean? The word has been used in the case of *Tamasic* attribute without thinking. It shelters lethargy and just as miseries do not leave when one supports of sin similarly sleep never leaves him. Since he loves his body and wealth, fear does not leave him. Just as sin of an ungrateful person is not mitigated, similarly grief resides in him perpetually because of his friendship with worldly things. Because he has tied himself to dissatisfaction, sorrow makes its abode within him. Discontent does not leave him until death. And arrogance also resides in him because attraction for youth, wealth and lust grow within him. He is always afflicted with fear, the enemy of the whole world. Just as death does not forget the body, similarly in a *Tamasic* individual, arrogance is perpetual.

Thus, the fortitude that has clutched the five failings (viz., sleep, fear, despondency, grief and arrogance) should be considered as *Tamasic* fortitude. (18:749-762).

Intellect decides about the three kinds of actions. The three kinds of fortitude then take the actions to completion. For example, even if one can see the path clearly after sunrise, the individual himself has to walk on the path by his own feet, but for that walk also it is necessary to have fortitude, i.e. the determination of mind. Thus I have told you about three types of fortitude and the three types of actions that are completed due to it. The fruit one gets from the action is called happiness. That is also of three types according to the nature of the action. I shall explain to you how this happiness in the form of fruit, becomes of three types due to the three attributes. (18:763-768).

Three Types Of Happiness

When a little spiritual happiness is gained, and continued spiritual practice in the same manner makes it grow until the sorrow for being in the body, vanishes, that happiness is the bliss of the Self. That bliss of the Self also is of three types. I shall tell you the characteristics of each of them. (18:776-777).

Sattvic bliss: In order to achieve that bliss of the Self one has to suffer in the beginning the pains of observing the rules of self-restraints, self control etc. When the strong detachment – which swallows all the likes and dislikes – develops, it uproots the binding (liking) to the heaven and the world. The weakness of intellect etc. gets severely mutilated while listening to strict discretion and observing strict austerities. Surge of the vital airs *Prana* and *Apana* is required to be swallowed through the *Sushumna Nadi* and all these efforts are required to be made in the beginning itself (of spiritual path). (18:781-784). The organs suffer while leaving the sense objects and feel as if it is the end of the aeon; but these pains are to be faced with detachment and courage. Thus, by suffering the pains in the beginning itself they achieve the highest kind of bliss. (18:787-788). Once the sense of detachment gets matured by the knowledge of the Self, all sorrows originating in ignorance, including the detachment, vanish. Intellect becomes one with the Soul and the mine of non-duality automatically opens up for it. In this way, the bliss, which is rooted in detachment and ends in the peace of Self-realisation, may be called *Sattvic* bliss. (18:791-793).

Rajasic happiness: The *Rajasic* happiness overflows when the sense-objects and organs come in contact with each other. (18:794). This happiness that nurtures the individuals is like the company of a confidence trickster or alluring company or a mime-acting that appears to be pleasant in the beginning but are harmful in the end. It exhausts the stock of happiness fast, destroys life and drains the wealth of merit. All sense pleasures that were enjoyed earlier look like a dream and what remains is only suffering sorrow. Thus in this life, this happiness results in calamities and in the after-life also it gives fruits like poison. Those who pamper their sense organs by sacrificing the righteous ways of living and through celebrating the pleasure orgies, strengthen the sins that lead them to hell. The worldly pleasures thus lead to ruin in the after-world. Worldly happiness, which is sweet in the beginning but leads to a bitter end, is *Rajasic* happiness. Do not even let it touch you. (18:797-805).

Tamasic happiness: The pleasure that is obtained from drinking the undrinkable, eating the uneatable, or in the company of a woman of loose morals, or by ruining others, snatching other people's wealth, or by listening to the praise from others, the pleasure that proliferates by lethargy or sleep and in the beginning and at end of which pleasure one misses the road to progress because of delusion, may be considered as *Tamasic* happiness. I am not going into its details because it is impossible. Thus I have clarified how, by the divisions of the action, the resulting happiness has also become of three types. (18:806-810).

No escape from attributes: Is there anything in this world apart from the doer, deed and the fruit thereof? The three attributes are woven in this triad. Therefore keep in mind that there is no object on this earth or in heaven, which is not bound by the attributes of nature. (18:811-813). No creature has escaped from the arrangement

of the attributes in this world. Therefore all objects in this world
are made up of these three attributes. It is these attributes, which
have turned one God into three (Brahma, Vishnu and Mahesh). It
is because of these three attributes that the three worlds (heaven,
earth and nether) were created and the four castes and their duties
have become different. (18:815-817).

DUTIES OF FOUR CASTES

The four castes: At the top of the four-caste system are the Brahmins.
The next two, *Kshatriyas* and the *Vaishyas* are of the same level
as the Brahmins because they are entitled to perform Vedic rites.
The fourth caste i.e. the *Shudras,* does not have the right to the
Vedas therefore its sustenance is dependent upon the first three
castes. Since it comes in close contact with the first three castes i.e.
Brahmin etc., it has been counted as a fourth caste. Because of their
contacts with the twice-born, *Shrutis* included *Shudras* also in the
caste system. *(see notes)* Thus, the caste system divides people into
four types. I shall tell you what the duties of the four castes are and
the nature of the duties. By virtue of these duties these four castes
escape the clutches of the birth and death cycle and attain God.
These duties are assigned to the four castes according to the three
attributes of nature. (18:818-825).

Attributes and castes: In this system the *Sattva* attribute has entered
equally in *Brahmins* and *Kshatriyas.* The *Rajas* attribute mixed
with the *Sattva* attribute has entered the *Vaishyas* while the *Tamas*
attribute mixed with the *Rajas* attribute has entered the *Shudras.*
Thus, mankind, which is basically one whole, has been divided into
four types by the three attributes. *Shastras* clarify the duties that
are separated due to the attributes. Now listen to which duties are
proper for each caste.[14] (18:828-832).

---

14 *This topic is only of academic value today. The qualities and duties mentioned
here are according to the tradition laid down by the Shastras followed until
the beginning of the British rule in India. Western education and new type
of professions has changed this. Today, these are not followed completely in*

The nine qualities of a Brahmin: Controlling the bodily tendencies and desires, the intellect meets the Self in solitude like a wife embracing her husband in private. This peaceful nature of the intellect is called *"Shama"* or *serenity* and all actions (fit for Brahmins) start from it. That which restrains the external organs by showing them the fear of the scriptural rules and does not let them turn towards unrighteousness is called *"Dama"* or *restraint,* and it is a helpmate to *"Shama".* It is the second quality of action. Ever thinking about God is called *"Tapas"* or austerity and is the third quality of action. This action has two types of *purity* or *"Shoucha",* the internal purity of the mind with pure emotions and the external purity of the body with good deeds. This is the fourth quality of this type of action. To tolerate all pains as the earth does is called *"Kshama"* or *forbearance,* which is the fifth quality and is sweet like the *"Panchama"* tone.[15] To behave in a straightforward manner with an individual who is against you is the sixth quality called *"Aarjava"* or *uprightness.* Understanding that behaving as prescribed in the scriptures leads to God-realisation is Knowledge and is the seventh quality of action. Steadfast unification of the intellect with the Supreme person by means of the power of knowledge of the *Shastras* or by meditation after the mind is purified is called *"Wisdom"* *(Vidnyan)* and is the eighth quality. And accepting what is prescribed by the *Shastras* is the same as *belief in God (Aastikya)* is the ninth quality of action and the action that has this quality is the true action. Thus, the action in which these nine qualities i.e. serenity etc., are faultlessly present is the natural duty of a Brahmin. (18:845-851). This string of nine jewels of the nine qualities is an ornament of a Brahmin and he is never without it. (18:854).

---

practice. Over time, education has drifted away from Vedas and Shastras. Education and jobs are closely linked making a family tradition obsolete in general. Engineering profession for example has trades that should belong to Vaishyas and Shudras but one finds engineers from all castes. Kshatriyas are no longer the only persons in Defense profession; we have people from all castes. Public Health was earmarked for those who have been termed traditionally as untouchables but we see people from all castes as Public Health Engineers.
15 *Equivalent to "G" scale of the western music.*

Seven qualities of a Kshatriya: Now I shall tell you what the proper action for a Kshatriya is. (18:855). He is strong like a lion who does not seek anybody's company while going hunting and exhibits inborn bravery without external support. This *bravery* is the first and best of the qualities of a *Kshatriya*. (18:856-857). To astonish the world by one's strength and qualities and not getting disturbed under any circumstances is the second notable quality known as *martial lustre* exhibited by *Kshatriyas*. Courage or *fortitude* is his third quality by means of which his mind and intellect do not experience fear, even if heavens come down. (18:859-861). Overcoming the emotional effects (joy, sorrow, fear etc.) resulting from many calamities and guiding the intellect to pass through them and obtain favourable results, is the fourth quality of a Kshatriya called *alertness*. Extreme *fighting spirit* is his fifth quality. He faces the enemy and avoids retreating from the enemy. This fifth quality is superior among all the qualities just as devotion is among the four worldly obligations of a person. (18:863-867). Giving limitlessly in charity as per people's wishes and needs is the sixth quality of a *Kshatriya* called *generosity*. (18:869-870). To protect and foster the subjects with love and to receive their services is the *sense of Godly duty* or *"Ishwarbhava"* *(Note: King is considered as representative of God)*. The storehouse of all power is this *sense of being God's representative,* which should be reflected in the behaviour of a *Kshatriya* and is the seventh quality, which is the king among all the qualities. A *Kshatriya* is adorned by these seven qualities. (18:871-873). The action that becomes sacrosanct by these seven qualities is the natural action of a *Kshatriya*. (18:878).

Qualities of a Vaishya: Now I shall tell you about actions proper for a *Vaishya*. (18:879). To make a lot of profit from farm, seeds and ploughs, in short, to live by farming, maintaining cattle, or buying goods cheaply and selling them at higher price are the natural actions of a *Vaishya*. (18:880-882).

Quality of a Shudra: The three castes *Vaishya, Kshatriya* and *Brahmin* are termed as *dwija* or twice born.[16] To serve them is only

---

16 *It is traditional for the members of the three castes: Brahmin, Kshatriya and Vaishya to undergo a ceremony called moujibandhan or thread ceremony after which they are formally entitled to study and to perform Vedic rites. This*

the true prescribed duty of a Shudra. There is no duty for *Shudras* other than serving the twice born. Thus I have told you about the actions proper for the four castes. (18:883-884).

Duties to be done as per caste entitlement: Just as joining the river is proper for rainwater and joining the ocean is proper for the river, similarly it is proper for a person to do whatever actions fall to his lot as per the rules of the four caste system. One's duties and entitlement as per one's caste should be understood from the *Shastras* and one should resolve firmly to do the natural actions as prescribed by them. (18:886-889, 891). A person who does actions in this manner, but laying stress on doing them gladly with body and mind without lethargy and without desire for fruits of the actions, does them exactly as prescribed by the *Shastras* and reaches the gates on this side of liberation (i.e. detachment), because he does not allow himself to be tainted either by not doing the prescribed deeds nor by doing the prohibited ones. He is therefore not affected by the ills of the worldly affairs. He considers actions with desire like shackles of sandalwood and does not even look at them. And because he gives up the fruits of the other actions namely the routine actions and thus nullifies them, he reaches the boundary of liberation. In this way he avoids the traps of sin and merit in this world and stands at the gates of liberation, detached. (18:893-894, 896-900).

IMPORTANCE OF DETACHMENT

Detachment – which is the boundary limit of all fortunes, the giver of Knowledge for attaining liberation and the endpoint of the labours of the path of action - is the fruit of the tree of merit and the guarantee for liberation. The bee i.e. the seeker, sits on the flower of detachment. That detachment is the dawn, signifying that the sun of Self-realisation is about to rise. (18:901-903). Thus, by observing the rules of prescribed actions he becomes entitled

---

is considered as being reborn as a person of that caste. Thus he is once born as a person in the world and second time he is born in the caste.

to liberation. Arjuna, performing this prescribed action is my one and only call and is the highest kind of service to Me, the Soul of everything. (18:905-906).

Prescribed duties puts burden on God: A faithful wife exchanges pleasures with her husband in all sorts of ways and the very same is her *tapas;* or a child has no means of life support except from its mother; therefore its righteous action is to serve her. (18:907-908). One should not abandon one's prescribed duties. When the prescribed duties are performed it puts an obligation on God. It is His desire that everybody should do appropriate duties prescribed for him. Therefore when these duties are done one doubtlessly attains God. (18:910-911). Not to default on behaving as desired by Him, is the highest service to Him. Doing anything other than this, is purely business. Therefore when prescribed duty is performed it does not amount to action. It amounts to obeying the commands of God from whom the five principles came into existence. That God wraps up the rags of ignorance to make puppet dolls of individuals and makes them play with the strings made of ego with the strands of the three attributes. God has pervaded the universe from inside as well as outside like the light from a lamp and when He is worshipped with the flowers of good deeds he is pleased. Therefore the Soul who is pleased with the worship confers upon him the grace *(prasad)* of detachment. In that state of detachment his attention is concentrated on God and he dislikes the entire world like vomit and all the pleasures in the world also appear to him like sorrows. Even before attaining the final achievement, he achieves oneness with God by his total attention to Him and becomes worthy of Self-realisation. Therefore, he who observes austerities for achieving liberation should practice own *Dharma* with deep faith. (18:913-922).

FOLLOW OWN *DHARMA*

Arjuna, though own *Dharma* (*Swadharma*) is difficult to

observe one should keep in mind the fruits one would gain from it. (18:923). Shall we not miss the bliss of liberation if we start to dislike our own *Dharma* because it is difficult? (18:926). Even if our mother is a hunchback, her love on which we survive is not so. (18:927). Even if *ghee* has better qualities than water can fish live in *ghee?* What is poison to the world is like nectar to the organisms living in it. Therefore, even though it is difficult to observe, everyone should do only what is prescribed for him and that which will liberate him from the worldly troubles. To adopt other people's behaviour *(dharma)* because it appears good, is like walking on your head instead of on your feet. Therefore Arjuna, is it not necessary to make a rule that one should practice one's own *Dharma* and avoid those of others? There is going to be a need for actions as long as Self-realisation has not been attained and doing any action will always be difficult in the beginning. (18:929-935).

When every action has its difficulties then why should we blame our *Dharma* for being difficult? (18:936). If doing even actions that we like involves labour, then how can we say that actions prescribed by *Shastras* are difficult? (18:945). Is there any fruit to be reaped other than sorrow when one accumulates sins by exerting one's organs and spending the time of our life? Therefore one should practice only one's own natural *Dharma* because it will mitigate your labours and fetch you liberation *(Moksha)*, the highest among the four obligations of man.[17] (18:948-949). Then pleased by the great worship of observing one's own *Dharma*, God destroys the *Tamas* and *Rajas* attributes from the mind and directs one's eagerness towards *Sattva* attribute resulting in the conviction that this earth and heaven are like poison.[18] The person then achieves the detachment of the type implied by the word *"Sansiddha"* used earlier (in the *Gita Shloka* No. 45) to explain the meaning

17 *(Dharma, Artha, Kama and Moksha) See footnote against Ovi No (12: 219-229)*

18 *Sadhana is to be practiced with the aim of not only of not having rebirth on this earth but also without the aim of attaining heaven where one stays only as long as merit lasts after which one is reborn on earth.*

of detachment. I shall now tell about how he becomes a seeker once this state of detachment is mastered and what he gains by it. (18:952-955).

BECOMING A SEEKER

Such a person is not caught in the web of worldly things like the body etc. His love for the world becomes dulled. He does not consider his sons, wealth and family as his even if they go by his wishes. Then his intellect scalded by the sense pleasures reverses into seclusion (i.e. becomes introspect). His conscience does not break the vow of not turning towards external objects. The seeker then grips his mind in the hold of oneness with God and turns its interest towards the Soul. At that time, his desire for the worldly things and for things beyond the world, vanishes. Therefore if the mind is controlled then desire also vanishes. Thus, the illusions about the realness of the world vanish and he comes to the state of true knowledge (of the Self). His past *karmas* are nullified by going through the process of enjoying or suffering for them and new *karma* is not created, because the ego of being the doer of the actions has already vanished. This state is called *"Karma-samya-dasha"* or the state of null *karmas*. When this state of null *karmas* is attained, he meets his Guru automatically. (18:956-966). Once he meets his Guru, his actions and his responsibility as doer stops. (18:968). The ignorance of the seeker is then destroyed by the blessings of the true Guru. (18:970).

State of actionlessness: Once ignorance gets destroyed then the triad of actions, the doer and the act of doing vanishes and karma is abandoned automatically. Thus, when the visible world is wiped away by destroying ignorance, which is the root cause of all actions, then the seeker realises that what he was endeavouring to know is he himself. (18:971-973). When ignorance goes, it also takes with it the worldly knowledge and what remains, is the actionless Consciousness. Therefore that state of pure knowledge is called non-doing (or actionlessness). He then remains in the state of his original form. The state of complete actionlessness is the *Siddhi* of actionlessness and is naturally the most superior among the *Siddhis*. (18:977-980). There is nothing more to be gained beyond the state of actionlessness. (18:983). This state is attained by the blessings of a true Guru. (18:984). Who can say that a person whose inclination has become steady in the Self by the destruction of duality, after listening, due to the fortunate advice of his true Guru has any action remaining to be done? Without doubt, such a person has nothing left to be done. (18:987-990). But it is not everybody that can reach that state. What a person, who has not yet been able to reach the state of Self-realisation should do is explained in the following. (18:991).

Getting ready to meet his Guru: The seeker should first burn in the fire of prescribed actions, using the fuel of actions-with-desire and prohibited actions the *Rajas* and *Tamas* attributes (i.e., burn prohibited actions as well as desire based actions Also, he should see that the desire for children, wealth and heaven should be under his complete control. The organs, which were exposed to various sense pleasures, should be controlled (*Pratyahar* or control of organs). And acting, as prescribed by his own *Dharma*, and making the offering of the fruits of the actions of his *Swadharma* to God, he should attain a steady state of detachment. He should work towards obtaining the means by which knowledge can grow and Self-realisation attained. If one meets his true Guru after being so prepared and the Guru gives advice on Self Realisation without reservations, (18:991-997) then in time he will gain the fruits. (18:999).

When one achieves detachment and also meets a true Guru *(Sadguru)* and discrimination takes root in his mind, then the mind, using that discrimination, decides that Brahman alone is real and all other worldly things are an illusion.

But the state of oneness with the all-pervading and the supreme Brahman is achieved only step by step in due time. This is the end of the path to liberation; the three states (of wakefulness, dream and sleep) dissolve in the thus attained Knowledge, in which the Knowledge itself dissolves; where Knowledge dissolves in itself the oneness of unification with Brahman vanishes and not even a trace of bliss of the Self remains; but which still remains as a remainder even when nothing remains, and the state of oneness with it (which is Brahman) is achieved step by step in due time.[19] (18:1001-1006).

The lamp of thoughts is lit by the oil of detachment and the seeker gets the treasure of the Self. The essence of the steps by which a seeker, who has become permanently worthy of enjoying this treasure of the Self achieves Self-realisation is what I shall tell you about now. (18:1008-1010).

STEPS TO SELF-REALISATION

That seeker reaches the banks of the holy waters of discrimination through the path shown by the Guru; he thus washes the dirt from his intellect. Then that intellect becomes pure and reaches its original state. Abandoning the conflict between happiness and sorrow the intellect gets engrossed in contemplation of the Self. By controlling the organs, he eliminates the five fields of pleasure to

---

19 *One may refer to the peace mantra in Ishavasyopanishad: Om Puurnnam-Adah Puurnnam-Idam Puurnnaat-Purnnam-Udacyate | Puurnnashya Puurnnam-Aadaaya Puurnnam-Eva-Avashissyate || Om Shaantih Shaantih Shaantih || The literal translation: That is infinite; this is infinite; From That infinite this infinite comes. From That infinite, this infinite removed or added; Infinite remains infinite. This is the definition of Brahman. Note that this state is not reached after the first experience of the Self but the Sadhak with continued practice must get the experience often until he is continuously in the Self-realized state. See Ovis (13:23-25) which elaborate on this point with an apt analogy: "And once the Knowledge thus gets completely ingrained in his mind then he becomes one with Me. But just as a person who has just sat down cannot be said to have been sitting around similarly unless Knowledge becomes fixed in a person, he cannot be called a person of Knowledge. Then he steadies his sights on the Brahman, the Object-to-be-known, which is the fruit of gaining pure knowledge".*

which the organs had given importance, brushing aside a life of Knowledge. On the strength of his *Sattvic* courage, the seeker tunes his purified organs to introspect the path of yoga. Similarly if he has to enjoy or suffer the fruits of the *karmas* of past lives he does not long for those fruits. In this way, giving up liking for good and dislike for the bad or harmful, he lives alone in a cave or forested hills where there is no disturbance from people. His pastime is to control the mind and the organs; his speech is silence. He is not aware of how much time passes in the contemplation of the *mantra* given by his Guru. And while eating he does not bother about three things, namely: to become strong, to satisfy his hunger and satisfy his taste buds. The satisfaction he gets by eating little has no measure. The body will die if hunger is not satisfied therefore he eats just enough to sustain life and that too in quantities that will not make him sleepy or lethargic. His body touches the ground only when he prostrates before the deity he worships; otherwise he does not lie on ground thoughtlessly. He moves his limbs only for getting food for the survival of the body. In this way he keeps his mind and organs under control. (18:1011-1029).

He does not permit his tendencies to reach the threshold of the mind. Then where is the question of expressing them in words? Conquering the body, speech, mind and external organs, he masters meditation. He constantly guards the steady interest in the Self-realisation awakened in him by the *Mantra* given by his true Guru. The customary way of meditation is to meditate in such a way that the process of meditation and the object on which he meditates, become one. For this one has to meditate until the process of meditation, the meditator and the object of meditation become one. Therefore the seeker, with his attention on attaining Self-realisation, resorts to the practice of yoga of meditation.[20] By pressing the joint midway between the anus and the genitals and thus contracting the anus, he practices the three postures (namely, the *Mula Bandha* posture, the *Jalandhar Bandha* and the *Odhiyana Bandha*) and unites the *pranas* thereby awakening his *Kundalini*.

---

20 See Chapter 6. . (6:192-210).

Clearing the path of the *Sushumna* nerve, he breaks through all the *Chakras* from *Muladhar Chakra* to *Adnya Chakra* and then releasing the shower of nectar from the *Sahasrar* (the thousand petal lotus at the top of the head), he brings the stream of the nectar down to the *Muladhar Chakra*. Then he makes an offering of his mind and the *pranas* to the consciousness active in the *Adnya Chakra*. While this power of *Kundalini* is being activated he continues his practice of meditation in the background. In order that the practice of yoga and meditation should continue uninterrupted, he has already befriended detachment, which accompanies him right from the beginning, until he attains the final unification with the Self. (18:1030-1043).

If detachment is present in a seeker of liberation until his tendencies dissolve in the Self then how can impediments come in his spiritual path? Therefore that fortunate person becomes worthy of Knowledge of the Self by practising yoga with detachment. Protected by the armour of detachment he rides the horse of *Raja yoga*, and holding the sword of meditation firmly in the grip of discrimination, he cuts through all difficulties, big and small, and marches in the dark battlefield of the world and wins the liberation. (18:1045-1049).

Enemies to be conquered:

First enemy-Body ego: Now, the first among the enemies, in the form of failings that have come to stop him in this battle and whom he has beaten, is the ego of the body (I-am-the-body feeling). This ego of the body does not leave you after killing you nor does it allow you to live properly after you take birth; it traps you and keeps you languished in the stockade of the body skeleton. But that brave seeker captures the fort of the body that is the shelter of this ego.

Second enemy-Strength: And strength is the second enemy he subdues. This enemy, i.e. strength, quadruples itself at the mention of sense-pleasures; it leads the entire world to the state of death. It is thus a basin of the poisons of the sense-pleasures and king of all failings. But how can it survive the blow of the sword of meditation?

(18:1050-1054).

Third enemy-arrogant pride: And the third traitorous enemy, which the seeker kills (by meditation), is the arrogant pride that makes a person feel happy when he gets the things he likes and shouts in that fit of joy. It makes the seeker go astray from the good ways and pushes him towards non-righteous ways, leaving him in the clutches of hell. And anger, the biggest of the failings that even the greatest of the *tapaswis* (observers of *tapas*) dread, arises from it.

Fourth enemy-lust: And the next failing is lust which grows more demanding the more you satisfy it. If you destroy it then anger also gets destroyed.

Fifth enemy-Parigraha: Just as the king makes the shackles to be carried by the very person for whose feet they are meant, similarly, *Parigraha* or the tendency to possess is the enemy which grows with possessions. It influences the seeker and introduces bad qualities in him and makes him dependent on family attachment. It has enticed even hermits into the company of people by means of activities like acquiring disciples, collecting books, building religious centres, exhibiting yogic prowess like *Khechari Mudra* etc. Even if he leaves home and goes to the forest then *Parigraha* manifests itself in the form of forest creatures and articles and pursues him even if he is naked. The seeker (my meditation) destroys the unconquerable *Parigraha* and enjoys the pleasure of having conquered the world. (18:1055-1066).

Therefore, the qualities like pridelessness etc. (See 13:201) now come under his command and offer him the kingdom of the true Knowledge (of the Self). And when he travels on the path of actions he is hailed by the three states of wakefulness, dream and sleep. Then the discrimination drives away the visible world and the state of yoga welcomes him. He is showered by *Riddhi* and *Siddhi*, the occult powers. And as the kingdom of unity with Brahman approaches near he finds the three worlds full of bliss. At this stage everything becomes equal and no duality is left which might have made him say that this is my friend and that is my enemy. In fact there is nothing left in the world which he can say belongs to him because he has become one with Brahman. Since he has embraced the entire universe, narrow feelings like attachments[21] are cast away. (18:1067-1075).

Worthiness to become Brahman: Thus, when the enemies are conquered and the realisation that the entire universe is unreal has been gained, the *Rajayoga* practice becomes automatically steady and he loosens the strong armour of detachment for some time. There is nothing left to be destroyed by meditation therefore he restrains his actions. (18:1076-1078). When attainment of Brahman approaches, his practice also stops. (18:1080). As soon as it is apparent that Self-realisation would soon be experienced, he does away with the means of spiritual practice; thereafter, the means for attaining spiritual realisation become progressively less and less – for they are no more needed. Then, when the detachment has reached perfection, the study of Knowledge matured and the fruits of yoga practice are seen in the form of peace pervading throughout his person, then the seeker is worthy of becoming Brahman Himself. (18:1083-1086). The unsteady nature of the river is seen only where it enters the sea; but the water which has become part of the sea remains calm. Similar is the relation between the *Siddha* who becomes Brahman and Brahman itself and by virtue of the pervading peace he soon attains Brahmanhood. But when instead of *becoming* Brahman a seeker *experiences*. Then it is called worthiness to become Brahman.[22] (18:1088-1090).

That person who has reached the state of worthiness of becoming Brahman gains cheerfulness of mind. (18:1091). The labours made for attaining Self-realisation are mitigated. This is the state that is gained by Self-realisation, which is well known by the term *Atma-bodha-prashasti* or serene cheerfulness. Because of being full of equanimity he neither grieves because something is lost nor desires anything in particular. (18:1094-1096). After

---

21 *Feelings like "This is mine" etc.*
22 *At this stage the seeker definitely experiences Brahman but has not become one with it. See Ovis (13:23-25) which elaborate on this point.*

he experiences Self-realisation, differences in anything he looks at, disappear. Because of this, whatever improper knowledge was gained during his erstwhile state, during the dream and wakefulness states, dissolves in ignorance. As Self-realisation increases, that ignorance also continues to decrease and dissolves into that Knowledge. (18:1098-1101).

Fourth kind of Devotion: As the knowable becomes less and less and the knower merges into Me along with Knowledge, all ignorance also vanishes. (18:1106). He then gains the fourth kind of devotion to Me wherein he cannot see anything other than Me; this devotion is called the fourth type because there are three other categories of devotion namely *Aarta* (distressed), *Jijnasu* (curious), *Artharthi* (desirous of wealth).[23]

Actually if you think about it, there is really nothing like devotion of the first type or the fourth type; that devotion is the name given to my natural state. (18:1111-1113). It is the same devotion which manifests itself as deep desire in an *Aarta* (distressed) devotee where the object of desire also is Me. In *Jijnasu* (curious) devotee, the same devotion becomes the desire for knowledge (the curiosity to know more.) The same devotion becomes the desire for wealth and wealth – which means everything – also becomes Me. (18:1119-1121). Thus this devotion to Me, because of ignorance, considers Me, the seer, as an object to be seen. *It is devotion to Me that is practised everywhere but the visible form imagined for Me is due to ignorance.* After the ignorance is removed, I am understood again as the seer. (18:1124-1125). Like the perfect moon on the full moon night, I am seen through the path of Knowledge also but in a different way. When I am thus seen, it is only I who gains Me and the seer also vanishes as a seer. Therefore Arjuna, this fourth type of devotion to Me is beyond the visible paths. (18:1127-1129).

You have already heard that the devotee who becomes one with Me with this Knowledge based devotion, becomes nothing other than Me because in the seventh chapter I have sworn to you that

---

23 See Ovis (7:108-109).

a person of Knowledge is My soul. In the beginning of the aeon itself I advised Brahmadeo through the *Bhagwat (Purana)* that this very same type of devotion is the best. Persons of knowledge call it "*Swa-Sanviti*" (Knowledge) and the Shaivaites call it *Shakti*. We call it "Extreme devotion". A *Kramayogi*[24] (*i.e. a yogi who progresses towards Self-realisation step by step.*) attains it at the time of becoming one with Me. Then he realises that it is I who has pervaded the whole universe. In this condition, detachment totally disappears with discrimination, binding with liberation and activism with renunciation. Just as the sky principle remains even after swallowing the other four principles, in the same way he remains aloof and attains unity with My pure and immaculate form, which is beyond the means and the goal and then enjoys the bliss of the Brahman. This experiencing of the bliss of the Brahman is like the distinct shining of Ganga even after it joins the ocean. A mirror kept before another mirror sees its own reflection. That is the manner in which the *Kramayogi* experiences the bliss of the Brahman. Even after the mirror is removed and the reflected image vanishes, the one looking into the mirror enjoys the bliss of the form of the Self in himself. This is similar to the feeling when one wakes up – the dream vanishes and the person realises that he is alone; and even when nobody else is there, he enjoys the aloneness. (18:1130-1141).

BEING ONE WITH ME

Some may say that there cannot be enjoyment after Oneness has been attained. (18:1142). But how can he who has not been one with Me know who I am? Then how can it be said that he is devoted to Me? Therefore that *Kramayogi* becomes one with Me and enjoys My form even without doing actions. (18:1145-1147, 1149). There may not be any action in non-duality but there is definitely devotion and that cannot be expressed in words but can be understood only from experience. It cannot be described in

24 Note: *not to be confused with Karmayogi who is the follower of the path of action. See later (18:1214-1218).*

words. (18:1151). When such a person, by previous influences utters anything or gives a call to Me then I respond to his call and it is as if it was I who made those utterances. When the speaker himself becomes Me then there cannot be any speaking and under these conditions silence constitutes my best praise. Therefore since it is only I that is speaking when he speaks, what is produced is silence and that silence is My praise. (18:1152-1154). In the same way whatever he sees through his eyes or intellect, that seeing pushes aside the object to be seen and shows instead the form of the seer himself. (18:1155). Thus, when the visible object disappears and is experienced as the seer himself, then even the consciousness of his being the seer, does not remain in that oneness. (18:1157). Thus, when the seer becomes one with My form and sees any object then that object and the seer both vanish along with the action of seeing. (18:1161). Once the seer becomes one with My form the visibility of the object, does not remain. This state in which the object is seen as well as not seen is my real vision. He experiences this vision with any object and he attains the sight that is beyond the visible object and the seer. And because he has entered the Self he is never unstable. (18:1163-1165). Because he has completely attained my 'form', i.e. Me, he becomes quiet (18:1166), and his coming and going stops; and that itself becomes pilgrimage to the non-duality that is Me. (18:1168).

He had gone away from Me because of his I-am-the-body feeling and now he has returned to Me; therefore this going and coming is his pilgrimage and he becomes My pilgrim. (18:1172). If due to the disposition of his body he started doing some actions then it is only I who meets him on the pretext of the action. Arjuna, in this state the difference between the deed and the doer vanishes and he himself becomes Me seeing Me through the Self. (18:1173-1174).

How can any action done after becoming one with Me become an action? If one does not maintain the ego of being the doer while doing action then all his actions become non-actions and that is the sign of My worship. Therefore Arjuna, even if he has done any action in prescribed way then it does not imply he has done any action, instead it becomes My superior worship. (18:1176-1179).

In this way whatever he speaks becomes My praise, whatever he sees becomes My vision and his walk becomes pilgrimage to non-duality that is Me. Arjuna, whatever he does becomes My worship. Whatever he thinks becomes My *Japa*, and the state he is in becomes My *samadhi*. He becomes one with Me through the yoga of devotion. (18:1180-1182). With his exceptional devotion he sees Me as the seer in everything that can be seen. He dances wildly with the knowledge that the visible universe apparent in the form of the field and the knower of the field in the three states of wakefulness, dream and sleep is all Me who is the Seer. (18:1185-1187). He knows that when he awakens then all emotions he saw in the dream were not different from himself. Similarly he experiences that what appears to exist and not exist is all himself who is the knower. He knows that I am the birthless, ageless, inexhaustible, and indestructible, without past and limitless bliss. He also knows that I am also immovable, not liable to fall down, infinite, incomparable, root of everything, formless as well as with form, bender of the ruling powers as well as the ruler, without beginning, indestructible, fearless, support of objects as well as the supported ones. He also knows that I am the master of everything, and that I am ever, natural, unceasing, everything and in everything and beyond all. That which is the most recent and also the oldest, with no form or with complete form, biggest or the tiniest, is all Me. That which is actionless, companionless and without sorrow is also Me. All things are in Me and I am in all things. Thus, I am the Superior Person.[25] I am without words, without ears, form or lineage. I am the uniform, independent and the ultimate Brahman. Thus, by becoming one with Me, he knows Me through his incomparable devotion and also realises that this knowledge is also Me. (18:1191-1200).

After the knowable has dissolved and only the knower remains, one who knows this is also the knower himself. Arjuna, he also realises that the power of Knowledge that knows this non-duality, is also Me. (18:1203-1204). When he knows that the one and the

25 *Purushottama.*

only Soul beyond the duality and non-duality is undoubtedly only Me and actually experiences it. (18:1205), then with the awareness of "I am he"[26] having dissolved in the bliss of the Self he enters My form. Therefore the reference to "he" becomes irrelevant and consequently reference to "I" also becomes baseless and he merges into My form. (18:1209-1210). Just as when one is subtracted from one, the remainder is zero, similarly when being and non-being are subtracted from each other what remains is Me. In that state it is meaningless to talk about the terms Brahman, Soul and God; and it is also meaningless to say that nothing exists. (18:1212-1213). Just as not speaking is as good as speaking a mouthful, realisation comes without the awareness of knowledge and ignorance. In that state realisation realises realisation, bliss enjoys bliss, happiness becomes happy, gain begets gain, brightness becomes bright and surprise dissolves in surprise; control of mind becomes silent, repose relaxes, and experience gets obsessed with experience. In short, he gains the pure fruits of becoming Me through the practice of *Kramayoga* (or the yoga of step by step progress). (18:1214-1218).

I am the crown of that emperor [27] of *Kramayoga* and in exchange for it he becomes the crown jewel of Knowledge. Or he becomes the expanse of sky above the pinnacle of liberation of the temple of *Kramayoga*. In these woods of the world, *Kramayoga* is the proper road that takes one to the town of unity with Me. Or, with the waters of knowledge with devotion, the seeker reaches the ocean of bliss of the Self which is Me, by the current of *Kramayoga*. Arjuna, I am telling this to you again and again because of the greatness of *Kramayoga*. Arjuna, I am not attainable by means of choosing a place, time or substance because I am naturally present in all, therefore no difficulties are faced in attaining Me. I can be attained easily by following the *Kramayoga*. (18:1219-1225).

---

26 Here "he" means himself i.e. the aspirant.
27 The Self-realized aspirant.

THE *GITA* SUPERIOR TO *SHASTRAS*

Shri Krishna says, "The Guru-disciple system has been established for learning how to attain Me. (18: 1226). Though I am always available, just as wealth present in the earth requires efforts to extract it, I can be attained only by certain means." (18:1228).

One may ask why Shri Krishna is talking about means after talking about the fruits so far. The excellence of the *Gita* lies in the fact that all the means suggested in it lead to attainment of liberation. The methods told in other *Shastras* are not necessarily all proven ones. (18:1229-1230). *Shastras* remove the grime of ignorance but beyond this they are not qualified to give knowledge of the Self. The place the *Shastras* have to go for proving their authenticity is the *Gita*. *Gita* guides the *Shastras* on proper path. (18:1233-1235).

Shri Krishna has discussed various methods for Self-realisation in detail in the earlier chapters of the *Gita*. But thinking that perhaps Arjuna might not have understood the subject by hearing once, Shri Krishna is telling the same thing again as a summary. And now that the *Gita* is nearing its conclusion he has tried to bring uniformity of objective between the beginning and the end, the reason being that various principles have been discussed in the middle parts to explain the various topics that arose during the discussion. Therefore somebody might say without considering the context of the earlier and later parts of the *Gita* that these principles are the main principles giving the essence of the *Gita*. Therefore we are ending the *Gita* by proving that the various principles are included in the consideration of the main principle. (18:1236-1242).

THE ESSENCE OF THE *GITA*

Destroying ignorance is the main topic of *Gita*, attaining liberation is its fruit, and the means for these two is Knowledge. This Knowledge has been discussed in detail in various ways in this book. Shri Krishna is telling the same thing again in a concise form. Therefore Shri Krishna has set upon to discuss the means for achieving the goal even if the goal has been achieved. (18:1243-1245).

Shri Krishna said, "That *Kramayogi,* by becoming one with Me with such dedication, remains so eternally. By worshipping Me with flowers of prescribed duties he gets faith in the knowledge of the Self by My favour. Once this faith is achieved then the devotion to Me grows and due to that devotion he becomes happy by becoming one with Me. He observes Me the Soul, illuminator of the whole world, as pervading everything (18:1246-1249). While he follows Me and takes shelter under Me with intellect, words and body, he may sometimes do improper deeds but just as when the stream of dirty street water and the big river are same once they meet the Ganges, once he has attained My knowledge, good and evil become same.[28] (18:1251-1252). The differences like good and evil appear only until one gets My all-pervading illumination. (18:1255). Therefore, as soon as he meets Me his *karma* in nullified and he occupies the seat of unification with Brahman. He achieves my eternal position, which is not affected by location, time or nature. All in all Arjuna, what gains will one who has gained My pleasure miss? Therefore Arjuna, surrender all actions in Me. (18:1257-1260).

Keep your attention in discrimination without abandoning the routine duties. It is with the strength of that discrimination that you will see My blemish less form which is different from action. You will observe that *Maya* in which all actions are rooted is far from you. You will find that just as there is no shadow without form similarly *Maya* also is not separate from the Soul. Once *Maya* is negated then total renunciation of all the actions *(karmas)* will occur without efforts. Once all karmas vanish then what remains is only soul. You now dedicate your intellect to it. This way your intellect will remain singularly united in Me. At that time your mind will abandon all other issues and be devoted to Me. Act rapidly

---

28 *This is only when he has finally become one with Him, not just after he experiences Self Realization.*

in this manner in order to see that by abandoning all subjects of contemplation the mind is concentrated in Me. (18:1261-1268).

When with this exceptional devotion your mind becomes one with Me you will receive my complete favour. Then the sorrows of birth and death, which all creatures have to suffer, become pleasurable however hard they may be. (18:1269-1270). How can he, whose I-am-the-body attitude has been completely destroyed by My favour, be afraid of the worldly matters? Therefore Arjuna, you will be saved from the downfall from the worldly matters, but if, under the influence of your ego, you ignore my advice then you will have to suffer the injuries caused by body awareness even after being liberated and being indestructible. In this realm of the body awareness there is not a moment's respite in suffering death at every step. If you do not listen to my advice then you will have to suffer terrible pains of death without even dying. (18:1272-1277).

If you despise discrimination and foster the ego and because of that ego, by using your own intellect, you called your own body as 'Arjuna', bodies of others as 'relatives' and the battle as 'sinful action' and became firmly determined that you will not fight, even then your inborn nature will make that determination infructuous. (18:1279-1285).

By your possessing the nature of a *Kshatriya* you have in you the inborn qualities like bravery, martial lustre, alertness etc.; therefore by virtue of these qualities of a *Kshatriya* your nature will not let you keep quiet without fighting. You cannot go against your nature because you are bound by these qualities. (18:1287-1291). A sick person does not like his illness nor does a poor person like his poverty but he has to suffer it due to his strong destiny. Due to the Divine power of God, the same destiny will not let you do otherwise. That God also resides in your heart. (18:1297-1298). That God has manifested himself by donning the ego of all beings. Through the veil of His *Maya* he singly moves the strings of 8.4 million shadows and makes them dance. He gives shape to everybody from Brahmadeo to a worm, according to its worth. And the creature for whom He sets up the appropriate body, occupies it with the feeling "I am this body". (18:1302-1305). It accepts the form of the body, which is separate from itself and sees itself in it. In this way, by seating the creatures on the contraption of the body, God moves the strings according to their *karmas*. The particular creature for which an independent string is allocated according to its pre-birth *karmas* moves according to that string. (18:1307-1309). Affairs of all creatures are carried by the power of God. (18:1311). Thus the same God, through basic nature, makes all creatures play and the same God is in your heart. Arjuna, the Self generated in your mind when you do not have the feeling that "I am Arjuna" is in fact His true form. Therefore that God will incite you for battle through your nature and make you fight even if you do not desire so. God is the Master of all and controls *Prakriti*. Therefore one should use one's organs to pleasurably do actions, appropriate to *Prakriti*. Therefore you leave the decision about whether you should fight or not, to *Prakriti*. Keep in mind that *Prakriti* is under the control of the God in your heart. (18:1314-1318).

Offer body, speech, mind and ego to Him: Merge into God by making an offering to Him of the body, speech, mind and ego just as the Ganga water merges into the ocean. Then you will attain complete peace by His grace and you will be engrossed in the Self with bliss of the Self. You will be the master of that indestructible state of the Self where creation is born, where repose takes rest and which the experience experiences. (18:1319-1322).

Gita the essence of Vedas: This science, well-known by the name *Gita*, is the essence of the Vedic literature and one achieves the priceless Self through it. Knowledge of the Self customarily known only as Knowledge, by praising which Vedanta became famous in the whole world, of which intellectual subjects are mere reflections and through which even I the Unmanifestable seer of all can be seen, is my secret treasure. But how can I hide it from you? Therefore Arjuna, I have given you this treasure because I feel the greatest sympathy for you. (18:1323-1327). I, the knower of all, having considered all aspects, have told you the true knowledge. Now you ponder on it properly and do what you consider proper.

The *Gita* is the Knowledge by which ignorance about the real nature of the world is destroyed and only I am seen in everything. I have explained this knowledge through the use of examples and similes. I have advised on the Knowledge of the Self in various ways. By that Knowledge shed the ignorance that creates confusion about proper and improper codes of behaviour (*Dharma* and *Adharma* respectively), which lead one to heaven or hell. (18:1388-1391). Just as only the dreamer remains when the dream goes away with the sleep, similarly nothing other than Me remains. Then with the idea that he is Me, the seeker becomes one with Me. Shedding the separateness from Me and realising the oneness with Me is what is called surrender. Once you surrender to Me you will become one with Me, therefore surrender to Me and be one with Me. (18:1396-1400).

How is it possible to surrender to Me as well as live as an individual at the same time? (18:1402). After you meet the God of the universe do not at all listen to the ominous talk that says 'binding of the worldly life does not go'. To serve Me by being one with Me is natural devotion. Gain knowledge through it. (18:1403-1405). After you surrender to Me by the realisation of non-duality you will not be touched by the issues of prescribed and prohibited actions. (18:1407). After becoming one with Me, is there any reason for anything else other than my all-encompassing form? Therefore do not worry about these things or about sin and merit. Understand that I shall become your sin and merit. Being separate from Me is the sign of binding to the *karmas*. That sin will be dissolved by knowledge about Me. Wise Arjuna, when you surrender to Me with undivided mind you will be one with Me and in this way automatically be free of all bindings. Accept Me and I shall free you by my light. Therefore there is no need for you to worry any more. Wise Arjuna, surrender to Me alone. (18:1411-1416).

So saying Shri Krishna embraced Arjuna by extending his right arm. (18:1418). It was just a pretext to impart to Arjuna that which the intellect does not understand and words cannot describe. Once the two hearts touched, the secrets from Shri Krishna's heart entered Arjuna's heart and by demolishing the non-duality He made Arjuna attain Self-realisation. (18:1420-1422).

Thus, Shi Krishna presented the holy Science of *Gita*, which all are entitled to read and which is the basic theme of the Vedas. Now, if you ask how you (i.e. Dnyaneshwar Maharaj) know that the *Gita* contains the basic theme of the Vedas, then the explanation is as follows. The same truthful God through whose breath the Vedas were born, is telling this science of the *Gita* on oath through his own lips. Therefore it would be proper to say that the origin of Vedas is in the *Gita*. (18:1426-1429). Just as a tree is contained in a seed, similarly the three Vedas are contained in the *Gita*. Therefore I think that the *Gita* is the root of the Vedas and I can also see it clearly. (18:1431-1432). I shall now clearly indicate where the three parts of the Vedas namely Action, Worship and Knowledge have been imprinted in the *Gita*. (18:1434).

Chapterwise Summary

In the first chapter is mentioned how the science of The *Gita* originated. The second chapter elucidates the *Sankhya* philosophy, which stresses upon Knowledge; this chapter is independently capable of leading one to liberation without any other help. (18:1435-1436).

Action: The third chapter makes the beginning discourse on the means for attaining liberation by persons who are in the grip of ignorance.

It advises an individual to avoid actions with desire and prohibited actions that bind one to the I-am-the-body feeling and do appropriate incidental and routine actions with care and with pure motives. Such actions are what Shri Krishna has recommended in the third chapter as constituting the Path of Action. (18:1437-1439).

Worship via Path of Action: Shri Krishna has then explained that once the individual starts pondering on how this performance of routine and incidental actions can free one from ignorance (of the Self) and thus reaches the threshold of being an aspirant he should offer all his actions to God (or Brahman). Whatever prescribed action occurs through body, speech or mind should be done as an offering to God. This expression of devotion to God through the path of action *(Karma Yoga),* has been discussed from the fourth chapter until the end of the eleventh chapter on the vision of the universal form. Thus in these eight chapters I have unveiled the section on worship discussed in the *Gita.* (18:1439-1445).

Path of Knowledge: The true knowledge, the knowledge of love, which is created through the devotion to `God and through the Guru-disciple system, is described in the twelfth chapter from the Shloka *"Adweshta"* (*Shloka* No 13) or in the thirteenth chapter from the Shloka *"Amanitva"* (*Shloka* No 7). Therefore the twelfth chapter has been included in the section on knowledge. In the four chapters from the beginning of the twelfth to the end of the fifteenth, the topic of discussion is the 'matured fruit of Knowledge' – hence these four make up the section on Knowledge.

Thus the *Gita,* which elucidates the three sections, is like a loveable *Shruti.* This *Shruti,* which contains the three sections, tells you loudly to gain the fruit of liberation. The class of ignorance, which is always inimical to the means of knowledge, has been described in the sixteenth chapter. That one should conquer this enemy with the help of the *Shastras* is what has been told in the seventeenth chapter. In this way, from the first chapter to the end of the seventeenth, Shri Krishna has discussed the Vedas created from his breath. The essence of all these chapters is contained in this pinnacle that is the eighteenth chapter. (18:1446-1455).

This dissertation named *Bhagavad-Gita,* which has been perfected in 700 *shlokas,* is the very form of the Vedas and is more generous than the Vedas. The Vedas are full of Knowledge but there is none more miserly because they speak only with the first three castes. Others like women, *shudras* etc., who suffer tortures from this world, are not allowed under their shelter. I feel that in order to remove these faults and with the intention of giving benefit to all, the Vedas have reappeared in the form of the *Gita*. Not only that, the Vedas are available to anybody through the *Gita* when its meaning is assimilated by the mind, by listening to it or by reciting it. (18:1456-1460).

BENEFITS OF THE *GITA*

He who always reads this *Gita* or remains in the company of one who reads it or distributes it to people by making copies of it, verily gives the food of the bliss of liberation to all. (18:1461-1462). This *Gita* gives away the bliss of liberation and peace to anyone without discriminating whether that person is good or bad creating peace in the world by gifting the bliss of the Brahman. By being afraid of the earlier criticism the Vedas entered inside the *Gita* and attained dazzling fame. For this reason Shri Krishna personally gave to Arjuna the message of the *Gita* which is the form of the Vedas and which enables one to savour them. (18:1464-1466). Making Arjuna as a pretext Shri Krishna has unveiled the *Gita* and emancipated the world and reduced the burden of worldly matters from people. (18:1470).

Shri Krishna said, "Because of your many meritorious deeds you have become worthy of listening to the *Shastra* of the *Gita* which is the best among all the *Shastras*. Therefore, understand the traditional method of behaviour according to this *Shastra* and perform accordingly with proper rituals. (18:1480-1481). When a disciple gets knowledge through Guru's pleasure, it becomes fruitful only if the customs of the (Guru's) sect are observed. I shall now tell you the appropriate tradition regarding this *Shastra*. (18:1484-1485).

This *Shastra* of the *Gita*, which you have acquired with great earnestness, should never be told to a person devoid of austerity.

And if he observes austerities but is unsteady in the devotion to his Guru then keep him away as Vedas have kept away or excluded *Shudras*. Or if a person observes austerities and is devoted to Guru and God but does not like to listen then too he does not deserve to listen to the *Gita*. (18:1486-1490). Now, if he observes austerities, possesses devotion as well as liking for listening but considers Me, who is the author of the *Gita* and ruler of all people, as an ordinary being or slanders Me or good persons, then also he is unfit to listen to the Gita. (18:1497-1499). The austerity, devotion and intellect of a person who slanders Me or my devotees are deceitful therefore even if such a person is devoted, intelligent and austere do not let him come in touch with this *Gita Shastra*. (18:1504-1505).

Therefore Arjuna, install the idol of the *Gita* in the heart of the superior devotee who has laid a firm foundation of austerity and built the temple of devotion to Guru upon it, installed a pinnacle of the gems of non-slander over it and kept the main door of that temple, (namely the desire for listening) open; then you will be like Me and come to My level of worth.

Because *Aum* – the single letter *Pranava* sound – was trapped inside the three monosyllabic letters *A*, *U* and *Ma*, that root of the Vedas has evolved further in the *Gita*. Or the *Gayatri Mantra* itself flowered and grew fruits in the form of *shlokas* from the *Gita*. He who explains the secret contained in the *shlokas* becomes one with Me after death. I love the devotee with My heart who explains the meaning of the *Gita*, even if he is separated from Me by his body. I like him more than a person of learning, an observer of ritualistic actions and an austere person. There is none dearer to Me than he who tells the *Gita* to a group of devotees on this earth. He who reads the *Gita* making his mind steady with the love for Me becomes an ornament in a gathering of saints. (18:1507-1517).

And the sins of one who with pure mind keeps faith in listening to the *Gita* by abandoning slander in whichever possible way, run away instantly as soon as words of the *Gita* fall in his ears.

(18:1529-1530).[29]

"Arjuna, now I am asking you whether the delusion in your mind caused by your ignorance about the Self has gone or not. Tell Me whether you now realise in yourself the sense of duty and and doing it with a sense of non-doer?" (18:1544-1545).

Arjuna who had become one with Shri Krishna now came to the worldly sense (18:1546) and said in a trembling voice, "I was under the delusion that 'I am Arjuna', but now by Your grace I am now freed from it. The Knowledge of the Self which You have given me has totally uprooted the delusion. (18:1563-1564). Oh Shri Krishna, Object of my devotion! I am prepared to obey any order coming from You. (18:1575)."

On which Krishna, mentally dancing with joy said to Himself, "I have now gained the best of all the fruits in the world in the form of Arjuna." (18:1576).

TRIBUTES TO GURU

I have composed this book in the form of *ovis* which are beautiful to sing or interesting even if they are not sung. In the *ovi* metre are strung letters, which give a taste of Brahman for the young and old. One goes into a trance just by listening to it; that being so, will not listening to its discussion cause an obsession? Even a simple reading of this book makes the learning bloom and one forgets about nectar in the presence of its sweetness. The perfected verse gives such satisfaction that listening to it gives more satisfaction than contemplation and meditation. This listening will impart bliss of the Self to the listener and all organs will be satiated. Persons of spiritual authority understand the secret of

29 *The philosophical part of Dnyaneshwari ends here. In its course it has covered several topics related to why and how to attain self-realization and become immersed in that state and hence liberation from Birth and Death cycles. Dnyaneshwar Maharaj concludes this great work by expressions of gratitude to his Guru Nivruttinath and the leading lights of the Nath Panth.*

the science of spirituality but others become happy even by skilful presentation of it. This is all the greatness of Shri Nivruttinath therefore this is not really my book but the result of his blessing. (18:1741-1750).

On some occasion, Shri Shankar spoke the spiritual knowledge into Parvati's ears. That knowledge was obtained by Matsyendranath who was hiding in the stomach of a fish in that sea of milk *(Kshirasagar)*. When Matsyendranath met the limbless Chouranginath at Saptashringi, the latter regained his limbs. Then, in order that he himself should enjoy the bliss of the *samadhi* without interruption, Matsyendranath gave his state of the yoga to Gorakshanath and installed him in his own position,[30] Gorakshanath being the only one in whom yoga could bloom and who could fight sense pleasures. (18:1751-1755). Then by tradition the bliss of non-duality, which has descended from Shri Shankar, was obtained from Gorakshanath by Gahininath. Seeing that people of the world are troubled Gahininath instructed Shri Nivruttinath to take up the tradition which had descended to him from Sri Adi Sankara and save these people immediately from the influence of the era of Kali.[31] Shri Nivruttinath was already compassionate by nature and in addition his Guru had instructed him therefore he immediately set upon to bring peace to the world. (18:1756-1760). By feeling pity for the distressed he showered peace on them on the pretext of explaining the *Gita*. At that time I was before him anxiously waiting for his favour therefore he elevated me to the position of fame. Thus he handed over the wealth of meditation to me through this book. Otherwise I have not studied, nor I have read and I do not know how to serve my master then how can I achieve the worthiness for composing this book. But in reality Guru Maharaj has given shelter to the world by composing

---

30 As chief of the Nath Panth. Matsyendranath, Gorakshanath, Chouranginath and Gahininath are four of the nine yogis (Navanath) of the Nath Tradition.
31 Note: Kali is the agent of strife and inspirer of strife in the present aeon known by its name Kaliyuga. Not to be confused with Kaali the form of Goddess Durga).

this book making me the incidental pretext. (18:1761-1765).

This book, which all you saints have caused to be completed through my hands so that it is useful to the three worlds, is incomparable. Only thing that now remains for me to do, is the service to you.

PRAYERS FOR THE UNIVERSE

Now, may the Supreme God who is the soul of the entire universe be satisfied by this discourse and grant me grace.

May the wicked shed their sinister outlook and

May they develop liking for good deeds and

May all individuals develop friendship with each other.

May the universe lose its darkness of sin and

May the dawn of righteous duties come and

May the desires of all creatures be fulfilled.

May the assemblies of devotees of God, who shower all that is auspicious upon this earth, meet all creatures.

These devotees are walking seeds of the wish-trees, living community of wish-stones or talking oceans of nectar.

May these saints who are (unblemished) like the moon without spots or sun without the scorching heat, be the friends and relatives to all creatures.

Why ask for more?

May all creatures in the three worlds be perfect and happy and

May every creature carry desire for ceaseless devotion to the Primeval Supreme Being. And,

May those who live by the support of this book gain happiness in this world and in the next.

On hearing this, Lord of the universe said,

"I have granted you this grace."

And by that boon Shri Dnyanadeo was very happy.

(18:1794-1802).

End of Dnyaneshwari
(The Philosophical Part)

Offered At The Feet Of My Guru Shri Shankar Maharaj

BIBLIOGRAPHY

(CV-MU) *Mahabharatacha Upasamhar,* by Vaidya C.V. (in Marathi), Surekha Prakashan.

(EP) *Encyclopedia Puranic* at URL: http://www.epurohith.com/encyclopedia.php?page=20&pedia_index=A

(GD-SS) *Shri Sai Satcharit* (Marathi) by Dabholkar Govind Raghunath (Hemadpant) Pub by Shri Saibaba Sansthan Shirdi. English Tr by N. V. Gunaji at URL http://www.saibaba.org/saisatc.html

(GP-B) *Bhagvadgita or the Song Divine* published by *Gita* Press Gorakhpur.(2007) pp 224.

(HW-LL) *Life before Life* by Helen Wambak, Bantam Books. NY.1979

(KP-MC) *Mahabharata Chronology* by Dr. K.N.S. Patnaik URL: http://www.hindunet.org/hindu_history/ancient/mahabharat/mahab_patnaik.html

(PB-VA) *India in the Vedic Age,* P.L. Bhargava; D.K. Printworld Pvt Ltd, New, Delhi (2001) 462pp

(RB-URL) *An article by Richard Baum* URL: http://richardtitlebaum.com/TheMother.html (date unknown)

(SK-TE) *True Experiences* by Swami Krishnanand, Pub.

Krishnanand Publication Committee, Shanti Ashram, Bhadran, Dist Anand, Gujarat. (1991)

(SR-B) *The Bhagvadgita* (English translation and notes) by Dr S.Radhakrishnan, Harper Collins India Ltd, (1993), 388p

(SY-HS) *The Holy Science* by Swami Shri Yukteshwar Giri, published by Self-Realization Fellowship, Los Angeles. California (1977) 78pp

(UP-CH) *Chandogya Upanishad* by Swami Swahananda published by Ramakrishna Ashram Mylapore. Chennai. (1980) pp 623.

(UP-BA) *The Brihadaranyaka Upanishad* published by Ramakrishna Ashram Mylapore. Chennai (1979) pp 515.

(UP-AI) *Aitareyopanishad* by Swami Sarvananda published by Ramakrishna Ashram Mylapore. Chennai (1978) pp 80

(UP-MA) *Mandukyopanishad* by Swami Sarvananda published by Ramakrishna Ashram Mylapore. Chennai (1976) pp 46.

(VL-AHR) *The Complete Book of Ayurvedic Home Remedies,* By Dr Vasant Lad pub by Three Rivers Press NY, (1999) 326 pp

(VS-DT) *Dattatreya Tradition* by V.V.Shirvaikar URL: http://vvshirvaikar.de/

(WG-AG) *Wikipedia Article on Agamas* at URL: http://en.wikipedia.org/wiki/Agama_(Hinduism)

(WK-SI) *Wikipedia article on Siddhi* URL: http://en.wikipedia.org/wiki/Siddhi

(WK-SD) *Wikipedia Article on Hindu Philosophy* at URL: http://en.wikipedia.org/wiki/Hindu_philosophy

(WK-TAT) *Wikipedia Article on Tatvas* at URL: http://en.wikipedia.org/wiki/Tatvas

(YD-YH) *Yogi Harinathji* by Yogi Dnyananathji, (in Marathi) published by Santkripa Prakashan, Pune 30 in the series Santacharitramala.(1982) pp 80. Pp 51.

Appendix 1

Dnyaneshwari *Ovis* Coresponding To *Gita Shlokas*

KEY- *Gita Shloka* No: *Ovi* Nos – *Ovi* No.

Chapter 1
First 84 *ovis* are dedicated to obeisance.

1: 85-87 2+3: 88-95 4: 96-98 5+6: 99-102 7+8: 103-108 9: 109-114 10: 115-120 11: 121-124 12:125-130 13:131-136 14+15+16:137-150 17+18+19:151-163 20:164-168 21+22+23:169-173 24+25+26+27:174-192 28+29+30:193-206 31:207-209 32+33+34:210-224 35:225-227 36:228-232 37:233-235 38+39:236-242 40:243-245 41:246-251 42:252-256 43+44+45:257-264 46:265-266 47:267- 274

Chapter 2

1: 1-5 2: 6-20 3: 21-29 4: 30-38 5: 39-51 6: 52-54 7: 55-63 8: 64-80 9: 81-83 10: 84-90 11: 91-102 12: 103-107 13: 108-110 14: 111-122 15: 123-124 16: 125-132 17: 133-135 18: 136 19: 137-138 20+21: 139-143 22: 144 23+24: 145-147 25: 148-151 26:

152-158 27: 159-163 28: 164-171 29: 172-176 30: 177-179 31: 180-190 32: 191-194 33: 196-200 34: 201-205 35: 206-207 36: 208-219 37: 220-225 38: 226-229 39: 230-231 40: 232-237 41: 238-244 42+43+44: 245-255 45: 256-259 46: 260-263 47: 264-266 48: 267-273 49+50: 274-277 51: 278-279 52: 280-282 53: 283-284 54: 285-290 55: 291-293 56: 294-296 57: 297-300 58: 301-302 59: 303-309 60: 310-314 61: 315-320 62+63: 321-330 64: 331-337 65: 338-341 66: 342-347 67: 348-350 68: 351-354 69: 355-356 70: 357-365 71: 366-367 72: 368-375.

CHAPTER 3

1: 1-5 2: 6-31 3: 32-44 4: 45-52 5: 53-63 6: 64-67 7: 68-76 8: 77-80 9: 81-85 10: 86-94 11: 95-100 12: 101-118 13: 119-133 14+15: 134-137 16: 138-145 17: 146-147 18: 148-149 19: 150-151 20: 152-157 21: 158-159 22: 160-163 23: 164-164 24: 165-168 25: 169-171 26: 172-176 27: 177-180 28: 181-183 29: 184-185 30: 186-191 31: 192-193 32: 194-201 33: 202-209 34: 210-218 35: 219-231 36: 232-238 37: 239-259 38: 260-262 39: 263-265 40: 266-267 41: 268 42: 269 43: 270-**276**

CHAPTER 4

1: 16-18 2: 19-26 3: 27-31 4: 32-40 5: 41-43 6: 44-48 7: 49-50 8: 51-57 9: 58-59 10: 60-65 11: 66-70 12: 71-76 13: 77-80 14: 81 15: 82-84 16: 85-88 17: 89-92 18: 93-102 19: 103-105 20: 106-107 21+22: 108-114 23: 115-118 24: 119-122 25: 123-125 26: 126-129 27: 130-139 28: 140-143 29: 144-145 30: 146-150 31: 151-154 32: 155-156 33: 157-163 34: 164-167 35: 168-170 36: 171-174 37: 175-176 38: 177-185 39: 186-191 40: 192-201 41: 202-205 42: 206-**224**

CHAPTER 5

1: 1-14 2: 15-18 3: 19-25 4: 26-28 5: 29-31 6: 32-33 7: 34-38 8+9:

39-47 10: 48-50 11: 51-70 12: 71-72 13: 73-75 14: 76-79 15: 80-82
16: 83-86 17: 87-92 18: 93-95 19: 96-102 20: 103-104 21: 105-108
22: 109-128 23: 129-136 24+25: 137-147 26: 148-150 27+28: 151-
157 29: 158-**180**

Chapter 6

1: 39-51 2: 52-53 3: 54-61 4: 62-66 5: 67-70 6: 71-80 7+8: 81-93
9: 94-104 10: 105-162 11: 163-185 12: 186-200 13: 201-210 14:
211-292 15: 293-344 16: 345-348 17: 349-352 18: 353-356 19: 357-
363 20+21: 364-368 22: 369-371 23: 372-374 24: 375-377 25+26:
378-382 27: 383-386 28: 387-390 29+30: 391-397 31: 398-403
32: 404-410 33+34: 411-417 35: 418-420 36: 421-429 37+38+39:
430-436 40: 437-440 41: 441-448 42+43: 449-456 44: 457-464
45: 465-473 46: 474-481 47: 482-**497**

Chapter 7

1+2: 1-9 3: 10-14 4: 15-18 5: 19-21 6: 22-28 7: 29-32 8+9: 33-39
10+11: 40-52 12: 53-59 13: 60-67 14: 68-102 15+16: 103-109 17:
110-118 18: 119-128 19: 127-138 20: 139-142 21: 143-144 22: 145-
146 23: 147-150 24: 151-157 25: 158-160 26: 161-164 27: 165-171
28: 172-174 29: 175-179 30: 180-**210**

Chapter 8

1: 1-3 2: 4-14 3: 15-29 4: 30-58 5: 59-68 6: 69-75 7: 76-80 8: 81-
85 9+10: 86-99 11: 100-111 12: 112-115 13: 116-123 14+15: 124-
151 16: 152-155 17: 156-159 18+19: 160-169 20: 170-178 21+22:
179-203 23: 204-219 24: 220-225 25: 226-237 26: 238-246 27:
247-260 28: 261-**271**

Chapter 9

1: 34-46 2: 47-56 3: 57-63 4: 64-70 5: 71-88 6: 89-97 7: 98-105

8: 106-123 9: 124-129 10: 130-139 11: 140-171 12: 172-187 13: 188-196 14: 197-238 15: 239-264 16: 265-268 17: 269-277 18: 278-295 19: 296-306 20: 307-327 21: 328-334 22: 335-343 23: 344-350 24: 351-354 25: 355-381 26: 382-397 27: 398-401 28: 402-406 29: 407-414 30: 415-424 31: 425-442 32: 443-474 33: 475-516 34: 517-535

CHAPTER 10

1: 50-63 2: 64-71 3: 72-81 4+5: 82-91 6: 92-103 7: 104-111 8: 112-118 9: 119-129 10: 130-140 11: 141-148 12: 149-152 13: 153-162 14: 163-175 15: 176-184 16: 185-186 17: 187-189 18: 190-205 19: 206-214 20: 215-220 21: 221-222 22: 223-224 23: 225-227 24+25: 228-234 26+27: 235-239 28+29: 240-246 30: 247-249 31: 250-258 32+33: 259-273 34: 274-280 35: 281-283 36+37: 284-295 38: 296-299 39+40: 300-306 41: 307 42: 308-335

CHAPTER 11

1: 44-68 2: 69-80 3: 81-88 4: 89-122 5: 123-140 6: 141-147 7: 148-153 8: 154-164 9: 165-196 10: 197-217 11: 218-236 12: 237-241 13: 242-244 14: 245-254 15: 255-265 16: 266-293 17: 294-306 18: 307-309 19: 310-314 20: 315-325 21: 326-331 22: 332-337 23: 338-352 24: 353-374 25: 375-391 26: 392-409 27: 410-422 28: 423-424 29: 425-426 30: 427-443 31: 444-450 32: 451-465 33: 466-471 34: 472-381 35: 482-490 36: 491-506 37: 507-513 38: 514-518 39+40: 519-536 41: 537-543 42: 544-560 43: 561-566 44: 567-578 45: 579-599 46: 600-608 47: 609-616 48: 617-622 49: 623-639 50: 640-662 51: 663-672 52: 673-681 53: 682-685 54: 686-695 55: 696-708

CHAPTER 12

1: 20-34 2: 35-39 3+4: 40-59 5: 60-75 6: 76-82 7: 83-96 8: 97-103 9: 104-113 10: 114-124 11: 125-140 12: 141-143 13: 144-150 14:

151-164 15: 165-171 16: 172-189 17: 190-196 18: 197-206 19: 207-229 20: 230-**247**

Cʜᴀᴘᴛᴇʀ 13

1: 7 2: 8-9 3: 10-28 4: 27-71 5+6: 72-184 7: 185-512 8: 513-593 9: 594-603 10: 604-615 11: 616-864 12: 865-873 13: 874-891 14: 892-912 15: 913-915 16: 916-926 17: 927-939 18: 940-959 19: 960-968 20: 969-980 21: 981-1021 22: 1022-1029 23: 1030-1036 24: 1037-1040 25: 1041-1050 26: 1051-1056 27: 1057-1068 28: 1069-1079 29: 1080-1083 30: 1084-1093 31: 1094-1119 32: 1120-1122 33: 1123-1128 34: 1129-**1170**

Cʜᴀᴘᴛᴇʀ 14

1: 41-51 2: 52-66 3: 67-115 4: 116-137 5: 138-147 6: 148-159 7: 160-173 8: 174-195 9+10: 196-203 11+12+13+14+15: 204-259 16: 260-264 17: 265-270 18: 271-278 19: 279-299 20: 300-319 21: 320-328 22: 327-335 23: 336-348 24: 349-361 25: 362-370 26: 371-403 27: 404-**415**

Cʜᴀᴘᴛᴇʀ 15

1: 72-143 2: 144-209 3: 210-266 4: 267-284 5: 285-307 6: 308-342 7: 343-360 8: 361-367 9: 368-372 10+11: 373-397 12: 398-400 13: 401-406 14: 407-420 15: 421-470 16: 471-525 17: 526-556 18: 557-558 19: 559-570 20: 571-**599**

Cʜᴀᴘᴛᴇʀ 16

1: 68-113 2: 114-185 3: 186-216 4: 217-264 5: 265-270 6: 271-280 7: 281-294 8: 295-313 9: 314-322 10: 323-329 11: 330-336 12: 337-347 13: 348-351 14: 352-356 15: 357-363 16: 364-376 17: 377-388 18: 389-404 19: 405-413 20: 414-424 21: 425-432 22: 433-444 23: 445-454 24: 455-**473**

CHAPTER 17

1: 34-48 2: 49-65 3: 66-75 4: 76-92 5: 93-104 6: 105-119 7: 120-124 8: 125-138 9: 139-153 10: 154-170 11: 171-184 12: 185-188 13: 189-200 14: 201-215 15: 216-224 16: 225-239 17: 240-241 18: 242-253 19: 254-265 20: 266-284 21: 285-293 22: 294-327 23: 328- 24: 354- 25: 369- 26: 380- 27: 405- 28: 414-**433**

CHAPTER 18

1: 87-97 2: 98-134 3: 135-144 4: 145-148 5: 149-165 6: 166-177 7: 178-183 8: 184-199 9: 200-211 10: 212-217 11: 218-232 12: 233-277 13: 278-313 14: 314-353 15: 354-376 16: 377-402 17: 403-460 18: 461-516 19: 517-528 20: 529-537 21: 538-548 22: 549-585 23: 586-594 24: 595-610 25: 611-630 26: 631-649 27: 650-662 28: 663-689 29: 690-698 30: 699-717 31: 718-723 32: 724-732 33: 733-744 34: 745-748 35: 749-771 36: 772-777 37: 778-793 38: 794-805 39: 806-812 40: 813-817 41: 818-832 42: 833-855 43: 856- 44: 880-884 45: 885-913 46: 914-922 47: 923-935 48: 936-955 49: 956-983 50: 984-1010 51: 1011-1021 52: 1022-1049 53: 1050-1090 54: 1091-1129 55: 1130-1245 56: 1246-1259 57: 1260-1268 58: 1269-1277 59: 1278-1285 60: 1286-1298 61: 1299-1318 62: 1319-1322 63: 1323-1340 64: 1341-1352 65: 1353-1389 66: 1390-1485 67: 1486-1506 68: 1507-1513 69: 1514-1523 70: 1524-1528 71: 1529-1539 72: 1540-1557 73: 1558-1586 74: 1587-1607 75: 1608-1612 76: 1613-1615 77: 1616-1630 78: 1631-**1810**

$\mathscr{A}$PPENDIX 2

NUMBER OF ORIGINAL AND TRANSLATED *OVIS*
DNYANESHWARI

		Gita Shlokas	Total *Ovis*	Used *Ovis*
Ch 1	Arjuna's Desponency	47	274	160
Ch 2	The Path of Knowledge	72	375	254
Ch 3	Path of Actions	43	276	169
Ch 4	Yoga of Knowledge	42	224	137
Ch 5	Renunciation	29	180	58
Ch 6	Meditation	47	497	300
Ch 7	Wisdom and Knowledge	30	210	145
Ch 8	The Imperishable Absolute	28	271	188
Ch 9	Sovereign Knowledge and Sovereign Mystery	34	535	337
Ch 10	Divine Manifestations	42	335	208
Ch 11	Vision of Universal Form	55	708	435

		Gita Shlokas	Total Ovis	Used Ovis
Ch 12	Yoga of Devotion	20	247	194
Ch 13	The Field and the Knower of The Field	34	1170	833
Ch 14	The Three Attributes	27	415	306
Ch 15	The Supreme Person	20	599	416
Ch 16	Divine and Demoniacal Endowments	24	473	377
Ch 17	Three Kinds of Faith	28	433	375
Ch 18	Release Through Renunciation	78	1810	1035
	Total	700	9032	5927

Dr. V. V. Shirvaikar

Dr V. V. Shirvaikar, born in Goa in 1933, had his primary and secondary education in Goa. He then studied at the Wilson College in Bombay and did his Master's degree in Nuclear Physics. He later joined the Bhabha Atomic Research Centre, Bombay where he was a research scientist, specialising in the Environmental Sciences, especially subjects related to safety from radioactive gaseous pollutants released from Nuclear plants, until his retirement in 1991. He did his Doctorate from University of Mumbai in 1972 while working at the Research Centre. He has authored several research papers in scientific journals, written several technical reports and guided research in his subject of specialisation. He was also connected with International Atomic Energy Agency, Maharashtra

Pollution Control Board, Bureau of Indian Standards and National Environmental Engineering Research Institute at Nagpur.

He developed high respect and an attraction towards Shri Shankar Maharaj when he happened to read the Marathi translation of *Towards the Silver Crests of Himalayas* and saw the photograph of Maharaj with his childlike face and remarkably big eyes. This attraction was fanned by Mr N. G. Date, a spiritualist from Malad (Bombay) who has been a catalyst to many in their spiritual path and with whom he came in contact by chance. Circumstances led to his being taken in his fold by Maharaj through another disciple in 1985, some 38 years after Maharaj took *Samadhi*.

Though Dr. Shirvaikar did initially keep in contact with the scientific work related to environment he now keeps himself busy with spiritual topics. He wrote several articles on spiritual topics for the quarterly periodical *Sai-Arpan* including a ten part series on Datta-Parampara and another ten part series on Teachings of Dnyaneshwari.

Dr Shirvaikar lives with his wife in Pune where he settled immediately after retirement from service. His two sons live in the USA.